P9-DED-451

Jossey-Bass Teacher

Jossey-Bass Teacher provides educators with practical knowledge and tools to create a positive and lifelong impact on student learning. We offer classroom-tested and research-based teaching resources for a variety of grade levels and subject areas. Whether you are an aspiring, new, or veteran teacher, we want to help you make every teaching day your best.

From ready-to-use classroom activities to the latest teaching framework, our value-packed books provide insightful, practical, and comprehensive materials on the topics that matter most to K–12 teachers. We hope to become your trusted source for the best ideas from the most experienced and respected experts in the field.

TRANSFORMATIVE CLASSROOM MANAGEMENT

Positive Strategies to Engage All Students and Promote a Psychology of Success

JOHN SHINDLER

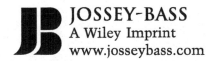

JOSSEY-BASS
A Wiley Imprint
www.josseybass.com

Copyright © 2010 by John Shindler. All rights reserved.

Published by Jossey-Bass
A Wiley Imprint
989 Market Street, San Francisco, CA 94103-1741—www.josseybass.com

No part of this publication may be reproduced, stored in a retrieval system, or transmitted in any form or by any means, electronic, mechanical, photocopying, recording, scanning, or otherwise, except as permitted under Section 107 or 108 of the 1976 United States Copyright Act, without either the prior written permission of the publisher, or authorization through payment of the appropriate per-copy fee to the Copyright Clearance Center, Inc., 222 Rosewood Drive, Danvers, MA 01923, 978-750-8400, fax 978-646-8600, or on the Web at www.copyright.com. Requests to the publisher for permission should be addressed to the Permissions Department, John Wiley & Sons, Inc., 111 River Street, Hoboken, NJ 07030, 201-748-6011, fax 201-748-6008, or online at www.wiley.com/go/permissions.

Permission is given for individual classroom teachers to reproduce the pages and illustrations for classroom use. Reproduction of these materials for an entire school system is strictly forbidden.

Readers should be aware that Internet Web sites offered as citations and/or sources for further information may have changed or disappeared between the time this was written and when it is read.

Limit of Liability/Disclaimer of Warranty: While the publisher and author have used their best efforts in preparing this book, they make no representations or warranties with respect to the accuracy or completeness of the contents of this book and specifically disclaim any implied warranties of merchantability or fitness for a particular purpose. No warranty may be created or extended by sales representatives or written sales materials. The advice and strategies contained herein may not be suitable for your situation. You should consult with a professional where appropriate. Neither the publisher nor author shall be liable for any loss of profit or any other commercial damages, including but not limited to special, incidental, consequential, or other damages.

Jossey-Bass books and products are available through most bookstores. To contact Jossey-Bass directly call our Customer Care Department within the U.S. at 800-956-7739, outside the U.S. at 317-572-3986, or fax 317-572-4002.

Jossey-Bass also publishes its books in a variety of electronic formats. Some content that appears in print may not be available in electronic books.

Library of Congress Cataloging-in-Publication Data

Shindler, John, date.
Transformative classroom management: positive strategies to engage all students and promote a psychology of success / by John Shindler.
p. cm.— (Jossey-Bass teacher series)
Includes bibliographical references and index.
ISBN 978-0-470-44843-4 (pbk.)
1. Classroom management. 2. Effective teaching. 3. Motivation in education. I. Title.
LB3013.S538 2010
371.102'4—dc22   2009026350

FIRST EDITION

PB Printing   10 9 8 7 6 5 4 3 2

About the Book

This book is your guide to creating the transformative classroom. It is a synthesis of what I have seen to be effective in the area of classroom management. It reflects my own experiences as a teacher, observations of hundreds of classrooms, my research, and the best ideas that I have read or heard. This book is intended for those who work with young people now or plan to. Practicing teachers, preservice teachers, parents, administrators, support staff, and coaches may all find it useful.

The content of the book is intended to cover the topic of classroom management comprehensively—from the practical techniques for achieving ease, clarity, and smoothness, to the more transformative techniques that will lead to student growth and development; from helping students with a habit of disruptive behavior to increasing each student's level of motivation; from the practical steps for developing classroom rules to a comprehensive system for creating a classroom community.

At the heart of the book is an examination of what it takes to create a psychology of success within our students individually and collectively. This concept, explained in Chapter Seven and revisited throughout the book, provides the framework for what is required to achieve transformative classroom management results.

I have been an educator for twenty-five years, from kindergarten to the university level. I have been in hundreds of classrooms and have taught thousands of students. When I reflect on what I have observed over the years, I find much of it perplexing. I have witnessed smart teachers who struggle with classroom management. I have observed skilled teachers who elect to use strategies that create more problems than they solve. And to this day I see too many great ideas that are seldom used.

I have concluded that what makes a teacher successful in one school is the same thing that makes a teacher successful in the next school. There is an operating assumption that classroom management is complicated because some things work with some kinds of students and some things do not. It is true that all students are unique and group dynamics, cultural backgrounds, and experiences vary—sometimes dramatically. But for the most part, sound ideas get positive results and unsound ideas get mixed results at best. Some ideas can seem promising but fall short of translating into effectiveness because at their core they are flawed. As a teacher, I used many of these flawed ideas and even defended them because I believed that they worked. But time, experience, and the chance to research and reflect (a chance that too few of us get) have given me a perspective that I did not have when I began my teaching career. Some of the insights in the book have come as sudden flashes of inspiration. Most have come from watching teacher after teacher apply particular practices and observing what occurred as a result.

I have found that not all ideas sold in the marketplace of classroom management strategies lead to desirable results. In fact, many of the most popular ideas result in more harm than good. For that reason, parts of this book are devoted to explaining why many of the most popular ideas in use today are flawed, and what to do instead.

In each chapter are reflections within the text that relate to the content immediately preceding it. Reading and reflecting on the material give readers an opportunity to process the information in more depth.

At the end of each chapter are journal prompts, which will help readers process what they have read. Some or all of these prompts may be assigned as part of a teacher education course to promote retention and provoke a deeper examination of the content.

Finally, each chapter includes at least two activities, which are intended to help those working independently or in groups to process the content of the chapter, synthesize material, or create components of a classroom management plan. Practical guidelines are offered for the development of such products as a classroom social contract, a process and participation assessment system, a set of logical consequences, and a series of technical management strategies.

This book rather quickly enters some relatively uncharted territory: the realm of teacher thought and mind-set. I have chosen to venture down this road for two primary reasons. First, the vast majority of our activity each day occurs between our ears. If we are intentional about what we do in the classroom, we will be much more effective. Second, I have found that what primarily keeps teachers from effectiveness or growing into the kinds of professionals that they would like to become is most often found in the domain of their thought processes and habits. What holds us up is not usually a lack of information or insufficient talent but patterns of thinking. The beginning of the transformative classroom will be a transformative mind-set on the part of the teacher. The book will guide the development of that mind-set as it outlines practical strategies for producing high levels of function and effectiveness within the classroom.

About the Author

John Shindler, Ph.D., is an associate professor of curriculum and instruction in the Charter College of Education at California State University, Los Angeles. His areas of expertise include school climate and culture, school improvement, teacher education, learning and cognitive styles, classroom management, and teacher leadership. Shindler is the chair of the Special Interest Group on School Culture, Climate and Community at the American Educational Research Association. He is cofounder and director of the Alliance for the Study of School Climate and author of several school climate assessment instruments and articles. Shindler is the developer of the Paragon Learning Style Inventory and author of several learning styles articles and resources. He is a former elementary, middle school, and high school teacher.

Acknowledgments

I first thank all of the teachers and students whom I have worked with, observed, and talked with over the years. You have all challenged me to grow. It would be impossible here to mention all of you or acknowledge your ideas, insights, and practices. That would take a whole book in itself.

I thank my friends and the members of my family, especially my parents, who have been exceedingly supportive. You have all been very patient with me through the more than five years of writing this book. Bruce Brown has been a pioneer, a mentor, and a dear friend. Finally, I could not have done this without the help of Trina, my wife and master editor. Her love, support, perspective, and encouragement have been invaluable.

I have had nothing but support and encouragement from my colleagues at California State University, Los Angeles (CSULA). Most notably, Albert Jones deserves a great deal of credit for the ideas in this book. We have spent countless hours talking about classroom management. The maturity of many of the ideas here is a direct result of his insights and wealth of knowledge. Clint Taylor has been a rock of support and an inestimable source of feedback. Kimberly Persiani-Becker provided a detailed review that significantly improved the book. I also thank the administration of CSULA for the sabbatical leave to complete my work.

I thank Kate Bradford at John Wiley & Sons for shepherding this project through to completion. I also thank the peer reviewers of the first two drafts, whose insights I noted and appreciated.

I recognize the contributions of the many great theorists and researchers in the field of education as well as some from outside the field. I deeply appreciate being able to draw from such a wealth of collective wisdom. This book owes a sincere debt of gratitude to the following giants: William Glasser, Carol Dweck, Richard Curwin and Allen Mendler, Jean Anyon, Alfie Kohn, Martin Covington, David and Roger Johnson, Eckhart Tolle, Rudolph Dreikurs, Mihály Csíkszentmihályi, Carol Evertson, and Carol Weinstein. I cannot imagine where we would all be without you.

Contents

Assessing Where We Are and Making Sense of the Inner Workings of the Classroom

1

Introduction to Transformative Classroom Management

In This Chapter

- Introduction
- Transformative classroom management
- Developing a guiding personal vision
- The progression of the book

This book offers strategies to make your classroom a place that changes lives for the better: *a transformative classroom*. It will demystify the process of creating a high-functioning classroom and will be your guide to creating the kind of class environment that you desire.

CASESTUDY

1.1

Ms. L's Transformative Elementary Class

What first strikes a visitor to Ms. L's urban public school third-grade class is the low level of anxiety and high level of confidence among the students, which allows them to take risks and express themselves. Today the students return to the classroom after recess and take their seats without any need for direction. After a smooth transition, the class is directed into a math lesson.

In contrast, the third-grade class next door comes back from recess somewhat rowdy and unfocused, and the teacher immediately begins to call out students who are misbehaving. The students finally open their math books after an extended transition.

(Continued)

During the lesson, only a few students volunteer to share their ideas because they worry that they will look incompetent, and the teacher interrupts the lesson many times to deal with misbehaving students.

Back in Ms. L's class, every student appears engaged and eager to share answers and ask questions when they are not clear about the material. The energy in the room is almost entirely focused on the activity, and no students feel the need to entertain themselves or their friends by misbehaving. Ms. L is calm and soft-spoken and refrains from any hint of negativity. She leads the lesson with questions that keep the students engaged and thinking critically, and there is a distinct flow to the activity. Throughout the lesson, the students look forward to being intellectually challenged.

If we had the ability to examine every classroom in every school, we would find that they vary dramatically from one another. We would find classrooms in urban, suburban, rural, public, and private schools, from every grade level and subject area, kindergarten through twelfth grade, that were functional and productive places. In the same sorts of schools, we would also see dysfunctional and unproductive classrooms. If we were to identify the variable in each class that was most responsible for the quality of the learning environment, we would find that it is we ourselves: the teachers. Our thoughts, values, and actions all have the effect of defining the climate and experience in our classes. Too few of us truly appreciate the ultimately powerful influence that we have, and we too often neglect to recognize that our classroom management choices can have a number of important effects:

- Promote community or fragmentation
- Lead to clarity or confusion
- Create a psychology of success or one of failure
- Be a liberating influence or perpetuate an unjust social class structure
- Foster a climate of motivation and joy or one of disinterest and drudgery

Researchers have found that classroom management actions and attitudes can be the difference between teachers having either a sense of job satisfaction and a feeling that their gifts are being successfully used or a feeling of burnout and unhappiness (Friedman & Farber, 1992). Moreover, how teachers approach classroom management will significantly determine the degree to which they feel successful and satisfied with their teaching (Fallona & Richardson, 2006).

READER NOTE

The reflections throughout each chapter offer you opportunities to reflect on the ideas presented in the text in relation to your own experience. They are a means by which you can process the content in the chapter in a practical and personal manner. Some of you may want to skip over the reflections on the first reading, especially if you are attempting to progress through the chapter at a quick pace.

REFLECTION

Survey a sampling of teachers to determine their levels of job satisfaction and levels of stress each day, and include a question about how successful they feel in the area of classroom management. Do you find a relationship between the two?

WHAT IS TRANSFORMATIVE CLASSROOM MANAGEMENT?

To understand what makes a classroom a transformative place, we might begin by examining the four case studies in this chapter. All four teachers have created what could be characterized as transformative classrooms. As you read about each classroom, notice their common attributes: clarity of purpose, self-responsibility, bonds among students, and an increasing level of function over time. In other words, they promote skills that are critical for success both in and outside the classroom.

CASESTUDY

Ms. R's Transformative High School Social Studies Class

Ms. R teaches social studies in an urban public high school that is considered low performing by most measures: its dropout rate is above 50 percent. But in Ms. R's class, students are working collaboratively. The students are from different cultures, neighborhoods, and cliques within the school, but in Ms. R's class, they function as a unified team. When this same group of students was observed the period before, they seemed to be mentally checked out and unruly. In that class, the teacher appeared to struggle with control, spending a lot of time raising his voice and threatening the students about what would happen if they didn't get to work. In Ms. R's class, in contrast, the students were entirely invested in the task and prepared when it was time to report their group's findings. Maybe the best words to describe the class are *trusting* and *respectful*. The students respect each other, their teacher, and their learning, and they know that their teacher trusts and respects them.

A transformative classroom functions to change for the better those who are within it—as individuals and as a collective. Transformative classroom management (TCM) is an approach that assumes that classroom management practices have a powerful long-term effect on student development and teachers' ability to be successful. It presumes that over time, high function is possible in any classroom; that some pedagogical and management practices lead to greater function, while others lead to greater dysfunction; and that if designed successfully, *any* classroom can be a transformative place.

TCM, unlike many other models, assumes that problems do not require reaction; rather, the sources of those problems need to be identified and altered. Problems within any class should not be viewed, as some would suggest, as a finite quantity of misbehaviors that need to be "dealt with" or "handled." Both functional and problematic or dysfunctional behaviors have explicable causes and in most cases are related directly or indirectly to teaching practices. Most problems are manifestations of predictable factors, including the interaction between teacher or school and the student, the systems in place, congruence between the expectations of the students and teachers, and the degree to which the class meets the students' basic needs. TCM places a special emphasis on perpetually working toward a better tomorrow.

| 1.2 | REFLECTION |

Have you seen classrooms that you would characterize as transformative? Reflect on the kinds of classroom management practices that occurred in them.

Figure 1.1 depicts the three domains of change within the TCM classroom. First, the transformative classroom supports each student's individual progression from irresponsibility and a "failure psychology" orientation to self-responsibility and a "success psychology" orientation: an internal locus of control, sense of acceptance and belonging, and growth orientation (Ayling, 2009). Second, the transformative classroom promotes the growth of the collective from its current state of function to one of greater function and ultimately into greater levels of community. Third, TCM endeavors to assist teachers in their own growth toward greater levels of self-awareness and a more effective and intentional set of practices, and it provides them the tools to become visionary leaders in the classroom.

DEVELOPING A GUIDING PERSONAL VISION

The process of creating a high-functioning transformative classroom begins by developing a vision of what you want to accomplish. To do so, it will be beneficial to take a few preliminary steps:

1. *Clarify your intention.* What do you specifically want? When you reflect on this question, it is useful not to let your thinking be overly restricted by what others tell you is possible,

	Movement and Growth From _____ → to → _____
Student	Failure psychology → Success psychology Irresponsible → Self-responsible Dysfunctional behavioral patterns → Functional behavioral patterns
Class or other collective	Dysfunction → Function Independent survival → A connected community Egocentric → Contributors
Teacher	Reactive or accidental → Intentional and aware Short-term survival → Long-term vision Manager → Leader

FIGURE 1.1. *The Domains of Transformative Classroom Management*

or not possible, or what you have become accustomed to through practice or observation. Allow yourself to conceive a vision that is guided as little as possible by fear and resignation and as much as possible by what you think is right. What kind of classroom would make you proud and would give you a sense of being true to your core values?

2. *Be purposeful about raising your level of awareness.* If you have not yet started teaching, you might want to observe a broad range of classes in a variety of schools. It is common for teachers to default to practices to which they were exposed themselves, so recognize that what you have seen to this point may have been a limited sample of what is possible. See what is out there. And if you do not see your vision operationalized within the classrooms that you observe, it may mean that you are in the position of making a significant contribution as a trailblazer. If you are currently teaching, this book will offer many opportunities to reflect on what you are doing and why. Exploring both your internal processing as well as your external situation will be useful. More effective practice begins with an examination of who we are and what we value, followed by taking stock of what we are doing and asking ourselves if it is getting us closer to our vision.

3. *Recognize that every practice has an effect.* Every choice you make shapes the overall classroom climate. Even the smallest action can have a profound impact on the behavior, motivation, and achievement of students.

Stick to Your Vision

Each of us possesses our personal vision of the ideal classroom. For most of us, that vision is rather ambitious and was part of what inspired us to work with young people as teachers, coaches, counselors, administrators, support staff, and paraprofessionals. Yet as we confront the realities of schools over time—the lack of motivation of many students, the discouraging attitudes of some of our peers, the difficulty of the job—many of us increasingly become resigned to relinquishing that ideal vision and make compromises that we never wanted to make out of a perceived need for survival or what seems to be practical necessity. However, what you want to accomplish is possible. You *can* get there. There are answers and pathways to making your vision a reality.

REFLECTION

1.3

Take a moment now or after reading this chapter to envision your ideal classroom. What does it look like? What is going on in it? How do you feel as the teacher?

GAINING PERSPECTIVE

Common sense and teaching experience are valuable, but in most cases, they alone are not sufficient in helping us succeed at translating our classroom management vision into a reality. Good intentions and common sense do not necessarily lead to good practice. If they did, we would see mostly excellent teaching and classrooms free of conflict and full of motivated students. And experience does not necessarily lead to improved practice over time either. If this were the case, we would observe that the most experienced teachers would be the most effective classroom managers. In some cases this is true, and the value of experience cannot be underestimated; however, in many cases, more experience simply leads to repeatedly applying the same flawed principles and practices day after day.

Moreover, adding isolated management strategies here and there may or may not result in improvements. We need to ask ourselves, "To what are we adding them?" Without a foundation that supports a positive strategy, the strategy itself may not bring about the positive effect that we desire, or even have a desirable effect at all. Having in place a sound set of guiding principles for action and thinking is necessary for independent practices to be effective and to function as part of an integrated whole. Furthermore, in most cases, our classroom management will be more positively affected by what we cease doing rather than something we add to our repertoire.

The Natural Condition of Classrooms

The natural condition of any classroom is functional, harmonious, satisfying, and productive. It exists beneath the various sources of dysfunction, stress, and strain in each classroom and is most often masked by the effects of ineffective management practices and the negative student reactions that result from them. Apathy, struggle, hostility, anxiety, inefficiency, and resistance, while common, are essentially unnatural conditions that are brought about by one or more dysfunctional ingredients present in the class. In other words, they are normal but not natural. The positive feelings that exist in any class—the love of learning, a desire to collaborate, the experience of achievement, inspiration, the joy of contributing, and growth—are all natural states. This is not to suggest that teaching is naturally easy or that an effort to promote a classroom that characterizes more of this natural condition will cause problems to disappear overnight. In most cases, the process of creating a high-functioning class is challenging and entails a great deal of commitment and effort. But the closer we get to it, the more normal that natural state becomes.

In addition, we need to be wary of advice that includes the phrase, "Well, it works." The fact is that anything can be said to "work." Every sound and unsound practice that is being used by teachers today is defended with, "It works." But the question should not be whether a particular practice works; the question to ask is, "Is this practice getting me closer to my long-term management goals and vision?" In many cases, justifying a classroom management practice based on the rationale that it works is often a smokescreen for using an ultimately dysfunctional practice only because it is familiar or convenient. Many popular strategies have genial-sounding names, such as *token economy, praise, behavioral charts,* and *reward systems.* However, as you will see throughout the course of this book, a close examination of these practices reveals them as having detrimental long-term effects. We might ask ourselves whether we are looking for practices that will sweep problems under the rug, lead to domestication rather than growth, deceive students temporarily, or make us feel better or justified. Or do we want our management practices to have long-lasting effects that change the lives of our students for the better? Isolated quick-fix strategies can be helpful for ameliorating problems, but in some cases, they can disguise the true source of a problem or, worse yet, limit the growth of the students toward more evolved behavior.

1.4 REFLECTION

How would you answer the question, "What does it mean when a classroom management practice 'works'"? Was it more difficult to answer this question than you first thought? Why?

Results from a study of twenty-one urban schools comparing the effects of different forms of classroom management practices found that transformative classroom management practices produced both a higher-quality school climate as well as greater student achievement when compared to other types of practice (Shindler, Jones, Williams, Taylor, & Cadenas, 2009). Appendix G outlines the results. Regardless of the grade or the neighborhood from which the students attend, the use of practices classified as transformative encouraged a wide range of desired outcomes including better student-teacher relations, better student-student relations, higher-quality instructional practices, and a more positive attitude and culture at the school. These effects were absent or demonstrated to a much lesser extent by the use of other more "traditional" methods.

THE PROGRESSION OF THE BOOK

The progression of this book is designed to be developmental, and all of the chapters are inter-related. The sequence of content is intended to support new teachers in the development of a personal classroom management plan and experienced teachers in the process of reforming and improving their classroom management practice. It begins with chapters intended to promote self-assessment and the development of a personal vision and set of intentions. It then offers a series of chapters that address essential elements of successful management, including the practical steps in creating a democratic classroom. This is followed by chapters that address specifically what it takes to achieve the qualities of a transformative class.

CASE**STUDY**   **1.3**

Mr. T's Transformative Elementary Class

Mr. T teaches fifth grade in a suburban public school. What an observer first notices is that he has given control of the class almost entirely to the students when it comes to making decisions and solving problems. He calls his class "Mr. T's Tribe." He commonly gives his class collaborative problem-solving exercises and simply watches from the sidelines. The self-directive skills that the students demonstrate are evidence of a great deal of training, practice, and reflection, but by this point in the year, Mr. T finds himself needing to intervene very little. One of his tools is a participation assessment system that incorporates a clearly defined rubric for high-quality behavior. After a couple of months, almost all of his students have developed the habit of working at the highest level defined in the system, which is characterized by a student finding ways to help others succeed. As a result, most of the students in the class have internalized the notion that their success is contingent on their ability to contribute to the group and support others.

Part One provides you an opportunity to assess your current beliefs and practices, form a vivid guiding vision, and set a path for improved practice. Chapter Two addresses how to move from less effective to more effective classroom practices. This chapter examines the nature of the effective classroom and what types of practices lead to function or dysfunction. Throughout the book, you will be encouraged to recognize the advantages of those practices that lead to increased levels of effectiveness and function, as well as the problems that are generated by the use of dysfunctional practices characterized by either teacher passivity or teacher domination.

Part Two begins in Chapter Three with an examination of the fundamental dynamics of the classroom environment, including the idea that "we teach who we are." This chapter looks at the nature of social and indirect learning dynamics and how to harness its power. Chapter Four compares common strategies for developing clear and shared classroom expectations, examines which strategies will be more effective in this process, and considers why shared expectations are the cornerstone to successful classroom management. Chapter Five addresses technical management: the strategies that promote a culture of listening and respect and ensure that every student is attentive, on task, and responsible and the entire class functions efficiently on a practical level. Chapter Six explores motivational strategies, and Chapter Seven looks at how to create a psychology of success in students. We will explore how each teaching act promotes or undermines students' psychological orientation to learning and achievement and the practices that are likely to produce each result.

Part Three begins in Chapter Eight with examining how to create a functioning democratic classroom. At the heart of any functional class is a set of common understandings and a sense on the part of students that they are responsible for being accountable and contributing to the collective. Through the development of a shared social contract, clear expectations, a sense of purpose, and a set of logical consequences, any class can achieve the qualities of a high-functioning democracy. In Chapter Nine, a distinction is made between punishments and logical consequences, and a process is outlined for developing logical and related consequences that will lead to more responsible student behavior and a stronger social contract. Chapter Ten outlines a system for implementing the social contract and promoting student responsibility, the key to a functioning democracy.

We begin Part Four by examining in Chapter Eleven the connection of instruction, assessment, and classroom management. The starting point for this discussion is the idea that teachers who are more effective pedagogically have fewer problems. In this part, we examine the relationship between how we teach and how it affects our management. Also, we explore how instructional and managerial choices work to either reinforce or liberate the social class structure and the students within that structure. Chapter Twelve presents practical ideas for leading and managing cooperative learning.

1.4 CASE STUDY

Mr. S's Transformative Middle School Math Class

In this urban public middle school, most students fear and dislike math. But Mr. S's math students bound into the classroom with a sense of positive energy. What a visitor notices first about the way that Mr. S teaches is that he uses questions many times more than statements. The students are responsible for doing the thinking and problem solving. The guided-practice activity today is hands-on and active: students use algebra tiles to work out solutions to problems. When Mr. S asks students to report their findings, all students eagerly volunteer—in contrast to many other classes where weaker students avoid involvement. It is clear that the expectations in this class are well established for those occasions when the student who is responding struggles. Students are entirely supportive of those responding, and Mr. S stays with the responder and helps the student work through his or her thinking. The result is a group of students who feel empowered and safe to take risks.

Chapter Thirteen, the first chapter in Part Five, addresses how to work with conflict and students who are considered difficult by some teachers. Conflict is a natural part of life in and out of the classroom and can be a source of growth or result in suffering. Some students come to us with habits that require a greater degree of intentional effort on our part than others. In Chapter Fourteen, we examine how to bridge the gap with students who appear disconnected and help students who have developed a pattern of negative identity learn to re-form the processes they have used to reach their goals and encourage them toward healthier, more functional behavior patterns.

Part Seven looks at how to synthesize the strategies outlined in the previous fourteen chapters into an approach for achieving a transformative classroom. Chapter Fifteen explores how to successfully implement a student-centered management approach and promote class-room community. Chapter Sixteen offers an in-depth exploration of the relationship between our thinking patterns and our effectiveness and job satisfaction. In many respects, the level of function or dysfunction in our classrooms will be a reflection of our own thoughts, attitudes, patterns, and beliefs. Here we discuss how to make our thinking an ally in the process of reaching our goals rather than a self-limiting hurdle.

A series of online resource articles related to specific issues in transformative classroom management is available at no cost to readers at trasformativeclassroom.com.

- "Developing and Implementing an Effective System for Assessing the Quality of Student Process, Participation and Behavior" provides an extensive step-by-step system for assessing investment, effort, and the process aspects of tasks. It explains why attempts to assess these kinds of outcomes must be sound and intentional or should not be attempted at all.

- "Why to Stop Using Colored Cards and Names on the Board Systems, and What to Do Instead" explains the many fundamental and practical problems related to the use of these popular behavior assessment systems. A sounder and more effective alternative is offered.

- "Competition in the Transformative Classroom" offers an in-depth analysis of competition in the classroom and provides an explanation of the difference between the healthy and unhealthy use of competition.

- "Moving Up the Continuum from a 4-Style Approach" will be helpful to those who find themselves relying on a dominating and teacher-centered approach. The 4-Style approach is characterized by a "boss" personality and relies to a great extent on personal confrontation with students. This style is explained in more detail in the next chapter.

The book finishes with a series of appendixes that include a question-and-answer session (Appendix A), a comparison of sound versus faulty management assumptions (Appendix B), an analysis of the use of the phrase "it works" (Appendix C), and analysis of the use of the term "the real world" (Appendix D), a catalogue of sources of classroom drama (Appendix E), an introduction to the Transform Your School schoolwide behavioral system (Appendix F), and results of a study demonstrating the effects of TCM on school climate and student achievement (Appendix G). Transformative classrooms can exist in isolation and can still be powerful as independent entities, but when an entire school adopts a transformative mind-set and set of practices, the burden for each teacher becomes lighter and the results become more profound.

In the next chapter we will examine the Teaching Style Matrix, and the four possible teaching styles, and classify classroom management strategies by their tendency to create more or less function and effectiveness.

> ## READER NOTE
>
> Each chapter in this book ends with Journal Reflections and Activities. These sections are intended to help you engage with key ideas in the chapter. A journal can be a valuable asset in processing your thinking more deeply. The activities may be helpful as you develop your own personal classroom management plan or teaching improvement plan.

Journal Reflections

- In what ways has school had a transformational effect on your life? What events were responsible for that effect? Why?
- What do you want to accomplish through reading this book?
- Have you ever been part of a transformative context—for example, in a classroom, team, group, project, or committee?
  - If you have not, the notion of creating one in your classroom may seem somewhat abstract. But as you apply the principles and practices from the book, you will begin to better recognize what it is.
  - If you have had this experience, what was it like? Many of those who have will tend to judge each successive context by that standard. This is very often true for students. Those who have been part of a transformative classroom are changed permanently. Reflect on why this is the case.

Activities

1. Develop a personal vision for your ideal classroom. Do not be too concerned for now about limitations that you feel are present in your school or the kinds of schools in which you see yourself working. Paint a detailed picture of how it looks and feels. What kind of work is going on? How does it feel in the class? What do teacher-student interactions look like? What is the climate in the room?
2. In a small group, discuss the following question: Do you see evidence of a transformational mind-set in schools in general? How do you explain your findings? What is either encouraging or discouraging this mind-set?

REFERENCES

Anyon, J. (1981). Social class and school knowledge. *Curriculum Inquiry*, *11*, 3–42.

Ayling, G. (2009). *Report of an adolescent transition, a possible intervention for the stress response and diseases in adult life*. Manuscript submitted for publication.

Fallona, C., & Richardson, V. (2006). Classroom management as a moral activity. In C. M. Evertson & C. S. Weinstein (Eds.), *Handbook of classroom management* (pp. 1041–1062). Mahwah, NJ: Erlbaum.

Friedman, I. A., & Farber, B. A. (1992). Professional self-concept as a predictor of burn out. *Journal of Educational Research*, *86*(1), 28–35.

Shindler, J., Jones, A., Williams, A., Taylor, C., & Cadenas, H. (2009, January). *Exploring below the surface: School climate assessment and improvement as the key to bridging the achievement gap*. Paper presented at the annual meeting of the Washington State Office of the Superintendent of Public Instruction, Seattle.

2

Classifying Approaches to Classroom Management and Moving Up the Teaching Style Continuum

In This Chapter

- Introducing the teaching style matrix
- Function versus dysfunction
- Raising the level of function and examining the roots of dysfunction
- Things to start doing
- Things to stop doing
- Examining the effects of our thinking
- Horizontal axis: Teacher centered versus student centered
- The four management approaches
- Comparing the advantages of a 1-Style versus 2-Style approach
- Moving up from a 3-Style approach

Each teacher has a personal style of teaching and classroom management, and much of the style will come from his or her own unique personality. However, a great deal of what we might call classroom management style comes from attitudes and pedagogical choices. In the domain of personality, each of us can find ways to translate our personal style into an effective teaching demeanor. Yet in the domain of choices and attitudes, some styles lead to substantially different outcomes than others (Harris, 1998).

REFLECTION   2.1

How would you characterize your teaching style or the style that you would most like to employ—or both?

13

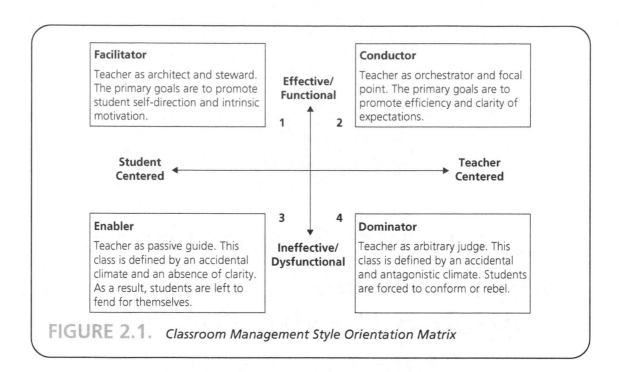

FIGURE 2.1. *Classroom Management Style Orientation Matrix*

In this chapter, we examine how the classroom management choices that we make, as well as our orientation to discipline itself, will determine the results that we will achieve. To help support this examination, it will be useful to incorporate a four-quadrant classroom management style matrix.

This classroom management style orientation matrix, depicted in Figure 2.1, has proven useful as a tool for classifying the management orientations and strategies teachers use (Shindler, Jones, Taylor, & Cadenas, 2004) and will provide one of the fundamental frameworks for the ideas and concepts in this book. The matrix is formed by the intersection of two continua or axes. The vertical axis of the matrix represents the level of effectiveness and function of the management practices. The horizontal axis represents a continuum of theoretical orientation defining each approach or style, from more student centered on the left to more teacher centered on the right. The intersection of these two axes produces four distinct teaching style quadrants. It should be noted that on the level of personality, any personal style could be fit into each of the four quadrants. However, as we will explore, each of the four styles represented by the quadrants produces dramatically different results in practice.

VERTICAL AXIS: EFFECTIVENESS AND FUNCTIONALITY

The vertical axis of the matrix is related to the continuum of effectiveness and function of the management practice. At the top of the axis are the most effective forms of practice, defined by high function, sound relationships, high levels of motivation, and high productivity. At the base of the axis are the least effective forms of practice, defined by low function, relationship dysfunction, low motivation, and a lack of productivity (see Figure 2.2).

What contributes to one's placement on this effectiveness continuum? When the classroom management performance of teachers in the field was examined, three factors were found to predict effectiveness (Shindler et al., 2004). These factors were related to the following three domains:

1. Orientation and dispositions

2. Teaching choices and practices

3. Thinking and assumptions

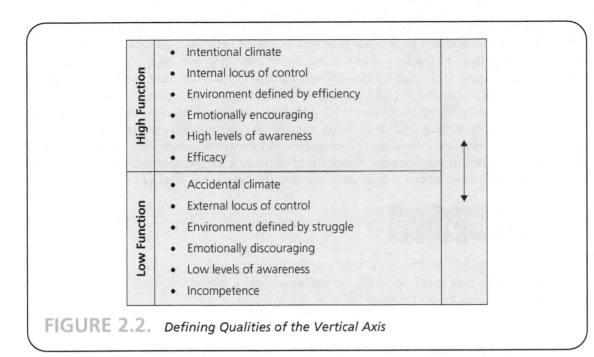

High Function
- Intentional climate
- Internal locus of control
- Environment defined by efficiency
- Emotionally encouraging
- High levels of awareness
- Efficacy

Low Function
- Accidental climate
- External locus of control
- Environment defined by struggle
- Emotionally discouraging
- Low levels of awareness
- Incompetence

FIGURE 2.2.   *Defining Qualities of the Vertical Axis*

First, effective teachers have an orientation to teaching that is defined by a sense of responsibility and intentionality. Second, effective management relates to a great extent to the quality of methods and strategies that teachers choose to incorporate and the effectiveness with which they are applied. In this chapter, we examine practices that lead up the continuum and others that leave one mired in the realm of ineffectiveness. Third, our attitudes, assumptions, and patterns of thinking substantially determine our ability to realize effectiveness and function. Each of these three factors is interrelated, but we will examine them independently.

Orientation and Dispositions

The degree of classroom management effectiveness and function were found to relate to the orientations taken by the teachers and their dispositions related to teaching (Shindler et al., 2004; Shindler, Jones, Williams, & Taylor 2009). High levels of effectiveness were related to the degree to which the locus of control of the teacher is internal rather than external and the level of intentionality of the system of management. Therefore, the peak of this axis represents practices that are less accidental or reactive and more systematic, deliberate, and reflective of an increasing level of teacher ownership for student outcomes. We examine both of these subfactors in more depth.

Responsibility and Internal Locus of Control. If you talk to a teacher who does an effective job of classroom management and possesses a high degree of self-efficacy, you will hear in his or her words the underlying convictions: "I believe it is about what I do" and "I am responsible for helping my students succeed" (Gettinger & Kohler, 2006; Henson, 2001; Yoon, 2002). The frame of mind that is expressed in this attitude is both internal—"Success will be dependent on the investment I make in my variable in the equation"—and responsible—"My job is to help every student succeed." Contrast this to the mind-set of a teacher who, after a sufficient amount of training and practice, still demonstrates ineffectiveness and experiences a high level of student failure. In most cases, the attitudes that these teachers express are both external—"There is nothing that I can do with these kids"—and irresponsible—"It is not my fault."

Greenwood (1990) found that teachers who believe that they, and other teachers in general, can motivate students to achieve give less evidence of stress and exhibit more internal locus of control than do teachers who believe that neither they, nor other teachers, can affect student performance. In a study by Guskey and Passaro (1994), the most significant predictor of teacher efficacy was the degree to which teachers assigned the cause of the outcomes in their class internally rather than externally. Although success in the area of classroom management will have a great deal to do with training and the methods we choose to employ, our underlying attitudes related to responsibility and locus of control will be the foremost determining factors in our success. Simply put, success is impossible without the mind-set that teachers are responsible for their students' learning and behavioral outcomes.

2.2 REFLECTION

Think about teachers whom you consider excellent. How would you characterize the language they use when they speak about their students and their profession? Does it reflect a more internal or external locus of control?

Intentionality and Consciousness. More effective teacher practices are demonstrated by those who know what they are trying to accomplish and how they intend to accomplish it. That is, they are intentional in their practice (Richardson & Fallona, 2001). This approach is in contrast to practices that are shortsighted, reactive, and unconscious and could be described as accidental. Intentional practice is characterized by efforts undertaken within a larger scheme that integrates each specific teaching act (Pajares, 1992). An accidental set of practices has no such coherence and amounts to little, if anything, beyond a series of disconnected strategies. This lack of vision creates a lack of confidence and a feeling of discontinuity in the students; in other words, they have a sense that they are part of a class that lacks leadership.

Effectiveness Versus Dysfunction in Classroom Management

Classroom management effectiveness is defined as a learning environment that promotes learning, motivation, and collective function. Classroom management dysfunction is defined as any event, behavior, pattern, feeling, or thought that prevents a teacher from being able to teach to his or her fullest potential or keeps the class from learning in the most liberated, satisfying, and effective manner.

Teaching Choices and Practices

Not all classroom management strategies will get you where you want to go as a teacher. Some will lead you up the effectiveness continuum, and others will keep you treading water or can even promote greater degrees of dysfunction. In this section, we examine practices that lead to the highest levels of sustainable effectiveness and those to avoid.

Management practices come in three types:

- Effective practices that we do that we would want to keep doing.

- Effective practices that we do not yet do, or do not do very well yet (that would affect improvement), that we would want to begin doing.

- Ineffective practices that we do but need to stop doing because they are limiting our success or in some cases actually leading us down the effectiveness continuum.

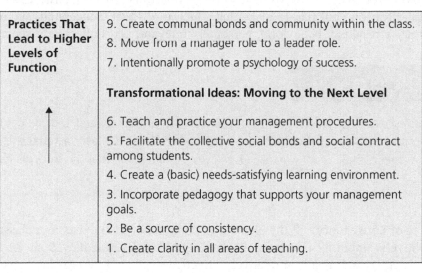

Practices That Lead to Higher Levels of Function	9. Create communal bonds and community within the class.
	8. Move from a manager role to a leader role.
	7. Intentionally promote a psychology of success.
	Transformational Ideas: Moving to the Next Level
	6. Teach and practice your management procedures.
	5. Facilitate the collective social bonds and social contract among students.
	4. Create a (basic) needs-satisfying learning environment.
	3. Incorporate pedagogy that supports your management goals.
	2. Be a source of consistency.
	1. Create clarity in all areas of teaching.

FIGURE 2.3.   *Management Practices That Contribute to Movement Up the Continuum*

Moving Up the Continuum to a More Functional Approach. As you examine the list of management practices that will contribute to movement up the continuum (represented in Figure 2.3), you will see few quick fixes on the list. Effective practices create a fundamentally more functional classroom and produce increasingly more effectiveness over time. They have the effect of empowering students and bringing out their best. Truly effective practices not only promote better student behavior but also help students become fundamentally better individually and collectively. The following six practices increasingly and sustainably raise the level of function in a class. In addition, three strategies for moving to the highest level on the effectiveness continuum are introduced.

1. Create Clarity in All Areas of Teaching   Most of the outcomes that you desire in your classes depend to a great extent on your ability to promote clarity within your environment. Clarity within the classroom has been found to correlate positively with student achievement, level of engagement, and student satisfaction (Hines, Cruickshank, & Kennedy, 1985; Shindler et al., 2009). And most classroom management dysfunction is related to a lack of clarity in some form.

The existence of clarity can be seen to mitigate dysfunction in four key areas. First, students need clear expectations. Without them, they are forced to guess. This can create a vacuum in expectations, which students fill with their own ideas of conduct. When we use abstract terms such as *responsibility, respect,* or *good behavior* without defining those concepts in a concrete and material way, these ideas remain abstractions. Much of what we call misbehavior is simply students guessing how to act in ways that we do not like (in other words, their guess was wrong). Second, you need to infuse a sense of intention and movement to the class. When the class experiences the deliberate movement toward a goal, they are much less likely to be bored or distracted, or feel their work lacks purpose. Third, students need to be given clear boundaries. Boundaries help students understand where lines exist (Bluestein, 1999). In their absence, problems arise. In part, this is due to the fact that inevitably students come to any class with a wide range of previously learned behavior and expectation for boundaries. Fourth, abstractions, such as respect, listening, effort, and responsibility, need to be operationalized, or they will remain abstractions. Many teachers complain that their students lack these traits, yet do not make the concepts concrete and practical for their students. Clarity can exist only in a concrete and observable world. Words can only point to behavior. Clarity therefore requires an intentional effort on your part to make that which is abstract, conceptual, and assumed into something that is concrete, behavioral, personally relevant, and collectively shared.

2.3 | **REFLECTION**

Recall the last class that you observed that you would call well managed. Did you get the sense that the students had a clear sense of the expectations? Recall the last class that you observed that you would consider poorly managed. Did you get the sense that the students had a clear sense of the expectations?

2. Be a Source of Consistency   If the element of consistency also exists in a classroom, things will run relatively smoothly (Evertson & Emmer, 2003). Even a flawed set of strategies, if applied consistently, will result in relatively effective results. How are classroom function or dysfunction and the idea of consistency related? First, the consistency of one's actions promotes or detracts from another's overall sense of whether a person is trustworthy. Part of being trusted by students is being reliable. When a teacher's decision-making process is perceived as too subjective or random, students lose trust, and that usually translates ultimately into a loss of commitment on the part of the student. Second, a teacher who follows through and consistently implements consequences is essentially making the concrete and practical statement that the class's social contract, class rules, bill of rights, or some other similar agreement is primary and the teacher's subjective interpretation is secondary. Third, reinforcing more functional behavior is necessary when teachers are working with a student or a class to help shape behavior. In many cases, even a small amount of contradictory reinforcement can undermine your efforts. Consistency helps clarify the cause-and-effect thinking you are trying to build. Inconsistency confuses it.

2.4 | **REFLECTION**

A useful principle related to consistency is that it is not the severity of the consequence that will make it effective but the certainty. Consider the consequences that we negotiate every day. Typically we take those that are certain more seriously than those that are more severe but less likely. For example, imagine if you were a driver who had a tendency to drive faster than the speed limit. Which intervention would be more likely to modify your behavior:

- Your car was equipped with a meter that fined you a dollar for every mile your car went over the limit?

- You knew that a patrol car on the route you usually travel to work gave $1,000 tickets to a handful of speeders each year?

3. Incorporate Pedagogy That Supports Your Management Goals   If you offer students a curriculum defined by monotonous tasks, mindless busywork, and exclusively teacher-directed learning, expect problems. Students involved in passive learning often use disruptive behavior to achieve a sense of control, engagement, satisfaction, and fun. Students who are engaged, challenged, and see real value to their work will be much more interested in learning than creating problems. Students who feel successful associate that success with the source: their teacher. When they are bored and unsuccessful, they associate that experience with the teacher as well. Teachers who accumulate positive associations over time are able to use that emotional capital later when they need to make requests.

4. Create a (Basic) Needs-Satisfying Learning Environment   If students' basic needs for power, competence, belonging, freedom, and fun are not provided for by their teacher, they will find other ways to meet those needs (Glasser, 1998). And often those other means include unwanted or problem behavior (Dreikurs & Cassel, 1974; Albert, 2003). If we look only at a student's actions from within the lens of whether this student is doing what we want, we have little useful insight for a solution to the problem when that student misbehaves. However, if we examine a student's actions within the lens of what basic needs the student is attempting to meet with this behavior, then we are well on our way to making sense of the problem and identifying solutions.

When you create engaging learning activities that create a sense of psychological move-ment in the class, a good portion of the reasons for misbehavior is removed and replaced with reasons for students to invest and enjoy their time in your class. Moreover, when students experience a curriculum as culturally relevant and meaningful to their lives, they are more likely to connect with it and less likely to express their sense of disconnection in acts of passive or active resistance.

5. Facilitate the Collective Social Bonds and Social Contract Among Students   The teacher is the primary force in the room that can help students become responsible to one another and develop a set of social bonds that support the group's capacity to function. Rules answer the question: "What am I supposed to do in here?" The social contract answers the question: "What, if I did it, would help the class function more effectively and best ensure my rights as a member?" Few students feel a sense of ownership over rules. However, bonds by their very nature are owned by those who share them and therefore are much more likely to lead to responsible behavior.

6. Teach and Practice Your Management Procedures   If students do not know how to behave, listen, transition from one thing to another, interact respectfully, work cooperatively in a group, resolve conflict, process failure, line up, perform when you leave the room, and so forth, it is the teacher's responsibility to train them in these things or to stop complaining if they do them poorly. Burden (2003) suggests that we should think about teaching classroom procedures in the same way that we think about teaching any other content. Chapter Five presents strategies, which we will refer to as technical management, for promoting this area.

REFLECTION   **2.5**

When you observe a class running smoothly early in the year, ask the teacher how it got to be that way. There was likely a lot of practice and intentional effort put toward the management in the first few days.

Transformational Ideas: Moving Your Management to the Next Level. As you become more skilled at recognizing and executing the six ideas listed above, you may find yourself ready to stretch your efforts toward a more advanced set of ideas for achieving effectiveness. These next three ideas represent avenues for not only reducing behavioral dysfunction but for helping your students transform their current level of functioning into one in which they can truly thrive.

7. Intentionally Promote a Psychology of Success   Three core psychological orientations of successful learners are an internal locus of control, a sense of acceptance and belonging, and a growth-oriented orientation to learning. We will survey these in depth in Chapter Seven. As you will recognize when you examine the factors that promote or detract from one's psychology of success, much of what is accepted as common discipline practice actually acts to elicit a failure psychology in students.

8. Move from a Manager Role to a Leader Role   As you progress through the book, you will be given ideas for thinking about classroom management as not simply a process of keeping students on task and motivated but to help them become self-responsible. Glasser (1998) describes the role of teacher leader as one who sets and models high expectations, encourages students to evaluate their own work, and promotes a climate of support and empowerment that is free of coercion.

9. Create Communal Bonds and Community Within the Class   Societal bonds answer the question, "What am I required to do, and what can I expect from others?" These bonds are critical for helping reduce problems and providing a functional environment. Moreover, when students experience their class as a community, they open up a wide range of new ways that they can grow both personally and collectively (Baker, Terry, Bridges, & Winsor, 1997). Communal bonds are characterized by the question, "What can I do to make the collective better?" As students increasingly take on this mind-set, there will be a corresponding decrease in the number of classroom management problems. Moreover, problems themselves become opportunities for growth. Developing community is discussed specifically in Chapter Fifteen.

2.6 REFLECTION

In what ways do you want your teaching and classroom management to have a transformative effect on your students?

Practices That Draw Teachers Downward on the Continuum and Eventually Lead to a Greater Degree of Dysfunction. Most ineffective classroom management practices are done intentionally by thoughtful teachers and staff members. These flawed practices often can be seen to lead to a greater level of dysfunction and, in many cases, unwanted by-products, yet often they are perceived to be "working" because they have an effect that appears to be desirable; in the short term and on the surface, they seem to be getting results. But as we will examine in this section and throughout the remainder of the book, these practices (Figure 2.4) erode the core foundation of effective classroom management and lead us down the continuum of effectiveness.

If we could separate out each of the hundreds of practices that we employ in a typical day of teaching, we could assess each independently. When we put them all together, they may all seem necessary and beneficial, but when we examine each in isolation, we can better recognize which ones are getting us where we want to go and which are not. Many of the popular but ineffective strategies in fact exchange one type of dysfunction for another: problems are not getting solved; they are simply changing form. As you survey the dysfunctional strategies that follow, ask yourself, "What dysfunctional state is being traded for what other dysfunctional state?"

Practices That Lead to Higher Levels of Dysfunction 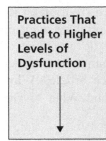	1. Trusting bribes and gimmicks to motivate students.
	2. Incorporating negative strategies, assuming they will eventually produce positive results.
	3. Using punishments or a pain-based logic in your discipline.
	4. Intermingling the personal with student performance.
	5. Involving those who were not involved.

FIGURE 2.4.   *Management Practices That Contribute to Movement Down the Continuum*

The "It Works" Fallacy

Beware of any phrase that includes the term "it works," such as: "This is the only thing that works with these students," or "Well, it works for me." In many cases, it can act as a rhetorical red herring. By definition, just about anything that anyone or any organization has done "worked" or "works" to produce some outcome. For example, a life of crime "works" for many people for a while. Trying to medicate problems temporarily "works" for the addict. For rich plantation owners, slavery "worked" in this country for 250 or so years. If we are looking to achieve greater levels of management effectiveness, the question should not be, "Does it work?" but, "Does it work to achieve a truly desirable outcome?" And even if the outcome seems to be desirable in the short term or within some narrow perspective, it may require a broader examination or a consideration of what that practice is producing in the long term to recognize its function or dysfunction. Appendix C explains this idea in more detail.

REFLECTION   2.7

Recall the last time you heard a teacher include the phrase, "That won't work with these kids." Do your own investigative research, and see if you can discover any teachers who are in fact succeeding with that strategy with similar students.

1. Trusting Bribes and Gimmicks to Motivate Students   Short-term fixes such as bribes and gimmicks may obtain an apparent desired outcome initially, but in most cases they erode the long-term quality of classroom discipline or motivation (Ryan & Deci, 2000). Bribes such as prizes for desired behavior, giving preferred activity time, rewarding students with inactivity (free time or avoiding work), stickers, stars, and devices, or gimmicks such as names on the board or colored behavioral charts seem like good ideas on the surface. But as you read further in the book, you will begin to recognize that each of these strategies actually does more long-term harm than good. Bribes, by definition, make the statement, "You need to be given something of no educational value to con you into doing something educational." Students' need for bribes will inherently grow as their intrinsic appreciation for learning will become suppressed. (In Chapter Six, we will explore how extrinsic rewards used purposefully can promote clarity of expectations as opposed to operating as bribes.)

Colored-card behavioral charts and names on the board work on the principle that public shame will modify behavior. Watching the student move his card from green to yellow after a misbehavior may be satisfying to the teacher and may even produce a repentant child in the short term but in the end, these strategies work against the development of responsible behavior and against the reduction of misbehavior. They are common and seductive, yet they create more problems than they solve. (See the online resource article "Why Not to Use Colored Cards and Names on the Board Behavioral Systems and What to Do Instead," at transformativeclassroom.com.)

2. Incorporating Negative Strategies, Assuming They Will Eventually Produce Positive Results
If you are waiting for your disappointment, complaining, lectures, guilt, shaming, put-downs, or any other negative actions (or, more accurately, passive and hostile inactions) to translate into better student behavior, it is a safe assumption that you will be waiting forever. These strategies may provide you with momentary relief from the feeling of responsibility and may even feel like action, but they are at best useless actions to which students become immune very quickly. Moreover, they are toxic and destructive influences that erode the motivation and emotional climate in the class (Shindler et al., 2009). The law of cause and effect dictates that every action will have an equal and opposite reaction. Thus, these negative actions will breed a corresponding negative response from students. This reaction exhibits itself in a wide range of manifestations of dysfunction ranging from apathy to conflict. We can't discard these practices soon enough! The remaining chapters offer positive and practical alternatives.

2.8 REFLECTION

Recall someone you knew who constantly told you what you did that was wrong. How did it make you feel? Was it motivational?

3. Using Punishments or a Pain-Based Logic in Your Discipline   The deliberate use of punishment presumes that enough pain administered to a student will result in the student's behavior change. This same logic goes for showing disapproval, put-downs, or anything else that implies the use of discomfort in an attempt to modify behavior or "teach a lesson." There are two problems with this logic. First, punishment does not do a very good job of teaching lessons, unless the lesson is how not to get caught or how to avoid the source of the punishment. Second, introducing more pain into the equation of a class environment inevitably creates a ripple effect that will manifest itself in such behavior as rebellion, displaced aggression among students, and negative identity promotion, as well as an increased level of fear and anxiety (Kauffman, 2005).

Chapter Nine examines why logical and related consequences are vastly more desirable alternatives to punishments for both changing behavior and encouraging more self-responsible thinking and actions on the part of the students.

4. Intermingling the Personal with Student Performance   It is tempting to try to encourage better student behavior with strategies such as personal praise, disappointment, affection, and withdrawal of affection. You may assume that these types of personal strategies will help you leverage your relationship with the students into better performance or behavior, but in the end, it will work against each of your goals: the relationship, the level of performance, and the quality of behavior.

When a student is given personal praise ("You are good because you have finished your work," or "I like you because you are behaving well") for desired performance or given personal criticism ("You are not good because you are not finished with your work" or "I am disappointed in you because of the way that you are acting") for undesirable performance, the line between self and actions is confused. A whole series of problems stems from this confusion. Let us briefly identify two of them. First, it results in a student who spends an unnecessary amount of time thinking about whether he has pleased the teacher rather than gaining satisfaction from the process of learning for its own sake. In the early grades, this is experienced as love and the loss of love depending on one's performance. In the later grades, this is experienced as the teacher's public comparison of students, playing favorites with those who perform better in their course or threatening to lower grades for students who "act up." Second, comingling the performance and the personal introduces an external and random or subjective logic into the class. The result is a diffusion of the clarity of classroom expectations and students' internal locus of control in which students think and act tentatively, always keeping one eye on the teacher, as opposed to developing their own sense of self-direction. This invites more misbehavior and collective dysfunction. Instead of learning to function for self-responsible reasons, students behave to please the teacher, that is, to the degree they want to please the teacher. What we achieve over time with these personalized strategies are students who behave well on days when they want to reward the teacher and not on days that they do not want to reward the teacher or have more powerful internal reasons (friends, the weather, bad moods, or meeting any of their basic needs, for example) to disregard their loyalty to them.

Assessing student participation can be a healthy and effective strategy. It can help clarify and reinforce student effort and investment in the process. But in most applications, it is used as a subtle or not-so-subtle form of manipulation. This must be done intentionally and thoughtfully or not done at all. The online resource article, "Developing and Implementing an Effective System for Assessing Behavior, Participation, or Process," available at transformativeclassroom.com, outlines a positive and effective system for assessing such areas as effort, behavior, process, and level of investment.

REFLECTION

2.9

When you observe teachers who seem to make the job look easy, do you find common attitudes among them? Conversely, when you observe teachers who seem to be perpetually unhappy and fighting against their students, do you find common ways of thinking among them?

5. Involving Those Who Were Not Involved Educator Albert Jones (2007) found that when we involve people who were not originally involved in the event of significance in discipline interactions, the result is a weakening of the disciplinary environment. A teacher who uses a lot of referrals to the office and administrative interventions makes the implicit statement that he or she cannot manage the class alone (Rausch & Skiba, 2004; Skiba & Rausch, 2006). In addition, the excessive use of office referrals has been shown to be related to a more negative school climate (Hellman & Beaton, 1986). Having parents involved in the learning process can be an invaluable asset in helping students succeed. However, teachers who outsource their own problems to the students' parents see their authority eroding (Skiba & Rausch, 2006). Certainly students sometimes must be removed from the classroom for the good of the whole, but this needs to be a last resort rather than a regular practice.

Involving those who were not involved shifts the locus of control away from where it can be most effective: the cause-and-effect relationship between the student's choices and our consequent actions. The result is a lose-lose outcome over time.

2.10   **REFLECTION**

Recall a teacher whom you have observed who sent a lot of students out of the room and regularly called parents requesting that they straighten out their children. Did that teacher have a well-managed class? Do you see a connection between the teacher's actions and the behavior of the students?

The Benefits of Moving Away from Short-Term Fixes   Commonly dysfunctional practices can be alluring and thus difficult to give up. But their use inevitably keeps us mired in the bottom quadrants of the matrix. As you work on moving away from short-term fixes, you will likely be tempted to resort to them in times of crisis. However, if you are ultimately successful in resisting their appeal and instead put your efforts into developing a set of effective long-term practices, you will increasingly notice the contrast between the outcomes of the less effective practices and the more effective replacements and recognize that the old practices were in fact keeping you stuck.

2.11   **REFLECTION**

If you are strongly attached to practices that I label dysfunctional, is that attachment related to where you learned these strategies? For many of us, these ideas may have been modeled by or suggested to us by teachers whom we respected, so it is understandable to have an attachment to them. But that is not sufficient reason to retain them and thereby keep hindering your own success. As you reflect on these practices more critically, you will likely recognize that while they may have been generally effective, there was a cost to using them.

How Your Thinking Can Promote Movement Either Up or Down the Continuum.   As Eckhart Tolle (1999) suggests, if we do not change the thinking that has created the problem-making conditions in our lives, even if our situation changes we will soon find a new set of problems to replace the old ones. Often just the way that we think can produce the experience of dysfunction, dissatisfaction, or unease. To a great extent, your classroom will be a projection of what is taking place in your mind. Your thinking can be a great ally in your efforts—or your own worst enemy.

Some types of thinking tend to lead down the effectiveness continuum toward dysfunction, and other types tend to encourage progress upward. At the heart of what will make you effective will be your ability to maintain your attention in the moment. A focus on the past will lead to blame or dwelling on what you did not like or wish you still had. A focus on the future will keep you desiring the future and wishing the present was different. This lack of acceptance of the present will make you not only less effective but less content. Taking the actions of students personally will lead to reactive behavior and make you less intentional and aware. Keeping your attention on what is important now (WIN) will lead to greater function as well as peace of mind. Feelings of negativity and disappointment are signs that you are personalizing the events in the room and have gotten lost in wallowing in the past or wishing for the future. As you become more effective at staying in the moment, keeping your attention on what you can do to improve your situation, and taking on an attitude of appreciation for your students, you will find that not only do you deal with problems more effectively, you have fewer to deal with in the first place. Chapter Sixteen examines the relationship between thinking and the quality of classroom management in more detail.

HORIZONTAL AXIS: TEACHER CENTERED VERSUS STUDENT CENTERED

The horizontal axis of the matrix represents the range of practices related to the locus of power, ownership, and fundamental goals for any class. This axis ranges from a very teacher-centered to a very student-centered orientation. Although this dichotomy represents a bit of an oversimplification, it offers a basic contrast in teaching philosophy, as you will see when we examine each of the subfactors—ownership, goals, and assumptions—in more depth.

Ownership and Power

In the teacher-centered class, the power rests primarily with the teacher, as does the ownership for decision making: the students need only follow instructions. In a student-centered class, the teacher takes on the role of guiding the students' efforts. Ownership for decisions, large and small, is given to the students whenever possible. This leaves the students with a higher burden for solving problems and making consequential choices. The question that best defines the contrast in this continuum is, "Who has their hands on the steering wheel of the class?"

Goals and Purpose

The underlying goal of a teacher-centered class is order. The underlying goal of a student-centered class is student self-reliance. In the teacher-centered class, success is defined by how well the students execute their responsibilities and the level of efficiency that exists in the learning environment. The rationale behind this thinking is that in an orderly and obedient classroom, there is less wasted time and more on-task behavior, which benefits everyone. So the view in a teacher-directed class is that the ends—students who are more productive more of the time—justify the means—teacher direction.

In the student-centered class, success is defined by the amount of personal and collective growth that students experience over the course of the term. The rationale behind this thinking is that when students are put in positions in which they must take ownership for their own learning and are expected to be self-responsible, they learn lessons that are as valuable as anything they can learn from the curriculum.

Basic Assumptions and Motivation

At the heart of a teacher-centered approach is the assumption that students must be managed because their nature is to misbehave. Basic to a student-centered approach is that students have an inherent desire to learn and improve. Therefore, in teacher-centered thinking, it is desirable to take a teacher-directed approach because the students need it. In contrast, the student-centered thinking would suppose that the reason that students might appear to need a teacher-directed class is that they have become dependent on them and are just lacking the opportunities to develop their own self-responsible nature.

As a result of these basic assumptions, a teacher-centered approach will have an inclination toward the use of extrinsic rewards. This approach finds rewards and punishments a very effective way to change behavior. Since the result is often more desirable behavior more of the time, the ends support the use of the means. A student-centered classroom resists the use of extrinsic rewards and punishments and views them as vehicles that rob students of their intrinsic motivation. This approach sets out to create a learning environment that is inherently motivating and relies on tapping into students' interests and meeting students' basic needs.

2.12 | **REFLECTION**

Where would you place your management orientation along the horizontal continuum? Are you more inclined toward a more student-centered or a more teacher-centered approach to classroom management?

THE RESULTING MATRIX: FOUR APPROACHES TO MANAGEMENT

When we position one axis across the other, we view four quadrants that characterize four very different approaches to classroom management and teaching in general. Throughout this book, each particular management approach or style is referred by its style number, 1 to 4, to represent each of the four quadrants of the matrix. Those at the top are 1-Style and 2-Style, and those at the bottom are 3-Style and 4-Style. Numbers are used only to distinguish quadrants, not to assign value. The orientation that is most your style and best for you will be left to you to decide: the 4-Style or dominator, the 3-Style or enabler, the 2-Style or conductor, or the 1-Style or facilitator. However, my intent is to persuade you very early in the book (if you ever needed persuading or have not been persuaded by now) that a 1- or 2-Style orientation will produce profoundly greater degrees of success for both you and your students.

As far as which orientation—2-Style or 1-Style—is more effective, I ask you to judge for yourself the approach that better fits your own personal teaching style and goals. A sound, healthy classroom with a fully functioning set of rules, responsibilities, and shared expectations can be achieved with either a 2-Style or a 1-Style management approach. But there are advantages and disadvantages to each orientation (see Figure 2.5).

4-Style or Dominator Management Approach

The essence of the 4-Style orientation is the teacher as boss. The teacher who uses this style feels compelled to dominate by both overt and covert means. Students in the class see quickly that they have only two choices: be obedient or rebel. Although there appears to be a high degree of intentionality to the 4-Style management practice due to the authoritarian display of power, a closer examination reveals much less intention in reality. Because the teacher

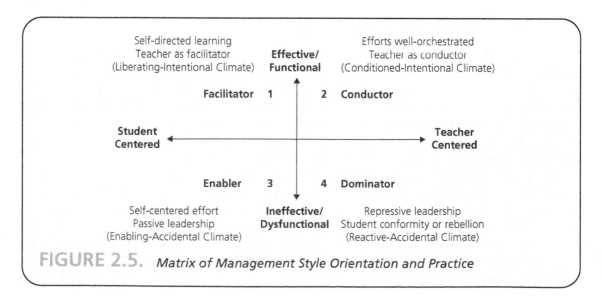

FIGURE 2.5. *Matrix of Management Style Orientation and Practice*

acts so frequently out of a reactive mode, students are seldom fully sure what to expect. The mood of the teacher has a great deal to do with the climate of the class on any particular day. Moreover, the 4-Style manager is typically a fan of extrinsic rewards, "sit and get" teaching methods, and the use of grading for the purpose of coercion.

At the heart of this management approach is pain-based logic. To attain his or her desired outcomes, the teacher resorts to the delivery of pain to students in the form of punishments, threats, anger, public humiliation, victimizing humor, putting names on the board, and shaming. As a result, the classroom takes on a combative and hostile climate. As the pain is exchanged between the teacher and the student, an increasing number of negative side effects occur, including a decrease in motivation, a lack of trust, an emotionally unsafe climate, and various acts of displaced aggression. An in-depth examination of the 4-Style approach and how teachers drawn to this style can move up the continuum is provided in the online resource article, "Moving Up the Teaching Style Continuum from the 4-Style Dominator to a 2-Style or 1-Style Approach," available at transformativeclassroom.com.

3-Style or Enabler Management Approach

The defining characteristic of the 3-Style manager is passivity. As a result, these teachers commonly experience perpetual disappointment that the students are letting them down. Teachers using this approach operate under the faulty assumption that if they make enough reasonable verbal appeals to students (rather than taking deliberate action or delivering meaningful consequences), the students will respond at some point with functional behavior. In most cases, teachers employing a 3-Style approach are acting out of the rejection of what they see as the unhealthy authoritarian 4-Style manager. Yet what they produce is often just as accidental and chaotic as what they are trying to avoid. And commonly, when 3-Style managers become too frustrated with their students' dysfunction and lack of respect, they react with episodes of hostility, which brings them even more inner conflict.

The fundamental problem is that teachers using a 3-Style approach preach self-direction and internal motivation yet do little to promote either. They confuse the need for structure with being controlling, which they see as objectionable. These teachers are typically well intentioned, but inherent in this approach is a lack of courage to lead. Their commitment to promoting student interests is noble, but over time, students learn that they can act as they please. As a result, anarchy and a high degree of social Darwinism become the defining qualities for the peer relations. Without intending to, teachers who use a 3-Style approach promote a rather unsafe emotional climate—thus their label: enablers. Cooperative learning and engaging hands-on activities that are the preference of the 3-Style approach increasingly descend into playtime and a chance for students to goof off as a result of a lack of clear direction and purpose.

REFLECTION

2.13

When you reflect on the easygoing and permissive 3-Style teachers that you have observed, what happened to their affect when things begin to go bad? Did the teacher stay easygoing? Did that permissive attitude translate into emotional safety for the students in the class? In other words, did you find that when the teacher did not worry about taking action, it translated into students' not worrying about what might happen to them?

Moving from a 3- to a 1-Style Orientation

If you have a strong commitment to a student-centered approach but realize that your efforts have led you to what you would characterize as a 3-Style approach, there is hope. And of all those who choose to pick up this book, you may be the one with the most to gain. It is likely that you have felt a temptation to adopt a 2-Style approach, yet the encouragement of others who find success with a more teacher-centered approach does not leave you entirely convinced or comfortable at abandoning your student-centered principles. You have likely had to endure a great deal of disparagement. No one gets criticized as much as the 3-Style teacher does. Because of what appears to be a very active (albeit hostile) approach by 4-Style teachers, people usually leave them alone. But for people like you, they typically feel freer to give advice.

Improvement of your situation begins with an examination of the essence of the vertical axis: intentionality and internality. Don't confuse taking action with being controlling. As you explore the coming chapters, you will discover how much planning and deliberate effort must go into helping students become self-directed. The methodological pathway is spelled out in detail in the following chapters.

2-Style or Conductor Management Approach

The most popular classroom management training in the past few years has been defined by the 2-Style orientation. Canter (1992), Wong and Wong (1991), Jones (2001), and many others would best be described as proponents of a teacher-centered approach. To characterize this style, Canter provides the useful term *assertive discipline* to distinguish an effective classroom manager from the passive (3-Style) or hostile (4-Style) approaches, which they identify as largely ineffective. The assertive 2-Style "conductor" builds his or her approach on logical consequences rather than personal attacks and negativity.

The conductor takes an intentional approach to management. A successful 2-Style approach begins early in the year with a period of training and education in rules, procedures, and consequences. As if under the command of an orchestra conductor, the class is trained to respond to directions in an efficient manner. The structure in the 2-Style classroom is evident. It is built on consistency and clarity. Out of this structure, the goals of a productive learning environment, respect, accountability, and positive relationships are constructed. The 2-Style classroom includes a heavy reliance on encouragement and rewards. The pedagogy in this approach tends to lean toward direct instruction but includes multiple methods that have been demonstrated to obtain results.

1-Style or Facilitator Management Approach

Relatively few teachers choose to take the path of the facilitator, or 1-Style approach. The ultimate goal of this approach is to create a class that is self-directed and manages itself. These teachers understand that to do this will take time, but they are willing to live with a little immediate unpredictability in order to achieve their long-term goals. These teachers' management goals are defined by an intentional promotion of the students' intrinsic motivation and sense of personal responsibility. Students in the 1-Style classroom grow in their ability to answer both the "What are we doing?" and the "Why are we doing it?" questions. An implicit understanding of community expectations is cultivated. To achieve this end, the 1-Style teacher makes a concerted attempt to help students recognize the value of functional and responsible behavior.

The 1-Style approach places emphasis on the process of learning over end products and on personal growth rather than the attainment of rewards or the students' success in relative comparison to other students. This orientation values long-term student empowerment over what might be considered methods that appear to be working in the short term. The goal is not merely to have the student appear to be on task, but to know that the learning is building toward a positive orientation toward learning itself. The pedagogical approaches that define the 1-Style orientation are typically constructivist, collaborative, and problem based. (See Figure 2.6 for a comparison of the four styles.)

REFLECTION   2.14

As you reflect on the differences between the 1-Style and 2-Style teaching approaches, it can be useful to bring in the metaphor of music. Which type of music would best characterize each style? For this exercise, I argue that jazz fits best as a 1-Style form of music and classical fits best as a 2-Style. Can either type of music be produced in a way that is masterful and sounds entirely effective and coordinated as well as beautiful? Certainly. So what does it take to play great classical music? Most likely we would need sheet music, well-trained musicians, a conductor, and practice.

What does it take to make great jazz music? Can it be done without a conductor? Yes. Can it be done without sheet music? Yes. Could four expert jazz musicians who had never met get in a room and play beautiful music? Very likely. So what is necessary to make that happen? It is the knowledge on the part of the musicians of how to play jazz—the "rules," so to speak.

As you compare the basis of 1-Style and 2-Style management, you might consider whether you want your classes to be well-conducted orchestras or a collection of students who know how to function in a coordinated manner without a conductor.

REFLECTION   2.15

Recall the most recent teacher you observed. Which style best characterizes his or her management approach?

Comparing the Advantages of a 2-Style Versus a 1-Style Management Approach

As you reflect on your own personal values and envisioning what you want to accomplish in your classroom, you may find yourself being drawn more to the 2-Style or 1-Style approach to management. Each approach is developed over the next several chapters, often side by side. Table 2.1 outlines a brief list of the advantages of each orientation.

REFLECTION   2.16

What would you anticipate to be the forms of resistance to using a 1-Style approach in a school characterized by a 4-Style environment? The experience of Erin Gruwell depicted in the movie and the book *Freedom Writers* (Gruwell, 1999) may be useful to consider as you reflect. The movie chronicled her efforts to instill a love of reading and writing in a group of students who did not originally value those activities, and resisted her efforts at first, but eventually became passionate writers.

	Student Centered	Teacher Centered
Effective/Intentional	**1-Style Approach** • **Facilitator** • Goal: self-directed students • Motivation: internal, build sense of self-efficacy • Clear boundaries • Build students' collective responsibility • Answers "Why are we doing this?" • Long-term goals (may be more challenging at first, but eventually becomes self-directed) • *Our class*	**2-Style Approach** • **Conductor** • Goal: on-task behavior • Motivation: external, positive reinforcement • Clear consequences • Build students' collective efficiency • Answers "What is expected?" • Short-term goals (the management should be in good shape by the second week) • *My class*
Ineffective/Accidental	**3-Style Approach** • **Enabler** • Goal: keep students happy • Motivation: student interests • Unclear boundaries • Students increasingly self-centered • Chaotic energy • Goals are vague (management problems happen early and are still happening at end of the term) • *The students*	**4-Style Approach** • **Dominator** • Goal: let students know who is boss • Motivation: avoid punishment • Arbitrary punishments • Students increasingly immune to coercion • Negative energy • Goals is to break students' will (students respond out of fear, but slowly increase hostility and rebellion) • *Those students*

FIGURE 2.6. *Key Characteristics of the Four Management Orientations*

TABLE 2.1. Advantages of the Intentional Management Approaches

Advantages of the 1-Style Approach	Advantages of the 2-Style Approach
Working toward a self-regulating system eventually.	Can get functioning system in place relatively quickly.
Increasingly empowered students over time.	Clearly understood teacher and student roles likely.
Promotes a lot of learning and insight into the skills necessary to participate in a democratic system.	Relatively simple to repeat each year and export to other teachers' classrooms.
The implicit structure becomes evident (and impressive) to others who are able to spend time in the class and appreciate the intention.	The overt structure of the system is readily apparent to administrators, parents, and other teachers.
Leads to high levels of teacher and student (needs) satisfaction.	Low stress on the part of teacher and students related to low ambiguity and chaos.

Can I Incorporate Practices from All Four Approaches?

Technically you can use practices that fit into any number of orientations; however, there is a cost. First, incorporating practices from the 3- or 4-Style orientation will have a destructive effect on a 2-Style- or 1-Style-based classroom plan and lead the user down the effectiveness continuum. Often without being aware of it, a very sound 2-Style or 1-Style teacher will use 4-Style orientation practices such as punishments, unhealthy praise, or public shaming (especially in the form of putting names on the board), and also without knowing it shift down the matrix, diminishing their ability to be more successful with their students.

Students cannot articulate in most cases that the use of particular practices feels contradictory and operates to send mixed messages, but they certainly experience it. And often when teachers are relatively likable and successful with their intentional forms of practice, it is difficult to measure the damage that 3-Style and 4-Style practices inflict on their classes.

Many teachers say, "I cannot decide between a 2-Style or 1-Style approach. Can I use some of each?" Incorporating a little from one and a little from the other is certainly workable. And certainly the main consideration in the process is to move the practice upward on the vertical axis. However, if you mix approaches, you may be sending mixed messages. A common example of a mixed-orientation message is allowing students to be self-directed in some cases and in other similar situations simply giving orders. This can send the message that sometimes you trust them and sometimes you do not. At first glance, this is probably how most teachers genuinely feel toward students. So what is the problem? Take a moment to reflect from the perspective of the student. What do you hear in that message? Is it trust? Who is steering the class? The students need to be clear as to your answer, or they will demonstrate their frustration. As you progress through this book, you will encounter ideas that will facilitate your decision to move in one direction or the other.

CONCLUSION

All teachers can have an effective teaching style. However, an effective classroom requires being intentional about the practices to employ as well as becoming self-aware of our own attitudes and orientation toward teaching and our students. Some teachers will be most comfortable pursuing the path of becoming a master 2-Style teacher. For others, a 1-Style will be the goal. Most important, the effort should be to move up the effectiveness continuum toward those practices and thinking that will lead to greater levels of function.

WHAT TO EXPECT IN THE REMAINDER OF THE BOOK

Look for references to the management style orientation matrix throughout the coming chapters. Many chapters incorporate the lens of the contrasting approaches of the 2-Style and 1-Style orientation to their topic areas. Chapter Fifteen is devoted to how to successfully create the 1-Style classroom.

In the next chapter, we examine the implicit level of the classroom environment. Before we begin to examine strategies and practices that will help you achieve the transformative classroom, we need to examine the implicit factors within the classroom that can support your efforts or hold you back.

Journal Reflections

1. What style of classroom management is most appealing to you at this time: 1, 2, 3, or 4? Why? Was the choice an easy or complicated one?

2. Does the school in which you currently work (or think that you may work in) align with your style choice? Do you see areas where there may be resistance or support?
3. Discuss two practices that you feel that you need to do more of (or include in your plan), and two that you feel that you need to do less of.
4. Have you considered the effects of your thinking on your teaching? What are areas of change that you feel might assist you in the process of growth as a teacher?

Activities

1. Match the following teacher behaviors (A–D) in the right column with one of the four teaching styles (1–4) in the left column (the answers are at the end of this section):

1-Style facilitator	Phrases that might be heard
	A. When are you ever going to learn?
	B. How are we doing so far?
	C. I like the way that you did that.
	D. I told you to stop that.
2-Style conductor	Possible response to misbehavior
	A. Ignores student
	B. Asks student to come up with a plan to cease the behavior
	C. Gives consequence
	D. Gives detention
3-Style enabler	Most common choice of instruction
	A. Effective direct instruction
	B. Lectures and tests
	C. Open-ended assignments with few guidelines
4-Style dominator	D. Projects with clear rubrics

---

2. In small groups, share with the other members of the group how you would classify and describe the most recent four teachers you have observed.
3. Discuss the following scenario in small groups (or reflect on it individually). Steven is a new teacher who wants to create a 1-Style classroom. Many of the teachers and the general culture at Steven's school would best be classified as 4-Style management. What do you see as Steven's challenges? What can he do? Will he need to conform to the culture of the school, or can he find ways to manage in the manner he feels is best?
4. Examine one classroom. In your analysis, what practices does the teacher need to do more of, and what does he or she need to do less of? Explain to the class or your small group how the problems in the class you have observed were in your analysis related to the practices of the teacher.

Answers to Activity 1: Phrase: A-4, B-1, C-2, D-3; Misbehavior: A-3, B-1, C-2, D-4; Instruction: A-2, B-4, C-3, D-1.

REFERENCES

Albert, L. (2003). *Cooperative discipline: Teacher's handbook*. Upper Saddle River, NJ: Prentice Hall.
Baker, J., Terry, T., Bridges, R., & Winsor, A. (1997). Schools as caring communities. A relational approach to school reform. *School Psychology Review*, 26(4), 586–602.
Bluestein, J. (1999). *Twenty-first century discipline: Teaching students responsibility and self-management*. Belmont, CA: Fearon.
Burden, P. (2003). *Classroom management: Creating a successful learning community*. Hoboken, NJ: Wiley.

Canter, L. (1992). *Lee Canter's assertive discipline: Positive behavior management for today's classroom*. Los Angeles: Lee Canter and Associates

Dreikurs, R., & Cassel, P. (1974). *Discipline without tears*. New York: Hawthorn Books,

Evertson, C., & Emmer, E. (2003). *Classroom management for secondary teachers*. Needham Heights, MA: Allyn & Bacon,

Gettinger, M., & Kohler, K. M. (2006). Process-outcome approaches to classroom management and effective teaching. In C. M. Evertson & C. S. Weinstein (Eds.), *Handbook of classroom management* (pp. 73–95). Mahwah, NJ: Erlbaum.

Glasser, W. (1998). *The quality school: Managing students without coercion*. New York: HarperCollins.

Greenwood, G. (1990). Relationships between four teacher efficacy belief patterns and selected teacher characteristics. *Journal of Research and Development in Education*, *23*(2), 102–106.

Gruwell, E. (1999). *The Freedom Writers diary: How a teacher and 150 teens used writing to change themselves and the world around them*. New York: Random House.

Guskey, T., & Passaro, P. (1994). Teacher efficacy: A study of construct dimensions. *American Educational Research Journal*, *31*(3), 627–643.

Harris, A. (1998). Effective teaching: A review of the literature. *School Leadership and Management*, *18*(2), 169–183.

Hellman, D. A., & Beaton, S. (1986). The pattern of violence in urban public schools: The influence of school and community. *Journal of Research in Crime and Delinquency*, *23*, 102–127.

Henson, R. (2001). A reliability generalization study of the Teacher Efficacy Scale and related instruments. *Educational and Psychological Measurement*, *61*(3), 404–420.

Hines, C., Cruickshank, D., & Kennedy, J. (1985). Teacher clarity and its relationship to student achievement and satisfaction. *American Educational Research Journal*, *22*, 87–99.

Jones, A. (2007, March). *Effective classroom management*. Paper presented at the Annual LAUSD Support Providers Training Workshop, California State University, Los Angeles.

Jones, F. (2001). *Tools for teaching*. Santa Cruz, CA: Fred Jones and Associates.

Kauffman, J. M. (2005). How we prevent the prevention of emotional and behavioral difficulties in education. In P. Clough, P. Garner, J. Pardeck, & F. Yuen (Eds.), *Handbook of emotional and behavioral difficulties in education* (pp. 429–440). Thousand Oaks, CA: Sage.

Pajares, F. (1992). Teachers' beliefs and educational research: Cleaning up a messy construct. *Review of Educational Research*, *62*(3), 307–332.

Rausch, M. K., & Skiba, R. J. (2004). *Unplanned outcomes: Suspensions and expulsions in Indiana*. Center for Evaluation and Education Policy. Retrieved August 23, 2008, from http://ceep.indiana.edu.

Richardson, V., & Fallona, C. (2001). Classroom management as method and manner. *Journal of Curriculum Studies*, *33*(6), 705–728.

Ryan, R., & Deci, E. (2000). When rewards compete with nature: The undermining of intrinsic motivation and self-regulation. In C. Sansome & J. M. Harackiewicz (Eds.), *Intrinsic and extrinsic motivation: The search for optimal motivation and performance* (pp 13–54). Orlando, FL: Academic Press.

Shindler, J., Jones, A., Taylor C., & Cadenas, H. (2004, April). *Does seeking to create a better classroom climate lead to student success and/or improved teaching? Examining the relationship between pedagogical choices and classroom climate in urban secondary schools*. Paper presented at the annual meeting of the American Educational Research Association, San Diego.

Shindler, J., Jones, A., Williams, A., & Taylor, C. (2009, January). *Exploring below the surface: School climate assessment and improvement as the key to bridging the achievement gap*. Paper presented at the annual meeting of the Washington State Office of the Superintendent of Public Instruction, Seattle.

Skiba, R. J., & Rausch, K. (2006). Zero tolerance, suspension, and expulsion: Questions of equity and effectiveness. In C. M. Evertson & C. S. Weinstein (Eds.), *Handbook of classroom management* (pp. 1063–1088). Mahwah, NJ: Erlbaum.

Tolle, E. (1999). *The power of now*. Vancouver, Canada: Namaste Publishing.

Wong, H., & Wong, R. (1991). *First days of school: How to be an effective teacher*. Mountain View, CA: Wong Publications.

Yoon, J. (2002). Teacher characteristics as predictors of teacher-student relationships: Stress, negative affect, and self-efficacy. *Social Behavior and Personality: An International Journal*, *30*(5), 485–493.

PART

2

Exploring the Nature of Classroom Dynamics and Student Motivation

3

Exploring the Fundamental Components of the Classroom Environment

In This Chapter

- Explicit versus implicit levels of the classroom
- We teach who we are
- Social frames
- Emotional bank accounts
- Teacher-student interaction language
- Power
- Implicit expectations
- Social learning model

Every school and every person inside the many classrooms exists as its own unique environment. It has its own feel, tone, and the way things are done. Although much of students' overall experience comes as a result of intended actions and plans, a substantial portion of what makes up the overall climate and experience of a class could be termed its implicit level or hidden curriculum (Eisner, 1984; Jackson, 1968). Haralambos (1991) defines the hidden curriculum as "consisting of those things pupils learn through the experience of attending school rather than the stated educational objectives of such institutions" (p. 1). The intentional or explicit level of schooling is made up of such factors as the stated rules and procedures, explicit expectations, and intended curriculum. By contrast, the implicit and commonly unconscious level is made up of unwritten rules, implicit expectations, social systems, the way power is manifested, and, to a great degree, the teacher simply "teaching who he is." In this chapter, we explore the nature and impact of this implicit and largely unconscious level of the classroom experience.

REFLECTION

3.1

What is your reaction to the idea that there are implicit-level factors operating in the classroom: "So what? So, things happen that are not planned," or "I don't understand them, so they can't be very important." As you proceed through this chapter, you will come to appreciate the power of this level of the classroom experience better. And as it is with natural laws, they operate whether we understand them or not.

THE CLASSROOM ENVIRONMENT

To begin to make sense of this dimension below the surface of any class, it might help to think about a trip down the hall of a local school. Let's imagine that we choose to examine three comparable classrooms, once at the start of the school year and then again a couple of months later. If the classes are truly comparable (for example, they are the same grade or subject area), it is likely that the three classes look very similar at the beginning of the term. As with any other new group, the students will behave in a manner consistent with their experience and past expectations. But if we return in two months, it is very likely that the three classes will now be dramatically different from one another.

3.2	REFLECTION

Observe a set of classes at the start of the year and then a few weeks later. What are the differences? How would you explain the causes? Is it the students, or the teacher?

What is the explanation for the differences? We could probably conclude the following:

- In the long term, the experience of the students in any classroom (in most cases) will have more to do with implicit factors than the explicitly stated wishes of the teacher. This experience is constructed and negotiated over time through the continuous interactions of the teacher and students.

- The environment will be defined primarily by the teacher and only secondarily by the students.

- The degree to which a class is more or less "intentional" as opposed to "accidental" is strongly related to the degree to which the teacher understands and is aware of the implicitly operating aspects of the classroom environment.

Creating the Weather in the Classroom

As Haim Ginott suggests, teachers "create the weather" in the classroom:

I have come to the frightening conclusion that I am the decisive element in the classroom. It is my personal approach that creates the climate. It's my daily mood that makes the weather.

As a teacher, I possess a tremendous power to make a child's life miserable or joyous. I can be a tool of torture, or an instrument of inspiration. I can humiliate, or humor, hurt or heal.

In all situations, it is my response that decides whether a crisis will be escalated or de-escalated and a child is humanized or dehumanized [p. x].

If we were to classify the various factors within any class, there are those that are primarily explicit, such as the curriculum, the rules, and the explicit expectations, and those that are

Degree to Which Area Can Be Concretely Evidenced	Component of the Overall Classroom Reality	Relative Level of Awareness
Explicit level: The factors in management that are obvious and concrete.	• Explicitly expressed and promoted expectations • Intentional messages sent to students • Explicit rules and procedures (technical management) • Class social contract and boundaries • Planned curriculum	Mostly deliberate and overt Processed and demonstrated on a conscious level[a]
Implicit level: The "hidden curriculum"—the factors in the class that are below the surface, but most often define the majority of the classroom environment.	• Social frames • How power is manifested • Emotional bank account • Teacher language • Teachers teaching "who they are" and what they value (for example, default tendencies, self-image, parent messages worldview) • Implicit expectations	Potentially above the level of awareness and managed intentionally Potentially below the level of awareness and operating accidentally

FIGURE 3.1. *The Explicit and Implicit Levels of the Classroom Environment*

[a] *The methods practiced on this explicit level can lead up or down the effectiveness continuum depending on how sound they are.*

more implicit, such as the social frames, the way power is manifested, and to a great extent the teacher teaching "who he or she is." (See Figure 3.1.)

The rest of this book is devoted to examining how to create an intentional classroom. But before we move into exploring how to achieve results on a mostly explicit level, it will be valuable to explore how to be more effective and aware at the implicit level. Although the typical class functions with a substantial lack of awareness of the underlying factors on this implicit level and how they operate, it does not have to be so. The more that you are able to develop an awareness of your classroom's implicit-level factors and take an intentional approach toward making them work to the benefit of everyone in the class, the less accidental and more functional your class will be.

EXAMINING THE IMPLICIT LEVEL OF THE OVERALL CLASSROOM ENVIRONMENT

An examination of the most fundamental components of the implicit level of the classroom environment begins with us, the teachers—teaching "who we are." This will be followed by how our words affect the class, the social frames that operate in the class, the principle of the emotional bank account, the way that power is manifested, and the many ways that social or indirect learning takes place in any learning environment.

We Teach Who We Are

It is said that "we teach who we are." If we recall our years of schooling and reflect on what we learned in each class, we would have to agree that as much of what we learned was related to who our teachers were as it was to what we studied. Recall the array of teachers you have had in the past. What do you remember about them? What stands out in your memory? A reasonable guess is that what you remember is more related to who they were as people than what they were trying to teach you. In fact, who they were taught you a lot. In some cases, it was how to be a good person or the kind of teacher you wish to be, or in some cases it was qualities that you have tried to avoid exhibiting and what not to do as a teacher.

Our teachers taught us something about being human. Some teachers we respected, and some we felt sorry for. Some inspired us to learn, and some seemed to us to be bent on killing whatever interest we had in learning. In a very tangible way, we are continuously teaching our values, culture, biases, politics, cognitive style, and a whole lifetime of mental conditioning in addition to the intended curriculum. No matter what we want our students to care about and what we want them to focus on, the truth is that they are continuously learning from who we are—or, more accurately, what our conditioning expresses about us when we teach.

Becoming Self-Aware of Our Default Tendencies and Unconscious Conditioning

If we are unaware of our default preferences or mental conditioning or unconscious tendencies, then we are essentially unaware of a whole host of things that we are teaching to our students. And we are each in our own way very predictable. We have tendencies, biases, values, and patterns that significantly influence our teaching. Is this a problem? The answer is usually yes. Commonly, unconsciousness leads to behavior we regret later. The more aware we are, the less predictable we are, and the less aware, the more predictable we are. So what is the problem with being a product of our conditioning and hardwired preferences that lead to predictable and knee-jerk reactive tendencies? The short answer is that our students are penalized. The long answer will become increasingly apparent as you read further into this book.

Most classroom management problem conditions are manufactured by the teacher. And that teacher usually has good intentions. So if most of us have good intentions but still create endless problems for ourselves, it follows that good intentions alone must not be sufficient. Successful teaching that includes effective classroom management must require a substantial level of self-awareness. Moreover, the higher the quality of our self-awareness is, the more focused our intentions can become. There are countless domains of thinking and behavior that are useful to become more aware of, and as we progress, we will discuss some of them. In this section, we focus on three of those areas: self-concept, cognitive style, and worldview.

Self-Concept. If we like ourselves, does that count for something? Conversely, if we don't really like ourselves or we feel uncomfortable in our own skins, what difference does that make to our teaching performance? The fact is that in many subtle and unconscious ways, we are perpetually teaching our self-concept and level of self-respect. Moreover, research shows that how we feel about and ultimately treat our students will inevitably be a reflection of how we feel about ourselves (Friedman & Farber, 1992). We will be better teachers if we like our students. If we feel good on the inside, it will show on the outside in a thousand ways that we may not even be aware of.

In addition, if we like and demonstrate a love of learning and enthusiasm for the material we are teaching, it will rub off on students. Cabello and Terrell (1994) found that when teachers were more enthusiastic about what they were teaching, students learned more.

REFLECTION

Recall the teachers who have engendered the highest amount of love and respect from you. Were they the teachers with the largest personalities? Or the teachers who thought they were the coolest? Or was it a teacher who expressed a care or respect for you as a person?

Cognitive Style. Research into cognitive preference (also called personality type, learning style, or temperament type) demonstrates that teachers' values are strongly predicted by their type on various cognitive dimensions. In a very real way we teach our cognitive type. Myers, McCauley, Quenk, and Hammer (1998) found that if teachers did nothing to alter their teaching—that is, they resorted to their default tendencies—the students who were less similar to them by cognitive preference were less successful, enjoyed the class less, and received lower grades, while the students who were more like them felt more successful and received better grades. Conversely, if the teachers were aware of their own cognitive style default tendencies and actively worked to be more responsive to the diversity of student needs, the students who differed from them in cognitive type approached the levels of success and enjoyment of students who were like them.

This is another dimension of teaching in which unconsciousness leads to the penalization of students. And just as we penalize students who are culturally different from us when we are not aware of our biases, we penalize students who are cognitively different from us when our lack of awareness leads to our defaulting to our hardwired tendencies. The online resource article, "Examining the Relationship Between Learning Styles and Classroom Management," available at transformativeclassroom.com, provides more information in this area.

REFLECTION

Recall a teacher in whose class you thrived. If you were to identify his or her cognitive style, would you say that you were similar? Do you think that had anything to do with the affinity and comfort you felt?

Examining Our Worldview. What are our basic assumptions about young people? What motivates them? What do they need? What characterizes the world that they are entering? Our answers to these questions will have a profound effect on how we teach (Fallona & Richardson, 2006). Moreover, it is likely that our worldview defines how we approach classroom management. If we have a dark view of human nature, we will expect the worst from our students. If we have a hopeful view of human nature, we will maintain faith in our students.

This book does not endeavor to answer the questions of human nature, but it is a certainty that what you believe to be true about the basic nature of your students will define your classroom. The classes of teachers who maintain a hostile view of the world take on qualities of coldness, competitiveness, and antagonism. The idea behind their basic philosophy is that if it's a cruel world out there, we might as well get used to it. The result is the penalization of the students in this type of class.

If our job is to create high-functioning students, we will not get there unless we create a school world that meets their personal and learning needs and fosters a psychology of success (see Chapter Seven). Moreover, we must recognize that "the real world" is created each day in our classroom. We are manufacturing the future by every act that we give rise to as a teacher.

Examining the Use of the Term *Real World*

Frequently we hear teachers refer to "the real world," as in, "That idea sounds nice, but it would not work in the real world." Initially it sounds as if it is coming from the voice of experience. Teachers who say this have been around the proverbial teaching block and can attest to how the "real world" works. But just as with the term "it works" (discussed in Chapter Two), we need to listen carefully to the messages beneath the words. It may seem harmless on the surface, but in essence, we are being instructed to adopt someone else's worldview. And it is a convincing rhetorical device. If someone states, "Boy, my students have a hard time being honest in class," we might think, "Gosh, that teacher is struggling with that issue in her class. Good luck to her." However, if someone declares, "In the real world, people will lie anytime they get the chance," we can come away convinced that it is a fact and, moreover, that we should stop trusting our current students and any of those we teach in the future.

In fact, the real world is rarely defined by adages that include the phrase "real world"; the use of "real world" usually indicates a jaded worldview that is fundamentally dysfunctional; and it is likely that students are paying the price for behavior that is informed by this view. We examine this term in detail in Appendix D.

3.5

REFLECTION

Recall the last time you heard a teacher make a suggestion to you that included the phrase "the real world." What was the context? In your estimation, what did the suggestion assume about the nature of students?

Teacher Language and Message Subtext

It has been said that words define our reality (Buzzelli & Johnston, 2002; Devitt & Sterelny, 1999). Herbert Kohl (2002) suggests that everything that is said and how it is said is significant and that "small things—comments, questions, responses, phrases, tone—often make a big difference in students' attitudes, not merely toward their teacher, but toward what their teacher teaches" (p. 145). The use of language in the classroom is a powerful influence and defines the very nature of how we make meaning.

This idea may sound rather abstract, so examine the language in any classroom. As you listen and observe, ask yourself these questions: "What is the purpose of the language used?" "What emotional climate is being created by the use of the language?" "Is the language used consistent with the nonverbal messages being sent?" In essence, you are asking what the subtext of the speech is. When you examine the words spoken by each of the three teachers represented in Exercise 3.1, assume that they all possess a desire for roughly the same explicit outcomes. Yet as you read their words, would you predict that their language exchanges would produce similar classroom environments?

EXERCISE 3.1

First, examine the following teacher language patterns. Second, classify and then develop a label for the types of language that are occurring in each case. Use any words you feel best for your labels. Next, as you reflect on each set of phrases, try to characterize the classroom climate that would be created with the use of each of these hypothetical language patterns.

Teacher A

- (After handing out an assignment) "I don't want to see all the sloppy papers that I saw the last time."

- "Stop talking or I will . . ."

- (After a wrong answer) "No, you guys aren't getting this."

- (Sarcastic responses on a regular basis)

- "I told you guys to get to work."

- "When are you ever going to learn?"

I'd label this language _____.
The effect on the classroom climate would be _____.

Teacher B

- (Gives directions but students keep talking) "Listen to me!"

- "There is too much noise in the room."

- (After directions are given, and students were not paying attention, and they do not do what the teacher wants) "Okay, I told you to keep the glue in the box until you get your paper ready" (students are still not listening) "Put the glue away, I said!"

I'd label this language _____.
The effect on the classroom climate would be _____.

Teacher C

- "Take a look at this group; see how they _____. That is a good example of the process we are looking for."

- "I know it is almost lunchtime, but let's stay with it for fifteen more minutes."

- (After some students were not attentive to directions) "Someone was talking, so I think I will start the directions over; I need 100 percent attention."

- (After an incorrect answer) "Okay, you seemed to be doing _____ and that would be right for that process, but what we were looking for was _____. Given that, do you want to try again?"

- (After a poor effort) "We have got to do a better job with this than last time. We need to get this stuff down by this week. We will need to have it for the test next week and for your projects."

I'd label this language _____.
The effect on the classroom climate would be _____.

Before we explore the language of each teacher, it is useful to recall that you did not know a great deal about any of the three teachers depicted in the exercise. You had only a small number of words from each of their classes. What could possibly be inferred from such a small amount of information? In fact, you inferred a great deal, and your assessment was quite likely right on the mark.

When asked to characterize the words of teacher A, you probably used terms such as *negative, hostile, condescending, antagonistic,* and *threatening.* Also you might have described the climate with words such as *combative, hostile, depressed,* and *nonmotivational.* If so, these would be accurate assessments. The climate in this class was quite antagonistic. Some students chose to withdraw, while others chose to engage the teacher in a power struggle. If we were to classify this teacher's language on the management style matrix, it would fall into the category of a 4-Style.

If we examine some of the phrases more closely, we can recognize why it was not difficult to see the eventual negative environment that the teacher created:

- "Stop talking or I will . . ." is a classic example of a threat. In essence, a threat sends two messages that never motivate students to learn: "I am hostile and unsafe" and "I am too weak or lazy to take any meaningful action."

- "I don't want to see all the sloppy papers that I saw the last time." This phrase is an example of chronicling failure—that is, the teacher points out to the students their past inadequate performance in a weak attempt to promote positive behavior in the future. This is very common, but like many other forms of negative recognition, it has no positive value. It is past oriented, does nothing to help support future behavior, and is weak and hostile.

- "When are you ever going to learn?" This phrase is a put-down. Like threats, put-downs demonstrate that the teacher is experiencing feelings of hostility yet is too weak to take constructive action. Even when said in jest, put-downs have a price. Humor can be a wonderful asset, but victimizing humor can work against building a safe emotional climate.

The descriptors that you used to characterize the language of teacher B likely included words such as *passive, timid, anxious, chaotic, frustrated,* and *ineffective.* Teacher B's words reflect a distinct lack of a sense of legitimate authority. Like teacher A, this teacher puts misguided faith in the use of negative recognition to achieve results. The passive nature of this teacher's approach would best be classified as 3-Style. The passivity can be seen through teacher B's words. "Listen to me!" could best be described as a plea. It implies a lack of an operating set of explicit boundaries or social contract. He or she is making the appeal, in so many words, of "listen to me if you respect me." This teacher's efforts demonstrate that relying on implied desire for respect rather than clear expectations typically results in frustration and disappointment.

It is likely that you had a much more favorable impression of the language used by teacher C. You likely characterized his or her language with such descriptors as *supportive, positive, respectful, effective, aware, nurturing,* and *deliberate.* And as you read the transcript, you assumed a safe and sane climate in the class. In examining the language of teacher C, you saw a desire for clarity. The words *we* and *need* reflect a class that is working together for positive goals. The subtext of teacher C's words could be characterized by the phrase, "I know that you can do it." There is a clear sense that this teacher's class operates at a high level on the effectiveness and function continuum.

If you were to sit at a table in the lunchroom with each of these teachers, it is likely that you would hear them express similar goals. Each would certainly desire a high degree of learning. They would all suggest that they had some behavioral challenges with some students, and all would, if given enough time, offer a well-conceived explanation for why they do what

TABLE 3.1. **Social Frame Development and Classroom Management**

Deference (Student)	Deportment (Teacher or Parent)
The student shows *responsibility*.	The student should receive corresponding *freedom*.
The student is *successful*.	The student should be *recognized*.
The student shows *loyalty* and *respect*.	The student should be shown *warmth* and *caring*.

Note: The frames are italicized.

they do. In other words, each would have a similar and very intentional plan for dealing with management on the explicit level. Yet given the recognition that each class would have an exceedingly different character over time, this example demonstrates the enormous power of words to define the classroom environment.

REFLECTION 3.6

The next time you are in a classroom, listen to the words of the teacher. How would you characterize the teacher's language? What is the subtext? What is the result for the students and the classroom climate?

Social Frames

At the core of any functional environment are implicitly operating social frames: culturally embedded, socially developed implicit roles and relationships that operate to help a society function (MacWhinney, 1999). In our society, as well as most others, at least three primary frames implicitly operate. They involve the deference (behavior) shown by a young person and the deportment (response) shown by a significant adult—a teacher or parent, for example. These three frames are outlined in Table 3.1.

REFLECTION 3.7

1. What do you think would happen if in any of the three cases in Table 3.1, a student showed the appropriate deference and did not get the expected response from the teacher?

2. What if the student were given the response without having shown the deference—for example, being given freedom without showing responsibility?

Collectively these frames operate to provide a society (or classroom) that makes sense and nurtures the young person's development. In a world that is governed by cause and effect and the boundaries supported by these frames, the young person is able to move through it with confidence and security. Without functioning social frames, young people are forced to adapt to a world of uncertainty and threat. They may grow in their ability to survive and cope, but they inevitably will experience a limited amount of joy and satisfaction in basic human needs. Each of the three frames is necessary for success, and they are good predictors of the sociopsychological health of any classroom.

Responsibility—Freedom. A healthy and functional classroom must promote a sound cause-and-effect relationship between freedom and responsibility. This relationship is fundamental to the development of a functional social contract, as we will discuss in Chapters Eight through Ten, and is at the core of how people develop responsibility. If this frame is operating successfully, young people are given greater opportunity to demonstrate their ability to use freedom to the extent that they have shown the capacity to use the freedom that they have been given. When a student does not demonstrate the ability to be responsible in certain situations, freedom and choices are limited until such time as the student is able to show the maturity and discretion necessary to earn them in the future.

When this frame functions poorly, corresponding problematic behavior is inevitable. Imagine a student who has successfully demonstrated responsible and trustworthy behavior and is given no corresponding freedom or choices. The predictable result is resentment and less interest in showing responsibility. In essence, the child will show us that if he is going to be treated like a child, he may as well act like a child. Conversely, children who are given limitless freedoms without ever demonstrating how to use that freedom in a responsible manner learn to be selfish and irresponsible.

Success—Recognition. The second frame deals with the relationship between achievement and recognition. Children should be given recognition when they try and are successful. When this frame is not functioning, we often find students who develop a failure psychology (see Chapter Seven) and a tendency to give up easily. In its most acute form, this may appear as a negative identity pattern in which the student is accustomed to and desires negative attention (see Chapter Fourteen) or a bottomless need for praise and affirmation. Many classroom management problems can be rooted back to students using what Dreikurs (1974) calls "mistaken goals" in the attempt to gain love and affirmation in ways that are disruptive to the class.

3.8 REFLECTION

It may be useful at this point to reflect on your own experience and how effectively social frames have functioned in your own life. Would you say that your parents gave you a healthy amount of recognition? Or did you feel that you were never quite able to measure up? Explore your present response to the past conditioning that you received from your parents. How does it play out in your classroom or current relationships?

In the classroom, promoting this frame aids students in learning about their own personal value and the value of their work. It also helps them make a positive cause-and-effect association between what they put into something and what they get out of it. When students are given praise and rewarded for little or no effort, they do not learn the intrinsic value of the task. The result is typically a student who views the situation with a sense of entitlement.

Loyalty—Caring. A functional class must be characterized by mutual respect between teacher and student (Pianta, 2006; Watson & Ecken, 2003). On the teacher's side must be a display of respect and caring, and on the side of the student is a sense of loyalty and respect to the teacher and the rest of the class. Research tells us that students work harder for teachers they like and respect (Hendley, Stables, & Stables, 1996; Pianta, 2006). And common sense tells us that students do not care what we know until they know that we care. As we walk down the hallway of any school and identify the classrooms in which there is a high incidence of classroom management problems or a low level of motivation, typically we also observe a corresponding lack of respect between the teacher and the students.

REFLECTION **3.9**

In many schools, especially at the secondary level, a number of students have lost faith in the third frame or with adults in general. Somewhere in these students' pasts, they tried to show loyalty and respect but in return received abuse and neglect. As a result, they are inclined to show little openness to engaging in a frame that has cost them in the past. This appears as a lack of respect and even hostility to teachers. If we want this frame to operate, we will not be able to simply respond because there will be no deportment to respond to. Therefore, we will have to initiate it. What strategies can you think of to help build this frame from your side of the equation?

The Classroom Emotional Bank Account

Related to the idea of social frames is the principle of the emotional bank account (Covey, 1989). In essence, this principle suggests that we are either depositing into or withdrawing emotional investments from our relationships. This principle operates continuously in the classroom as well. When we satisfy students' basic needs, demonstrate real care for them, promote their success, make them feel positive about themselves and what they can do, and recognize their gifts and efforts, we make deposits. And since we can withdraw only what has been deposited, if there is nothing in the bank, we will be rather limited when we need to make a withdrawal. For instance, when we ask students to make an exceptional effort, do something challenging, be unusually patient, take emotional risks, think beyond their self-interest, or be tolerant of annoyances that we feel will lead to their growth, we make withdrawals (see Figure 3.2). The evidence of the amount of investment may never be explicitly discussed, but it will be readily apparent in any class. On the positive side, it takes the form of students working hard because they feel that they "owe it to the teacher." On the negative side, it takes the form of students' doing the minimum and acting largely out of self-interest.

REFLECTION **3.10**

Joy is a teacher who likes to get a lot done. She is demanding of her students and is a no-nonsense kind of teacher. She does a lot of lecturing and challenges her students to listen and excel on her tests. Because she expects attention, she usually gets it, but as the period goes on, the level of side conversation and off-task behavior increases. How could Joy use the principle of the emotional bank account to be more effective?

Social frames and the principle of the emotional bank account operate whether or not we are aware of them or understand how they work. Therefore, they can operate either entirely accidentally or entirely intentionally—that is, we can be very deliberate about cultivating them to the benefit of our students. Maintaining some conscious attention and intention related to how each area is functioning will lead to better outcomes. In addition, it is beneficial to use each idea as a tool for periodic classroom climate self-assessment. When things in the class

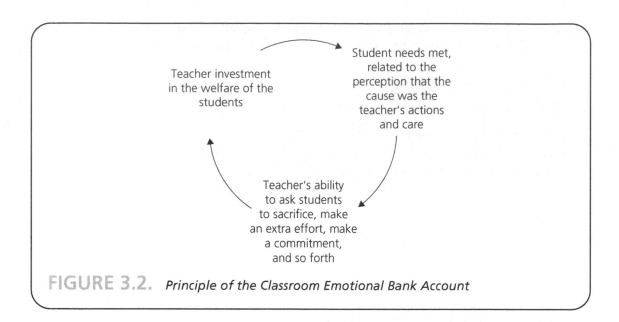

FIGURE 3.2. *Principle of the Classroom Emotional Bank Account*

feel a bit off, we can ask ourselves, "Which of the frames is not functioning as well as it could?" or "What have I invested in the emotional bank account lately?" As you reflect on your answers to these questions, you will likely think of possible adjustments to make to your teaching practices or thinking. Social frames will be revisited in more detail in Chapter Seven as we assemble a recipe for a success psychology.

Power in the Classroom

Interrelated to the use of language and social frames, the use of power defines the implicit level of the classroom reality to a great degree (Buzzelli & Johnston, 2002). Jackson (1968) highlighted the use of power as a fundamental component in his landmark analysis of the hidden curriculum in the book *Life in Classrooms*. Power is difficult to observe, but can be seen in its effects. We might infer that on a fundamental level, power is the force that makes things happen. Moreover, feeling some degree of power is a basic human need. As we will discuss in more detail in Chapter Six, if students' individual or collective need for power is not met, they will exercise it in one form or another.

You too have a basic need for power as a human being and are no less inclined to "correctively" react if you are not experiencing a healthy feeling of control. So in an operational sense, the more each member of the classroom society is getting the need for power met, the more potential there will be for power to exist in the class.

Real Power and the Paradox of Power. As teachers, it is tempting for us to think in terms of being powerful. However, true power is internal—within us and within each of our students. Our real power lies in our ability to act consciously and intentionally rather than to give in to reactivity and unconsciousness. What many call power is usually inner fear being projected outward in a manner that seeks to dominate and control. Therefore in practice, trying to "be powerful" usually leads us toward a desire to force our students to surrender to our authority, which will eventually lead to either rebellion or conformity—neither of them desirable.

It may be more useful to think of power as a force rather than a trait. So if power is the force that makes things happen, what can we do to create more of it? We want to raise the level of power and awareness in our students and then channel that power toward positive and productive outcomes. So in a sense, the more power we give away, the more power exists. This is the paradox of power (Fitzclarence & Giroux, 1984). Our use of authority can help us gain the power to achieve desirable outcomes. But it is granted to us by our students, and it will exist only to the degree that they see that it is leading to a greater good. If we ask, "What can I do to appear more powerful?" we will get lost. In most cases this chain of thought will lead to unconsciousness, power struggles, and resistance. Instead, asking ourselves, "What forms of power can I give to students [that they have shown that they are ready for] that will make the class more productive and functional?" (the responsibility-freedom frame) and "How can I help raise the level of awareness and inner power in my students?" will lead to seeking effective ways to empower students and improve overall function and effectiveness.

Teacher Authority as Power

Since the teacher is in the role of the manager of the class, he or she has power in another form: the authority to influence student behavior. This could be termed *teacher authority.* Teacher authority is, in a sense, the right to ask others to do something. As teachers, we need to ask students to do many things in a day, and we need to make those requests from some basis of authority. Without it, we would have little efficacy. In examining classroom interactions, French and Raven (1959) identified five basic forms of teacher authority: attractive/referent, expert, reward, coercive, and position/legitimate. Each must operate to some degree, but some will be emphasized and used more than others for most of us. These forms are explained in more detail at the online resource site for this book, transformativeclassroom.com.

REFLECTION

3.11

What does real power look like in a classroom? Use the definition that real power is related to that which makes things happen—most important, student motivation and learning. In your experience, what are those things? Also, have you seen evidence of the paradox of power?

The Power of Unspoken and Implicit Expectations. Consider how your expectations affect your class as a collective and your students individually. Do you treat boys differently from girls? Do you have different expectations for students given differences you may perceive in their socioeconomic backgrounds? Most teachers would say that they do not, but as we examine research by Anyon (1984), explored in more depth in Chapter Eleven, the reality of what takes place in schools generally suggests that we have very different expectations for students depending on their socioeconomic status. As a result, we treat students of different groups very differently.

If we ask most teachers what their explicit expectations are, we tend to get somewhat similar responses. However, if we examine what expectations students hold, we see dramatic differences. So how are expectations communicated? The answer is rather complicated, but involves verbal and nonverbal messages that are inferred and processed by students. As noted earlier, we teach who we are. And we can assume that who we are and what we value will be communicated one way or another. Our likes, dislikes, biases, worldviews, culture, politics, assumptions about class, gender, ethnicity, and so forth influence how students experience our class.

Pygmalion in the Classroom

The effects of implicit expectations can be seen clearly in a notable study conducted by Rosenthal and Jacobson (1968), "Pygmalion in the Classroom." In the study, teachers were given the list of their students for the next term. On the list, some students were identified as rising stars and were said to be gifted and were predicted to show a greater degree of progress and performance than the other students. In actuality, the students were randomly chosen from the class list. Can you guess what happened when the students were tested at the end of the term?

3.12 REFLECTION

What did you predict happened in the "Pygmalion in the Classroom" study? Why do you make that prediction?

If you guessed that over time, the rising stars were shown to have significantly outperformed their classmates, you are correct. The researchers demonstrated that the expectancy and subsequent differential treatment of the teachers created a variable in the learning experience that produced a powerful outcome.

What are the lessons of this research? First, examining the implicit level of the classroom reality, especially as it relates to expectations, helps us see that good intentions are often not enough to keep us from sending harmful or limiting messages to our students. The teachers in the Pygmalion study no doubt had good intentions for all of their students, yet their lack of self-awareness resulted in a dramatic difference in the way that they treated them. Second, we want to consider how we could project the kinds of expectations that could promote the success and success psychology (see Chapter Seven) of all of our students. In other words, we want to treat all of our students as rising stars.

3.13 REFLECTION

Given that the students in the Pygmalion study were randomly sampled and did not know that they were identified as rising stars and the teachers were not instructed to do anything different with them, how can you explain such a dramatic difference in performance over time? How would you guess they treated the students who were identified as rising stars differently?

What Is So Problematic About the "Accidental Classroom"?

When we accept a high level of unconsciousness and an "accidental" quality in our classrooms, the typical results are a correspondingly high degree of classroom dramas, psychological games, and implicit rules that students feel forced to negotiate. When they have to spend a large amount of time trying to negotiate this underlying set of rules, the typical result is that they remain stuck in survival mode and are not able to move into more fully functional states of mind. The result is a group that stays in a rut of self-protectionism, never able to move toward greater levels of growth or function. Moving up the effectiveness continuum requires exchanging the accidental quality of the class with one defined by intentionality.

HARNESSING THE POWER OF SOCIAL OR INDIRECT LEARNING

Social learning theory implies that we can learn from situations by making inferences from what we observe (what happens to others) without having to be directly involved (Salomon & Perkins, 1998). Consider the following two situations:

1. As we drive, we observe a car on the side of the road that has been pulled over by the police. We make the decision to slow down as we deduce that this same fate could happen to us.

2. We observe person A act in a way that impresses person B (whose respect and admiration we desire). We note that person B responds positively when person A talks about travel. The next time we interact with person B, we find opportunities to bring up the topic of travel.

These two situations are examples of the principle of social, or indirect, learning: lessons were learned indirectly through observation rather than through direct experience. We can see this same principle being demonstrated in the classroom. In fact, it is happening almost continuously. Most of what we learn about what is appropriate or what should be avoided we learn indirectly. For example, at some point, we likely experienced being in a classroom situation in which a fellow student made a remark or answered a question that a teacher reacted to in a publicly critical manner. Recall your thought process and subsequent behavior at the time. Along with almost every other student in the class, your reaction was likely to think something to the effect: "I am not going to let that happen to me." And as a result, you may have determined that it was not worth the risk of volunteering ideas in the class and to be more careful about how you responded in the future. Although the teacher did not directly criticize your answer, your response to the event may have been nearly as profound as if it had happened to you personally. Whatever lesson you took away from the incident, it is likely that you used what you observed to guide your future behavior.

Bandura and the Bobo Doll

Albert Bandura is a leader in the field of behavioral psychology and social learning (1971, 1986). One of his famous experiments involved groups of children and a plastic clown called the Bobo doll. In this experiment, he gave each group of children the same verbal directions: "Don't touch the doll, and go play with the toys." Behind the researcher was a video screen that showed various video scenarios. In one, the children on the screen went past the doll and began playing with the toys. In another, the children aggressively attacked the Bobo doll. In the first case, the children imitated the children on the video and walked past the doll to play with the toys. In the second case, the children disregarded the verbal directions but followed the aggressive modeling. The researchers went on to show students a variety of other kinds of modeling on the video screen and then observed the effects. Students who watched violence in any form were more likely to treat the doll aggressively than did the students who watched nonviolent material. The researchers concluded that the power of modeling (indirect or social learning) was in some cases more powerful than direct instruction.

REFLECTION

3.14

Reflect on your experience as a student. Can you recall situations in which you changed your behavior as a result of something that you observed happening to someone else but did not happen to you directly?

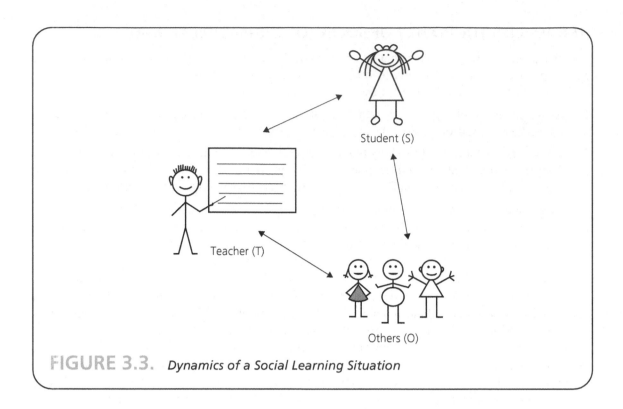

FIGURE 3.3. *Dynamics of a Social Learning Situation*

The interaction described in the example of the critical remark characterizes a dynamic that could be described as teacher (T) and student (S) interaction with an audience of others (O). As we examine all of the potential dynamics in Figure 3.3, a series of principles emerges. Here we examine what each of these principles looks like in the classroom. Throughout the rest of the book, these principles will be highlighted with icons in relation to their practical applications. In each icon, the arrow shows the direction of the influence in the event, and the dotted lines show the indirect learning or observation.

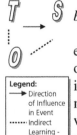

Legend:
→ Direction of Influence in Event
······· Indirect Learning - Observation

Principle One: The students as a collective learn lessons indirectly from the interactions between the teacher and particular students.

When we interact or intervene with one student or group of students, we have an audience eager to learn what we model. What we do sends a message to the rest of the class. As the other students observe our treatment of one student, they make decisions related to how to act in the future based on what they observed. These lessons lead to the students' judgments about many things. First, they learn to what degree they feel we can be trusted. Do we keep our word? Do we act rationally? Are we approachable? Second, students learn about our level of reliability. It is rare to find a group of students who are not highly concerned (if not obsessed) with fairness. They want to know whether we are consistent. Do we have favorite students in the class? Do we act unpredictably?

3.15 REFLECTION

Recall a situation in which you felt that a teacher had favorites. What information did you use to infer that this was the case? Did the teacher ever say directly that these students were his or her favorites? If not, what led you to the conclusion that there were favorites?

Third, students learn about the soundness of the social contract (or rules, boundaries, expectations, or a code of conduct). The level of integrity of the social contract (as we will examine in detail in Chapters Eight through Ten) is based on whether it is administered without prejudice as perceived by the students. When students perceive their teacher treating each of them with the same level of regard, being equitable and fair, and being true to the tenets of the social contract, they learn to trust not only the teacher but the operating principles of the class. This trust leads to a sense of emotional safety and security. Without this foundation of trust, little of what could be considered transformational will be possible.

REFLECTION   3.16

Recall a class in which you felt there was a great deal of inconsistency along with perceived differential treatment. How did it make you feel? Did you feel emotionally safe? How did you and the other students compensate for the teacher's inconsistency and the feelings that it engendered within you?

Principle Two: For some students, peers may be a more significant source of influence than the teacher.

For many students, impressing peers may represent a larger need than meeting the expectations of the teacher, especially if the student has an unmet need for love or belonging.

You may have one or more students who seem to be fixated on peers as their reference group and seem much less concerned about your expectations for their behavior. This need for peer approval seems to be strongest in the middle school years. For some teachers, this can even lead to an avoidance of students of this age. But while you cannot significantly change their needs or alter their cognitive developmental patterns, you can creatively work with the situation to the benefit of everyone.

First, you need to stop taking offense at what appears to be a lack of respect for adults—you, in this case. Continue to model respect, and expect it from all of your students.

Second, you need to make a genuine connection with the student. Send the message to these students that they are liked, needed, and believed in.

Third, you need to help these students contribute. If the students are put in situations in which they are able to contribute to the welfare of others, they will be in a better position to meet the need for belonging and self-efficacy, as well as meet the teacher's need for a student who is responsible. For instance, you might give them small leadership roles, such as passing out papers or setting up an activity. And when they do, you need to make it clear to them that you appreciate what they are doing for the "good of the class."

REFLECTION   3.17

What is your first instinct with a student who seems to be uninterested in meeting your expectations but is very attuned to what classmates think? Is it to teach this student a lesson by being emotionally distant in return or to be passive-aggressive toward him or her until he or she changes? What is the likely result of these responses? In your judgment, do they lead to a change in the student's behavior?

Principle Three: We need to encourage popular and influential students to support group goals.

Often we have students in our class to whom other students look as a model or to set the dispositional tone in the room. For many of these students, power comes from popularity and their place at the top of the social hierarchy. For others, it comes from being a large and dynamic personality. For still others, it comes from having persuasive skills and charisma beyond their years, and thus the ability to influence the opinions and decisions of the group. If these students take on a sense of entitlement or decide to work against the goals of the group, they will create a political problem that can have a divisive effect on your ability to teach and lead.

There are ways to support these influential students' being positive forces in the class as opposed to our political opponents:

- Let these students know that you like and respect them and recognize their influence. But there is no place for a sense of entitlement, and in your class, influence comes with some responsibility.

- Help these students recognize how to be positive leaders in the class. It may help to point out cases in which you have already seen them do things that demonstrate positive leadership. Concrete examples will make the idea of a position of responsibility less threatening if it is new to them.

- Remember that they are still kids—even the center on the basketball team, the prom queen, or the child of the mayor. For some, this student will bring back memories of students who intimidated us, looked down on us, or irritated us when we were in school. Do not blame the student or yourself for having these feelings. Simply recognize that you are the leader today, and let the past go.

- Help these students recognize that it feels better to be a positive leader than someone who has to play a game of defending their sense of entitlement. It may not be what popular culture is telling them, but when they look inside themselves, they will see that it feels a lot better.

3.18 REFLECTION

Recall how popular students acted when you were in school. Were they leaders, or did they project a sense of entitlement? What did the teachers in the school do to encourage their behavior in either of these directions?

Principle Four: Students learn through indirect observation what behaviors have an effect on the teacher.

3.19 REFLECTION

Recall a class in which a student or two learned that saying or doing certain things could get a reaction from the teacher. What was the response from the rest of the class? What did they consequently do as a result of what they had observed?

Very quickly, students learn what affects their teachers. They learn what we like, what sets us off, and what they can do to gain more power. For example, think about a class in which one or more students learned that if they asked the teacher questions about his personal life, latest vacation, or favorite athletic team, the teacher obliged by rambling on about that subject and therefore spent less time on the material related to the course. This teacher-conditioning process can be innocuous, or it can have substantially destructive effects. In an extreme but rather common case, students can train the teacher to allow them to become apathetic, unmotivated, and comfortable with adopting a failure psychology. In this case, they have conditioned the teacher to treat them as "falling stars" rather than "rising stars," and the teacher has allowed the training to become a conditioned attitude. Case study 3.1 shows one example of how students can do this.

CASE STUDY

3.1

Students in a college-level psychology class once decided to discover how effective they could be at modifying the behavior of a guest instructor. They came up with a plan without giving away what they were doing or letting the instructor in on the experiment. Through the use of either smiling and laughing or frowning and yawning as their forms of reinforcement, they were able to behaviorally modify the instructor's actions. By the end of the period, he had been conditioned to lecture from the far corner of the room with his arms folded.

Understanding this principle is necessary to maintain adequate awareness of the many influences that condition us each day. Are we allowing students to push our buttons? Are we getting hooked into power struggles? Are we leading or being led? A useful strategy for dealing with student manipulation is to raise it to the level of awareness and make it transparent. For example, in the case of the students asking spurious questions, we may want to respond, "I know you guys want to keep asking questions about what I thought about the game to keep from getting started, but we need to start now. If we have time, we can talk about the game later." In the case of the students wanting to quit, a response is, "I hear you telling me that you cannot do this, but I have seen you do it before, so let's all do our best and make the effort and see if we can get it. I am betting you can."

Principle Five: One times one can sometimes equal thirty. Using the social learning mechanism to your advantage in instruction.

Indirect learning can have a powerful effect on the quality and engagement level of our instruction. Our management will be more effective when we model skills and consider indirect learning dynamics in discussions, questioning, and feedback. Two of the many powerful indirect learning strategies are the use of public positive recognitions and of questioning to keep students cognitively on the hook:

- *The power of positive recognitions.* When we give feedback to one student privately, we deliver information to that one student. When we give positive feedback to a student publicly, we have delivered indirect information to every student in the class. This strategy provides both more concrete as well as more abundant feedback. The next chapter follows up on the idea of positive recognition in more detail.

- *Keeping students cognitively on the hook.* When we ask an individual student a question, we engage one at a time. If we do this on a regular basis, the students learn that they are off the hook when we are engaging someone else. No matter what we tell them, the message is that they are a passive audience until it is their turn. By altering this strategy somewhat, the dynamics change dramatically. Part of the solution to keeping students cognitively on the hook is the purposeful use of asking questions. Evertson, Anderson, Anderson, and Brophy (1980) demonstrated that more effective teachers asked more and more purposeful questions when compared to less effective teachers. For example instead of responding to a student with, "Yes, that is correct. Good job," you could instead triangulate that answer to the whole class by asking, "Interesting. How do you think she arrived at that answer?" We explore this technique in more detail in Chapter Eleven.

3.20	### REFLECTION

Recall a time when your teacher went around the room and called on students one at a time in a fixed pattern. What were you thinking about as other students responded? Was it related to the academic material? Did you feel accountable or engaged in the learning process?

Principle Six: Make tomorrow better as a result of what you do today.

Using the social learning model in decision making can often help us judge the benefits of any particular practice. It can be very useful to ask ourselves the question, "What indirect learning will result from my present actions?" What may seem like a good idea for today or for one student may in fact not be so effective in the long term or may result in some undesirable indirect learning for the group. In fact, many strategies that prove to be effective in the long term are based on counterintuitive reasoning and may even seem to have limited use on the surface. Therefore, you might want to ask yourself the following questions when considering a strategy: "What are students learning from the repeated use of this strategy that I am considering?" and "What am I likely to experience more of in the future as a result of the social learning that takes place?"

Many of the strategies described in this book may seem as though they are somewhat indirect and may involve more of long-range focus than those to which most of us are accustomed. However, many of the strategies that appear to have an instant impact actually have substantial negative side effects when examined in light of their indirect or long-term effects. It is tempting to do what works today. Nevertheless, being committed to transformative results and not simply convenience requires remaining intentional and maintaining a long-range view.

The following strategies may seem on the surface and in the short term to be effective, but in the long run they tend to teach unwanted lessons and as a result promote unwanted outcomes (the chapters noted address the issues):

- Bailing out students who act pathetic or helpless (Chapter Fourteen)
- Hovering over and giving a disproportionately high amount of attention to misbehaving students (Chapter Ten)
- Dissolving groups that cannot get along (Chapter Twelve)
- Asking for excuses (Chapter Eleven)
- Encouraging tattletales (Chapter Eleven)
- Appeasing students through deals and bargains (Chapter Eleven)
- Giving inactivity as a reward or activity as a punishment (Chapter Ten)
- Taking an authoritarian (4-Style) approach with a defiant student (Chapters Thirteen and Fourteen)
- Using personal nonspecific praise (Chapters Six and Seven)

- Using public shame in the form of names on the board or colored-card systems (explained in detail in the online resource article, "Comparing Behavioral Assessment Systems and Why Descending-Levels Models Are Not Effective," available at transformativeclassroom.com)

REFLECTION

3.21

How many of these strategies have you used? Do you still use them? Before reading the explanations for why they have undesirable effects in the coming chapters, predict what those effects might be.

We will revisit the social learning model often in the following chapters because it helps bring a fuller perspective to any classroom event. Considering our actions within the perspective of indirect learning can help us be more effective. In the following chapters, the T-S-O icon signals a social learning model reference.

CONCLUSION

Practicing conscious awareness allows us to act more intentionally and less reactively. Awareness of the hidden curriculum and the more implicit aspects of the overall classroom environment lead to moving more of our teaching above the line of conscious recognition and into the intentional realm. Chapter Sixteen revisits the idea of how our thinking and level of awareness affect our ability to be successful and experience more peace of mind throughout the day. The next chapter explores how to promote effective, intentional classroom expectations.

Journal Reflections

1. Is the notion of a hidden curriculum new to you? What portion of the curriculum do you feel is implicit or hidden? Why?
2. When you reflect on the idea of "teaching who you are," what feelings does it evoke?
3. Recall an event that resulted in a profound life lesson that you learned indirectly. What implications does this event have for your teaching?
4. Do you feel that most teachers adequately consider what the long-term and indirect and social learning effects of their management strategies will be? Explain your answer.

Activities

1. In small groups, complete exercise 3.1 on your own, and then discuss the labels you used for each teacher with the other members of your group. Did you find that you characterized the effects on the classroom environment in a similar way for each teacher?
2. As a class (or in your small group) discuss the implications of each of the three social frames. It may be helpful to recall your thoughts from reflection 3.8. Here are some guiding questions to assist you.
   a. If a student is in the situation in which he or she acts very responsibly but is given no corresponding freedom or self-determination from the adults, what is the likely result? Contrastingly, what if a student has acted irresponsibly but is still given the same amount of freedom and license as the students who acted responsibly?

b. If a student has worked hard and done all that the adults in the situation have asked but is not given the corresponding recognition, what is the likely result? Contrastingly, what if a student has made little or no effort and is nevertheless rewarded and praised excessively?

c. Sometimes developing the loyalty-caring social frame can be difficult. Often students have learned not to trust the adults in their lives. What can we as teachers do to promote our end of the bargain to initiate the health of this third frame? What would you say to a teacher who says that it is not important that the class feel any loyalty or caring to one another or the teacher?

3. In groups, discuss the implications of social learning theory. In the most recent class that you observed or taught, give an example of the indirect learning that you observed. Offer the others in the group one idea for a practice that seems useful but that you now recognize to be of limited value given its social learning model implications.

REFERENCES

Bandura, A. (1971). *Social learning theory*. New York: General Learning Press.

Bandura, A. (1986). *Social foundations of thought and action*. Upper Saddle River, NJ.: Prentice Hall.

Buzzelli, C. A., & Johnston, B. (2002). *The moral dimension of teaching: Language, power and culture in the classroom*. New York: Falmer Press.

Cabello, B., & Terrell, R. (1994). Making students feel like family: How teachers create warm and caring climates. *Journal of Classroom Interaction*, *29*, 17–23.

Covey, S. (1989). *Seven habits of highly effective people*. New York: Simon & Schuster.

Devitt, M., & Sterelny, K. (1999). *Language and reality: An introduction to the philosophy of language*. Cambridge, MA: MIT Press.

Eisner, E. (1984). No easy answers: Joseph Schwab's contributions to curriculum. *Curriculum Inquiry*, *14*, 201–210.

Evertson, C. M., Anderson, C. W., Anderson, L. M., & Brophy, J. E. (1980). Relationships between classroom behaviors and student outcomes in junior high mathematics and English classes. *American Educational Research Journal*, *17*(1), 43–60.

Fallona, C., & Richardson, V. (2006). Classroom management as a moral activity. In C. M. Evertson & C. S. Weinstein (Eds.), *Handbook of classroom management* (pp. 1041–1062). Mahwah, NJ: Erlbaum.

Fitzclarence, L., & Giroux, H. (1984). The paradox of power in educational theory and practice. *Language Arts*, *61*(5), 462–477.

French, J.R.P., Jr., & Raven, B. H. (1959). The bases of social power. In D. Cartwright (Ed.), *Studies in social power* (pp. 150–167). Ann Arbor: University of Michigan Press.

Friedman, I. A., & Farber, B. A. (1992). Professional self-concept as a predictor of burnout. *Journal of Educational Research*, *86*(1), 28–35.

Ginott, H. (1972). *Teacher and child*. New York: Avon Books.

Haralambos, M. (1991). *Sociology: Themes and perspectives*. London: Collins Press.

Hendley, D., Stables, S., & Stables, A. (1996). Pupils' subject preferences at key stage 3 in South Wales. *Educational Studies*, *22*(2), 177–186.

Jackson, P. W. (1968) *Life in classrooms*. New York: Teachers College Press.

Kohl, H. (2002). Topsy-turvies: Teacher talk and student talk. In L. Delpit & J. Dowdy (Eds.), *The skin that we speak* (pp. 145–161). New York: New York Press.

MacWhinney, B. (1999). *The emergence of language*. Mahwah, NJ: Erlbaum.

Myers, I., McCauley, M., Quenk, N., & Hammer, A. (1998). *Manual for use: Myers-Briggs Type Inventory*. Palo Alto, CA: Consulting Psychologists Press.

Pianta, R. C. (2006). Classroom management and relationships between children and teachers: Implications for research and practice. In C. M. Evertson & C. S. Weinstein (Eds.), *Handbook of classroom management* (pp. 685–709). Mahwah, NJ: Erlbaum.

Rosenthal, R., & Jacobson, L. (1968). Pygmalion in the classroom. *Urban Review*, *3*(1), 16–20.

Salomon, G., & Perkins, D. (1998). Individual and social aspects of learning. *Review of Research in Education*, *23*, 1998, 1–24.

Valli, L. (1992). *Reflective teacher education: Cases and critiques*. Albany, NY: SUNY Press.

Watson, M., & Ecken, L. (2003). *Learning to trust: Transforming difficult elementary classrooms through developmental discipline*. San Francisco. Jossey-Bass.

4

Promoting Clear and Shared Classroom Expectations

The Cornerstone of the Effective Classroom

In This Chapter

- What are classroom expectations?
- Where do expectations exist?
- Levels of classroom expectations
- Why be concerned with intentionally promoting classroom expectations?
- Strategies that are most effective at intentionally promoting clear, positive, and shared expectations
- Examining classroom expectations within the 1- and 2-Style classroom management approaches

WHAT ARE CLASSROOM EXPECTATIONS?

In any classroom, expectations are always present. Whether they were promoted intentionally or unintentionally, whether they exist in the minds of students consciously or unconsciously, they are there continuously defining the classroom. Students use their expectations to answer the questions in the class. These include the practical questions such as:

- What are the directions for this activity?
- How am I being graded on this project?
- What would happen if I decided to get off task?

    And they include the larger questions, such as:

- Do I find the learning in which I am involved meaningful to me?
- Does the teacher respect me?
- Am I emotionally safe in this class?

It is useful to recognize that all teachers are constantly projecting expectations, and all students are continuously interpreting the expectations for any situation (Hargreaves, Hester, & Mellor, 1975). Things that are said and done, patterns of action, body language, and tone of voice all send out information that students invariably interpret. Over time these interpretations lead students to construct answers to their questions and make judgments about what they understand is expected within the class. Put simply, students learn to expect through what they have experienced and observed in the past.

WHERE DO EXPECTATIONS EXIST?

Indispensable to the transformative classroom is the presence of intention and awareness. The means to achieving these qualities is dependent on the teacher's ability to develop clear and shared expectations among the members of the class. In fact, any classroom's expectations exist only to the degree that they are clear and shared. In the effective class, students know where things are going, how they fit in, and what is expected of them, and they trust that others do as well. Yet Wentzel, Battle, and Looney (2000) found that half the students they studied reported not knowing what the teacher expected.

The idea that expectations exist as shared concepts and ideas seems rather abstract. However, an examination of a few classroom situations will help validate this view. For instance, most of us have observed a class in which all the students seemed to know what was expected of them with very little telling on the part of the teacher. And we have observed classes in which there were long lists of rules on the wall and the teacher made constant pleas for orderly behavior, yet the majority of students seemed to be working off conflicting scripts, and the energy in the class could best be characterized as divergent and chaotic.

4.1

REFLECTION

Recall classes that you have observed that seemed to have a shared sense of purpose and direction. What do you think contributed to that environment?

So how do you create a classroom in which your students are all in congruence about those practical classroom realities that would work to their benefit? In this chapter, we examine various strategies for creating intentional expectations.

TYPES OF CLASSROOM EXPECTATIONS

Before we look at how to go about promoting shared intentional expectations, it is useful to make some distinctions about the types of expectations that operate within any classroom and the ways that this idea will be used throughout the following chapters. The expectations within any class can be classified from least to most conscious or conspicuous, beginning with unconscious expectations, followed by explicit but unwritten expectations, and, finally, written rules, classroom constitutions, or social contracts.

Previously we examined the idea of unconsciously conveyed expectations and noted that teachers do not need to try to communicate their biases, preconceptions, and motives, which nevertheless affect what they say and do (Weinstein, Gregory, & Strambler, 2004). Recall the Pygmalion in the classroom study (Rosenthal & Jacobson, 1968) in which teachers were told that some of their students were rising stars. These teachers were entirely unaware that their implicit expectations were having such a dramatic effect on how they were teaching. Moreover, research has shown that students whom teachers like get better grades in their classes (Pianta, Hamre, & Stuhlman, 2003).

Because of the powerful effect that expectations can have, recognizing and making a deliberate effort to bring unconscious expectations to your conscious awareness is critical. Although it is possible to project primarily intentional expectations to students, keep in mind that you will struggle to promote healthy and functional explicit expectations if you have a substantial number of unexamined dysfunctional expectations operating like computer viruses to corrupt your intentional efforts.

The number of expectations that could potentially exist in any classroom is countless. If you began to list all the behaviors that you desire from your students, you could identify hundreds. So while it is tempting to try to capture all of your expectations in a set of written rules, that would ultimately be counterproductive. Therefore, you need to make a distinction between the mechanisms for achieving some basic ground rules and principles and promoting the endless number of other expectations that you want students to hold. Later we examine the process for creating and implementing a formal social contract. While the social contract will include all levels of expectations in principle, in practice it will focus primarily on the formal guiding principles in the class. It will include the basic rules that the class has agreed to follow and the logical consequences when students choose to violate those rules. For example, the social contract may include a rule related to being on time and a consequence for being late. The rule will include an expectation (there is a value to being on time), but it is formalized when it is termed a rule (for example, "When you are late, the consequence for violating that rule is that you will lose the opportunity to do. . .")

In this chapter, we examine how largely unwritten expectations are promoted. While the development of the social contract will act in concert with your efforts to promote classroom expectations in general, our classroom management efforts will be more successful when we take a systematic approach to the development of the countless numbers of unwritten expectations within the class.

REFLECTION
4.2

I recently heard two teachers talking early in this school year, each lamenting that they struggled to get the kind of learning outcomes that they wanted because of some student misbehavior. One of the teachers said that he did not feel he should have to actively help the students behave better because "they should be able to do that by now." The other teacher took the position that part of his job was to support more functional behavior on the part of his students.

Which teacher would you guess had fewer behavioral problems as the year progressed? What are your thoughts about each teacher's position?

A whole host of benefits come with intentionally promoting clear and shared classroom expectations. A survey of the research demonstrates many that would be largely anticipated— for example:

- Students know what to expect and understand the learning tasks better (Wentzel, 2006).
- The class runs more smoothly with less confusion (Grusec & Goodnow, 1994).
- Students have a clearer sense of what it takes to perform (Hines, Cruickshank, & Kennedy, 1985).

However, other benefits of clear expectations are less obvious:

- Expectations that are clear and shared are essential to help foster the cause-and-effect relationship between actions and consequences that is at the heart of functional frames, an effective social contract, and the logic to the reasonable and related consequences for that contract. Without clarity and a shared understanding, consequences feel arbitrary. The result is that they will have less benefit, be experienced as more punitive, and result in more resentment and less behavior change.

- The absence of clear expectations will create practical problems and an environment of uneasiness in the class that will lead to confusion, frustration, and hostility when expectations clash.

- An intentional approach to promoting expectations helps them become more concrete and meaningful. When expectations exist as words (or even less effective privately held assumptions), they remain abstractions. They must be operationalized to be effective.

- Expectations help the class interpret events and actions as examples or nonexamples of "things that are making us better." For example, a funny comment can be either hurtful or act to amuse the group. The clarity of the expectation provides a means for helping members of the group understand which it is. The result is that students feel more liberated to act and are less fearful that what they do or say will be unwanted or unacceptable to others.

- A foundation of clear and shared expectations is essential for creating a 2- or 1-Style classroom. In the absence of clear expectations, the teacher-centered class will inherently manifest 4-Style characteristics, and attempts at student-centered management will descend into a 3-Style environment.

4.3   REFLECTION

Examine an environment in which there is a lot of anger, resentment, and pain giving. Do you find a desire on the part of those involved to create clear expectations? If they are tired of the frustration but have developed a habit of attack and retaliation, you will notice that the expectations are rather vague, and the parties like to keep it that way. Why do you think this is?

As teachers, the more deliberate and intentional we are about promoting our classroom expectations, the more effective we will be. Moreover, the expectations that guide the class will be those that are desirable and lead to the mutual benefit of teacher and student.

INTENTIONALLY CREATING POSITIVE EXPECTATIONS

Some strategies demonstrate a greater capacity to promote quality behavior than others. The most effective intentional strategies promote in the minds of students a sense of clarity of the expectation and positive associations with the desired behavior implied in the expectation.

If we were to evaluate the effectiveness of the most commonly incorporated strategies according to their ability to create positive expectations, we would observe a substantial variation in effectiveness. An approximation of the effectiveness ratings for each strategy is offered in Figure 4.1.

Each of these strategies is examined in more depth in the following sections, beginning with the most effective and progressing to the least.

Purposeful Action

Purposeful action on the part of the teacher is rated at the top of the list for the simple reason that actions really do speak louder than words. No matter what we say, students learn about our class from what we do. In a sense, words are technically action, but in an operational

Practice	Clarity Rating	Affect Rating	Overall	What They Promote Related to the Management Effectiveness Continuum	↕↔
Purposeful action • Consistency • Follow-through	+	+	****	Strategies that do a great deal to create cause and effect clarity and positive associations related to expectations	
Positive recognition	+	+	****		
Clarifying statements, directions, and mantras	+	N+	***	Use promotes movement up the effectiveness continuum	↑
Clarifying questions	+	N+	***		
Expectation cues	+	+	****		
Debriefing	+	N+	***		
Written expectations	+	N	$**\frac{1}{2}$		
Personal recognition or praise	N N+	N+ N	* *	Strategies that do little to promote expectations and create inconsequential or confusing emotional climates	
Warnings	N–	N–	*		↔
Requests	N–	N–	$\frac{1}{2}$	Use promotes little movement up or down continuum	
Negative recognitions	N–	–	$\frac{1}{2}*$	Strategies that do very little to promote clarity and do a great deal to create negative associations with the desired behavior	
Irrational or negative actions	–	–	0		↓
Threats and put-downs	–	–	0	Use promotes mostly movement down the effectiveness continuum	
Assessing behavior	NR	NR		Strategies that vary greatly depending on how they are used	

FIGURE 4.1. *Ratings of Common Management Practices Related*

Note: Rated from most (four asterisks) to least (no stars) effective.
Key: + = Demonstrates high levels of effectiveness in this area. N+ = Demonstrates some effectiveness.
N = Is neutral or inconsequential. N~MI = Does a bit more harm than good but has an effect. ~MI = does mostly harm. NR = No rating; can vary from + to – depending on how they are used.

sense, they can also be perceived as inaction. Actions demonstrate that we are committed to our words. Actions take more effort than words, so students learn what we value and who we are by what we make the effort to do. Inaction sends a powerful message as well. When we fail to follow through on our agreements or responsibilities, we undermine the cause-and-effect relationship between choices and consequences in the class and shift the locus of control away from the student (internally) to ourselves (externally). When we complain, as opposed to take action to change the problem, we show students that we are more interested in image management than the quality of the learning in the class. *Note:* The following icon represents a reference in the text to the social or indirect learning model introduced in the Chapter Three.

Our actions are the primary means by which we promote the responsibility-freedom social frame in the class. These lessons are learned in most cases through indirect or social learning. For example, when a classroom expectation is collectively understood (for example, about following directions, showing respect to other students, or fulfilling one's student responsibilities) and students successfully meet it, we can take action to give the students more freedom or self-determination related to that expectation. Positive recognitions are also useful, as we will discuss later, but a change in practical action will have an even greater effect on the development of the expectation. Conversely, when we have set up an expectation that implies that if the student does not do A, then as teacher we are responsible to do B (deliver a consequence or support the student's efforts to improve his or her behavior) and do not follow through, the concrete and observable message to the students is that the expectation is weak or nonexistent.

4.4 REFLECTION

Recall teachers whom you have had in the past or have observed recently. Contrast teachers who tended to take action and followed through on agreements versus teachers who did a lot of telling but seldom took action. In which classrooms were the expectations clearer? Which strategy was more effective at changing behavior?

Positive Recognition

Positive recognitions are incidents in which the teacher points out that something that is happening or has happened is beneficial for an individual student or the class as a whole. What is being positively recognized or encouraged can take the form of good ideas, quality performance or effort, behavior that meets important expectations, or any other behavior judged to be valuable.

Positive recognitions have a powerful effect. However, we need to distinguish them from what I term *personal recognitions* or *praise*. Positive recognitions highlight behavior, whereas personal recognitions or praise call attention to the agent doing the behaving. Praise, by its nature, leads to dependence on an external source and is not readily associated with learning. Positive recognitions create clarity of the task and encourage the student's own internal goals and interests.

Consider an example related to listening. A common phrase that many primary teachers use is, "I like the way Maria is listening." Compare that phrase to, "It's great that we are listening so well. Notice how much easier it is to. . ." The first phrase may sound like a positive recognition at first, but examine it more closely. What do students infer when they hear it? Maria will hear something to the effect, "The teacher likes me because I am being good." The other students likely hear, "The teacher likes Maria because she is being good." It does little to create clarity of the expectation or reinforce the need for the expectation. Personal recognitions are more effective than negative recognitions such as mentioning who is not listening, but they run the risk of having negative effects associated with praise by operating as an emotional extrinsic reinforcement of persons, not behavior (Kohn, 1999).

Consider the phrase, "I see this group has taken care to organize all the ideas that they brainstormed before they started to create their poster; this will help the quality of their end result." This is an example of a positive recognition of behavior—in this case, the collective behavior of a group. Notice the specificity of the feedback. The effect will be that it will feel positive and encouraging to those who received the recognition, but it does not sound personal, and it will have the effect of modeling that quality performance to the other students.

Positive recognitions can be focused primarily on the collective or on particular individuals or groups. There are advantages to each level of attention. Following are some advantages of recognizing a collective accomplishment:

- The group feels that in a sense, it has won as a team. This experience will help develop communal bonds within the group.

- The members of the group are given the chance to recognize that it is possible to trust that others will do their part as they do their part.

- The focus of the reinforcement is more readily associated with the accomplishment of the behavior rather than personalities.

Although these emotions experienced by the members of the recognized group are subtle, they can have a powerful cumulative effect. The group feels a progressive sense of pride and cohesion as their efforts are acknowledged. With time, the group begins to associate collective function with fulfilling the need for belonging. In addition, the growing level of trust generates acceptance and a feeling of emotional ease.

REFLECTION

4.5

Recall a situation in which you found yourself working with a group of people with whom you worked well and grew to trust. What was your level of anxiety in this situation? How about your acceptance level of what was taking place?

Now recall a situation where you found yourself working with a group you did not trust very much. Where was your level of anxiety throughout the process? How critical were you of the final outcomes in each case?

When we evaluate the use of positive behavioral recognitions of collective behavior in relation to our two principles for judging the quality of expectation-promoting strategies (see Figure 4.1), why it is so effective becomes more evident. Collective positive recognitions have the effect of identifying behavior specifically and therefore making expectations clear and concrete. In addition, they act to meet students' basic needs for power, competence, and belonging and create a positive association with the expected behavior. Over time, their use promotes a steady progress up the continuum of management effectiveness to greater levels of function.

Pedagogical Suggestion

If generating the language for your positive recognitions is not coming easily, the following phrases may be helpful general examples:

"This group just ___. That is a great idea that I had not thought of."

"I am seeing people doing a good job of taking the time to ___ before they ___."

"I love the creative ways that we are approaching ___."

"I appreciate that you are putting so much care and attention into ___. It will pay off when we ___."

"Do you remember that we had trouble with this two weeks ago? Now see how well we are doing."

Recognition of individual or individual group behavior has these advantages:

- The teacher can specifically recognize a particular behavior that he or she wants other students to model.

- The teacher can recognize a student or group publicly in a way that can be motivating to the student or group.

- The teacher can use the recognition to shape a behavior or help a student recognize a skill, ability, or accomplishment.

Recall the social learning model from the previous chapter: the power of positive recognition becomes more evident. When you recognize a behavior or academic performance demonstrated by a particular student that exemplifies quality effort or thinking or clarifies the requirements of the task, the effect is that the other students have information that they can use. When we silently observe and evaluate student performance on a task, we tend to learn a great deal about what would help the students do better. Students work in isolation, and we gain the benefits of insight as we monitor their learning. When we make audible what we have observed in the form of positive recognitions of high-quality efforts and task clarifications, the students gain the benefit of our insight.

For example, instead of walking around the room and giving students simple task completion feedback, such as, "You have five minutes left," or making praise statements such as, "Good job," you will have a much greater impact if you find concrete behaviors to recognize that will teach the class as a whole lessons. Examples are, "I notice some groups deciding on who is going to take on each role before they get into the task. Good idea! It will make your job easier as you continue." The use of public positive recognitions has the effect of being both a powerful teacher of the collective and an emotionally satisfying form of encouragement, or what we might term healthy praise to those being recognized.

4.6   REFLECTION

If you do not already provide your students with frequent and intentional positive recognitions, you may want to take part in some active research in this area. For an hour or so, find as many opportunities as you can to make positive recognitions. After the hour, note the degree to which the students show a clear understanding of and investment in the task. Also note the effect in the room. Does it feel more positive and focused?

Clarifying Statements, Directions, and Mantras

A clarifying statement is one in which the teacher (or sometimes a student) states the necessary behavioral expectation—for example, "We are making sure that we are getting all the notes we need to present our ideas in a couple of minutes." This kind of statement does not assume that anything is happening or is not happening currently. It is not a positive or negative recognition. It is simply a neutral clarification stated positively.

Clarifying statements work like focusing a lens. They do not change the picture or interpret it. They just help students refocus their efforts a bit more intentionally. When the teacher uses a clarifying statement such as, "We are all giving Sandra our undivided attention right now" (because Sandra is sharing an answer with the members of the class), there is no judgment about what is not happening, praise for what is happening, or new information. It is just a statement to help focus the expectation lens more clearly. It affirms the expectation was already understood but may have been a little fuzzy.

Providing good direction in any activity is critical. And as the use of clarifying statements, expectation mantras, and positive recognition acts to further define any task, we have powerful tools for making our learning targets clear and "standing still" (Stiggins, 2001) without the need for constant explanations or negativity. The next chapter offers a systematic method for giving directions that promotes accountability and a culture of responsibility.

Finally, a highly effective but underused strategy for clarifying expectations is the stating of expectation mantras. Mantras, repeated phrases that help shape a desired behavioral expectation, act on the conscious level as clarifying statements and on the unconscious level to condition thinking. An example of a mantra phrase is, "In this class, we [listen to one another attentively, take care of our equipment, say only life-giving statements to one another, raise our hands when we have something to say, persist and stay positive without quitting or getting negative, learn from our mistakes and move on quickly, and so on]." No matter how familiar or unfamiliar the content of the mantra statement is to the students, how accurately it represents the current state of affairs, or how trite you think you may sound saying it, give it a chance to work. Mantras work to the extent that they are stated repetitively.

Regardless of the students' existing level of performance in relation to any particular behavior, mantras act to raise the level of quality of that behavior in the direction of that expectation. For instance, if you inherit a class that demonstrates a habit of disrespect, it will be effective to employ the mantra, "In this class, we do a great job of listening to each other and respecting one another's opinions." While at first it may sound a bit odd to the students (because they see evidence that this is not currently accurate), over time as they hear it repeated and as you reinforce respectful behavior and show no tolerance for disrespectful behavior, you will see behavior change. The mantra begins to become internalized. Moreover, your use of the mantra sends a message to your students that you believe in them, will accept only the best they have to offer, and will not give up on them.

Over time you will see behavior change and also a change in their self-concept related to the particular expectation. Ultimately the evidence that a mantra has been substantially internalized will be when you begin to hear students say it as they interact with one another.

Clarifying Questions

Clarifying questions ask students to reflect on their actions in relation to an operating behavioral expectation. For example, the question, "Looking at the clock, at which stage of the process should you be right now?" has the effect of prompting the students to consider their level of progress in relation to the amount of time that they have to complete the task. When compared to clarifying statements, clarifying questions have the effect of eliciting not simply recognition of the expectation but also subjective interpretation. To illustrate the difference, it may help to consider an example of each type of statement related to the same expectation:

- *Clarifying statement:* "Make sure you are all doing a good job of your cooperative group roles."
- *Clarifying question:* "How would you say you are doing in fulfilling your cooperative group roles so far today?"

Each statement will have the effect of focusing the expectation lens. Neither is judgmental or distracting. However, it is instructive to reflect on what types of thinking each will elicit. The clarifying statement effectively brings awareness to the task, and the clarifying question adds the dimension of promoting reflection. In the clarifying statement, few students will hear the implication related to the quality of the task. Mostly they will just hear, "Make sure you are on task." In the clarifying question, the students are encouraged to consider the quality and effectiveness of their efforts to a greater degree.

The decision as to whether to use a question or a statement depends on the situation. But a general principle might be to use questions more frequently when the expectation has already been shown to be clearly understood and demonstrated at least once. Before then, it will likely be more frustrating than useful.

Expectation Cues: Telling Versus Expecting

When you tell students what to do, you are in essence keeping them dependent on your instructions to perform. As classroom expectations become more internalized, you can begin to simply expect and then recognize rather than tell. You can accomplish this with the use of expectation cues: key words that represent a broader series of behavior. (Cues are discussed in more detail in the next chapter.) A good example of a cue word is *ready*. If you operationalize the concept of *ready* successfully, the result is that this one word can represent an extensive set of knowledge, skills, and dispositions. Consider the following two statements:

- *Telling:* "I want you all to get ready to go."
- *Expecting:* "I am looking for a group that looks ready."

In the first statement, the students are told clearly what they need to do, and if they understand what *ready* means, it will function as an effective request for them to act. In the second statement, the implicit assumption is that the students already know what *ready* means, what is required to meet the expectation (in this case, to move with a sense of urgency to get prepared for a new activity), and what the potential consequences might be for meeting or not meeting the expectation.

The difference depends on how the cue (cause) is supported by consequences (effect). If there is some advantage or benefit to being ready when the teacher says he is "looking for a ready group," the students will move with a sense of urgency. What is the benefit, advantage, or consequence for being ready? It could be getting to go first or some other privilege, a common understanding that time is of the essence, or the awareness that being ready demonstrates respect to the other members of the class.

Within the 2-Style approach, "ready group" competition is a powerful technique. Even if the reward is small (for example, getting to go first), students will act quickly to get ready. However, it has the effect of defining the purpose of getting ready quickly as getting to go sooner. Within the 1-Style approach, it may be effective to incorporate competitive incentives early in the year, and as students begin to internalize the value of the expected behavior, weaning them off the extrinsic incentives over time.

If you are working on incorporating a 1-Style approach, it will be helpful to progressively tap into more intrinsic forms of motivation for meeting expectations as the year goes on, such as the realization that it shows respect to the other members of the class.

When is it best to use expectation cues rather than directions? As with the choice between clarifying statements or questions, it is best to be as direct and concrete as possible at first; then as the expectation becomes better understood conceptually and practically, use expectation cues the majority of the time to get the best results.

Debriefing

Debriefing with your students after an activity can be a powerful method for clarifying the expectations within that activity (Roth, 2002). It is especially effective for clarifying concepts and skills that could benefit from being operationalized. For example, you may have an expectation that groups will use active listening during a cooperative learning activity. But the concepts and skills related to active listening are rather abstract and unfamiliar to most students; debriefing can help make them more concrete and behavioral. In this case, you might ask students, "Who can share an example of a member of their group who did an especially good job of active listening?" Once they identify the person, encourage the students to be very specific about what that group member did in behavioral terms, as well as the benefits the group experienced as a result of that member's actions—in this case, being good active listeners. Debriefing can be useful to clarify a broad range of expectations, from what makes for an effective procedure to the elements that define quality for a product or performance. When you debrief, you are in essence using the effectiveness of positive recognition yet making it even more powerful because it requires students to generate the concrete examples of the concept themselves. Moreover, positive recognition by peers is typically more rewarding than when it comes from the teacher. When we examine the potential of debriefing within the lens of our two principles for what makes expectations effective, we find that it is highly effective at promoting both clarity and positive feelings related to the behavior.

At its essence, debriefing is an inductive exercise in identifying the concrete, specific ingredients to a concept of task. In practice, it can take many forms, so you can use it however it best suits the needs of the situation and the nature of the task. Debriefing can be especially powerful when used after a cooperative learning exercise or to help clarify abstract terms used to define high-quality behavior or participation.

Stolovitch (1990) offers a six-step process for debriefing following highly interactive activities that moves from more concrete and practical to more abstract and general:

1. *General discussion and decompression.* Set the context for the kinds of concepts and skills that you are going to debrief.

2. *Generation of factual information from the activity.* Help the students recall what happened in concrete, specific, and behavioral terms. These recollections will act as data for your inductive examination.

3. *Drawing inferences from the factual information.* Ask the students to interpret the data by posing questions to facilitate the process of interpretation, such as, "What did they [you] do that made you label their actions as effective?" or "When you did . . ., what was the effect?"

4. *Identifying generalizations and unifying principles.* Help students create generalizations from their inferences. Again, this will be best facilitated with questions, such as, "So given what we have concluded about what worked, what overall principle can we draw from our experience?"

5. *Identifying how skills can be transferred to other situations.* Once students have developed a set of working principles that help promote effectiveness in one context, help them see how those same principles can be applied to other contexts. For example, you might ask, "How could you use the principles for conflict resolution within your cooperative learning groups on the playground?" or "We have generated a set of principles for giving written feedback in our peer writing process. Is there any part of that that we could apply to the process of verbal feedback in our class discussions?"

6. *Looking for real-world applications.* Help connect the skills and concepts from the classroom context to the outside world and the students' daily lives. This process could be as simple as asking them to think about how this applies to what they experience outside the class or what is going on in the world, or as complex as relating the discoveries within this process to other assignments or service-learning projects.

Taking just a minute or two to debrief after an activity can pay for itself many times over in the clarity that it creates and the processes of inquiry and reflection that it promotes. When used repetitively for the same kinds of activities, it provides students with opportunities to reflect on and then apply the skills that they learned as a result of previous episodes of debriefing. In addition, it provides each student with the opportunity to positively recognize others (or themselves) or be positively recognized, which reinforces the behavior and builds community as well. Used effectively, debriefing can contribute to a needs-satisfying classroom climate, as well as produce clearer expectations.

REFLECTION

4.7

Reflect on situations in which you were positively recognized by your peers for demonstrating a skill or action in a group context. How did it make you feel? How effective was it in reinforcing the skill or action?

Written Expectations

Putting expectations in writing is helpful for many reasons and should be included whenever possible. The clarity provided by written directions can spell out the task for all learners more effectively and may be essential to students who are not strong auditory learners or are second language learners. Be careful, however, not to assume that written directions are sufficient to clarify and support your expectations. When words are conspicuously displayed in the class, students will read them many times over. However, if the actions in the class do not support the words, even the most dramatic and catchy posters will quickly become invisible. This is true for both directions for tasks and for broad behavioral expectations.

If we were to examine two groups of students who were given a task where one group had written directions and the other did not, which group would you predict would do a better job of the task? The answer may seem obvious, yet how often do we trust verbal directions when written directions would have saved a great deal of misguided effort, the need to repeat what was said, and frustration for both teacher and students? For early grades, putting directions at work centers or on the board is a highly effective practice. For upper grades, giving individual students or groups assignment task sheets and rubrics will result in a much higher-level product in the end, as well as a more focused process along the way.

There are other ways as well to use the written word to clarify your expectations:

- Use the walls to help convey your messages.
- Display student work early in the school year, and let them know it is their space.
- Use bulletin boards to make a statement or provide information.
- Put up your favorite sayings, quotes, and messages.

Personal Recognition or Praise

"I like the way Brandon is sitting" is an example of a personal recognition statement. These statements have become more popular in the past decade as a way to reinforce desired behavior without being negative (Wong & Wong, 1991; Canter, 1992). It is true that they are more positive than a negative recognition such as, "I am waiting for Brandon to sit quietly before I can begin." So on that score, they produce overall a more positive effect on the association with sitting quietly. But if we examine personal recognitions more closely, we will recognize that they are essentially a form of praise (discussed in the next chapter). What we are saying is that the *student* is doing something we like. On the surface the affective message seems to be supportive, but examined more closely, as is the case with any praise, the affective association is not with the act (in this case, sitting quietly) but with the student. Therefore, other students do not experience a positive association with sitting. They may even develop a negative reactive association with it. It can in the end represent something that certain students ("of whom I am jealous") do. So as a student, my choice to sit now includes the considerations for both my feeling about the students who are being praised as well as how much I desire the affection of the teacher on that day. In terms of clarity, personal recognitions are not especially strong either. Because the association is with the student being praised, there is little sense of cause and effect between the behavior and any resulting consequence.

4.8

REFLECTION

Evaluate the power of personal recognition or praise. Observe a teacher who uses it as the primary source of clarifying expectations. What do you notice? Do you see a high level of clarity? How about the quality of affective association with the expectations? It is quite possible you will notice that it becomes less powerful over time, and at some point, the teacher will (misguidedly) turn to something negative in an effort to gain more control. In your observation, could this frustrating cycle have been avoided by using a more effective strategy for clarifying expectations for desirable behavior?

Warnings

Warnings are a familiar technique to everyone. They are used to tell us something is coming up of which we need to be made aware, or that we did not get it right this time and had better do it right the next time. Time warnings or change-of-activity warnings are valuable techniques that help students prepare for a change in activity. They support the clarity and emotional ease in the room.

The "I'll let it pass this time" type of warning has a much more confusing effect on the quality of classroom expectations. A teacher who gives a warning to the class or a student that an action was problematic and that this time nothing will happen but next time it will is sending the message that an expectation needs to be respected. Warnings are typically effective at making the teacher feel a little better for a little while, but not at changing behavior or clarifying expectations. In fact, if they are expressed in an angry or frustrated tone, they can exacerbate the undesirable behavior.

A warning is intended to portend an action, but it is in itself an action. Or, rather, it might be better to say that it is a conspicuous and deliberate inaction. It sends the message that in this class, the cause-and-effect relationship between behavior and consequences is weak or that the teacher does not have the energy or courage to follow through. If the teacher makes warnings a routine intervention, students learn to assume that they get a free pass the first time they choose to cross a line (Bluestein, 1999). Students do not need to be malicious to learn quickly that they are able to take advantage of any system that gives them a buffer between their choices and accountability for those choices.

4.9

REFLECTION

Test this principle yourself. Consider your own response to a condition in which you know that the police always give one warning to drivers not wearing a seat belt versus a condition in which they give tickets to all nonbelted drivers without warnings. Would your behavior be affected?

Warnings are not usually useful. Yet when a classroom expectation is new or is in place only for a particular event, warnings can be a useful consideration to those who did not understand the direction or expectation well. Warnings in this case are a courtesy that says, in effect, "We are all doing our best and acting with good intentions, but we are human and need reminders of what is expected. So let me do you a favor and explain what we need to be doing at some future time." But given that many of the expectations that we have are for things that we do on a regular basis (lining up, participating in class discussions, turning in work on time, cooperating within the group, and so on), a reminder is seldom called for. In these cases, warnings water down the cause-and-effect relationship between what is expected and what happens when expectations are met or not met. A mere warning today makes the clarity of the expectation a little weaker for tomorrow.

Requests

Requests are cases in which the teacher asks the students to do something and holds the assumption that they will do it. In practice, a request alone will have little effect on promoting an expectation. However, what happens afterward within the context of the request has a significant effect. For example, if the teacher asks the class for attention, expects them to be listening, does not speak until they are attentive, and follows up with consequences if there is not 100 percent attention, students learn that the request is meaningful. If the teacher requests attention, does not get it, and then begins to talk anyway, the students quickly learn that the teacher really does not have an expectation of being listened to. And when the request comes in the form of a plea such as, "I want you to listen to me," students learn that the teacher's requests are essentially meaningless (and maybe even pitiful).

Requests differ from directions in that they ask, whereas direction and clarifying statements tell. This difference can be rendered inconsequential if students learn that when we ask them to do something, we are actually giving them directions. For example, students may learn that when their teacher says, "It is time to stop, so I want you to put away your books and open your journals," she means that there is now an expectation that they make the transition from one activity to another, it is not optional: they need to move with a sense of purpose, or there will be a consequence. Keep in mind that for students whose parents do not phrase directions as requests, this can be confusing. In most cases, students can adjust to the style preferences of the teacher, but the teacher does bear the responsibility of effective communication and making expectations clear to students of all cultural groups. Teachers should be careful not to penalize students who are not able to infer that they use requests when they are actually giving directions or commands.

4.10 REFLECTION

What type of language and inflection did your parents use when they wanted you to do something? Did it take the form of a polite request, was it more of a straightforward command, or was it something more neutral? What would you predict the result would be if you were to use this same type of style with children who were used to something quite different? Have you seen firsthand examples of this?

New teachers especially should keep in mind an important principle involving the use of requests as related to expectations: *never make a request that students do something they are already expected to be doing.* An expectation implies an understanding between parties, and part of that understanding involves consequences (effect) for when students choose not to meet the expectation (cause). When the teacher makes a further request instead of taking the action that is implied by the expectation, the students learn that there is no cause-and-effect relationship between their actions and the consequences for those actions. Consequently, the particular expectation becomes weakened. Moreover, they learn that when the situation requires it, the teacher will not follow through but will instead use a passive tool such as a further request.

Negative Recognitions

A negative recognition is any message from the teacher that identifies a particular behavior that he or she wants stopped. It could also be referred to as the "chronicling of misbehavior." Negative recognitions can take the form of comments to individuals, such as, "Cornell, I want you to stop bothering Mahfouz." Or they can take the form of comments to the collective, such as "It is getting too noisy in here," or "Shhhh!"

As with warnings, negative recognitions of unwanted behavior may seem like action and in the short term make the teacher feel that he or she did something to address the problem. Yet over time, the net result is that the expectations in the class get weaker and the climate in the class grows more negative. Using negative recognitions to achieve clarity of expectations is like drinking salt water to quench a thirst: there is a momentary sense of resolution, but whatever is done is actually worsening the problem.

If we evaluate negative recognition of behavior using a two-part standard that sound expectations come from strong cause-and-effect relationships along with a positive association with the behavior expected, it fails both parts. First, as with warnings and threats, pointing out unwanted behavior is essentially conspicuous inaction. We are showing in a very public manner that we are too lazy or weak to take any meaningful action. The cause-and-effect relationship created in this case is when students misbehave but the teacher does nothing (while pretending to do something). Because there is no meaningful action, the students quickly learn to tune out the message that comes with the inaction.

Second, consider what negative recognition does to the association with the behavior. Imagine that the behavior is well-done small group interaction. A typical negative recognition might be something like, "You guys over there! Quit socializing and get to work!" How has the teacher created a positive association with the desired task? The distressing fact is that the group (and indirectly the whole class) just heard the teacher say something to the effect, "Socializing is what you want to do, and this task is not very enjoyable, but you are supposed to do it because I am in charge and I decide what we do here." The teacher has just contributed to the students' perception that the work was not enjoyable, thus creating an even more negative association with the task. The intention of negative recognition is founded in pain-based logic: *if I give you pain (shame, guilt, or disappointment), you will change your behavior.* This logic will not only lead to a negative climate and depressed motivation, but will undermine the process of creating clear expectations.

REFLECTION

4.11

Reflect on the effect of the use of negative recognitions and chronicling of behavior and chronicling of student failure by the teachers whom you have observed. What was the effect on the class? What was the effect on the clarity of the expectations in the class? Compare the language of this teacher to one who relied more extensively on the use of positive recognitions. What did you find?

Threats and Put-Downs

"If you guys don't stop goofing off before I get over there, you are all going to be in trouble." On the surface, a threat such as this can appear to be a powerful tool to encourage behavior. However, recall the qualities that give an expectation its power and consider whether threats meet those qualifications. By its nature, a threat is hostile and passive. It sends the message that the teacher is willing to externalize his or her negativity but is too weak to take any meaningful action. Is it apparent to you why threats were rated with no asterisks in Figure 4.1

for their ability to promote intentional expectations? They are, however, rather effective at creating the implicit and unintentional expectation that the teacher is not an emotionally safe being and is lazy as well. As a result, they have the effect of leading a class downward on the effectiveness continuum toward greater levels of dysfunction.

Put-downs work with a similarly superficial but faulty logic: if I tell you enough times and in strong enough terms how inadequate you are, you will change. Do you recognize the pain-based logic in this thinking? Unfortunately, most of us have a great deal of day-to-day experience with put-downs. They do have power. They cause us to retreat or avoid. They have the power to destroy relationships and deflate the motivation of others, but they have little to no value in promoting desirable expectations or changing behavior for the better. Like threats, they are hostile and passive. The pain and hurt that you see on the face of the person you just put down is likely the tip of the iceberg. Almost certainly there is a great deal more under the surface. And sooner or later, all the pain that a teacher gives out will come back in some form or another—multiplied by the number of students in the class.

4.12 REFLECTION

Have you seen an example of the principle of the tortoise and the hare played out in a school? Is it always the most talented and charismatic who have effective management? What is it that leads to effective management, if not simply talent?

Assessing Behavior

Using a system for assessing student behavior can have a profound effect on improving the expectations for quality behavior. Used intentionally and systematically, it qualifies as an effective source of clarification, creates positive associations with expected behavior, and communicates positive recognitions. Used unsystematically and carelessly, it can at best be ineffectual and at worst create a negative association with the behavior being assessed. And when it is structured as a deficit model, such as a names-on-the-board or colored-card system, it acts as a systematic process for delivery of negative recognitions. The online resource article "Developing and Implementing an Effective System for Assessing the Quality of Behavior, Participation, or Process," available at transformativeclassroom.com, examines a step-by step process for constructing a system that teachers at any level can use to help support healthier and more functional class behavior.

Expectations and Management Style Orientations

The following short phrases characterize each of the four management style orientations as they relate to expectations:

1-Style: "How does it feel when we [meet the expectations for the class]?"

2-Style: "I need you to [meet the expectations of the class]."

3-Style: "There is not enough [behavior that is meeting my expectations]."

4-Style: "There is too much [behavior that is not meeting the class expectations]."

Over time the strategies that you use for communicating your expectations are greatly responsible for defining the climate in your classroom. Your choices can promote a climate that is functional and positive or one that is reactionary and negative. As characterized in Case Studies 4.1 and 4.2, the strategies that may appear useful in the short term for producing a compliant class may not ultimately produce the clarity and behavioral consistency that you desire. Conversely, if applied consistently, sound strategies for promoting clear and positive expectations will in the long term achieve the result of a class full of students who know what is expected of them and are inclined to demonstrate that behavior.

CASE STUDY

4.1

The Tortoise and the Hare: Elementary School Example

Elsa and Alberto are new elementary-level teachers. Elsa has been a teacher's assistant and is very comfortable in a school environment. Alberto is a quiet person with a soft voice and has not had much experience with students. Elsa comes across as confident and capable. She likes to present an affectionate and caring persona to her students. She also likes to use personal approval and disappointment to modify behavior with such phrases as, "I am having trouble hearing," "It makes me sad when we say things to each other like that," and "It will make me happy if we all do our best on this project."

This year Alberto has committed to using fewer personal appeals and more clarity-building strategies. He is attempting to use a lot of positive recognitions, clarifying statements, and expectation mantras. Early in the year, some students continue to test the class boundaries and seem to be expecting him to get upset and show his displeasure at their misbehavior. However, he refuses to fall into that pattern and instead takes those students aside and explains to them that if they act responsibly, they will receive more rights, but if not, they will lose rights and privileges. The class gradually responds, realizing that these policies are leading to better behavior and a sense of enjoyment in the class. Alberto is better than the teacher they had the year before who spend a great deal of time threatening them and telling them what not to do. Alberto finds that he has bonded with his students without the need to use praise and disappointment. He recognizes that the students can tell that he really likes them, and on an unconscious level, they appreciated that he was empowering them. He makes it about their growth, not about him.

After two months, Elsa is still required to express a lot of approval and disapproval. Some days things go smoothly, while on others, students seem to be immune to her pleas to "be good." Every couple of days, she seems to need to give a lecture about how the quality of behavior and effort should be better than it is. After the same period of time, Alberto finds that he does very little asking. Students seem to know what is expected and rely on their own understanding of the rules rather than his approval or disapproval. He also notices that his personality is emerging, and he feels increasingly confident. He is able to use humor and lightness and does not feel the need to put on a hard shell to send a message that he is the authority in the room.

In the parable of the tortoise and the hare, the more talented hare lost the race to the less gifted tortoise due to overconfidence and lack of effort. In this actual case,

(Continued)

Alberto, like the tortoise, did not rely on his personality, common sense, charisma, or talent; he relied instead on effective technique that he executed faithfully. Elsa may have been the more gifted teacher, but because she made her class about herself and used giving and withdrawing affection to produce results, her students did not learn self-responsibility.

4.2   CASESTUDY

The Tortoise and the Hare: Secondary School Example

Byron and Kara are secondary teachers. Byron is what many refer to as "born teacher." He has been a substitute for a year and has gotten used to using his commanding and persuasive personality to get students to behave. Kara has spent a great deal of time at night worrying about whether she has what it takes to be a good teacher. Byron is beginning his student teaching, and Kara is in her first year as a full-time teacher. Byron uses a good number of personal statements and communicates his pleasure and disappointment. He uses phrases like, "I would expect better work from high school students," or "This level of noise is making it hard to teach," or "I like it so much better when everyone is listening and on task."

Kara does not have a large personality or a lot of experience, but she is committed to creating clear and positive expectations. She finds that using positive recognitions, clarifying statements, and expectation mantras feels somewhat unnatural, but she nevertheless sticks to her principles and refrains from using personal or negative feedback. At first, her students test her and respond slowly to only being given clarifying language: they almost seem to be asking for negative recognitions and shaming. However, over time, they begin to get used to the way that she talks to them and prefer it to the teachers who seem so negative all the time.

After two months, Byron is still dealing with a lot of inconsistency. Every couple of days, he needs to give a lecture about how the quality of behavior and effort should be better than it is. He is finding himself shifting the blame for the dysfunction onto the students, especially a few who consistently misbehave. Byron settles into a pattern of using a mix of positive, personal, and negative forms of feedback in varying amounts. But over the course of the year, the behavior, the level of focus with activities, and the quality of processes and procedural execution by his students remain inconsistent and often leave him disappointed

Kara is finding that her expectations have become very clear to her students, and the anxiety level in the room is very low. She notices that the better she becomes at giving clear feedback during tasks, the better the products she receives from the students. Her favorite mantra is, "In this class, we always put the time into preparing and making the effort so we know the products will be great." What she discovers is that with each project, her students internalize that mantra (as well as the many others that she uses), and she sees the quality of their work getting progressively better. She also realizes that she was able to make it past the first three weeks of school without resorting to going negative.

After two months, Kara notices that the challenges that she experienced in the first few weeks have mostly disappeared. She is struck by how much she is now able to accomplish with her students. She finds that she is able to be creative in her lesson planning (she worried that she would not be able to after hearing so many horrifying stories), because she worries little about overcoming the resistance that so many teachers complain about.

This true story is another example of the parable of the tortoise and the hare. Byron appeared to possess more of the qualities that we associate with an effective secondary teacher, yet in the long run, his personalized methods of creating expectations produced mixed results. In contrast, Kara was more effective with her technique and refrained from giving in to the temptation to use negative strategies, and in the long run she was more successful.

2- AND 1-STYLE MANAGEMENT ORIENTATIONS IN RELATION TO THE INTENTIONAL DEVELOPMENT OF CLASSROOM EXPECTATIONS

Both 2- and 1-Style management approaches require the promotion of the qualities of clarity and positivity in how classroom expectations are developed. Moreover, each approach needs to be undertaken intentionally and deliberately. Yet given that the goal of each will be different, they require somewhat differing strategies, which will ultimately lead to different results. The essence of a 2-Style approach to expectations is the clarification of the respective roles, duties, and responsibilities of both the teacher and the students. The ultimate goal of this approach is for students to become experts in understanding and exhibiting the behavior defined by the expectation—as defined by the teacher—to demonstrate that they are a functional part of the class.

The essence of a 1-Style approach to expectations is the development of the students' sense of collective responsibility toward promoting the common good. Because the common good of any group evolves over time with the needs and development of the group dynamics, the expectations will need to evolve as well. Therefore, in the 1-Style class, helping students understand what the expectation is intending to accomplish can be as important as the fact that the expectation is known and is being shown. The development of a student-owned social contract, shifting the focus of technical management from execution to recognition of value, periodic class meetings, and negotiating boundaries are among the strategies that will promote of the goals of the 1-Style classroom. These and other techniques for promoting a self-directed class are examined in detail in subsequent chapters.

A technique that can be effective in supporting expectations within a 1-Style management approach is boundary setting (Bluestein, 1999): the process in which the teacher and students work together to find the most desirable and workable standards for any particular situation. Its effectiveness varies dramatically depending on how it is led. If it takes the form of random complaints, changing expectations after the fact because of students' pleading, or is generally characterized by selfishness or laziness, it will be counterproductive. It will lead the 1-Style classroom toward the realm of the 3-Style classroom. However, when students respond with a sense of responsibility to being empowered with a substantial amount of control over the expectations in their class, boundary setting can work as a means to increased student ownership as well as clarity of expectations.

For example, if you find that students are having trouble completing a regularly assigned task in the time that you typically give them, you might take the opportunity to ask how you as a collective might solve your problem. The potential solution could take any number of forms that would work for you and that the students would find acceptable to them as a group. After the boundary-setting exercise, a new expectation has emerged for the situation. The outcome may help solve the problem, and more than that, the process will have had a powerful effect on the development of 1-Style classroom goals and the clarity and effectiveness of the new expectation.

As we will discuss in Chapter Fifteen, if you are committed to a 1-Style approach but have inherited a group of students who are unfamiliar with being empowered with a high level of self-direction or engaging in democratic participation, it may be necessary to begin operating early in the year by using a 2-Style approach and gradually work toward a more internalized and self-directed 1-Style approach. Any class can learn to be self-directed and exhibit a clear understanding of shared behavioral expectations. For all students, this environment represents a context in which there is the greatest potential to have their basic needs met. Nevertheless, for some students, gaining an operational knowledge of and internalizing the value of many of the basic expectations for being a functional member of a self-directed classroom community will require a great deal of intentional instruction on the part of the teacher.

CONCLUSION

No matter what your personal vision of an ideal classroom is, you will be successful achieving your goals to the extent that you are able to promote clear and intentional expectations. Shared expectations must serve as the cornerstone. The following chapter addresses technical management: the domain of management that addresses such areas as creating effective procedures, directions, transition, and gaining 100 percent attention from students. High-quality technical management is built on clear and positive expectations.

Journal Reflections

1. In your experience, what methods did adults use to express to you that they wanted or did not want you to engage in a particular behavior? Were they effective?
2. In what situations would you use warnings?

Activities

1. Examine a classroom, or recall one that you have observed recently. Does the teacher use more positive or more negative recognitions of behaviors? What is the result in your analysis?
2. In small groups, discuss the use of personal praise versus encouragement or positive (performance) recognition. Then classify the following phrases as either praise or positive recognition:
   - "I like the way Alicia is listening."
   - "I see groups locating all their research before they start writing their reports."
   - "That looks like a good idea."
   - "Good job, Sven!"

- "We've done so well transitioning from one presentation to the next. Wonderful!"
- "I'm so pleased with the way the papers turned out."
- "Jorge, that's the way to set your feet early to hit that forehand!"

REFERENCES

Bluestein, J. (1999). *Twenty-first century discipline*. Torrance, CA: Fearon.

Canter, L. (1992). *Lee Canter's assertive discipline: Positive behavior management for today's classroom*. Los Angeles: Lee Canter and Associates.

Grusec, J. E., & Goodnow, J. J. (1994). Impact of parental discipline methods on the child's internalization of values: A reconceptualization of current points of view. *Developmental Psychology*, *30*, 4–19.

Hargreaves, D. H., Hester, S. K., & Mellor, F. J. (1975). *Deviance in classrooms*. London: Routledge.

Hines, C. V., Cruickshank, D. R., & Kennedy, J. J. (1985). Teacher clarity and its relationship to student achievement and satisfaction. *American Educational Research Journal*, *22*, 87–99.

Kohn, A. (1999). *Punished by rewards: The trouble with gold stars, incentive plans, A's, praise, and other bribes*. Boston: Houghton Mifflin.

Pianta, R. C., Hamre, B., & Stuhlman, M. (2003). Relationships between teachers and children. In W. Reynolds & G. Miller (Eds.), *Handbook of psychology: Vol. 7. Educational psychology* (pp. 199–234). Hoboken, NJ: Wiley.

Roth, W. (2002). Becoming in the classroom: Learning to teach in/as praxis (Chap. 2). In D. Lovoie & W. Roth (Eds.), *Models of science teaching preparation*. Amsterdam: Springer Netherlands.

Rosenthal, R., & Jacobson, L. (1968). Pygmalion in the classroom. *Urban Review*, *3*(1), 16–20.

Stiggins, R. (2001). *Student involved classroom assessment* (3rd ed.). Upper Saddle River, NJ: Prentice Hall.

Stolovitch, H. (1990). D-FITGA: A debriefing model. *Performance and Instruction*, *29*(7), 18–19.

Weinstein, R. S., Gregory, A., & Strambler, M. J. (2004). Intractable self-fulfilling prophecies: *Brown* vs. *Board of Education*. *American Psychologist*, *59*, 511–520.

Wentzel, K. R. (2006). A social motivational perspective for classroom management. In C. M. Evertson & C. S. Weinstein (Eds.), *Handbook of classroom management* (pp. 619–643). Mahwah, NJ: Erlbaum.

Wentzel, K. R., Battle, A., & Looney, L. (2000, March). *Teacher and peer contribution to classroom climate in middle school: Relations to school adjustment*. Paper presented at the annual meeting of the American Educational Research Association, Seattle, WA.

Wong, H., & Wong, R. (1991). *First days of school: How to be an effective teacher*. Mountain View, CA: Wong Publications.

5

Effective Technical Management

Promoting a Culture of Listening, Respect, and Efficiency in the Classroom

In This Chapter

- Creating a culture of listening and respect
- Promoting 100 percent attention
- Effectively giving directions
- How to foster efficient classroom procedures
- Beginning and ending the day (or period) effectively

5.1

REFLECTION

A parent, colleague, or administrator at your school peeks in the window of your classroom and watches what is going on for thirty seconds or so. If this person had yet to see you teach, has he or she now made a determination as to how effective you are as a teacher? What information did this person use?

Consider how others form their initial impressions of you as a teacher. What evidence do they use? It is likely not how knowledgeable you are, or the quality of the relationships that you have formed with your students, or even your students' academic performance. Their impression is probably going to be formed as a result of their perception of the levels of control and attention that they observe existing, or the technical management of the class. So, valid or not, technical management—the efficiency and practical organization of the class—determines to a great extent how teachers are judged as teachers by others as well as by students (Doyle, 2003). In addition to succeeding at making a good impression, research has demonstrated a great number of compelling reasons to become an expert at the technical strategies of managing a classroom:

- *Your stress level.* When you struggle with students less, you have more energy to put into more creative matters (Friedman & Farber, 1992).

- *The students' stress level.* When the students feel that there is a smoothness and momentum to the class, they tend to relax more (Friedman, 2006).

- *Much more gets done in a day.* When time is not wasted dealing with inattention, following up on directions, and corralling students during transitions, there is more time for learning and whatever else you want to accomplish (Doyle, 2003; Emmer, Evertson, & Anderson, 1980).

- *You begin to develop a culture of listening.* Over time students become more comfortable with a climate of respect for others' ideas and appreciate the value of being attentive (Elias & Schwab, 2006).

- *You have a starting point to master a 2-Style management orientation or transition to a 1-Style set of practices.* Without a fundamental structure to the technical aspects of management, efforts to incorporate a more student-centered approach most often take on more of a dysfunctional 3-Style appearance rather than a well-functioning facilitative 1-Style (Cartledge & Milburn, 1995).

EXAMINING THE PRINCIPLES OF TECHNICAL MANAGEMENT

The most effective strategies for technical management can be some of the most unnatural and counterintuitive practices one comes across. Principles such as 100 percent attention, being absolute, resisting the temptation to use negative recognitions, and taking action rather than offering explanations for what should be better are not what we do naturally in the world outside school. They are probably not what our common sense tells us to do. However, following our natural inclinations in the area of technical management typically leads to a perpetual wrestling match with students when it comes to attention, following directions, and carrying out procedures. This wrestling match is at best an added stressful element to the job, and at worst a source of great pain and suffering, and even the reason that many leave the profession. "Why am I wasting my breath and making all this effort if they never listen to me? Is it supposed to be this hard?" The answer is that it is not—if we accept that some practices are simply more effective than others in this area. Transformative technical management practices may not feel instinctive initially, but they become natural over time and, more important, help you bring about the outcomes that you desire.

5.2 **REFLECTION**

Think of technical management as similar to housekeeping. We do not all have the same need for a house that is clean and neat. Some people feel stressed with an expectation that everything needs to be neat and sanitized. Others feel stressed when there is more than a little mess. So just as with keeping up a home environment, when it comes to the level of attention, the efficiency of the transitions, and the orderliness of routine procedures, we all have a different ideal. What is your expectation in this area? What kinds of issues give you stress?

Whatever your ideal vision is in the area of technical management, you can achieve it with enough time and the right techniques. Whether it is a class that moves with precision and order, a relaxed class, or a class that runs itself, what you want is possible. But you do need to have a vision to work toward. Therefore, the first step in the process of achieving effective technical management is to create a picture in your mind related to what you can live with—and then accept nothing less. Over time, regardless of grade level, students will adjust to your expectations, whatever they are.

If the idea of being intentional and determined about what you expect is a new one, you may need to reflect on the importance of your role as the leader in the class. If this does not come easily, an encouraging realization may be that your ability to project leadership qualities will make a significant difference in how much your students learn. Self-doubt, fear, a dismissive attitude toward the need to be intentional in this area, or the thought that you do not want to be seen as being on a power trip will all lead to a lose-lose situation in your classes. There is only one person who can be the leader in the class: you. Each class presents different needs and degrees to which they need to be supported in their efforts to be a functional and considerate collective (Emmer & Gerwels, 2006). Without effective technical management, you will get little else done. Your students will be the losers, and you will perpetually feel as though you are unsuccessful, no matter how well you are doing in the other aspects of your teaching.

Whether your goal is to be effective with a 1- or 2-Style approach, you need a solid foundation of technical management. There will be significant differences in what effectiveness will look like in each case. But without sound technical management in place early, no matter how noble your intentions, your classrooms will start to resemble a 3-Style or 4-Style environment.

At the heart of effective technical management is a culture of listening. It may not appear to be critical on the surface. Nevertheless, a culture of listening will lead to other essential qualities, such as respect, self-control, awareness, valuing one another's ideas, and building bonds within the group.

The 100 Percent or 50 Percent Principle

Most of us come into teaching not having expected 100 percent attention in our interactions with friends and family, so it is probably not a familiar interaction pattern. But keep in mind that this situation is different. You have not been hired to professionally help your family members grow into successful learners. Also, students are most often not fully mature in their social behavior. Many teachers do not believe that expecting 100 percent attention will have a significant effect on their classes. They see too many other more substantial problems and outcomes to worry about expecting everyone to listen. But what teachers find when they do commit to expecting 100 percent attention is that it is possible and that a good proportion of their other problems disappear when students begin to be attentive to one another.

There are very few classes in which there is a moderate level (80 to 90 percent) of attention. Examine a number of classes for yourself. Either you will observe nearly all the students listening in all the situations they should be, or you will find that lots of students are not paying attention and that the collective level of attention in the class varies greatly from activity to activity. The reason is that attention tends to be a 100 percent or somewhere around 50 percent mechanism. It makes sense when you recall the social learning diagram.

Social and Indirect Learning Dynamic (Revisited)

If we apply listening as the behavior in this social or indirect learning dynamic, what we find is that the other students (O) learn the expectations and consequences for listening from watching what happens when another student (S) is not listening. Observe the interaction (shown by line a in the icon). The other students (O) draw conclusions related to what happened to the student (S) (line b), and then make assumptions about what the teacher's (T) expectations are (line c) for other members of the class as well.

Recall our examination in the previous chapter related to how students develop their expectations. Words in these situations will have a much less significant impact when compared to what students learn from observing a teacher's actions. You can test this principle by observing the effectiveness of asking students to be quiet. If you do nothing except ask—you take no action—invariably students will learn that your words are not meaningful. Those who use continual requests for attention rarely achieve high levels of attention. By using very few words, students can learn from your actions that you need their attention. For example, consider a case in which the teacher (T) asks for 100 percent attention, and the student (S) chooses instead to talk to another student. If the teacher takes action (delivers a consequence), the other students (O) learn that the expectation is real. However, if the teacher keeps talking or engages in an ineffectual act such as negative recognition, saying *shh-shh,* or asking for attention, the public message to the members of the class (O) is that it is okay, or at least possible, to talk when the teacher is talking. As a result the other members of the class (O) become much more likely to engage in the same type of inattentive behavior.

As this cycle repeats itself, the expectation in the class is quickly reduced from 100 percent attention to only those who feel like it. This number varies from class to class, but it will include students who attend out of a sense of personal obligation or previous training. As we examine the mechanics of this situation, it becomes evident that you will have 100 percent attention as long as you are absolute about the expectation and follow through with consequences for lack of attention. If you are less than absolute, you will experience less—and, over time, significantly less.

5.3 REFLECTION

Have you seen the 100 or 50 percent principle displayed in a classroom that you have observed? What kinds of strategies did the teacher use in the 50 percent classroom? What strategies did the teachers use who attained 100 percent attention?

Another important and often overlooked aspect to the 100 percent attention expectation is that hands should be free as well. In some cases, with certain groups of older or more mature students, this is less significant. But for most students most of the time, equipment, supplies, balls, and anything else that is going to be a distraction should be left on the desk or the floor for the duration of the directions or explanation. This can be a simple intervention for such problems as pencil tapping, bouncing balls, or playing with the learning manipulatives while attention is required.

Culture of Listening

A culture of listening begins with the students' perception that the teacher is absolute about attention. This perception can be supported only by the reality that the teacher *is* absolute. That means the teacher always expects 100 percent attention; when someone is talking and there is anything but 100 percent attention, the teacher must stop and take action. The action itself does not have to be dramatic or severe (more on this later), but it does need to be automatic and consistent. The same principle must apply to any member of the classroom community who is authorized to speak.

A culture of listening goes far beyond telling students to listen to the teacher. It means showing respect to anyone who is sharing and expecting 100 percent attention and respect when you are speaking. It will take a while for students to adjust to this climate if they have been used to environments where there was little attention to or accountability for listening, but they will increasingly come to appreciate it. You will notice that it is catching hold when you observe students waiting for others to stop and listen before speaking, and when you notice that students speak more purposefully and confidently since others are attentive to what they have to say.

A simple yet effective way to send the message that you require 100 percent attention is to wait for all students to be attentive. If a student or two is not listening fully, you might stop giving directions and wait for the student. It can be even more powerful to restart your directions from the beginning (for example, "I notice we are not all listening. I will start again"). The use of shame and embarrassment is tempting, but avoid this because it is counterproductive. Also, do not refer to students who are not listening (negative recognitions); instead, restate the expectation (clarifying statement). If one student is demonstrating a habit of poor attention, privately give that student a logical consequence. The message to the whole class is, "There will never be a time when anyone is talking and it will be okay not to be listening." The message to a student with a habit of poor listening needs to be, "Very soon you will find a way to be an excellent listener, so let's start now. Tell me what you are going to do to make sure that you will always be listening and getting the most from your learning."

On a technical level, promoting a high level of attention is critical to your ability to meet your student learning outcomes. While this is of great value in and of itself, promoting a culture of listening has a deeper value: it fosters in each student increased levels of respect for the ideas of others. As students grow in the ability to attend and come out of their own ego-centered thought processes, they increasingly awaken to the world around them and are present to the moment. Research supports what many teachers report anecdotally—that students today are increasingly bored, apathetic, and self-centered (Twenge, 2006; Yazzie-Mintz, 2007). The starting point for bringing about positive change is helping them learn the value of being attentive to the world around them and creating a culture of listening and respect in the classroom. The skill of attentiveness is one of the greatest gifts that teachers can give their students.

Using Attention Cues

To initiate directions or signal the need for students to shift their focus from some other state to 100 percent attention requires using some type of attention cue. The most effective cues are those that are symbolic rather than literal. For example, if you wanted to gain the attention of the class, you could say, "Okay, class, it is time for you to stop what you are doing and give me your attention." This would work, but it takes a lot of time to say all those words, and the more words that are used, the less likely it will be that the message has an impact. You can accomplish the same goal more effectively, and with less time, by using a cue—for example, simply say, "Eyes and ears." You can use any word, signal, or sound to signify the rather involved message that you need all students to be 100 percent attentive.

Over time, the cue comes to represent all that is involved within the expectation related to what it means to demonstrate quality attention and take on the demeanor of a participant within a culture of listening. For younger students, clapping a rhythm and having the students respond with the same rhythm can be effective. In a physical education setting, a whistle can be a good choice. Some teachers find that silently raising their hand is an effective cue. At the secondary level, a cue word is typically effective. There are many types of cues that are used to good effect. Find one that works for you and your students. Table 5.1 outlines some common cues and their pros and cons.

TABLE 5.1. **Pros and Cons of Some Common Attention Cues**

Type of Cue	Grade Level	Pros and Cons
Bell or sound	Any	+ Works well to develop an autonomic response − Need to carry it with you or move to where it is − Relatively artificial
Whistle	Any (great for physical education and other activity- based situations)	+ Works well to develop an autonomic response − Need to carry it with you or move to where it is − Relatively artificial
Hand clapping (for example, teacher claps a rhythm and students respond in kind)	Preschool to grade 4	+ Works well to develop an autonomic response + Student response adds the dimension of recognition and being "tuned in" + Easy to do − Less appropriate for older students
Chanting (for example, teacher chants a phrase, such as, "1, 2, 3 eyes on me," and students respond with a response, such as, "1, 2, eyes on you")	Preschool to grade 4	+ Works well to develop an autonomic response + Active on the part of the student + Easy to do − Less appropriate for older students
Turning the lights off and on	Preschool to grade 6	+ Works well to develop an autonomic response. − Lights are not always readily available − Relatively artificial.
Counting down (for example, teacher begins to count down from 5 to 1)	Preschool to grade 8	+ Clear signal + Can be good for transitional changes − Why give students five seconds to do something they could do immediately if they wanted to, such as stop and listen? − Promotes the use of all the time given to get attentive
Hand raised (for example, teacher raises his or her hand and waits and students also raise their hands to show they are ready)	Any	+ Clear signal to anyone who can see you + Symbolic + Active + Relatively natural interaction − May not be visible to all students
Cue word (for example, "eyes, eyes and ears," "listen up")	Any	+ Works well to develop an autonomic response + Easy to use − Not as interactive as clapping or chanting for younger students

5.4

REFLECTION

The effect of a good attention cue is a lot like the effect of your phone ringing. Reflect on what happens to you physiologically when your phone rings. How does it affect your state of mind? Compare that state of mind to when you hear someone else's phone ring. What is the difference? Have you ever heard a ring that is the same as yours from another phone? How did your response vary as compared to if that phone had had a different ring?

An effective attention cue elicits a response that is as much on the level of the unconscious as it is on the conscious mind. Therefore, it should possess autonomic as well as behavioral qualities.

Autonomic Response. There should be a behaviorally conditioned response to your cue. Students should respond in large part because it is automatic and unconscious, and less because they are making a situational choice. The power of the conditioning will come from:

- The value associated with what comes after the cue
- The consistency of the expectation to listen
- The consistency of the consequences for failure to listen
- A positive association with performing the behavior

If the teacher expects 100 percent attention at all times, gives valuable and brief comments after each cue, has effective consequences when there is not 100 percent attention, and does not abuse the use of interrupting students by repeatedly stopping and starting them or asking for attention for long or unnecessary explanations, the cue will have power. However, if the teacher is inconsistent in the expectation of attention—he or she talks when other students are talking, has few consequences or resorts to negativity when all the students are not listening, or abuses the power to require attention—the cue will have little power. To test these principles in action you might compare two classes in which there is a cue used: one in which 100 percent attention is obtained and one where it is not. What is the difference?

Behavioral Qualities. The most effective cues are those that exist symbolically (a word, a sound, or a signal) and/or behaviorally (an automatic response such as clapping a response or a chanting a refrain), not as verbal information (Elias & Schwab, 2006). They should not occupy conscious energy in the students' minds. They trigger within the students an internal mechanism in which they raise the class's level of attention, focus, and awareness. And they should become antecedents to a shift in mental state, discussed in the next section.

5.5

REFLECTION

What attention cues have you observed teachers using? Were they effective?

FIVE STATES OF STUDENT ATTENTION

Students typically are asked to exhibit at least five states of attention, although they can be in only one of them at any particular time. Each has its own mental state requirements. The use of a cue helps in shifting from one state to another.

1. *One hundred percent attention.* In a fully functional culture of listening, whenever the teacher is giving explicit directions or another student is volunteering ideas, all members of the class should be listening attentively ("We have all got our eyes and ears up here and our hands free," or "We are all giving Esther our undivided attention.")

2. *Casual (optional) attention.* Often the teacher or a student spontaneously makes a comment while the class is engaged in a task. The comment has value to the whole, but the teacher did not think it was worthy of stopping the class formally ("I see some really good examples of categories that groups are using to classify their items," or, "Are we all making sure that we are doing a good job of executing the role that we have been assigned?").

3. *Students are free to talk at a reasonable level about the learning task* ("I should be hearing groups brainstorming ideas for their poster at a conversational level so that we can all hear ourselves think," or, "It is great to be talking as long as it is about the assignment").

4. *Students are free to talk about anything* that is considered appropriate for a classroom ("I need you guys to hold tight for a couple of more minutes, so it is okay to talk, but we need to stay in our seats until the bell rings").

5. *Students are required to be quiet* so that others are able to work in peace but are not necessarily required to be attentive. ("We all need to be completely quiet until everyone is done with the test. You are free to read or work on the homework, but we have to wait on any conversation until everyone is done").

It is essential that students know exactly what the expectation is for the current state of attention and what behavior is appropriate for that state. You might be surprised how many students are not sure what level of attention or amount of interaction is appropriate at any given time. Early in the year, it may be useful to be explicit when you change state and add expectation language to any set of directions—for example, "[Give directions], and since we are working independently, I should hear only occasional quiet voices when you are asking each other questions; other than that, it should be pretty quiet."

5.6 **REFLECTION**

Observe a class where there is a great deal of anxiety and confusion when students are working independently or the teacher is making casual comments. Would you say that the students are clear as to what the expectation is for the required state of attention? Observe a class where there is a great deal of ease and focus. Do these students have a clear sense of the expectation for their state of attention?

Employing Cues Effectively

Attention cues work only if they are used purposefully. Here are some recommendations for employing them effectively:

- Use cues to move only from attention states 2, 3, 4, or 5 to state 1.

- Never use a cue to gain attention during state 1. The expectation is that there is 100 percent attention already. The use of a cue indicates the change of a state of attention, so when there is no change in state, the use of a cue is not only redundant, but weakens the power of the cue and the person facilitating the action. If there is an expectation for 100 percent attention and one or more students are talking, a consequence, not another cue, is called for. How to redirect attention is addressed in the next section.

- Use consequences to help reinforce cues, such as stopping and waiting, proximity, and personal consequence implementation, for those who demonstrate a habitual problem with attention. Remember that stopping and waiting or starting over is a consequence if done calmly, but if you add disappointment, a lecture, or any other forms of negativity, it becomes punishment. Adding punishment elements shifts the locus of control away from the students and creates a negative association with the act of listening—neither of which is a desirable outcome.

- The cue will work to the degree that you project absoluteness. Assume that it will take time for the cue to become part of the conditioning of the class. It may require practice, deliberateness, and the repeated use of consequences, but eventually the cue will be a natural part of the class procedure.

Redirecting Attention in State 1

The average teacher spends a great deal of time addressing students who are not listening when the expectation is 100 percent attention. Common sense tells us that when a student is not listening or is talking to another student, the teacher needs to point that out and tell them to stop and listen. This natural inclination is understandable, but it will most likely perpetuate the problem (Sanford & Evertson, 1981). Likewise, interventions such as saying *shh-shh* or asking for attention will prove ineffective. Doyle (2006) found that the result is usually an increase in the assumed need, and subsequent increased use of these types of responses by the teacher to the point that they become unconscious reactions. We keep asking, but they keep talking.

 If we examine the dynamics of the situation, the ineffectiveness of these types of efforts to redirect attention becomes apparent. Recall the previous discussion of how expectations are developed intentionally as a result of clarity and a positive association. Redirecting students who are supposed to be attentive is essentially reinforcing the expectation. A negative recognition such as, "Lara, stop talking and listen," has a number of negative effects: it sends out negative and weak energy to the group (we did not take any action but essentially just complained about Lara publicly); it is distracting and wearing to the others; and it does not change behavior. In fact, it trains students to become dependent on reminders from the teacher to stop side talk. Likewise, saying *shh-shh* in essence is saying, "Shut up. I am out of ideas and am not going to take action, but listen anyway." When we use these types of negative recognitions to put out fires, we feel that we are addressing the situation, but the evidence in front of us is plain: the fires keep popping up. Exploring our efforts within the social and indirect learning dynamic, it is clear why. We are not taking positive action or promoting the quality of the expectations.

CASE**STUDY**

5.1

Ted and His Unconscious Habit of Saying *Shh-Shh*

Ted was a talented first-year high school teacher who cared deeply about his students. He had a good rapport with students and consistently designed engaging lessons for them. He was optimistic about every phase of his teaching except the idea of gaining attention; he had accepted that it was impossible. When I observed him, I quickly noticed that when he began to give instructions or lectures, his students would engage in side

(Continued)

conversations, and Ted would say *shh-shh* to get their attention. On our first meeting, I counted over fifty times that he said *shh-shh* in one class period. When I pointed this out to him, he was surprised. He was unaware that he was saying it. It had become an unconscious habit and, in both of our estimations, an ineffective strategy. I asked him to consider the use of more effective techniques such as to use a cue, wait for attention, and when necessary clarifying statements, such as, "I need all eyes up here right now."

A week later, I observed Ted again. He was down to ten *shh-shhs* per period, and things were looking better. After a couple more weeks, he kicked his habit completely and found that his class was listening to one another and to him. Once he changed his expectation of what was possible and made some adjustments in how he gained attention, he achieved dramatic improvement in his management. He commented that he had not recognized how much stress he felt as a result of wrestling with his class for attention until he did not have to and noticed how much easier it made everything else.

To redirect attention, it may be helpful to begin by taking on the internal mind-set and projecting the external expectation that soon the need for redirecting attention will become increasingly less necessary: "In this class we are all respectful listeners." Next, make an assessment of the level of legitimate power that you are projecting. Is a feeling of inadequacy holding you back from being able to lead? Do you fear the discomfort of confrontation with some students? Finally, you need to take effective action:

1. *Use simple, active consequences.* Stop and wait for 100 percent attention. This is especially important when one student is talking and the others are expected to be attentive. To support this expectation, ask the student to wait for the others to be attentive (or start again if they were interrupted) and comment to the class, "Hold on, Soma. Let's wait until everyone is listening attentively to your answer. Thank you. Try again."

2. *Use clarifying statements.* Instead of negative recognitions ("Terrik is not listening"), clarify the expectation with statements such as, "We are all listening attentively right now." It is also effective to use positive recognitions such as, "We are all [or almost all] doing a great job of tuning in right now." But avoid personal praise for students who are on task. Comments such as, "I like the way Miguel is listening," sound like positive recognitions, but they are not. The words "I like the way" shift the locus of control (externally) to us and what we like or do not like. The result is a weakening of the expectation.

3. *Use proximity.* Move around the room. Proximity is not a consequence and should not be used to intimidate students. However, it is a reminder and shows the class that you are aware of what is going on.

4. *Use substantive logical consequences.* Students who do not get the hint from clarifying statements, proximity, and actions such as your stopping need to be held accountable for their choice to violate the expectation or social contract. Items 1 through 3 are all essentially hints to students to do better. They project positive action and absoluteness, but they are limited. Students who show a lack of respect for others by their inattention need to accept responsibility for that choice.

CASESTUDY

Karina and Her Tendency to Put Out Fires

Karina was a student teacher in a second-grade classroom. A well-organized and no-nonsense type, she was a bright student and expected to do well in student teaching. When I observed her for the first time, she was well prepared and looked confident, and she was a success on nearly all levels. Yet she struggled with holding the students' attention and keeping them from getting off track, especially when they were reading on the rug.

On our first meeting, I counted and found that she was making about four negative recognitions for every positive recognition. I could see her trying to put out fires when a student would stray off task. She used phrases such as, "We are waiting for Jessy," and, "Paolo, stop talking and pay attention." In addition, she used the cue that she had established for gaining attention ("One, two, three, eyes on me") whenever the students began to lose attention. The more she recognized the negative behavior and used her cue (inappropriately), the more she encouraged the unwanted behavior and created a negative, even desperate, atmosphere.

After the lesson, which was very successful apart from the level of attention, she felt like a failure. I helped her focus on the positive in what she did and encouraged her to change the ratio of positive and negative recognitions; use her cue to gain attention and use a redirecting clarifying statement only when she did not have 100 percent attention; and deal with her two chronic problem students individually.

In the next visit, Karina was successful at creating a better ratio and used her cue appropriately. By the end of the quarter, she had eliminated the negative recognitions and found that they were entirely unnecessary. She had begun the quarter doing what her instincts told her to do (let the students know when they were doing something they were not supposed to be doing). She finished the quarter recognizing that she simply needed to create clarity, expect 100 percent attention, and follow through with consequences when she did not get it. In addition, she found that she was much happier promoting positive energy in the class than feeling like the "listening police."

REFLECTION

In your estimation, what percentage of students in the typical classroom (or gym or art room), listen to, understand, and then carry out the teacher's directions effectively?

EFFECTIVELY GIVING DIRECTIONS

Having an effective process for giving directions is critical. Most teachers hold the belief that there is no way to expect all students to hear and then follow directions, so they settle for a relatively ineffective process in which they give directions, repeat them to those who were not listening, and then go around and discover that several students did not understand the task correctly. The starting point for achieving 100 percent attention is believing that it is possible to achieve and maintain an absolute commitment to it; the same is true for the expectation that directions can be followed correctly by all students all of the time (with the exception of students who have substantial processing disabilities). We need to approach giving directions with the expectation that they happen once, all students make the effort to understand them, and they are followed.

Here is a systematic procedure for giving directions that will lead to more students being on task more of the time and support a culture of listening:

- *Step 1:* Always begin with a cue to gain 100 percent attention.

- *Step 2:* Use a finish word (for example, *Go! Now! Start!*). After gaining 100 percent attention, explain that the students should listen and be still until they hear the finish word. The finish word allows the students to relax and listen and to know that they do not have to move until they understand fully. It provides the teacher the assurance that the students will listen and not start moving before you have completed the directions. Until the finish word, they need to be in processing mode, in the moment, not too far off in the future just yet.

- *Step 3:* Give the directions. Be clear. Give both the purpose and the specifics necessary to execute the task, that is, keep both the abstract (the point of the lesson) and concrete (what the students will do) student needs in mind. Your directions and cue will be strengthened by your ability to make the directions concise and imbued with a sense of urgency and positive expectancy.

- *Step 4:* Call for any questions. This seems like a formality, but it is a critical step in this process and paramount in your effort to develop a culture of listening. Students typically do not ask questions when they have them, so send a consistent message beginning on the first day of class that when you ask for questions, you really expect them to ask until every student understands. This will likely take time and will be an adjustment in their thinking. Most students have learned that it is better to ask later than to look stupid in front of the whole class. You must remove the threat from asking questions and send the message that all members of the class community need to be patient and respectful of those who are asking questions. An effective message to send is, "I must not have explained the directions perfectly; help me know what I did not explain very well." A clear expectation should develop that everyone wins when the group as a whole comprehends. It will help to send the message that "it is likely that if you have a question, others will have that same question, or will at least benefit from your having asked it." One of the many practical strategies to support the process of confirming what we understand and what we still need to understand is to have students explain the directions to a neighboring student. As they attempt to explain them, they will better recognize what is clear and what is still fuzzy.

- *Step 5:* Use random checks to enhance accountability. For example, after giving the directions and then asking for and responding to all questions, randomly select one student to check understanding by asking a question such as "Okay, Jorge, what are the groups supposed to do first?" In this example, let us assume that Jorge's response reflected good understanding. At that point you have a reasonable assurance that Jorge's level of understanding reflects the whole group's, so you can move on to the finish word ("Good! Okay. Go!"). If Jorge does not know or struggles to explain the piece of the direction, assume that the process of explaining the directions is not yet complete. Jorge's lack of understanding gives you the information you need to be effective as you try to explain the confusing parts again, and it sends the message to the class (O in the social learning model) that any of them may be the student who is asked in the future (S) and they need to be ready.

These checks should be shame-free and truly random. If the student whom you ask for an accountability check does not have the information, avoid the temptation to add negativity (external) to the student's sense of irresponsibility (internal). You can say something to the effect, "Not exactly, Jorge. Hmmmm, I must not have done a very good job explaining that part. I will try again." The power will come from the effect this strategy will have on each student's sense of accountability; adding shame will only create needless fear. A student who cannot answer correctly indicates that he did not understand the directions fully; more important, it indicates that he did not ask about the part that he did not understand. A failure of understanding is not the student's fault, but the failure to ask is. In a culture of listening, students learn that it is not about trying to avoid looking dumb (a failure orientation); it is about making the effort to get what is needed to learn (a growth-oriented orientation).

- *Step 6:* When all questions have been asked and the accountability checks have produced evidence that students really do understand, it is time for the finish word ("Okay, go!").

The overall direction-giving sequence should progress something like this:

1. "Eyes." Wait for 100 percent attention.
2. "When I say go, . . . !"
3. "I need you to [give the student complete directions]."
4. "Are there any questions?" Answer all questions.
5. "So, Jorge, what is the second thing we need to do?" If he gives the correct answer, move to step 6. If he gives the incorrect answer, restate the directions, and repeat the random accountability check.
6. "Okay, go!"

So what if after doing all of that, as you are circulating, a student says, "I don't get it" or "What are we doing again?"? In these cases, use your response to teach a lesson to this student and all the others observing with an eye on the future. Your message should not be about your anger or disappointment and should not shame the student for not listening; it should be about accountability. So although it will be counterproductive to project disappointment, it is damaging to your long-term efforts of supporting self-responsible students and a culture of listening if you enable the problematic behavior. Therefore, do not simply repeat the directions to students who were not listening. They had a chance to ask questions about what they did not understand earlier, and they did not take it. To give them the directions again (unless they have a special difficulty with auditory information) is to send them and the rest of the class the message that if they do not listen the first time, you will bail them out. Instead you might suggest gently that they ask another student (one who was listening) to explain the directions.

Expect this process to be effective rather quickly, but it will take time to change old habits. So it may be a few weeks before you sense that they trust that you are not going to go back to what they may have been used to or that they have to be truly accountable and attentive. As the expectation for accountability and quality membership in a listening culture grows, students will begin to increasingly support one another to be attentive and respectful. They will increasingly take on the role of stewards of the culture of listening.

Because not all students process directions verbally, the degree of on-task behavior and the quality of learning will be better if you have directions and procedures in writing before you begin any activity. Clarity and accountability are greatly improved by posting directions outlining the task of your regular class procedures as well as for learning centers, computers, group projects, lab stations, and anything else that may be misunderstood. Written words are not a substitute for the process of creating shared expectations, but they are an asset to that effort.

In your efforts to promote more effective behavior in students it is useful to examine your internal reactions for clues for what is working and what you need to change. Examine the following sequence of events:

Sequence A: Problem → inaction → problem remains → distress → negativity

Sequence B: Problem → action taken → change → ability to positively recognize behavior

You will notice that sequence A ends in some form of negativity. It could be disappointment, anger, frustration, or self-doubt, and it could remain internalized (the student feels distressed and guilty) or might be externalized to your students through shaming, lecturing, punishing, or withdrawal of affection. In nearly all cases, when you find yourself being negative, you will discover that you can trace it back to an earlier inaction on your part. As we examine how best to shape students' more effective and functional behavior, it is useful to maintain a mentality of positive-active (sequence B) rather than negative-inactive (sequence A). We explore the sources of negativity in more depth in Chapter Sixteen.

5.8　REFLECTION

Recall a situation in which you or a teacher you observed felt disappointed or frustrated by the behavior of a group of students. Was there a point in which you or they could have had the students practice, redo, or learn to do a better job of the skill that was lacking?

TRANSITIONS, ROUTINES, AND PROCEDURES

Sanford and Evertson (1983) found that 15 percent of the time in an average class is spent in transitions between activities. Moreover, the quality of the transitions has been found to set the tone for the subsequent segment (Arlin, 1979). The keys to smooth, stress-free, day-to-day procedures and transitions from one activity to another are practicing and shaping the desired behavior and relying primarily on positive feedback. The routines, procedures, and transitions in your class can be as efficient and effective as you wish, but it will depend on how intentional and dedicated you are. Following these guidelines will help you achieve your goals:

1. *Create a routine for each kind of transition.* When it is time to go from one location in the room to another or to change from one activity to another, the students assume that it is supposed to happen in a certain way, in a certain amount of time, with a certain outcome. Most of the stress for the teacher or students comes from differing expectations. If a situation presents students with the need to interpret what is expected, they will. Don't allow yourself to be disappointed by behavior resulting from their interpretation if the expectation was not clear. Instead, make it clear early in the school year. Create a familiar routine for each regular procedure in the class.

2. *Model any procedure or routine that is new to students.* Often simply demonstrating what a procedure looks like in action can help some students execute it (Cartledge & Milburn, 1995). Using a student or group of students to model can be even more powerful than doing it yourself. Once it is modeled, use positive recognitions to help reinforce the concrete behavioral aspects of the task.

3. *Practice procedures and transitions.* The time that you spend practicing routines and transitions will pay for itself many times over the course of the year (Yinger, 1979). As much time as needed in the early part of the term should be spend practicing procedures.

4. *Use time to help structure the expectation of the transition.* First, give students a time warning shortly before the end of the activity to help them mentally make the transition and better prepare for an efficient physical transition—for example, "In two minutes, we will be presenting our findings. What do you need to do to be ready?" Second, use a time limit to help clarify the expectation for how long things should take. For example, you might ask the students, "How long should it take for us to put what we have away and be ready for the next lesson?" Here you might take suggestions from the class, but choose one that helps support a reasonable goal. In this example, let's assume that one minute is plenty of time for all students to complete the task. So your direction may sound something like the following, "[Cue], we need to stop now and move on to doing the lesson. We should be able to do that in one minute. Any questions? [Process the questions.] Go!"

5. *Implement consequences for when the procedure does not meet the expectation.* The best consequence by far is having the students do the procedure again. When you redo, repeat, or practice what needs to improve, you are being active and, just as important, are in the position to be positive and recognize the achievement. Success will come from being active and positive. So that means there are some major mistakes to avoid:

- Being disappointed if the students do not make the transition within the allotted time. This would be passive and hostile.

- Doing nothing and ignoring that the class did not meet the goal. It sends the message that you do not follow through.

- Telling the class that they must do it better next time. A lecture is not action and is not only empty but weak.

6. *Recognize the class's accomplishments.* Especially early in the year, it is critical to demonstrate appreciation for taking care and making the effort when lining up, transitioning, cleaning up, rearranging things, going from place to place, putting away equipment, or any other routine tasks. Over time, you may want to shift your focus from how well they are meeting your expectations (2-Style approach) to how valuable it is for them (1-Style approach). For example, after the students have just transitioned from one activity to another quickly and efficiently, instead of saying something such as, "Great job; that was our best transition yet," which defines the 2-Style approach and would be an excellent phrase at the start of the year, a more 1-Style phrase might be, "Did you notice how effectively we just transitioned from A to B? That really shows that you are becoming a self-directed group of people, and it helps us get more done in a day." Notice that the first message was focused on the teacher and the second on the students.

REFLECTION 5.9

Recall a situation where you or a teacher you observed asked students to transition from one activity to another without any guidelines or expectations. What happened? Did you see any evidence that the students took the opportunity to meet some of the basic needs that had gone unmet (for example, power, love, fun, or freedom)?

An effective technique for promoting urgency and positivity into transitions is to make them into a game. This is especially effective with younger students. One of our graduate students has her students move from place to place as "fast" animals, such as "fast turtles." This infuses the activity with a sense of creativity, urgency, and fun. Another student suggested the use of music in transitions. To reinforce the time aspect, she played a piece of music for a set amount of time. The expectation is that the transition needs to be completed before the music ends.

You might challenge more mature students to take ownership of the efficiency of their transitions, procedures, and routines and ask them what they could do to make the time more effective. It is essential, especially early in the year, to let the students know what benefits their increased efficiency will have. This may start as a tangible incentive (perhaps something fun at the end of the period with the time saved), but ideally move to more intrinsic values, such as a show of respect for one another and their learning and the joy of solving a problem collaboratively.

Procedures

To achieve an effective system for common procedures, use the same logic: (1) teach the procedure, (2) practice it until it is sufficiently demonstrated, (3) use positive recognitions of any behavior that is close to the desired goal to shape and guide the effort toward achieving the "complete behavior," (4) celebrate successes with genuine positive appreciation when done well, and (5) provide more opportunities for practice if not done well and (6) positive recognitions when they get there. We will examine two examples of procedures that you might commonly face: at the elementary level, the need for students to line up and travel in a line efficiently, and at the secondary level, a preparation exercise for a lab activity.

Asking students to line up to go somewhere can be a continuous headache or an enjoyable experience. Table 5.2 compares case examples of two common class profiles and how lining up is dealt with in each.

TABLE 5.2. **Effectiveness of Lining-Up Strategies According to Classroom Climate Condition**

Negative Classroom Climate	Positive Classroom Climate
The class begins the year unable to line up effectively.	The class begins the year unable to line up effectively.
The teacher warns them that it "must get better."	The teacher has the class practice lining up on the first day of class until they have produced a perfect line.
When students are out of line or pushing, the teacher points them out (negative recognitions): "Kaida, you get back in line, or I am going to have you pull your card."	Each time the class lines up, the teacher is encouraging and projects a positive expectation: "Let's see if we can make an even more perfect line today."
When the students return from a trip to the library where they could not stay in line and were pushing and noisy, the teacher shames and lectures them.	When the line breaks down on the way to the destination, the teacher calmly tells the class to turn around and head back to the class. The teacher then clarifies the expectation, offers an encouraging message, and asks the students to try again.
The teacher gets in the habit of standing behind the line and physically moving students into place and shifts students who cannot get along to the back of the line.	The teacher stands at the front of the line and uses humor and positivity to promote a perfect line. He or she may look down the line and make the comment that the line is "about 99 percent perfect and almost 100 percent perfect" (as the students try to get even straighter and quieter).
The teacher regularly gets angry and threatens the students that if their line does not get better, they will have to stay in and miss the chance to go to their intended destination.	The teacher decreases positive recognitions over time and increases reflective questions to the students such as, "How does it feel to have perfect lines and have all the other classes admire how disciplined you are?" thus shifting the locus of motivation from external to internal.

You may deem less need for students to act in a uniform manner at the secondary level. Nevertheless, the principles for achieving efficient procedures are going to be essentially the same. If the students demonstrate that they do not have the skills to be responsible in a given situation, they do not need lecturing; they need to learn to be responsible. Your message to secondary students should be, "When you *show* it [responsibility], you will *get* it [opportunity, freedom, choices]": "When you show you can take care of the new equipment, you will be able to use it." "When you show that you can work collaboratively, you will get more opportunities to work with others." Eliminate disappointment and any other forms of negativity, and instead use encouragement and positive recognitions of behaviors that are close to the desired goal, along with meaningful consequences. In most cases, the best consequences in this area are lost opportunities for a set amount of time.

A good example of an effective intervention at the secondary level is a case in which the teacher asks the science class to complete a pre-lab before moving on to doing the formal lab activity. In this case, three or four groups successfully completed the pre-lab on Monday. The consequence is that they are able to move on to the lab on Tuesday. However, one group did not do an adequate job of the pre-lab.

REFLECTION   5.10

What would you do with this class at this point? The common response is to ask them to do better next time. Would this be effective?

The common reaction is for the teacher to be negative, lecture the students on how important it is to do a good job on the pre-lab, and threaten that if they do not do a better job in the future, they will not be able to do the lab. This intervention will most likely lead to a perpetuation of the problem and the teacher's disappointment level. In other words it is lose-lose.

Instead, the teacher in this case used active-positive logic. The teacher told the group that they needed to spend another day on the pre-lab doing a better job with it. During this time, the teacher was positive and encouraging and did not shame or exacerbate the students' unhappiness by making them feel guilty. The students did complain and act mistreated, but as the locus of control was maintained with the students, this reaction dissipated rather quickly. At the end of the day and in the weeks following, the teacher was able to recognize their accomplishments. The behavior was changed, and the teacher was able to remain supportive and positive. It was a win-win outcome.

Beginning the Period. One of the biggest time wasters can be taking roll. Use the rule never to take instructional time away from class to take roll. You might want to use a seating chart, or a student role monitor, or have the students engage in a regular activity that allows you two minutes to take roll. But find a system for identifying missing students that is stealthy and effective. There should never be a need to call roll after the first couple of days of school.

Dismissals. As with any other procedure, you need to develop a user-friendly simple system for dismissing students. For most grades (especially through middle school), it is effective to use the concept of "ready group," or "ready student." The concept of "ready" will need to be established (for example, materials away, sitting down, attentive). At first, you will need to explain it to the students. But soon you can use some form of incentive to encourage ready behavior. For example, you might say, "We need to go [or line up, or take part in an activity]. I am looking for a ready row [or table]." It will not take long before the students make the effort to demonstrate ready behavior given the incentive that being ready will lead to getting to go earlier. There are many benefits to having students attempt to get ready as opposed to just knowing it is time to go: students are in a better position to listen effectively to last-minute directions; you are assured that materials are away and are not in the unpleasant position of asking students to come back and clean up or do it yourself; and students associate the end of the period with a determination by you that things are ready to end for now, rather than the bell which has no relationship to the lesson.

Having a student of the week do the dismissals is a way to foster student leadership and illustrate the idea that because the expectations in the class are so clearly understood by all that eventually any member of the class society can manage the simple procedures in the social contract. Your implicit (and, if you so choose, explicit) message to students related to technical management procedures is that "we all know what it looks like when it is working, we all accept that we need to practice when it is not, and we all benefit when it does work."

The Problems with Warnings

Using warnings is tempting in the process of developing classroom technical management procedures. In the short term, they help us feel that we are being fair and informative. Over time, though, the result of warnings tends to be a degradation of both the clarity and consistency of the expectations. Warnings tend to weaken the cause-and-effect relationship between what is expected and what happens if the expectation is not met. When A happens, B will follow. In essence, a warning has the effect of putting a gap between the cause and the effect. Moreover, giving a warning often sends the message that you would rather not take action if you can avoid it.

5.11 | REFLECTION

Reflect on the role of warnings in your own life. How much effect have they had on your behavior when compared to actual consequences?

ADVANCED PRINCIPLES TO SUPPORT YOUR TECHNICAL MANAGEMENT

To help support the emotional climate that you believe will be most helpful to accomplish a particular student learning outcome, you might consider the impact of the emotion you are projecting. Therefore, a useful principle is mirroring the affect that you want to see from your students. That is: let your face and emotions support the disposition that is most needed by your students. If you want them to be serious, express a serious affect. If you want them to be relaxed, speak in a calm tone and relax your face. What affect would help the class best at the time? Is it being businesslike, fun, focused, or confident? Provide it yourself, and watch the change in them.

Another useful principle is never to teach a new concept or content and a new procedure at the same time. If you are working with new content or a new concept, make sure that you process it in a familiar manner. If you want to introduce a new procedure for processing ideas or concepts, let the students work with familiar content. That way, they are able to focus on what you intended and are not confused by two novel variables. For example, if you want to introduce a new concept attainment procedure, use a familiar concept. And if you want to introduce the next math concept, use a familiar strategy.

As is the case with so many classroom management efforts, we can use our feelings of disappointment or negativity to help us improve our practice. Feeling negative about the level of attention, the transitions, or the quality of following directions is a clear sign that we need to be more intentional about that area. So feeling frustrated or disappointed is a signal to be more purposeful about taking action the next time the situation arises or, better yet, take action (that we may have been procrastinating or avoiding) now to change the problematic condition.

If we recall the cause of our negative feeling, it is almost a certainty that the negative feeling could have been avoided if we had taken action earlier. Most of the emotional negativity teachers experience is a result of a repeated absence of follow-through. The solution to effective technical management, as well as an avenue to a sense of peace and confidence, is to empower the students with the skills they need to demonstrate the desired behavior successfully. It will promote both sanity and effectiveness to take an active-positive mind-set and approach and use such strategies as requiring the students to practice it until they understand rather than allowing ourselves to wallow in a passive-negative mind-set. It may take a while to reach a level of effectiveness that feels stable, internalized, and worry-free, so it will feel like work at first. But if you are taking action to improve the situation, you will not feel the negativity. And success is energizing, whereas failure and resignation are draining and deflating. Chapter Sixteen sets out ways to cut the strain and negativity in our minds and classrooms.

1-STYLE TECHNICAL MANAGEMENT

Table 5.3 outlines the difference between 1- and 2-Style approaches to technical management. Both styles share a core set of principles, such as consistency, clarity, positivity, and active and strong teacher leadership. In the 2-Style, the teacher continues to be the primary locus of the decision making, whereas in the 1-Style, students increasingly become the source of decision making when it comes to technical management. In the 2-Style classroom, the students know plainly what to expect from the teacher, and clarity is created as a result of the teacher's use of action, follow-though, positive recognitions, and giving and removing freedoms in response to the level of responsibility shown by the students. In the ideal, the 2-Style classroom is characterized by a well-choreographed set of routines and procedures, orchestrated by the teacher.

TABLE 5.3. The 2-Style and 1-Style Approaches to Technical Management

2-Style Approach	1-Style Approach
Goal: absolute consistency and efficiency.	Goal: self-direction and training your way out of the leadership role.
Teacher directs activities with students and is very clear about what is expected.	Teacher develops rituals and expectations that students internalize.
The end of the year looks much like the second week: orderly and efficient.	By the end of the year, the teacher has shifted responsibility to the students.
Students learn that procedures are approached consistently with a regular pattern and structure.	Students begin to see the purpose behind procedures, so that over time, they act increasingly with their own internal motivations.
A poor procedure requires more practice and more meaningful consequences.	A poor transition calls for a discussion of why it should improve, and then practice of what is decided alleviates the problem.
Students show attention because the consequences are clear and automatic.	Students attend because they appreciate the idea of mutual respect for those speaking.

In the 1-Style classroom, the difference is not so much how it appears on the surface but the source of motivation to act on the part of the students. While effective 1-Style technical management may begin much like that of the 2-Style classroom, there is a shift in the locus of decision making over time. Chapter Fifteen discusses in more detail how to shift from a 2- to a 1-Style form of management, but the key will be in assisting the students in understanding why their efficiency has essential value (Elias & Schwab, 2003). For example, the elementary teacher may begin to reduce the number of reinforcing comments about the students' quality line behavior and replace them with less frequent statements to the effect, "How does it feel to do a great job of lining up, and what are the benefits to each of you?" These types of questions help the students recognize that behavior such as quality listening, efficient transitions, and following directions are not done simply to please the teacher, but have a fundamental value to the members of the class: more time spent on task, self-respect, mutual respect, acting in a coordinated fashion, increased responsibility, the skill of listening, and a greater sense of internal locus of control. As the year goes on, the teacher withdraws overt displays of power and provides increasing amounts of power and responsibility to the students as they show the ability to use it wisely. Cartledge and Milburn (1995) describe this shift as the key to transitioning to what they call the self-monitoring stage of functioning.

Over time, the leadership for the behavior comes increasingly from the students as they take personal responsibility or are given the role of leader. Using student leaders for lines, transitions, and routine procedures works well at the elementary level. Using student leaders for attendance, paper collection, dismissal, and group work tends to be effective at the secondary level. The rule in the 1-Style classroom is that if students are intelligent enough to perform a leadership task, they should be the ones doing it.

Teachers still need to make a great many executive decisions and provide the vision, so their main job is to help guide the students' knowledge and awareness. The most effective means for this are positive recognitions and clarifying questions. For example, after a high-quality transition, the teacher may ask the class, "Do you remember that we could not do that two weeks ago?" or "I keep track of how well we transition, and I add that time to our choice time on Thursdays." When a class is doing a particularly good job of being attentive and respectful to one another, the teacher may comment, "Stop a second, and think about how nice it is to know that others are listening to you." Or ask, "Do you miss the days when we had such trouble listening?"

1-Style technical management takes more time to master when compared to that of 2-Style, and it may not be as neat and clean in the growth stages, but the extra time and effort 1-Style takes is worth the student outcomes it fosters. But unless you are really committed to doing what it takes to achieve the benefits of self-directed and other-centered students, there will not be enough internal motivation to persevere, so adopting a 1-Style approach is usually going to lead to frustration and potential failure. If you remain committed to these ideals and are willing to keep your eyes on the prize, the benefits can be substantial.

CONCLUSION

While many of us view technical management as a necessary evil, our ability to be successful and get the most from our students often depends on it. Moreover, how we approach the very ordinary tasks of gaining attention, giving directions, and teaching procedures can have a powerful long-term effect on the degree to which students develop a sense of the importance of their work, respect for one another, and the ability to be present and in the moment.

The next chapter explores the area of student motivation. The various techniques for promoting both intrinsic and extrinsic motivation are examined. However, the motivational climate and the success of the strategies discussed in the next chapter are greatly affected by the ability of the teacher to promote shared expectations and sound technical management as we have discussed here.

Journal Reflections

1. What is your expectation when it comes to technical management? What type of class would be more stressful for you: one in which you felt there was too much order or one in which you felt there was too much slack?

2. Do you see yourself being more of a 1- or 2-Style technical manager? Will you maintain the same expectations throughout the year?

Activities

1. Describe the types of cues that you plan to use, as well as some of the consequences that you will implement when you do not have everyone's attention. Also, do you have a finish word that you like? Discuss with your group why you made the choices that you did. Have you seen them being effective in action?

2. Do some action research of your own. Observe at least two teachers for an hour or two. Count the number of times that each teacher uses negative recognitions for inattention (for example, "I am waiting for . . ." Shh-shh! "Please be quiet, Jason; you need to listen"). Now count the number of times that students talk when there is an expectation that they are not supposed to. Is there a relationship? *Advanced idea:* Count the effective interventions. Observe whether the teacher uses clarifying statements. What effect do you observe these interventions having on the level of attention?

REFERENCES

Arlin, M. (1979). Teacher transitions can disrupt time flow in discussions. *American Educational Research Journal*, *16*, 42–56.

Cartledge, G., & Milburn, J. F. (1995). *Teaching social skills to children and youth: Innovative approaches* (3rd ed.). Needham Heights, MA: Allyn & Bacon.

Doyle, W. (2006). Ecological approaches to classroom management. In C. M. Evertson & C. S. Weinstein (Eds.), *Handbook of classroom management* (pp. 97–126). Mahwah, NJ: Erlbaum.

Elias, M. J., & Schwab, Y. (2006). From compliance to responsibility: Social and emotional learning and classroom management. In C. M. Evertson & C. S. Weinstein (Eds.), *Handbook of classroom management* (pp. 309–341). Mahwah, NJ: Erlbaum.

Emmer, E. T., & Gerwels, M. C. (2006). Classroom management in middle and high school classrooms. In C. M. Evertson & C. S. Weinstein (Eds.), *Handbook of classroom management* (pp. 407–437). Mahwah, NJ: Erlbaum.

Emmer, E. T., Evertson, C. M., & Anderson, L. (1980). Effective classroom management at the beginning of the school year. *Elementary School Journal*, *80*, 219–230.

Friedman, I. A. (2006). Classroom management and teacher stress and burnout. In C. M. Evertson & C. S. Weinstein (Eds.), *Handbook of classroom management* (pp. 925–944). Mahwah, NJ: Erlbaum.

Friedman, I. A., & Farber, B. A. (1992). Professional self-concept as a predictor of burn out. *Journal of Educational Research*, *86*(1), 28–35.

Sanford, J. P., & Evertson, C. M. (1983). Time use and activities in junior high classrooms. *Journal of Educational Research*, *76*, 140–147.

Twenge, J. (2006). *Generation me: Why today's young Americans are more confident, assertive, entitled—and more miserable than ever*. New York: Simon & Schuster.

Yazzie-Mintz, E. (2007). *Voices of students on engagement: A report on the 2006 High School Survey of Student Engagement*. Bloomington, IN: Center for Evaluation and Education Policy.

Yinger, R. J. (1979). Routines in teacher planning. *Theory into Practice*, *18*(3), 163–169.

6

Examining Motivational Strategies

What Makes Your Students Care?

In This Chapter

- A comparison of extrinsic and intrinsic motivational methods
- Common extrinsic strategies
- Motivational strategies that have variable effects
- An examination of intrinsic motivation
- Motivation and psychological movement

The field of human motivation is a complex and expansive domain, not lacking in motivational experts or approaches. This chapter offers a limited survey of several classroom motivation strategies and sets out theoretical and practical perspectives for each.

REFLECTION

6.1

What do you think of when you hear the term *student motivation?* Is it the result of something that the teacher adds to the equation or something that the student brings to the situation?

INTRINSIC VERSUS EXTRINSIC MOTIVATION

The idea of classroom motivation often carries with it strategies that are used to provide incentives for students do something or do it with greater intensity. Yet motivation is not always something that is added to the situation. It can be something that comes from within us (Ryan & Deci, 2006). While making an absolute distinction can be tricky or difficult, we might refer to some motivators as coming from the outside, or being *extrinsic;* and others coming from within, or being *intrinsic.* Extrinsic forms are those in which there is something added that comes from an external agent, such as a reward from the teacher (Alberto & Troutman, 2003). Contrastingly, intrinsic forms tap into internal sources. These forms of motivation may

TABLE 6.1. Comparison of Intrinsic Versus Extrinsic Motivation

Love of Learning—Intrinsic	Desire for Reward—Extrinsic
Assumes the learning activity itself is satisfying	Assumes that an extrinsic motivator is necessary
Transferable to other contexts and situations	Not transferable outside the context in which the reward is present
Can take time to support and cultivate	Can be relied on after only a short period of introduction
Primarily process focused	Primarily product focused
Implies that the learning or task itself has value and meaning	Implies the learning or task is a means to an end (the reward)
Natural condition	Manufactured condition
Has long-term benefits	Benefits are short term
Promotes a mentality that is useful when transferred into the context of building relationships	Promotes a mentality that may hinder the inclination to invest in the relationship-building process
Promotes ever-increasing levels of self-motivation	Promotes an ever-increasing need for rewards
Can be difficult to rely on with a new group of students who are not accustomed to using these sources of motivation	Can be useful for motivating a behavior that is unfamiliar or unformed

reflect the meeting of a basic need or can come from an inner source of satisfaction such as personal fulfillment. Table 6.1 outlines some of the fundamental distinctions between intrinsic versus extrinsic sources of motivation.

Table 6.1 shows that the advantages of extrinsic motivational techniques include their ability to help initiate and shape behaviors and that they can be relied on after only a relatively short period of introduction. In comparison, supporting the development of students' intrinsic motivation will have substantial long-term advantages. Over time, students with a more intrinsic motivational orientation, working within a needs-satisfying environment, will tend to outperform those who have become accustomed to extrinsic rewards, reinforcement, and incentive (Dweck, 2000; Glasser, 1990; Ryan & Deci, 2006).

While it is true that there are few absolutes in the field of motivation, it may be helpful to classify various motivational strategies into those that are more extrinsic and those that are more intrinsic. Given that at any one time a multitude of motivational influences exists inside and outside any learner, it is still useful to examine each strategy independently. In the following sections, we'll examine many of the most common intentional strategies used in schools to motivate students. These strategies (outlined in Table 6.2) are divided into those that can best be characterized as extrinsic, those that encourage intrinsic motivation, and those that will have a variable effect depending on how they are applied.

6.2 REFLECTION

As you examine the most popular forms of motivation used in the classroom, reflect on your own classroom experience with each. Which forms of motivation did you find effective? Were they typically those that could be classified as intrinsic or extrinsic? In your mind, what were the benefits and problems of each type?

TABLE 6.2. Common Classroom Motivational Strategies

Form or Strategy	Advantages	Disadvantages
Group A: Motivational strategies best characterized as extrinsic or external		
Grades and rewards	Tangible, familiar, motivating to students who value them. Similar to monetary motivators in that they work as rewards.	Shift focus away from learning goals. Increased levels of the reinforcement may be necessary to maintain effect. Can rob students of intrinsic sources of motivation.
Incentives	Can be useful to define valued outcomes or processes. Help clarify the focus of the effort.	Can lose their value over time if used repeatedly. Students may expect them after a while.
Personal praise	Feels good. Works to make student work harder. Works in the short term.	Can be addictive. Can reduce student's internal locus of control. Can be manipulative.
Punishments, shaming, and threats	Works in the short term. Motivates students who are used to that technique. Can help clarify the boundaries in a class.	Can promote students' merely avoiding getting caught. Does not inspire high-quality behavior. Can create hostility and resentment.
Public recognition	Can reward behavior and effort that may not be rewarded by peers. Feels good to recipient.	Can reinforce preexisting "haves" and "have-nots." Requires consistency and thought.
Phone calls home	Can alert parents to patterns of which they may not have been aware. Demonstrates a commitment to the student's success. Positive calls can have a profoundly positive outcome.	Sends the message that the teacher may not be able to handle the student alone. Parents may not be helpful, may be the cause of the problem, or may be enablers of the problem. Acts as public shaming. Can appear as a sign of weakness.
Group B: Strategies that can promote extrinsic or intrinsic motivational mind-sets depending on how they are applied		
Positive reinforcement	Helps shape the desired behavior. Can be done quickly, efficiently, and without much cost or planning. Can provide useful feedback for self-improvement.	Can create a dependence on the teacher's energy to motivate. Is external. If in the form of praise, essentially extrinsic.
Assessing behavior or effort	Can promote high-quality behavior and effort. Begins working fairly quickly. Helps promote the concept of good behavior. Can reward effort and process outcomes.	Can be very manipulative. Can make students dependent on an external evaluation of their behavior. Can be a tool for favoritism and bias.
Competition	Can raise the level of interest in the activity. Can bring the team aspect into an effort. Comparison is motivational to those who aspire to the top. Brings a "game" feeling to work.	Comparison can shift focus away from the quality of the effort. Breeds fear of failure. Promotes shortcuts and cheating to get the prize. Creates winners and losers.
Teacher relationship	Can send a message that the student is valuable, accepted, and special. Can help students care about academics. May be the only thing that some students respond to.	Takes time and energy. Can produce students who become excessively needy. Can work against students' developing more internal sources of motivation.

(continued)

TABLE 6.2. **Common Classroom Motivational Strategies (Continued)**

Form or Strategy	Advantages	Disadvantages
Instructional design	Can promote a context in which students are engaged, self-directed, feeling successful, invested, and empowered. Can create a context where success leads to a love of learning and self-efficacy.	Can promote a context where students learn that schoolwork is mostly meaningless and irrelevant to their lives. Can reinforce the learning process to be an artificial exercise that involves little critical thinking or a sense of purpose.
Avoiding penalties	If negative consequences are built into a context of a social contract and clear set of expectations, students learn not only to be responsible but also that there is a clear cause-and-effect relationship between their choices and their opportunities.	If negative consequences take the form of punishments, lectures, threats, or public humiliation and shaming, students learn to avoid the external agent of the penalty but do not learn any meaningful lesson. Is founded in pain-based logic.
Group C: Motivational strategies best characterized as intrinsic or internal		
Self- improvement	Promotes intrinsic motivation. Helps students clarify their own goals and desires. More long-lasting sense of satisfaction.	Takes a lot of time to promote. Students who are used to more external motivation may not trust its value.
Increased responsibility	Can create cause and effect between responsibility and freedom. Can increase responsible behavior.	Have to give away power to students. Creates more unpredictability in many outcomes.
Problem-solving and inquiry-based learning	Can promote greater resourcefulness. Can promote an emphasis on process. Motivational to students when they solve the problem or reach the goal.	Can be messy. Potentially less teacher control of outcome. Requires a great deal of intention and planning.
Basic needs-satisfying environment	Allows students to experience inner sources of satisfaction. Activities feel inherently meaningful and as though they are going somewhere psychologically; as a result, there is little experience of boredom. Promotes student creativity and sets the stage for communal bonds among students.	Requires the teacher to be aware of students' needs. Requires teacher to be purposeful and skilled at instructional design and classroom management. Teacher cannot entirely control other students who may undermine the quality of the environment.

EXTRINSIC MOTIVATION TECHNIQUES

This section examines what could be considered the leading principally extrinsic motivational strategies used in classrooms historically: grades, rewards, incentives, praise, punishments, positive reinforcement, and phone calls home. This section also includes recommendations for applying these strategies in a manner that produces beneficial and effective results.

Grades

Grades are the most prevalent example of formal extrinsic motivators used in schools. Their primary purposes are to provide a concrete representation of either the completion of a task or the quality of a performance and act as an incentive for later benefits and opportunities. As representations of the level of quality performance, grades have only a symbolic meaning. They only represent something of value (quality work, scores on a test, or assignments completed, for example) and have no inherent value. Therefore, in practice, grades become more effective when they are clearly related to a meaningful outcome (Reeve & Deci, 1996). This is why grading systems that incorporate more authentic measures, such as performance assessment rubrics, are more motivational than more artificial uses, such as a total of the number of correct responses on a worksheet. Moreover, the way that a grade is derived can help it become more meaningful and tap into an intrinsic source rather than being entirely an extrinsic reinforcement (Reeve & Deci, 1996).

Grades also act as an incentive. As students progress in their academic careers, grades have the effect of creating future opportunities. These opportunities vary greatly depending on several variables: importance to parents or schools and scholarship or financial aid opportunities, for example. Moreover, only some students are much more influenced or even aware of these incentives. As a result, grades are a more motivational influence on some students than others. A survey of a typical high school will support the wide discrepancy in how students view the importance of grades. And teachers who rely primarily on students' being motivated by grades are commonly frustrated with the number of students who are unaffected by the threat of a poor grade if their performance does not improve. In most cases, students who see a relationship between their grades and their ability to reach their personal goals will be most influenced by this source of motivation and therefore more concerned with the grades that they receive.

However, students commonly see grades as something "given" to them by the teacher (the external agent). Too often they view grades as a representation of their aptitude, ability, or even self-worth rather than the quality of their investment. Although this is rarely the intention of the teacher for giving the grade, it is common for students to perceive the grade as such. So, for example, a student who gets a C on a paper may perceive that grade as a reflection of himself or his ability in that subject. Given this reaction, he finds himself in the position that he must respond to the level of the grade by either accepting or rejecting it as an accurate reflection of his ability. Although these two responses—accepting the grade as consistent or rejecting it as inconsistent—may appear somewhat different, they are similar in that neither will motivate the student to do better in the future. If the student views the C grade as consistent with his academic self-concept, he will find no need to do any better or adopt any different strategies in the future. If the student perceives the grade as inconsistent with his academic self-concept, he will likely feel shame, confusion, and inadequacy along with resentment toward the teacher. Even if there is a great deal of intensity to the emotion connected to this second response, if the cause is viewed as external and the student does not feel that his grade reflects concrete and constructive feedback, there will be little or no motivation to change future behavior. The result is the all-too-familiar phenomenon: the student becomes used to getting Cs. As we will discuss throughout this chapter and the next, there are very effective strategies for helping the student desire excellence. Giving more Cs is not one of them.

REFLECTION

6.3

Recall your response to various grades that you received as a student. Did they motivate you to do better? Did you view them as including a personal component (the teacher either liked or did not like you)? Did they confirm or conflict with your expectation and academic self concept?

Chapter Eleven discusses how the assessment of meaningful and clear learning targets will produce better student performance and higher-quality behavior. When students recognize that their grade results from a valid representation of their performance as assessed in relation to meaningful criteria, they are more likely to experience the assessment process as meaningful and as something that leads them on a clear pathway to achievement (Reeve, 2006).

Rewards

Another common extrinsic motivational strategy, used primarily at the elementary level, is to give tokens and other prizes to students who perform a desired behavior. These act as concrete representations that something of value has been accomplished. Therefore, they are intended to act as the reinforcement in the process of operant conditioning, a technique that originated in the field of psychology called behaviorism and is most associated with one of its pioneers, B. F. Skinner (Skinner & Belmont, 1993). In operant conditioning, the operant—or desired behavior that is being conditioned—is reinforced by an extrinsic reinforcement or reward (Alberto & Troutman, 2003). In this case, the operant is the act of desirable behavior on the part of the student, and the extrinsic reward is the token or prize (Reeve, 2006).

Incentives

Incentives can take many forms—for example, prizes at the end of the week for successfully performing a task or refraining from an undesirable behavior, group privileges for being first or best, or rewarding students who do well on one task the chance to opt out of a further task. They concretize the nonverbal bargain: "If you [the student] do something that I [the teacher] have determined is good, I will give you something that you should like." In this way, incentives can be helpful in clarifying what is desirable behavior. At their best, they can help promote good habits and shape more functional patterns of action (Hickey & Schafer, 2006). For example, if a mother provides a child an incentive to make her bed every day, the child may become comfortable with that behavior and continue it throughout her lifetime, even after the incentive is no longer present. In the case of healthy behaviors that become intrinsically satisfying once they become habits, this can lead to positive long-term benefits. However, with any extrinsic reward, we must question whether the incentive has contributed to the development of good behavioral patterns or has just bribed students to do something that they would not have done without the bribe and will not do once the bribe has been removed. And if over time the students do not experience any internal satisfaction from the behavior being induced, the incentive will eventually lose its power.

6.4 **REFLECTION**

Recall situations in which you were given rewards for doing a task others wanted you to do or to do better. Were you motivated? What is your association with that task today?

One popular incentive strategy is that of preferred activity time (Jones, 2000). This sets up the bargain that if the student applies herself acceptably to an academic task now, she will be given the opportunity to do something that she really likes to do later. On the surface, this strategy works: it motivates the student to do what it takes to attain the preferred activity. However, this strategy has two undesirable by-products. First, although it may work in the short run, like other bribes it will lose its effect over time, and students will eventually return to their previous level of motivation for the academic activity. Moreover, they will become accustomed to the bribe and likely demand it. Second, it will reinforce the principle that the work that is being done in the academic time is undesirable. If we bribe students with a preferred activity, we actually generate the previously unconsidered question, "Preferred to what?" What is the association that we are creating? Is it that academics are inherently unenjoyable? Although this strategy is attractive, consider its costs and long-term effects. And if you feel you need to bribe your students to engage in learning, you may want to consider the alternative of making the learning activities in your class engaging and inherently motivating.

REFLECTION

6.5

Reflect on the following parable:

There was once a man who lived by a park and worked the night shift at the factory. During the day, he liked it quiet so that he could get some sleep. He lived alone and did not like children very much. So when the children began to play ball at the park and make lots of noise, he became angry. He tried to ignore the noise but could not. As he reflected on his dilemma, he was struck by a cunning plan.

The next day, he went to the field and addressed the children. He told them that he loved the sound of their play and that it reminded him of when his children were young (neither was true). Then he told them that if they came to play faithfully, he would pay them each a quarter. The children were pleased, to say the least, and thought the man was the greatest. The next day, the man arrived and paid each child a quarter. He did the same thing the next day. The children were very happy. The next day he arrived right on time, but gave the children some bad news: he loved to hear their voices as they played and it made him so happy, but he did not have much money and could pay them only a dime each. The children were a little disappointed, but agreed to come back and play for the smaller amount.

As promised, he paid them a dime for the next three days, but on the fourth day, he again had some bad news. He told the children that he really hoped that they would come out and play, but that he was out of money and could no longer pay them. At this, the children were very upset. After a quick conference, the children decided that they could not play if they were not going to be paid, and they left, never to return.

The man went home and was able to sleep in peace and quiet that and all other afternoons.

Do you think the story represents a valid reality? Can you think of an example of this same principle in your own experience?

Punishments

The desire to avoid undesirable conditions can be motivating, so punishments can have the effect of changing behavior. As we will discuss in more detail in Chapter Nine, avoidance of a punishment is based in fear and founded in a pain-based logic. The source or feeling of fear can be alleviated in a great many ways, but only one of these is to change behavior to achieve or improve the behavior others desire. Others include avoiding school, avoiding the teacher, giving up, self-destructive behavior, or changing the definition of failure to success (see Chapter Fourteen for more on the student with a negative identity). Like extrinsic rewards, punishments lose their effect over time (Kauffman, 2005; Landrum & Kauffman, 2006). Moreover, they do not support more positive forms of motivation or behavior because they offer no pathway to success, only a source of discomfort for failure.

However, if the consequential penalty is natural or logically related to the misbehavior and is associated in the student's mind with his own choices, then it can have the effect of supporting real learning at the same time as it represents a disincentive to misbehave (Reeve, 2006). And as we will examine in Chapters Eight through Ten, developing logical consequences is a critical feature of creating a classroom social contract that helps students become more responsible and the class more functional.

Positive Reinforcement

When asked about their favorite motivational strategies, most teachers and preteachers respond by saying something to the effect that they want to be "positive" and use a lot of "positive reinforcement." On the surface, this is encouraging, especially when compared with the possibility that they would rely heavily on strategies defined by destructive criticism, shaming, pain-based logic, and coercion. However, not all positive reinforcement is the same or will have the same effect (Lerman, 2003).

Positive reinforcement describes a wide range of practices, including the use of extrinsic rewards, praise and approval, encouragement, having positive expectations, being warm and accepting, using positive recognitions, providing increased opportunities, and using systems for rewarding quality behavior (Landrum & Kauffman, 2006). These all share a couple of features in common: each is given purposefully and is controlled by the teacher and therefore external to the student. But they will have dramatically different effects on student behavior and motivation. I have already outlined the differences in the effects of different extrinsic reward strategies. Some of what we might refer to as positive reinforcement can remain largely external, while other forms can lead to the development of more intrinsic sources of motivation. I make this distinction throughout this book, but it is especially compelling when it comes to the use of praise—a practice that is widespread but largely misunderstood and misused.

Healthy Versus Unhealthy Praise. Encouragement can take many forms. While we want our students to feel appreciated, the language that we use to show that appreciation can have dramatically different effects (Deci, Koestner, & Ryan, 1999). Many people, in and outside education, use the term *praise* to refer to generically supportive messages to students. As we examine the term *praise* and the common uses of what might be considered praise, we will see that different types of messages have very different effects on both the student being praised and the class as a whole. Ultimately we might compare what is commonly referred to as praise—essentially external personal messages—to a healthier and more effective alternative: internally focused positive performance recognitions.

Problematic Praise Messages. What is commonly referred to as praise is at its essence a personal comment from the teacher that conveys the message that the student is being or acting in a manner that pleases the teacher. For example, the teacher who says, "Good work, Nasi," or "I like the way Anders is working," is using messages that sound encouraging on the surface, and the intention *is* to encourage good behavior. But these types of messages have potentially negative effects.

Messages such as "What a good boy," or "Quinh-xiao is doing such a good job," have the effect of essentially giving "love" for obedience. The message they send tells the students that the teacher gives affection to those who please her or him. In fact, these messages are very external: they originate from the wishes and desires of the teacher. The net result could be best characterized as the use of the teacher's affection as an external reward. This type of message, in comparison to what was referred to in the previous chapter as positive recognitions, is significantly less effective in the effort to clarify appropriate behavior or promote learning. In fact, in the long run, personal praise can promote a dependent and helpless pattern of thinking in students (Dweck, 2000). If we are attempting to create externally motivated "affection addicts," then this form of praise is an effective means. If we include disappointment for behavior that displeases the teacher, we can be even more effective in creating dependent "failure fearers" and students who are easy to manipulate. As we examine the effects of praise more closely, we can see that the negative effects reach beyond the object of the praise to the class as a whole.

REFLECTION

Have you observed a teacher who used a great deal of personal praise? What was the effect?

Effect of Praise on the Student Being Praised. As we will discuss in the next chapter, both academic achievement and academic self-concept are strongly related to the degree of internal locus of control (LOC) that a student possesses (Ayling, 2009). Internal locus of control is essentially the mentality that our thoughts and actions have consequences. And if we do certain things such as apply ourselves to our learning, we learn more. When we make students dependent on any external reinforcement, we rob them of that internal LOC. Any external reinforcement is addictive, but the addictive quality of praise is special. Students long for love and acceptance. A teacher who says phrases such as, "Good boy, Darius," is giving the student her affection as a personal reinforcement, and the implicit pact is that as long as Darius does what pleases her, she will continue to give Darius that reinforcement. The natural result is that the student learns to approach each task with the mind-set, "I wonder if the teacher likes what I am doing?" He increasingly loses touch with his own sense of value, sense of satisfaction for the learning, interest in creativity, and internal locus of control. If the teacher adds a message of disappointment when Darius does not do what she desires, the cycle of addiction is complete. Not only does Darius begin to increasingly crave the desired messages, but he increasingly fears withdrawal of the feeling he gets from those messages. Over time, he begins to act and behave in ways that he has interpreted are most likely to achieve his desired dose of praise.

As we grow in our understanding of how the brain operates, the better we recognize that the chemical reactions within the student's brain are much the same for praise as they are for drugs such as opiates. If we take a step back and examine student behavior within the praise-intensive classroom within this addiction framework, the clear parallels become evident.

Some might say that if we are going to successfully teach students, making some of them dependent on praise may be a necessary evil in the pursuit of getting them to learn. This might be a legitimate argument if praise were useful in helping students learn. But it is not. As we discussed in Chapter Four, personal praise is far less effective than positive recognitions of performance. Praise is nearly useless in helping students understand the task in a more meaningful way and robs students of their internal LOC. Consequently it produces increasingly passive learners over time (Deci et al., 1999).

 Influence on the Class as a Collective. The stated intention of praise is to send a message to a student or a class that a desirable behavior has been performed. As we discussed in the previous chapter, a message is effective in promoting a behavioral expectation that succeeds in developing clarity of the desired behavior and promotes a positive association with that behavior. Let's examine the effectiveness of the use of personal nonspecific praise on those two counts.

When we say, "Good job, Terrance!" we assume we are positively reinforcing Terrance's behavior. But what actually occurs? In essence, the rest of the class hears us say, "I like Terrance," or "I like the way Terrance is working." The rest of the class hears nothing to help them understand why we like the way Terrance is working or what constitutes a successful performance—which is what they need. The net effect of the message is that the class heard another example of their teacher expressing what they already knew: that he or she has a positive view of Terrance.

This praise is promoting the addictive cycle described earlier within the class as a whole. Students learn from watching the teacher giving praise for behavior that pleases her or him. Therefore, if the students want some of that praise, they need to focus on pleasing the teacher. Over time we create a class of students who try to appear good. Their locus of control has shifted externally, they become less interested in what they are learning and more and more interested in what the teacher thinks of them, and they begin to equate success in school with the amount of praise they get each day. All of this leads to a psychology of failure, as we will discuss in the next chapter.

Another effect of praise on the collective is that as it becomes more desirable and more addictive, it becomes a scarce commodity for which students must compete. Observe the dynamics of a classroom society (or any other society with a scarce resource) where an artificially induced high demand for praise has been created. The result will be competition (Reeve, 2006). Students' perspectives will shift to whether they are achieving more or less praise relative to the others. If they are receiving more, they will (probably erroneously) view themselves as succeeding in school. If they are not receiving as much, they will (also falsely) view themselves as losing the praise game. Those who are winning have an incentive to gloat. Those who are losing have an incentive to fight back. This is frequently exhibited in the antagonism projected at those who are viewed as favorites of the teacher.

As is the case with any other scarce resource, those who do not have the skill or will to attain the resource by playing by the rules (attempting to become a "good" girl or boy) will attain a counterfeit version by another means. For example, if I cannot get the attention praise brings by finishing my work, I can get attention by disrupting others' work. The counterfeit commodity I achieve may not sound as sweet as praise, but it still feels like attention. And as we will discuss in Chapter Fourteen, the opposite of love is not hate but indifference. Many students would much rather get attention by misbehaving than by being ignored. If we have set up the rules so that good behavior receives praise (external reinforcement shown as the teacher's love) and bad behavior receives disappointment (external punishment shown as the withdrawal of love), we should not be surprised when a student shows the resourcefulness to get the need for attention (counterfeit love) met by making his or her own rules ("give me real love, or I will get attention on my own terms").

Although we often view these students as "problem students," we should give them credit for finding an ingenious solution to the problem situation in which they found themselves. In addition, as we examine the effects of our use of praise, we can see that we essentially created the conditions for the problem by the implicit rules that we created in the class.

Unhealthy Praise Messages

- "Love" given for obedience
- External and addictive
- Your value, not the student's
- Nonspecific, noneducational feedback
- Combined with the overuse of disappointment, becomes highly manipulative or addictive

Healthy Encouragement Messages

- Behavior, not student, praised
- Authentic and spontaneous
- For accomplishment or effort
- Based on student's own goals

- Show appreciation
- Public attention to underappreciated student
- Combined with the use of authentic emotional investment, can show caring by the teacher

REFLECTION   **6.7**

Recall a recent case in which you observed a teacher, coach, or parent praise a child. Using the distinctions outlined in the lists above, would you classify it as more on the healthy or unhealthy side?

Phone Calls Home

With all that teachers do in a day, it is often difficult to find the time or energy to make calls to parents regarding their sons and daughters. However, if you survey teachers who do make the effort to call, they will most likely tell you that it is time well spent. Nevertheless, all calls home will not have the same effect. Following is a list of ground rules for home phone calls that will help them become a worthwhile intervention:

- *Make many positive calls for every critical call to a home.* In fact, eliminating the critical calls altogether is best. It is a common and understandable practice to save your energy for remediation. However, it is usually a mistake. There will be situations in which a parent should know that a student in your class has developed a pattern of behavior that you want to work together to change. These calls can be effective. But they send the implicit message that you as the teacher are unable to solve the problems in your class independently. However, a phone call home to the parents of a student who has demonstrated a dramatic improvement in the quality of participation or has made a remarkable contribution will have a profound effect in the short and long terms. First, it acts as an intermittent positive reinforcement. Second, it promotes a collaborative and supportive relationship between you and the parent. Third, it makes the school, you, and the student all look good, which is welcome in the cycle of learning. Finally, it demonstrates to the student that you freely choose to recognize his or her effort, even when it is not required of you. It shows that you do not take this student's progress toward high-quality behavior for granted.

- *Be specific about what you observed of the student in your call.* General praise or criticism is rather useless. The phone conversation will be more effective if the parent has a copy of your class's expectations that you sent home earlier in the year. Be specific, and emphasize one or two areas that you observed the student demonstrate well. For example, if you have noticed that the student is now making a much more consistent level of effort than in the past, give an example of the past behavior and then of the current behavior. Then describe to the parent what you see as the benefits the student is experiencing as a result of this improvement. When making a call regarding a behavior pattern that needs to change, be constructive and have a plan for how the change will best come about.

- *Make regularly scheduled calls.* If forgetfulness or lack of time are problems, consider setting aside a time each month or midterm to make calls home. Start with calls to homes of students whose effort level you would characterize as especially good or poor.

- *Be respectful and professional.* Show appreciation for the parent's contribution and the complexity of raising a child. Never talk down to parents, and never feel a need to apologize or be submissive (note this especially for some younger teachers). This contact will in many ways define their impression of you and the school as a whole.

6.8

REFLECTION

Recall situations in which a teacher called home to talk to your parents. What was the effect on your relationship with that teacher? Did the contents of the phone call have an effect?

MOTIVATIONAL TECHNIQUES WITH VARYING EFFECTS

Some motivational strategies can be classified neither as inherently effective nor ineffective, desirable nor undesirable, but vary depending on the way that they are applied. These techniques include teachers using their relationship with the students as a motivational tool, the assessment of behavior, classroom competition, the instructional models that are used, and the use of occasional external reinforcement. This section will describe the types of applications of each of these techniques that will lead to more sustainable and internal student motivation and what types of applications to avoid.

Teacher Relationship

The saying that "students do not care what you know until they know that you care" is both intuitively obvious and supported by research. Relationships are at the heart of the 1-Style classroom, and they begin with the teacher's emotional investment. Your ability to develop community, a psychology of success, and outcomes that would qualify as transformative will be dependent on your ability to show that you have a genuine positive regard for your students and that you believe in them.

A good relationship begins with good intentions. Many teachers describe looking back at their early years of teaching and recognizing that when their attempts were clumsy and even ill advised, their positive intentions and desire for the welfare of their students produced a great deal that was positive. Love can overcome bad strategies to a great extent when it comes to motivating children. But it does not undo a mistake, and it does not always lead to success. Some of the best-intentioned and brightest teachers leave the profession because the love they had for their students and for sharing their subject was not returned by the students. Here are suggestions for how you can get the most from teacher-student relationships:

- *Show unconditional positive regard for students.* Separate your acceptance of them as people from their behavior and their achievement. There is never a time when withdrawing positive regard (love) achieves a lasting positive result. This frees you to be honest and objective with your feedback related to students' work and behavior.

- *Being a friend is fine; being too familiar is not.* The idea that teachers should not "smile until Christmas" is ill conceived (Shindler et al., 2003). But being a buddy runs the risk that students will misunderstand your position and role, and you will lose position authority.

- *If your class is about you, you will struggle to create healthy relationships with your students.* It is easy to fall into the mind-set that you are going to pretend that you are invested while in reality you are uninvested emotionally. It may be helpful to recall the Pygmalion in the classroom phenomenon. Can you treat all of your students as rising stars?

- *Avoid the trap of using excessive personal praise, disappointment, and rewards for good behavior.* It indicates that your motivations are rooted in your own needs rather than those of your students. It may seem effective, but beware of creating a classroom full of reward addicts.

- *Be careful of using humor.* Using humor can be motivating and can keep students engaged and on your side. But be careful not to use victimizing humor. Self-deprecating humor, recognizing absurdities, having fun with your own mistakes and surprises, and tasteful jokes can be effective ways to bond with your students and show that you care enough to account for their basic need for fun.

- *Make the effort to take an interest in your students as individuals.* Knowing about them, their interests, and what they are doing outside of your class can have a powerful effect.

REFLECTION

6.9

Reflect on a teacher who had an effect on you. What was it that he or she did? Did you feel empowered or valued? Why?

Assessing Behavior

Most teachers at some point consider the idea of assessing student behavior. Many end up incorporating it on a minimal level, many others are turned off by its potentially manipulative properties, some use behavioral assessment systems that do more harm than good, and very few take full advantage of its transformative potential. There are two online resource articles devoted to using student behavioral assessments effectively and explaining why you should not use undefined "action points" or deficit model systems such as colored behavioral charts or names on the board ("Assessing the Quality of Student Process, Participation, and Behavior" and "Why to Stop Using Colored Cards and Names on the Board Systems, and What to Do Instead" can be found at www.transfomativeclassroom.com). Used purposefully, assessing process and participation can have a dramatic effect on the quality of process investment, effort level, or any other behavior included in a well-developed system. It can be a useful adjunct to the class's social contract and democratic operating procedure. Used unsystematically or as a deficit model, it can have a harmful effect that may be invisible but profoundly destructive. A thoughtful implementation can promote the intrinsic sources of motivation on the part of the students. Used carelessly, it can feel like just another external source of teacher oppression and domestication.

Figure 6.1 depicts the conceptual difference between shame-based behavioral assessment systems, such as colored cards or names on the board, and ascending-levels rubrics defining quality behavior. In essence, in the colored-card systems, negative behavior is the focus and as a result is reinforced and perpetuated. In the ascending-levels rubric, the focus is an ever-improving level of quality.

Competition

By definition, competition creates a scarcity of rewards and a sense of urgency to obtain that reward. This can certainly be motivating to many students. Used wisely, competition can increase the level of intensity and fun in an activity. Used unwisely, it can create a whole host of negative side effects, such as increasing students' fear of failure, increased cheating, overemphasis on end results rather than process, increased mistrust among students, promoting the advantage of the advantaged, and creating an unsafe emotional climate in the class.

Because competition is such a widespread motivational strategy and because its use can have such powerful effects, an additional resource article online is devoted to the examination

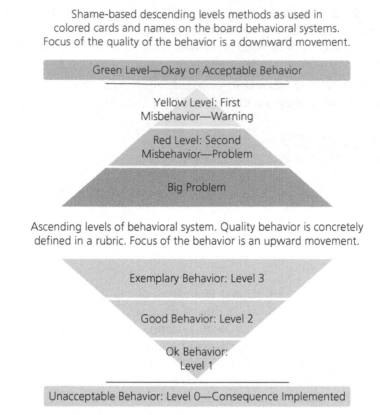

Shame-based descending levels methods as used in colored cards and names on the board behavioral systems. Focus of the quality of the behavior is a downward movement.

Green Level—Okay or Acceptable Behavior

Yellow Level: First Misbehavior—Warning

Red Level: Second Misbehavior—Problem

Big Problem

Ascending levels of behavioral system. Quality behavior is concretely defined in a rubric. Focus of the behavior is an upward movement.

Exemplary Behavior: Level 3

Good Behavior: Level 2

Ok Behavior: Level 1

Unacceptable Behavior: Level 0—Consequence Implemented

FIGURE 6.1. *Psychological and Behavioral Movement Promoted by the Two Contrasting Behavioral Assessment Systems*

of what it is and how it can be used most effectively (see "Competition in the Transformative Classroom" at www.transformativeclassroom.com). Here are the differences between healthy and unhealthy competition.

Healthy Competition

- The goal is primarily fun.
- The competitive goal is not valuable or real; examples are trivia contests, short-term competitions for a solely symbolic reward, and lighthearted challenges between groups where there is no reward and it is characterized that way.
- The learning or growth goal is conspicuously characterized as valuable.
- The competition has a short duration and is characterized by high energy.
- There is no long-term effect from the episode.
- All individuals or groups see a reasonable chance of winning.
- All students understand how competition works in their classroom.

Unhealthy Competition

- The competition feels real. The winners and losers will be affected.
- The competitive goal or reward is valuable or real; examples are long-term point systems, competition for grades, grading on a curve, playing favorites, and awards for skill-related performance.
- The learning task is characterized as a means to an end (winning the competition).

- Winners are able to use their victory as social or educational capital at a later time.
- Competition implicitly or explicitly rewards the advantaged students.
- Over time students develop an increasingly competitive mind-set.

Instructional Design

In Chapter Eleven, we will examine the relationship between instructional choices and the effect on management and motivation. It is likely that the most significant factor in achieving a class that is working hard and with care is the teacher's selection of the type of work that students are doing. Conversely, when there are motivational or behavioral problems, most often the type of instruction is the main culprit.

REFLECTION

6.10

Recall a teacher who created especially engaging lessons. What was the effect on student motivation? Did the teacher need to use a lot of extrinsic rewards to get students to care about their work?

Adopting a More Intentional and Effective Approach to the Use of Extrinsic Behavioral Reinforcement

It is a well established fact that human behavior can be conditioned by environmental stimuli (Landrum & Kauffman, 2006; Reeve, 2006). While we can debate the extent to which behavior is externally conditioned or has its source in more internal drives, as educators we need to recognize the power of environmental conditioning. If we examine an effectively managed classroom, we will see a teacher who understands behavioral principles (Landrum & Kauffman, 2006). That does not mean the teacher will overuse extrinsic conditioning or even rely on it as a motivational strategy, but we will understand that the forces of behavioral conditioning are operating continuously.

The starting point to making sense of behavioral conditioning is to understand that in a conditioning situation, something acts as a focal event, action, or operant and then something happens afterward to reinforce it (Landrum & Kauffman, 2006). For example, if we wished the family dog to consistently fetch a stick that we throw, we might give the dog a treat each time he brought back the stick, but only if he brought back the stick. In this case, the dog learns that when he does the desired behavior (brings the stick back), he will get a doggy treat. Yet it is important to remember that in one's efforts toward behavioral conditioning, especially when it relates to humans, little or none of the actual conditioning or learning that actually occurs will necessarily resemble the intended conditioning or learning. For example, the intention of most punishments is to create a disincentive related to the unwanted action. But what is actually learned is much more complex and typically takes the form of a disincentive to interact with the source of the punishment (person meting out) or the creation of a new set of skills to get around the punishment in the future (Kauffman, 2005).

Under examination, the popularity of extrinsic rewards is understandable; however, consider as well the reasons their by-products are considered undesirable. In most cases, they work in the short term to motivate behavior. But there are several questions to ask before using extrinsic reinforcements:

- Is the motivation to perform the behavior increasing, or just the motivation to obtain the reward?

- Will the schedule of reinforcements be sustainable? Or will a greater amount of reinforcement be needed in the future (see the discussion on weed pulling later in this chapter)?

- What is ultimately being learned?

- Like the man in the story about the noisy children, are we replacing an internal source of motivation with an external one and as a result extinguishing our students' intrinsic motivation?

If you are attempting to develop a student-centered 1-Style classroom, the frequent and sustained use of extrinsic rewards will be inherently counterproductive. They will work against the development of such outcomes as self-responsibility and the inclination to reflect on what will lead to one's personal growth or the common good of the group—dispositions that are essential to the 1-Style classroom (Kohn, 1999; Ryan & Deci, 2006). Or they can be part of a very effective teacher-centered classroom and assist the teacher in developing a 2-Style approach in his or her effort to promote more efficient student behavior (Reeve, 2003).

For those who feel compelled to include extrinsic forms of reinforcement among their motivational strategies, it may be helpful to consider the following guiding principles for using them effectively:

- Relate the reinforcement to a clearly identified desired behavior. The primary focus should be on accomplishing the desired behavior rather than attaining the reward.

- The closer in time the attainment of the reward is to the desired behavior, the stronger effect the reinforcement will have.

- Intermittent or random schedules of reinforcement will be more powerful than regular and predictable schedules of reinforcement.

- Reinforcements that are given after the display of an expected behavior will be more effective than arrangements and deals made before the desired behavior is performed.

- Avoid putting students in situations in which they are competing for rewards, especially meaningful rewards. Use competition only when all students are in an equal position to display the behavior if they so choose. Rewarding effort, good choices, cooperation, and other things that students can control can be effective at attaining more of those behaviors. But competition that includes rewarding winners for ability, personality, parental support, or academic performance will undermine the level of motivation in the class and can even backfire with many students when it comes to the desired behavior change.

Following these guidelines will not lead to higher levels of intrinsic motivation, but they will likely be effective in changing behavior in the short term. Moreover, they will help reduce the dependence of students on rewards and make it easier to remove them over time. When we do gradually remove the reinforcements, we should be left with a substantial amount of new "learned behavior" and only a minimal amount of "withdrawal" from the students who have developed a dependency on the reinforcement.

Following are three examples of typical but problematic uses of extrinsic rewards followed by a more effective strategy in the same situation:

Typical but problematic: "If you all do your work, I will give the class a prize on Friday." *Problems:* The reward is too far removed in time; the probability is that a reward is going to be needed for every desirable behavior; and when Friday comes, you will likely be in a difficult spot. It is a certainty that some students will have met their end of the bargain and others will not.

Better idea: "You have just spent the entire period focused on a task; that is the first time you have all been able to do that. I am going to give you all [an extrinsic reward or removal of a negative reinforcer]." This is a better way to put it because it was random and immediate and will promote behavior change. The students know what they did, so they will repeat it. They will not expect the reward but will exhibit behavior that they understand may be reinforced. They learned that when they did that particular behavior, the teacher will reward them.

Typical but problematic: "The group that does the best job of. . .at the end of the day will get a prize." *Problems:* This is competitive, and there will eventually be some resentful students; the work is done in anticipation of the prize (that is, the prize is primary and the purpose of the behavior is secondary); and the reinforcement is not well connected to any particular repeatable behavior (good reinforcement promotes the repetition of desired behavior).

Better idea: "I asked you to put away your reading books and take out your math book. This table did it right away without being asked again, so they will be the first in line to go out to recess." This is better because it will change behavior: the other tables will be much quicker in the future, anticipating that something similar might happen again; it reinforces your expectations—real learning took place in a very concrete example; it was immediate and clearly related both in time and causality; and the focus is on the expected behavior first and the reward second.

Typical but problematic: A token economy or arrangements where students get points for certain behaviors and the points are added up for some reward at the end of a certain period. *Problems:* The behavior was done primarily for extrinsic rewards. This is essentially paying students to do what they should be doing and what we want them to love to do for its own sake. This choice destroys both of those goals. The schedule of reinforcement is continuous, and continuous reinforcement leads to a gradual decrease of motivation. It ends up creating a lose-lose decision: "Do I increase the reward to maintain the motivation level, or do I slowly watch my students begin to demand an extrinsic reward for everything and increasingly avoid behaviors that are not rewarded (including just about everything that we want them to care about in our class)?"

Better idea: If you are committed to the use of a point system:

- Use it for a short duration at the start of the year (three weeks or less).
- Use it to clarify your expectations. Relate your reward system to the critical expectations that are necessary for the class to function, such as listening, cooperation, and efficient procedures. This process may be useful when attempting to shift from a 2-Style to a 1-Syle classroom.
- Use only random or intermittent reinforcement schedules. Random is the better choice. That is, students realize what the desired behavior is supposed to be (working cooperatively, listening, being on task, raising hands), but they do not know when the reinforcement will occur. If you compare the level of the desired behavior in a random reinforcement condition versus a fixed condition, you will be amazed at the difference.
- Give points and take points away without warning. Warnings always weaken reinforcements.
- Do not give a large amount of attention to the points. Attach your emotion to the accomplishment of the behavior rather than the attainment of the points.
- The ultimate reward cannot be meaningful or substantive. It cannot relate to grades, your affection, or something of real material worth. In fact, simply achieving the most points can be enough of a reward in and of itself and may be a preferable reward in your effort to emphasize that the process was the point, not who won or lost.

- Make it a game for fun and mutual entertainment, and focus on how it is leading to behavior change. Again, the extrinsic is always presented as a material reminder of something of real and intrinsic value, such as learning or becoming a better class.

6.11 REFLECTION

Recall a situation in which you were rewarded with points or prizes for certain behavior. Do you remember if you won or were rewarded with prizes? Do you remember what you were asked to do to achieve those rewards? Which memory is more powerful? What does your memory tell you about the source of your motivation to perform?

INTRINSIC MOTIVATIONAL TECHNIQUES

Intrinsic motivation, according to Ryan and Deci (2006), is the inherent propensity to engage one's interests and to exercise and develop one's capacities.

Intrinsic motivational techniques cannot be as easily explained as separate techniques or strategies when compared to extrinsic techniques. Like any other successful methodology, they must be developed intentionally, but a holistic approach is most effective. Much of the process of promoting intrinsic motivation involves the removal of barriers to students' abilities to access their inner motives and satisfiers. Rewards, pain-based motivators, meaningless tasks, learning in isolation, and a lack of support all act to block intrinsic sources of motivation. For a student's intrinsic sources of motivation to grow, the learning context must support them.

It may be most instructive and practical to examine many intrinsic motivational ideas within a single structure: that of basic needs. Inquiry and problem-based learning, increased responsibility, and achieving personal growth all make much more sense by examining them within the context of how they meet basic needs. Yet when students experience a needs-satisfying environment, they think of it less as a source of satisfaction and more as a context for being more fully alive. Reeve (2006) describes it this way: "When [students' basic needs are met] however, students do not typically say, 'I feel competent' or 'I feel autonomous.' Instead, they say, 'that is interesting,' 'that is fun,' or 'I enjoyed doing it.'"

Unlike extrinsic forms of motivation, intrinsic forms are less about adding something. For instance, intrinsic basic needs simply exist, and we all possess them. During the school day, either they are met within the context of the learning environment or students will be forced to meet them in alternative ways. In some cases, the alternate means students use to meet their needs manifest as disruptive behavior and problems for the teacher or unhealthy habits for the student.

Basic Needs

Each of us has fundamental basic needs that we must find a way to satisfy (Glasser, 1980). If we are unable to satisfy them, we experience some type of dissonance. While theorists vary slightly when identifying the core areas (Curwin & Mendler, 1986; Glasser, 1980; Reeve, 2006), the basic human needs for love and belonging, power, competence, freedom, and fun seem to be inherent and universal.

These basic needs exist inside and outside the classroom. The evidence that a student comes from a home in which his or her basic needs have been met is usually quite apparent. Most likely these students are confident, centered, and trusting. The time spent at school can often have an even more determinant effect on students' ability to meet their basic needs than their time away from school. The activities in which they are engaged are more structured, limiting their ability to meet their needs more naturally, and in many cases, meeting one's needs is more challenging at school. As a result, we discover that students find numerous creative ways to get their needs met during the school day. Quite often these means become labeled as inappropriate behavior.

Teachers have no choice but to recognize that students have basic needs and that those needs will manifest themselves. Most students have the ability to deny their needs for a short period of time, but to do this day after day would be intolerable. More important, students should not have to endure a school environment that denies their basic needs. A critical ingredient to successful classroom management is to initially view all problems through the lens of basic needs. For some teachers, this may require a paradigm shift, and for others, it may help clarify their perspective. For example, if we look out at our class and see frustrated expressions, a common (but highly ineffective) response is to view that reaction as inconvenient to us and our plans. A more effective reaction, and one that will lead to a solution, is to ask ourselves, *What basic need is lacking right now?* When we view student misbehavior and unconsciously use the lens of thinking we need to let them know that their behavior is inadequate, a management dead end will result. When we examine the behavior or emotional climate in class through the lens of basic needs, problems become illuminated, diagnosis gains coherence, and solutions become more evident.

When basic needs are not being met, the reactions by the students (their coping mechanisms) can take internal or external form. As we examine each basic need in the following sections more closely, these reactions become more evident, as does how each basic need can be met in the classroom.

Love and Belonging. All of us need to feel that we are loved and are a wanted part of a group. The desire to be accepted by the group is considered by many theorists as the fundamental human drive (Dreikurs, 1974). Moreover, our sense of self-acceptance is greatly influenced by factors within our environment. If we feel perpetually unloved, alienated, or isolated, common internal reactions are a sense of guilt, worthlessness, loneliness, and lower self-esteem. Common external reactions include acting out, overachievement, clowning, and pleasing. Teachers can give students a greater sense of love and belonging by recognizing their unique qualities and talents, creating an emotionally safe community environment, and showing genuine care and respect.

Power. Each of us needs to feel that we have some control over our destiny. If we do not experience a sense of agency in our lives, we feel helpless. As we discuss in the next chapter, a sense of power is fundamentally related to the development of an internal locus of control. Those who feel that they lack power can become withdrawn and passive-aggressive, and they may rebel or act with hostility. Teachers can give students a sense of power by refraining from 4-Style management strategies and giving them choices, responsibility and opportunities for leadership, and ownership for the development of class procedures and the social contract.

Competence. We all want to feel a sense of self-efficacy. We need to feel that we are capable and have something valuable to contribute. Much of our identity is connected to what we can do and how well we can do it. If we feel useless, unvalued, incompetent, or unappreciated, common internal reactions are losing motivation or a sense of inadequacy, and common external reactions are bragging, acting overly competent, seeking attention, and excuse making. Teachers can give students a greater sense of competence by focusing on progress and not products, removing conditions in which comparisons among students are used, recognizing incremental achievement and original ideas, expressing high expectations, and helping students achieve the goals they have set for themselves.

6.12

REFLECTION

Recall a situation in which you felt very competent. How did you act? How would you describe your level of motivation? Conversely, recall a situation in which you felt little, if any, sense of competence. How did you act? How would you describe your level of motivation?

Freedom. We all need to feel that we are autonomous and have freedom of choice. We must feel a sense of liberation to be able to express our individuality. Common internal reactions are feeling too restricted or imprisoned and becoming withdrawn or resentful, and common external reactions are fighting back, active resistance, and seeking paths around authority. Teachers can help students experience freedom through supporting autonomy and creativity; avoiding personal praise and disappointment; validating differing viewpoints within the class; and fostering the attitude that the teacher does not have, and need not have, all the answers, and that everyone makes mistakes.

Fun. We all need to have fun and experience wonder and joy. Fun may be difficult to define. What is fun for one person may not be fun for another. Yet we all feel the need to experience enjoyment and whimsy. If we are put in a repressive or tedious environment, common internal reactions are boredom, frustration, and daydreaming, and common external reactions are making one's own fun, engaging the teacher in off-task games, and hostility. Teachers can promote students' sense of fun by the use of humor, providing opportunities for creative play, making learning engaging and interesting, and a thoughtful use of healthy competition.

6.13

REFLECTION

The word *fun* draws different reactions from those in different positions. Sometimes the idea that learning needs to be fun can feel oppressive and fill us with guilt or disdain for those who tell us to make things more fun (such as our students). But take a closer look at the idea of fun. What makes you happy? What feels like fun? When do you see a look of joy on the face of your students? Fun need not involve big laughs and a party. How could you meet your students' need for fun without betraying your values as a teacher?

The Results of Meeting Basic Needs

The conditions that meet basic needs have the effect of promoting intrinsic motivation, and vice versa. When we assist students on a path of personal growth, we inevitably meet their needs of power and competence. When we give increased responsibility, we are not so much adding something or giving something to the student as we are allowing the basic needs for power, contribution, and belonging to be fulfilled and the student to bloom. And as we examine the effect of instruction on motivation in Chapter Eleven, it will be evident that creating a learning context in which basic needs are met is a more effective means to achieving student motivation than bribing students to do work they find meaningless and unsatisfying.

CONSIDERING MOTIVATION AS MOVEMENT OR FLOW

Recall a class, team, or committee, for example, that consisted of a series of meetings in which you felt consistently motivated and eager to take part in the activity. In this situation, would you characterize what was going on as "going someplace"? Now recall another situation in which you felt your participation was out of a sense of obligation. In other words, you were just putting in time, and as a result, you found yourself finding ways to entertain yourself that may not have been part of the stated agenda. In this second case, how much psychological movement did you feel the situation provided? In other words, how much did you feel that there was a flow (Csikszentmihalyi, 1991), or that things were going somewhere and you were part of that movement? It is a good bet that it was very little. Recall what you did to meet your needs and entertain yourself.

Examining these two situations should give you some insight into the reality of your students and the needs they bring to your class. If there is not a sense of movement in your class, it is very likely that your students will create that movement with behavior that may appear to be a problem. And as we discussed regarding socially constructed reality, these problem behaviors could go in the category of problems manufactured by the teacher. You cannot expect the same level of behavior from powerless, joyless, bored students as you would from students who are going somewhere that they feel is meaningful to them. We as teachers "make the weather," and regardless of whether we are aware of it, we create more or less psychological movement in our class.

Psychological movement has two factors: the direction of the movement and the rate at which the movement takes place. Figure 6.2 depicts this concept.

Clarity of the Goal

The sense of movement that a group feels will be related to how well the goal of the activity (or series of activities) is internalized. But all goals will not achieve the same outcomes or kinds of motivation. For example, consider the two cases you examined from your own experience. Which case held more intrinsic interest to you? It is a good bet it was the first one, which you felt was going somewhere. Be careful when selecting your goals. It may be helpful to examine Table 6.2, the chart of motivational strategies, earlier in this chapter for some ideas. It is highly likely that the goals that ultimately lead to extrinsic rewards will not last as long or maintain their effectiveness over time as those rooted in sources of internal satisfaction. Again consider the event that you recalled for the first case. How would you characterize your goals?

Amount and Schedule of Reinforcement

The rate of movement will vary to the degree that there is reinforcement for the attainment of that goal. This reinforcement can be external or internal and about a tangible product or a clearly satisfying experience. And given what we know about reinforcement, we can assume that the more intermittent the schedule of that reinforcement is, the stronger it will be. In addition, the more closely the reinforcement is related in time and logical relationship

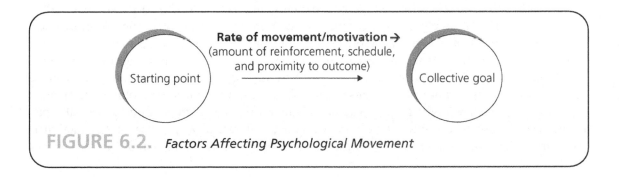

FIGURE 6.2. *Factors Affecting Psychological Movement*

to the achievements necessary to attain the goal, the more effective it will be. For example, if immediately after successfully playing a tune on the piano we are reinforced, we will be more motivated to keep practicing. That reinforcement could be extrinsic (money or praise for example) or intrinsic (a sense of satisfaction or the joy of making a wonderful sound), yet in both cases, our motivation in the future will be related to how immediate and substantial the reinforcement is.

Comparison Case Examples

A case example might help clarify the principle. Imagine you were given the task of pulling weeds. For most of us, the task alone is not inherently reinforcing, so we would likely do it only for payment. Let's say we are getting paid as our reinforcement, and assume that we agreed to do the work for fifty dollars a day. What would our motivational level be for our first day? Assume that we were paid the same amount no matter what our rate or quality. What would happen to our motivation? In comparison, let's say that we were paid per weed. How would that affect our level of motivation? What if our supervisor stopped by every once in a while and gave us a bonus if he or she observed an exceptional level of effort? All of these variables would affect our level of motivation. They would not change the stated goal, but they would affect our psychological sense of movement toward that goal.

Now consider this case from another perspective. We might ask as a result of the motivation provided in each condition whether we are more or less likely in the future to engage in weed pulling without being paid. And what will the result be to our motivation to take part in work that is similar to weed pulling? This example illustrates that with a well-conceived plan of reinforcements, we can increase motivation by manipulating the reinforcement schedule and the clarity of the goal. But while we can obtain a high level of motivation in the short term with an extrinsic type of goal such as the one described, we have to ask what the long-term cost of any motivational program would be.

Now let's paint a picture that may look similar to the one that you envisioned earlier in the situation in which you felt that things were going somewhere. You would characterize the goal of the work as very meaningful and very clear. You knew what you were aiming for, and you had a desire to attain the goal. But why? Possibly you were being given an external reinforcement, but it is also likely that you saw value to the work. It was relevant to you. The reinforcement could simply have been seeing progress toward your goal and the feeling of getting better or accomplishing something. And if there were others involved, part of the reinforcement may have been the feeling of working together to achieve a common goal.

When we examine the activity in any classroom, we can quickly determine if there is a feeling that things are going somewhere and whether there is momentum. Do the students know where they are going? Is there something satisfying about the goal and the steps along the way to achieving it?

As we consider our basic needs, think about how the satisfaction of getting needs met affects one's level of motivation and a decreased necessity to engage in what Dreikurs (1974) calls "mistaken goals": goals that give us a sense of satisfaction and psychological movement but are unhealthy for all concerned. As you examine the idea of self-theories (Dweck, 2000) and the development of a growth orientation to work in the next chapter, consider how one's orientation to the task can create more or less of a psychological sense that one is going somewhere in the effort. If we find joy in the getting there and experience learning as a means to growth, we will feel a deeper sense of motivation. But if we feel that the goal is just a means to an end (we want to feel a sense of relief, avoid failure, make sure others are pleased, or something else), we will only experience a limited degree of motivation as we take part in the task. Those who know where they are going and feel a deep sense of satisfaction in the getting there rarely feel bored. Teachers who look out at a sea of bored faces know that students do not know what the goal is, do not care about the goal, or view the work simply as an obligation.

CONCLUSION

Putting the elements of this chapter together, consider using the lens of success psychology as a way to think about what makes a task satisfying, motivational, and something that you would do without a lot of external reinforcement. A practical guide to the development of a success psychology within a class is outlined in the following chapter.

Journal Reflections

1. Would you say that your education to this point has been defined more by intrinsic or extrinsic forms of motivation?
2. As you examine your education and the classrooms that you have observed recently, would you classify them as basic-needs-satisfying places?

Activities

1. In small groups, discuss your example of a situation that you felt was going somewhere. What made it feel that way? Why was it different from other educational situations you have been in?
2. Examine a class other than one that you are teaching. Identify anything that you consider a problem: lack of control, boredom, inattention, conflict, hostility, alienation, or something else. Given these problems, can you recognize the unmet basic needs that are at their root?
3. As a class, discuss the story of the man who wanted to take a nap. Do members of the class see the principles of this parable manifested in classrooms that they observe?
4. Create a section in your classroom management plan or teaching improvement plan that addresses motivation. In a few pages, outline the principles and strategies you will use to support the motivational levels in your class—for example:

   - Why will your students be motivated in the short term? In the long term?
   - How would you characterize your motivational style?
   - Why will your students care about the work that they are doing?
   - Why will your students care about each other?
   - What effect do you want your motivational strategies to have on your students?

REFERENCES

Alberto, P., & Troutman, A. (2003). *Applied behavioral analysis for teaching* (6th ed.). Upper Saddle River, NJ: Merrill/Prentice Hall.

Ayling, G. (2009). *Report of an adolescent transition: A possible intervention for the stress response and diseases in adult life.* Manuscript submitted for publication.

Csikszentmihalyi, M. (1991). *Flow: The psychology of optimal experience.* New York: HarperCollins.

Curwin, R., & Mendler, A. (1986). *Discipline with dignity.* Alexandria VA: ASCD Press.

Deci, E. L., Koestner, R., & Ryan, R. M. (1999). A meta-analytic review of experiments examining the effects of extrinsic rewards and intrinsic motivation. *Psychological Bulletin, 125,* 627–668.

Dreikurs, R. (1974). *Discipline without tears.* New York: Hawthorn Books.

Dweck, C. (2000). *Self-theories: Their role in motivation, personality and development.* Lillington, NC: Psychologists Press.

Glasser, W. (1990). *The quality school: Managing students without coercion*. New York: HarperCollins.

Hickey, D. T., & Schafer, N. J. (2006). Design-based, participation-centered approaches to classroom management. In C. M. Evertson & C. S. Weinstein (Eds.), *Handbook of classroom management* (pp. 281–308). Mahwah, NJ: Erlbaum.

Jones, F. (2000). *Tools for teaching: Discipline, instruction, motivation*. Santa Cruz, CA: Jones Publishing.

Kauffman, J. M. (2005). How we prevent the prevention of emotional and behavioral difficulties in education. In P. Clough, P. Garner, J. T. Pardeck, & F. Yuen (Eds.), *Handbook of emotional and behavioral difficulties in education* (pp. 429–440). Thousand Oaks, CA: Sage.

Kohn, A. (1999). *Punished by rewards: The trouble with gold stars, incentive plans, A's, praise, and other bribes*. Boston: Houghton Mifflin

Landrum, T. J., & Kauffman, J. M. (2006). Behavioral approaches to classroom management. In C. M. Evertson & C. S. Weinstein (Eds.), *Handbook of classroom management* (pp. 47–71). Mahwah, NJ: Erlbaum.

Lerman, D. C. (2003). From laboratory to community application: Translation research in behavioral analysis. *Journal of Applied Behavioral Analysis*, *36*, 415–419.

Reeve, J. (2006). Extrinsic rewards and inner motivation. In C. M. Evertson & C. S. Weinstein (Eds.), *Handbook of classroom management* (pp. 645–664). Mahwah, NJ: Erlbaum.

Reeve, J., & Deci, E. L. (1996). Elements of the competitive situations that affect intrinsic motivation. *Personality and Social Psychology Bulletin*, *22*, 24–33.

Ryan, R. M., & Deci, E. L. (2006). Self-determination theory and the facilitation of intrinsic motivation, social development and well-being. *American Psychologist*, *55*, 65–78.

Shindler, J., Taylor, C., Jones, A., & Cadenas, H. (2003). *Don't smile 'til Christmas: Examining the immersion of new teachers into existing school climates*. Yearbook for the American Educational Research Association Urban Teaching and Learning SIG, Los Angeles, CA.

Skinner, E. A., & Belmont, M. J. (1993). Motivation in the classroom: Reciprocal effects of teacher behavior and student engagement across the school year. *Journal of Educational Psychology*, *85*, 571–581.

Promoting a Success Psychology in Students

In This Chapter

- Exploring what constitutes a psychology of success
- Promoting a growth versus fixed ability orientation
- Promoting acceptance and belonging in the classroom
- Promoting an internal locus of control in students
- Indicators that you are making progress in fostering a psychology of success

7.1

REFLECTION

To begin this chapter, reflect on the following questions:

- Why do some students feel confident academically and persist in the face of challenge?
- Why do some students experience high self-esteem?
- Why do some students love to learn and reflect a high level of motivation without the need for extrinsic reinforcement?
- Why do some classes have a sense of movement to them?

There *are* answers to these questions, and interestingly, the answers are related. At the heart of what creates intrinsic motivation, self-esteem, confidence to take risks, a sense of social responsibility, and a love of learning is what could be termed a psychology of success. This chapter outlines a theoretical framework and a set of practical guidelines for promoting a psychology of success within the classroom. It also illustrates what teachers, parents, and coaches should avoid doing—behavior that has been shown to promote what could be termed a psychology of failure.

At this point, many readers may be thinking, "Sure, it would be great to promote a better climate and a success psychology in my class, but I have a lot to accomplish each day. I really don't have the time to put much attention into this area." This is an understandable concern. However, the development of a success or failure psychology is not so much about adding things to class to make students feel better about themselves; it is about understanding the effects of teaching choices. Creating a success psychology is fundamental to promoting high-quality classroom management and student achievement. In a study conducted in urban public schools, the presence of success psychology–promoting practices was highly correlated with student achievement scores and school climate quality (Shindler, Jones, Williams, Taylor, & Cadenas, 2009; see Appendix G).

Each action on our part is either promoting or undermining our students' psychology of success. As we progress in the chapter and operationalize this concept, why this is and which actions will produce which effects should become more apparent.

A COMPARISON OF TWO CLASSROOMS

To better understand the practical implications of the conceptual idea of success psychology, it may be useful to examine two hypothetical classrooms.

In class A, students feel little sense of belonging. They view their class as a place to get their work done, to fill a day or a period. They have friends but few, if any, meaningful bonds with the other students in the class. Students experience some good days and some bad days, but feel they have little control over the events that contribute to each. They try to do what they are told and avoid getting into trouble when they feel a need to break a rule here or there. Some students feel pretty smart and try to maintain that standing, while other students see themselves as not as smart and become relatively comfortable with getting lower grades and giving up on the more difficult tasks. As the year goes on, these patterns become entrenched with modest variation. By the end of the year, the same subgroups of students show low motivation, the same subgroups are getting in trouble, the same subgroups are getting academic recognition, and the class has settled into a well-established social pattern defined by a series of cliques and a well-entrenched hierarchy.

In class B, students feel accepted and as though they are part of a community. They take risks and express themselves. They feel a responsibility for their learning and to the group as a whole and take the other members' needs and feelings into account before they act. Most of the time, they are very involved in their work, are seldom bored, and become increasingly confident at persisting in the face of difficult work. The more they learn, the more they grow in a sense of personal empowerment. They grow to love learning for its own sake and have little need for prizes, rewards, or incentives. Students in this class do not see themselves as being in competition with other students or feel a need to be better than others, so they find it easy to be encouraging to one another. They see learning as a journey and encourage their classmates' success along with their own.

7.2 **REFLECTION**

Have you observed or been a part of classrooms such as the two described here? Have you thought about what made them so different? In your opinion, does a climate like that described in class B develop by chance?

Classes such as class B do not come about by accident. They require a great deal of intention, awareness, and knowledge of what it takes to get there. As a result they are rare. Classes such as class A can come about by "accident" or, more accurately, by the unexamined actions of the teacher. Unfortunately, these types of classrooms are not at all rare. It may seem obvious, but it is useful to reflect on the fact that in both cases, the teacher was trying to do something. Moreover, it is likely that teachers who produce each of these types of classes have good intentions for what they wanted to accomplish. So given the great disparity between these two classes, what can we conclude?

There is in fact no real world when it comes to school. Classrooms are what we make them (Huberman & Middlebrooks, 2000). Teachers make the weather, and that weather is the psychological climate in the class (Ginott, 1972). To succeed in creating a climate that more closely resembles class B rather than class A, you must accept a few principles. First, the climate in the class is manufactured by you, the teacher. Second, not all sources of motivation get the same results. Third, intrinsically motivated students did not get that way by accident. They have been systematically encouraged to become so.

THE THREE FACTORS OF SUCCESS PSYCHOLOGY

As we examine the idea of a success psychology, we can see a whole series of ideas rooted in a common phenomenon. The concepts of self-esteem, achievement psychology, intrinsic motivation, movement psychology, and success psychology are all characterized by the same fundamental components. A substantial amount of research indicates that all these orientations lead to academic success (Auer, 1992; Benham, 1993; Dweck, 2006; Klein & Keller, 1990; Rennie, 1991). When we pare the research down to its fundamental components, we see three factors that make up a psychological orientation toward success:

- Growth versus fixed ability orientation as related to one's self-efficacy
- A sense of belonging and acceptance versus isolation and worthlessness
- Internal versus external locus of control

The following sections describe each of these areas briefly and are followed by a table of practical teaching strategies categorized as promoting or undermining these factors in the classroom.

PROMOTING A GROWTH VERSUS FIXED ABILITY ORIENTATION

Carol Dweck and her colleagues in their research over the course of thirty years have developed a useful paradigm for examining academic self-concept, achievement, and motivation. They demonstrated in a series of studies with students (Dweck, 2000, 2006) that future success is not as much the result of talent or current level of achievement as it is the result of the orientation or cognitive strategy one uses to approach learning tasks. Research and common sense support the notion that the level of one's sense of competence (or self-efficacy) will relate to the level of self-esteem (Davis & Peck, 1992). We of course want students to experience healthy levels of self-esteem. However, the different cognitive strategies that one might choose to use to attain that sense of competence will not accomplish the same result, especially in the long term. Dweck offers a useful lens for distinguishing two contrasting cognitive strategies for feeling competent and how they have dramatically different results over time.

Two Views of Intelligence

Dweck consistently discovered as she examined students in various classrooms that they seemed to have one of two perceptions relating to the nature of their ability and intelligence. Most classes had a balanced portion of students from each orientation. One group of students had what Dweck termed a fixed ability theory of intelligence and ability. These students viewed their ability as something set and stable. They viewed themselves as smart or not smart. They believed they were good at this or that they were not. As a result of this view of the nature of their intelligence, these students developed a pattern of behavior defined by trying to look smart and avoid looking dumb. Their highest desire was to accomplish tasks successfully and prove their ability to others. They held the belief that if they were successful, that would demonstrate that they were smart or talented. So they sought tasks that would make them look good to others and maintain their conception of themselves as competent, and they avoided tasks they viewed as difficult.

7.3   REFLECTION

As you reflect on the cognitive orientation described above, do you recognize this pattern in yourself? Most of us do. Can you think of a situation in which you wanted to succeed so that you would not feel "dumb"? Why did you fear failure in this situation? Why does failure feel so painful?

The other group of students possessed what Dweck referred to as a growth orientation. This group viewed intelligence as something that was developed over time rather than being a fixed quantity. These students perceived learning and the attainment of knowledge or skill as coming from investment in the process of learning. Every opportunity to take part in learning was an opportunity to get better. They approached the task not by asking what the outcome would say about them and their ability but by what they could take away from the venture.

Two Corresponding Reactions to Failure

In one study, Dweck (2000) assessed the reactions of students in two groups to a failure condition. In the study, the students were given seven math problems that were relatively simple and three that were unsolvable. When confronted by failure, students with the fixed ability orientation dealt with it by assuming that there was nothing they could do further. They became frustrated and gave up quickly. Their assumption was that their ability was not enough to overcome the difficulty of the tasks, and so they felt helpless. After experiencing this failure, they quickly began to demean their ability and intelligence and reported that they perceived the whole of their effort as unsuccessful, even though this was in fact a disproportionate assessment. Dweck (2000) labeled this conditioned reaction the "helpless pattern."

The group of students who reported a growth orientation when faced with a failure condition immediately began to consider the various ways that they could approach the task differently. They persisted in the task until they were told they had to stop. Throughout the task, they used self-instruction and positive self-talk to motivate and guide themselves through the challenging task. When the task was over, they did not view any part of it as a failure but felt that they had merely run out of time. Dweck (2000) labeled this conditioned reaction the "mastery-oriented pattern."

7.4   REFLECTION

Reflect on a situation in which you experienced failure. How would you characterize your reaction: Mastery oriented or helpless? Do you see these patterns in your students, players, children, and friends? In your estimation, what effect would each approach have if employed consistently over a lifetime?

All students need to feel a sense of self-efficacy and confidence, but what can appear to be confidence can often be a fragile belief that in a particular situation, one is better than those around them or "good enough" for what they are asked to do. If competence and confidence are perceived as coming from "how good we are" at a task (related to innate ability), then we tend to give up quickly and protect our egos in the face of failure. Over the course of an academic career, this leads to a pattern defined by a fear of failure and a great deal of anxiety associated with the adequacy of one's performance. As we examine the concept of a psychology of success, the strong relationship between a helpless pattern and a psychology of failure will become increasingly evident.

It is common for many of us to realize that we have spent most of our academic life holding a fixed view of ability and as a result have been driven by a fear of failure. Some of us may even glorify the motivation that fear provided and the high test scores that it produced. Let me offer a few thoughts. First, students with a fixed ability orientation tended to score increasingly lower than their growth-orientation peers. This was especially true over time. The achievement gap between the two groups was shown to grow over the years. Second, while fear of failure (and its cognitive sibling, pain-based logic) may provide some motivation, it cannot lead to a success psychology, and in fact will lead in the opposite direction. The sooner that one lets go of one's pain-based logic patterns, the better. Third, many of us need to accept that our parents and their parents probably reared us to have at least some fear of failure. However, just because we may have turned out fine in the end does not mean it was a strategy that we want to pass on to those we care for. It is wise to learn different, healthier ways to motivate our students.

REFLECTION 7.5

Did your parents try to motivate you with fear of failure by the use of shame, embarrassment, guilt, or comparison? How do you view the use of these strategies today?

Promoting a Growth Orientation in the Classroom

While students come to us with an orientation of either growth and mastery or fixed ability and helplessness that can be already deeply conditioned, it is important to recognize that what we do in the classroom will have a profound effect on which orientation is developed. What we choose to do in our classrooms will promote one orientation or the other. We can foster growth patterns and help students break helpless patterns, or create a climate where fear of failure is the pervading motivational force. In fact, we can assume that most of the hundreds of teaching choices that we make each day are contributing to one or the other.

Table 7.1 offers a list of practical strategies to promote a growth-oriented orientation in your students as well as the class as a whole. It is juxtaposed with practices to be avoided that would have the effect of promoting a helpless pattern.

REFLECTION 7.6

Observe a classroom or reflect on one that you have witnessed recently. Would you classify the practices in the class as promoting more of a mastery-oriented or a helpless pattern? Would you suppose that the teacher was consciously aware and intentional about doing one or the other?

TABLE 7.1. Teaching Practices That Promote a Growth or a Fixed Ability Orientation

Promoting a Growth-Oriented Pattern	Promoting a Fixed Ability/Helpless Pattern
Give learning goals (goals related to how much one is going to learn).	Give performance goals (goals related to measuring the ability of the participant).
Focus on means and processes.	Focus on ends and products.
Focus on effort and application.	Focus on ability and intelligence.
Challenge stereotypical beliefs about various groups' typical ability and intelligence.	Reinforce stereotypical beliefs about various groups' typical ability and intelligence.
Give operational feedback and positive recognitions (see Chapter Six) related to process aspects of the task.	Give personal praise (see Chapter Six) and feedback related to how good at the task or intelligent one is.
Assess what is most important. What you assess on a daily basis defines your classroom concept of success. Complete the following sentence, "If I could only assess _____, I would have a better class." Consider a way to assess the idea that you put in the blank (see Chapter Eleven).	Assess only what you can count. Rely on worksheets and tests, and make sure students understand that the points are what is important.
Encourage students to make mistakes and take risks. Project trust while challenging students to stretch beyond their comfort zones.	Encourage students to avoid mistakes. Model mistakes as deserving of self-criticism. Project a lack of trust in their resources.
Have high expectations for all your students, and catch them being good. Do not accept low self-estimations, especially in the areas of effort and process. All students are capable of total effort, and total effort in the process leads to good outcomes.	Use language in your feedback that implies that some students are more talented than others. Speak in terms of students being good at this or that. Encourage students to stick to what they currently believe they are good at and avoid that at which they are weak.
Help students stay in the moment as they work. Do not encourage them to interpret their past as failure but only as opportunities to learn and grow, and help them not to define themselves by past failures or successes. Help them focus on what they are doing and enjoy the process, and allow the outcomes to work out, reducing stress and promoting creativity.	Remind students constantly about what and how they have failed in the past and how they need to worry about the future. Speak only about the end result of the work as being important.

PROMOTING A SENSE OF BELONGING AND ACCEPTANCE WITHIN THE CLASS

This second factor within the framework for a success psychology reflects the degree to which any member feels wanted and part of the group, and the degree to which one likes and accepts one's self as one is. The more one feels accepted and acceptable, the more one will be able to express one's self, act authentically, and be fully present to others (Osterman, 2000). Self-acceptance is in contrast to self-aggrandizement or a compulsion to please. A sense of belonging and acceptance is essential to a young person's mental health and ability to trust and take risks (Inderbitzen & Clark, 1986). It comes in part from accepting messages from those the student respects, a positive and accepting attitude and self-talk, experiencing emotional safety, and feeling a part of a community. Research has shown a relationship between a sense of belonging with acceptance and self-esteem (Davis & Peck, 1992; Katz, 1990; Osterman, 2000; Washinawotok, 1993). Moreover, building a sense of classroom belonging and the sense of self- and peer acceptance has been shown to promote higher achievement (Dembrowsky, 1990; Rhoades & McCabe, 1992; Washinawotok, 1993). For those who endeavor to employ referent or attractive power as a significant means to motivate students and gain respect, the notion of creating a class with a high level of belonging is immediately appealing. Much of the climate created in any classroom in this area will come from the affect of the teacher. If you project an accepting affect to students and express a value for bonding as a class, the effect is liberating and needs satisfying. And in your efforts to have a transformational impact on students, your emotional investment can have a profound result. How you feel about your students will be critical, and what your students believe about the degree to which you care about them and the quality of the relationships in the class will define their sense of acceptance and belonging to a great degree (Osterman, 2000). Also, what you do will have an equally profound effect. It may seem counterintuitive at first, but you need to recognize that you can love and care about your students and at the same time do a great deal to undermine their sense of acceptance and belonging. In other words, it is possible to have good intentions and great affection while unconsciously using strategies that create dependence, a sense of competitiveness, and mistrust within the class.

REFLECTION

7.7

Have you observed a class in which the teacher expressed a lot of caring and affection for the students, yet the result was a class in which students never learned to trust one another and gained little self-confidence? Conversely, have you observed a class in which the teacher took a very businesslike approach but created a high degree of community and group cohesion? How would you explain what you observed?

Some of us come to this profession by value of personality (being more introverted or logical minded, or both). The common perception is that while teachers who are not predisposed to being highly emotional and warm may be good teachers and effectively manage their classes by relying on expert and legitimate authority, they will be at a great disadvantage when it comes to creating a climate of acceptance and belonging. This is simply not true. While it is true that if a teacher projects indifference to students, effectiveness will suffer and will meet few students' needs to feel liked and accepted, it is also true that acceptance and care can be shown subtly and demonstrated in countless ways without being displayed dramatically. It might be more gradual, but it is possible. As we have observed, any teacher's feelings, values, and thinking will come out in his or her actions eventually. If we like our students, they will know it, and if we do not, they will know that as well. However—just as important for the more reserved teacher—it is useful to keep in mind that creating a class defined by acceptance and belonging will be more a function of what one chooses to do (combined with what to choose to refrain from doing) rather than of temperament or personality.

Table 7.2 outlines a set of instructional practices that will promote or undermine the sense of acceptance and belonging for individual students and entire classes.

7.8 REFLECTION

Choose one class in which you were a student to examine. As you read each entry in Table 7.2, which set of practices better characterized this class? Did you feel the effect on your sense of acceptance and belonging at the time as a result of the practices that were used in the class?

TABLE 7.2. Instructional Practices That Promote or Undermine a Sense of Acceptance and Belonging

Promote a Sense of Acceptance and Belonging	Undermine a Sense of Acceptance and Belonging
Demonstrate unconditional positive regard for all students. Eliminate any perception that your liking and acceptance are related to the students' performance or behavior. Send a clear message: "I like and accept you 100 percent the way you are. That means no matter what grade you get, what level of effort you display, or what kinds of positive or negative consequences you receive (and the fact that I like and accept you will not help you to avoid responsibility, or imply that I am not going be honest or critical)."	Combine your like or dislike of students and your treatment of them. Make sure that they know that the students you like will receive benefits, so it is worthwhile to try to get on your good side. Use praise and disappointment to reinforce this relationship.
Use cooperative structures where interdependence and interreliance are unavoidable. Cooperative learning activities are useful for promoting collaborative skills (see Chapter Twelve).	Isolate students by using exclusively independent work. Frown on students working together.
Use assigned roles, assigned grouping, and rotation of grouping in cooperative work. Students need to work with and rely on each member of the class, not just their friends.	Allow students to develop cliques and subcultures. Let them choose their own groups or partners early and consistently.
Do not accept put-downs in any form, especially negative self-talk. Demand and model positive interactions and respect 100 percent of the time. Create a culture of respect and listening (see Chapter Five).	Do nothing, or give only lip service to students who put down and disrespect others. Accept that "kids will be kids" and turn the other way when you see acts of oppression and abuse. Assume that the level of attention will never be perfect. Allow students to be inattentive to one another.
Keep all assessment private. Avoid comparisons of any kind between students at all cost. Help students refrain from putting their performance in a relative context. Help them instead work to their own standards and the standards of excellence as defined by the assignment. Rubrics help here.	Make students' grades public, and make public comparisons among students' work. (Grading on a curve may be the single most destructive practice to the sense of acceptance and belonging in a class.) Use student-to-student comparison to "motivate" both high- and low-achieving students.
Engage in a limited use of "healthy" competition for inconsequential outcomes. (See online resource article "Competition in the Transformative Classroom" for ideas for using competition in a healthier manner at www.transformativeclassroom.com.)	Force students to compete for "real" rewards (your love, grades, status, privileges, or any tangible rewards).

(continued)

TABLE 7.2. Continued

Promote a Sense of Acceptance and Belonging	Undermine a Sense of Acceptance and Belonging
Appreciate differences, and recognize the unique gifts of each of your students. Make a deliberate effort to let students share their stories, talents, and work. For younger grades, "who I am" poems can be one of many valuable tools for doing this.	Show your preference for a few of your favorite students. Point out the ways that these few students are praiseworthy. Avoid letting students share their outside school life in class.
Be real, approachable, and caring, and validate students' feelings. Take the opportunity to share who you are.	Express a disinterested affect, and let students know that you are there because it is your job to be. Or pretend to be friendly and present, but never make the effort to appreciate your students.
Find ways to make the students the teacher (through peer tutoring, writing partners, leadership of daily activities, or presentations and jigsaw instruction in which students teach each other the lesson content, for example). Let the students know it is "their class." Get out of their way as often as possible, and let them own the class.	Keep command of your class, and treat the students as though they are too immature and irresponsible to contribute to the class. Make sure they understand that it is "your class," not theirs.
Be deliberate about making sure all students are allowed to contribute. Find conspicuous and systematic ways to ensure that students are called on randomly and all students have an equal opportunity to volunteer.	Call on students who have been reliable responders in the past. Avoid the others unless you feel the need to call on them to shame them for not paying attention or doing their reading.
Build a sense of community within the class (see Chapter Fifteen).	Allow the class to become an "accidental culture" defined by cliques, winners and losers, and emotional self-protection.
Use a sound and collectively developed social contract (see Chapter Eight). Create a sense of clear cause and effect between actions and consequences. Help students trust you by being consistent, fair, and clear.	Be a 3- or 4-Style teacher. Allow the class to be defined by a crime-and-punishment or a free-for-all mentality. Use a lot of anger and reactivity to keep the students on their toes.

PROMOTING AN INTERNAL LOCUS OF CONTROL WITHIN STUDENTS

This third factor in the definition of success psychology is defined by one's sense of internal causality and orientation toward personal responsibility. The more our locus of control (LOC) is internal, the more we feel that our destiny is in our own hands. In contrast is an external LOC or an orientation that views cause as an external factor and one in which life happens to us. An internal LOC, which can be defined as the belief that we are the author of our own fate, comes from having a causal understanding of behavior and effect. It is learned from freely making choices and taking responsibility for the consequences of those choices. Through responsible action and accountability for those actions, young people learn to attribute the cause of success or failure internally. Consequently, they feel a sense of power and responsibility and are able learn from life experience. Another term for *internal locus of control* is *personal empowerment.*

7.9

REFLECTION

If you had superpowers and could guarantee that a young person would grow up with a sense of either high intelligence or high responsibility, but only average at the other, which would you choose? Why? Are you thankful that no one has to make this choice?

Research has drawn a strong relationship between levels of student self-esteem and sense of an internal locus of control (Fitch, 1970; Hagborg, 1996; Klein & Keller, 1990; Sharidan, 1991). Moreover, studies have shown repeatedly that students with higher degrees of internal locus of control demonstrate higher levels of achievement (Auer, 1992; Bar-Tal & Bar-Zohar, 1977; Tanksley, 1993; Wang & Stiles, 1976). In fact, high levels of internal LOC have been shown to be an even more significant predictor of achievement than intelligence or socioeconomic status (Hagborg, 1996). In addition, higher internal LOC has also been shown to mediate the stress response (Meaney, 2001).

Instructional behaviors that promote an internal locus of control and empowerment are rooted in developing a clear understanding of cause and effect. Students should learn that their achievement is directly related to their behavior, especially their level of effort. A requisite to seeing this relationship is providing students with choices and expecting accountability for those choices. Table 7.3 outlines instructional practices that can promote or undermine a student's internal locus of control.

7.10

REFLECTION

It has been said that the more control you give up, the more you get in the end. Do you agree with this statement? For teachers who resist encouraging the internal locus of control in their students, what do you think they feel that they will lose? Do you agree?

THE EFFECT OF INSTRUCTION

The methods of instruction that you use will have a significant impact on your ability to be successful in developing this area of your students' psychology. Providing engaging instructional activities and frequent opportunities for students to synthesize and construct their own knowledge will increase your ability to achieve a success psychology environment in your class. Chapter Eleven offers pedagogical strategies that will complement your efforts to promote a climate of success in your class.

THE RELATIONSHIPS AMONG THE THREE FACTORS

As you have examined each of the three areas, you will have discovered that efforts made in any one of the three areas will help to encourage the other two. Each of the areas complements the others. In fact, they come from essentially the same source and are all food for our basic human essence. A growth orientation will lead to more self-acceptance and the desire for others to succeed as well. And as students become more self-accepting and realize their place within the group, the more empowered they will ultimately become. As they become accustomed to a climate characterized by these qualities, they recognize that they have no interest in going back to a classroom where they are absent.

TABLE 7.3. **Instructional Practices That Promote or Undermine an Internal Locus of Control**

Practices Promoting an Internal LOC	Practices Undermining an Internal LOC
Give students choices over that which affects them. Promote the social frame related to freedom and responsibility by being conspicuous and deliberate about giving more choices and freedom to the members and the class as a whole when they demonstrate the ability to use that freedom responsibly. Increase the opportunities for the students to make choices to the extent practically possible.	Be a dictator in the class. Avoid giving students choices of any kind. Assume that students are too immature to make choices about that which will affect them. Be unclear and reactive about why freedoms are given or taken away. In general keep the class about "you."
Use clear, concrete, and specific performance objectives and assessment targets. Make the learning targets clear and standing still. Incorporate well-designed, concrete, specific rubrics whenever possible.	Keep your grading criteria vague and mysterious. Let the students know that you plan to use subjective criteria in which you "know good work when you see it," and make them have to guess what you are looking for.
Find opportunities to assess the process and other student-owned behaviors when possible. Students do not often have control over their ability, but they do have 100 percent control over the degree to which they apply themselves. Teachers who assess the process manufacture a success psychology (see also Chapter Eleven).	Assess only the finished product, never the process. Directly and indirectly find ways to equate grades with innate ability. Rely mostly on tests and worksheets.
Give students voice and ownership of the classroom social contract, rules, expectations, and consequences. Ensure that consequences are clear and related. If students then violate the social contract or break rules, follow through with consistently applied automatic and related consequences while avoiding punishments (see Chapters Eight and Nine).	Autocratically lay down the rules for the class, and then be random and inconsistent in your implementation of them. Use a subjective and arbitrary rationale for when and why you give consequences and punishments. Assume that a pain-based logic will work when you need to shape up the class. Let students know that when they upset you, you will punish them (refer to the 3- and 4-Style teachers in Chapter Two).

Recall our exploration of motivation in the previous chapter. It should become apparent that internal psychology and motivational disposition are related. In other words, the more that students possess a psychology of success, the more likely it is that they will experience intrinsic forms of motivation. And if we promote the ingredients of a success psychology within the class, we will be encouraging intrinsic motivation. Contrastingly, if we have created students who have adopted a failure psychology, we will see a corresponding lack of motivation on their part. So when we look out at that class of students who are apathetic and unmotivated by anything except bribes and punishments, we can safely bet that what they have experienced to this point has manufactured this psychology of failure in them. And when we observe a class in which the students demonstrate self-responsibility, intrinsic motivation, and a feeling of being connected, we know that their previous teachers have had a lot to do with this.

INDICATORS OF PROGRESS IN FOSTERING A PSYCHOLOGY OF SUCCESS

In the process of making an intentional effort toward promoting a success psychology in class, you will notice some signs that changes are occurring. While it may be somewhat difficult to see a psychological orientation changing directly, you can see evidence of the transformation in behavioral indicators. Expect most change toward a success psychology to take time, but since these changes are rooted at such a deep cognitive level and provide a fundamental source of needs satisfaction, they tend to have a lasting impact. Some of the most revealing indicators that this change is occurring will include:

- *Increased healthy risk taking.* This is a result of students' feeling supported by the group and releasing the fear of failure. When students do not fear that making mistakes will lead to ridicule by others or self-condemnation or shame, they feel free to take chances and think and behave creatively.

- *Increased expressiveness and participation.* Expressiveness is the result of students' feeling encouraged by the group and little, if any, concern for making mistakes or looking bad. More students raise their hands and contribute as a result.

7.11   REFLECTION

Reflect on situations in which you are not afraid to take risks and express yourself creatively, and then contrast those in which you feel timid and repressed. Do the ingredients of the psychology of success offer insight into why you feel so different in these situations?

- *Reflection of higher levels of effort.* This is a result of the students' internalizing the cause-and-effect relationship between effort and success. Students learn that they get much more out of their learning when they put more into it. They grow in their appreciation of the fruits of their labor as well as the joys of self-discipline.

- *Less blaming and externalizing.* Students develop an increasing sense of personal responsibility and more self-acceptance. They begin to recognize that blaming is antithetical to their growth in self-responsibility and self-awareness.

- *More self-responsibility and self-motivation.* As students realize that school is an opportunity, not simply a chore, and feel a greater sense of empowerment, they begin to pursue learning for its own sake and not as a result of being coerced or bribed.

- *Less use of vocabulary such as "I can't do this" and more positive internal talk.* This comes from a greater sense of personal empowerment and the reduction of the helpless pattern thinking, as well as the modeling and support of classmates who are growing in the same ways.

- *Little or no indication of boredom.* Boredom comes from minds that are not in the moment. As students learn the joy of investing in the task, they allow themselves to be in the moment to a greater degree. Add to that a decrease in the need to use all the mental energy that is required to be self-protective as a result of being in a threatening environment, and you have a more peaceful mind. A peaceful mind does not obsess about the past or stress about the future. It can be present and aware. And a mind in the moment is more productive, creative, and less easily bored. Hunter and Csikszentmihalyi (2003) found that students reported being 31 percent more engaged when they were involved in an activity that was personally satisfying to them.

- *Intrinsic motivation and a love of learning.* As students become accustomed to a natural state of learning, free of the fear of failure, free of social repression, and fundamentally empowering, they take on their natural state and feel the satisfaction of their intrinsic drives.

- *A feeling the class is going somewhere.* There will be an increasing sense in the room that the participants feel that the activities possess a natural movement or flow

(Csikszentmihalyi, 1991). This comes from the experience of goal attainment as a result of being part of meaningful and needs-satisfying activities.

7.12	**REFLECTION**

Recall the question from the previous chapter where you were asked to reflect on a life situation in which you felt that things were going somewhere. Was it characterized by the three factors described in this chapter?

RESEARCH ON THE EFFECTS OF APPLYING A SUCCESS PSYCHOLOGY FRAMEWORK

The pedagogical and motivational protocol for promoting success psychology outlined in this chapter was used as a treatment variable in a study by Ayling (2009). Eighty-nine adolescent study participants were given pre- and postassessments of LOC and self-esteem. Initial ratings of LOC and self-esteem were low in the majority of cases. The subjects were then taught by teachers in a school that adopted the use of the protocol for creating a success psychology (Shindler, 2003). Within four months, 90 percent of the subjects had shown a significant increase in both self-esteem and LOC. The results of this study support the anecdotal evidence that had been gathered previously, indicating that classroom practices can produce significant and long-lasting effects in students' locus of control and self-esteem.

CONCLUSION

Using the lens of success psychology can provide a useful tool for examining the quality of almost any human context. In the classroom, it offers a practical assessment device for checking on the health and functionality of students. Moreover, it can provide a useful window internally into your own emotional health at any time. If you are not feeling that your work and relationships are nurturing a success psychology within you, you will not be as effective or content as you might. So you could make it a regular practice to ask yourself how you are doing cultivating each of these three areas in and out of the classroom. When something is not going well, it can usually be traced back to one or more of the areas. If we as teachers do not feel empowered, loved, or as though we are learning, it will be difficult to be as effective as we could be in promoting those things in our students.

At the heart of the transformative classroom is a psychology of success. When we empower students to find their true nature and inner sources of inspiration, we encourage within our class the natural condition that exists beneath the dysfunction and fear among any group of students. The transformative path is defined by a countless number of small, practical choices. Operationalizing the concept of success psychology provides a set of guiding principles for making those choices. The following chapters offer additional ideas for creating a healthy and productive classroom that contributes to a psychology of success within a class.

Journal Reflections

1. Observe a classroom for a period of time. Note how many of the teacher's choices you would judge to promote a success psychology and how many you would judge to promote a failure psychology. Note the reaction of the students. What conclusions did you draw from your observations?

2.   Reflect on your personal conditioning as it relates to an orientation toward success or failure. What in your experience do you feel is encouraging a success psychology within you? What is your current inclination to promote such an orientation in your students (or potential students)? What factors or experience do you feel may be limiting you?

Activity

1.   Divide the class into six groups. Each group takes a separate topic and creates a separate list. One group takes as the topic "things that teachers do to promote an internal LOC" and another group the topic "things that teachers do to undermine an internal LOC." In the same way, divide into pros and cons the ideas of "acceptance and belonging" and "growth orientation," so that all six groups have one side or the other of a topic. Have each group brainstorm as many items as they can and then share them with the whole class. Alternately, if there are only enough participants for three groups, each group can brainstorm both the "promote" and "undermine" lists. It can be useful to provide each group with an overhead transparency or flip chart and a pen.
2.   Alternatively, this could be done in a graffiti cooperative model where each group gets one sheet of paper labeled with one of each of the six topics. Groups move together around the room, adding elements to each list. Using different colored pens is optional. Set a time limit. At the end of the time, groups present on their original topic, incorporating the items that have been added.

REFERENCES

Auer, C. J. (1992). A comparison of the locus of control of first and second grade students in whole language, basal reader, and eclectic instructional approach classrooms. *Dissertation Abstracts International*, *53*(11), 38–56.

Ayling, G. (2009). *Report of an adolescent transition, a possible intervention for the stress response and diseases in adult life.* Manuscript submitted for publication.

Bar-Tal, D. B., & Bar-Zohar, Y. (1977). The relationship between perception of locus of control and academic achievement. *Contemporary Educational Psychology*, *2*, 181–199.

Benham, M. J. (1993). *Fostering self-motivated behavior, personal responsibility, and internal locus of control*, Eugene, OR: Office of Educational Research and Improvement. (ERIC Document Reproduction No. ED 386 621)

Csikszentmihalyi, M. (1991). *Flow: The psychology of optimal experience.* New York: HarperCollins.

Davis, L. E., & Peck, H. I. (1992). *Outcome measures—school climate: Curriculum and instruction.* Paper presented at the annual meeting of the Mid-South Educational Research Association, Knoxville, TN. (ERIC Document Reproduction No. ED 353 335)

Dembrowsky, C. H. (1990). *Developing self-esteem and internal motivation in at risk youth.* Practicum paper. (ERIC Document Reproduction No. ED 332 130)

Dweck, C. (2000). *Self-theories: Their role in motivation, personality and development.* Lillington, NC: Psychologists Press.

Dweck, C. (2006). *Mindset: The new psychology of success.* New York. Ballantine.

Fitch, G. (1970). Effects of self-esteem, perceived performance and choice on causal attributions. *Journal of Personality and Social Psychology*, *44*, 419–427.

Ginott, H. (1972). *Teacher and child.* New York. Avon Books.

Hagborg, W. J. (1996). Self-concept and middle school students with learning disabilities: A comparison of scholastic competence subgroups. *Learning Disability Quarterly*, *19*(2) 117–126.

Huberman, M., & Middlebrooks, S. (2000). The dilution of inquiry: A qualitative study. *International Journal of Qualitative Studies in Education*, *13*, 281–304.

Hunter, J., & Csikszentmihalyi, M. (2003). Positive psychology of interested adolescents. *Journal of Youth and Adolescence*, *32*, 27–35.

Inderbitzen, H. M., & Clark, M. L. (1986, April). *The relationship between adolescent loneliness and perceptions of controllability and stability.* Paper presented at the annual meeting of the Southeastern Psychological Association, Orlando, FL.

Katz, L. G. (1993). *Distinctions between self-esteem and narcissism: implications for practice.* Perspectives from ERIC/EECE, Monograph Series, No 5. (ERIC Document Reproduction No. ED 363 452)

Klein, J. D., & Keller, J. M. (1990). Influence of student ability, locus of control, and type of instructional control on performance and confidence. *Journal of Educational Research*, *83*(3), 140–146.

Meaney, M. J. (2001). Maternal care, gene expression and the transmission of individual differences in stress reactivity across generations. *Annual Review of Neuroscience*, 4, 1161–1192.

Osterman, K. F. (2000). Students' need for belonging in the school community. *Review of Educational Research*, *70*(3), 323–367.

Rennie, L. J. (1991). The relationship between affect and achievement in science. *Journal of Research in Science Teaching*, 28(2), 193–209.

Rhoades, J., & McCabe, M. E. (1992). *The cooperative classroom: Social and academic activities.* Position paper. (ERIC Document Reproduction No. ED 363 583)

Sharidan, M. K. (1991). Self-esteem and competence in children. *International Journal of Early Childhood*, 23(1), 28–35.

Shindler, J. (2003). *Creating a psychology of success in the classroom: Enhancing academic achievement by systematically promoting student self-esteem.* Retrieved October 11, 2008, from www.calstatela.edu/faculty/jshindl/cm.

Shindler, J., Jones, A., Williams, A., Taylor, C., & Cadenas, H. (2009, January). *Exploring below the surface: school climate assessment and improvement as the key to bridging the achievement gap.* Paper presented at the annual meeting of the Washington State Office of the Superintendent of Public Instruction, Seattle.

Tanksley, M. D. (1994). *Building good self-esteem for certain fifth grade children through cooperative learning, individualized learning techniques, parental involvement, and student counseling.* Practicum paper. (ERIC Document Reproduction No. ED 367 095)

Wang, M., & Stiles, B. (1976). An investigation of children's concept of self-responsibility for their learning. *American Educational Research Journal*, *13*, 159–179.

Washinawotok, K. (1993). *Teaching cultural values and building self-esteem.* Practicum paper. (ERIC Document Reproduction No. ED 366 470)

3

Developing a Functional Democratic Classroom Society

8

Creating Collective Classroom Bonds with a Social Contract

In This Chapter

- What are social and communal bonds?
- What is a social contract?
- Steps in implementing the social contact

This chapter explores the nature of social and communal bonds. It is the first of three chapters dealing with the practical and theoretical issues related to creating and maintaining an effective social contract and provides a step-by-step process for developing a working classroom social contract.

Many teachers today want to create what could be characterized as a "democratic" classroom. Others aspire to have classrooms that function as "learning communities." This trend toward seeking classroom structures that endeavor to empower students rather than simply control them is an encouraging development. The good news for these teachers is that over time and with effective leadership, any class can be a functional democratic society. And with a little more time and a clear understanding of what it takes to empower students to value and commit to the common good of the group, any class can begin to take on the characteristics of a community. Both require a great deal of awareness of what is standing in the way of one's success and a dedicated intention and commitment to doing what it takes to make it happen.

WHAT ARE SOCIAL BONDS?

Social bonds or social contracts are explicit and implicit agreements made between individuals in any group to help clarify what they should expect from one another (Scheff, 1997). The group can be as small as two people or as big as the population of a country or, of course, even the planet. For example, we enter into an agreement with our governments in which we pay some taxes and can expect some services in return. Likewise, when we walk down the street, we have some confidence that others will refrain from harming us if we refrain from harming them. In these examples, the agreements are fairly clear; however, there are times when what it means to fulfill our part of the bargain or what behavior constitutes violating the social contract can be more ambiguous.

As we know from living in a modern society, laws do not guarantee that citizens treat one another fairly or act as good democratic participants. In fact, laws are just the beginning of creating what could be called a well-functioning democratic society. This is also true in the classroom. Rules do not make a democratic classroom, no matter how well the teacher enforces them. A democracy is more. At the heart of a working democracy are well-defined, collectively owned social bonds: the implicit and explicit agreements among the members of the collective that create mutual understanding and trust. The intentional development of a social contract (also called a behavioral covenant or bill of rights) can help clarify those agreements. A well-functioning social contract promotes a well-managed class and provides students with an invaluable education in democratic participation.

WHAT ARE COMMUNAL BONDS?

Whereas social bonds answer such questions as, "What must I do to fulfill my part of the social contract?" communal bonds answer the question, "What can I do to make the collective better?" Societal bonds are at the root of what make most of our daily interactions smooth and reasonable. Communal bonds more often reflect friend and family relationships and are at the root of why we feel part of something greater than ourselves (Scott, 1988). It is difficult to have sustainable communal bonds without well-functioning social bonds in place.

As you begin to develop your vision for your ideal classroom and management style, clarifying the kinds of bonds you want operating in your classroom is useful. Social bonds are essential for any 1- or 2-Style classroom to create a sense of safety, clearness, and efficiency (see Figure 8.1). But achieving more substantive levels of group cohesion, a high-functioning 1-Style classroom, and transformative outcomes requires fostering communal bonds among students. In this chapter, we focus primarily on how to create the well-functioning social bonds that are required for a successful democratic society and return to the idea of community in Chapter Fifteen.

8.1 REFLECTION

What proportion of classes that you observe would you characterize as democratic? How many would you describe as true learning communities?

WHAT IS A CLASSROOM SOCIAL CONTRACT?

At minimum, a classroom social contract outlines how each group member will keep from infringing on the rights of the others (Curwin & Mendler, 1986; MacNeil, 1980). A more empowering social contract outlines what members can do to promote improvement for themselves and their class. The classroom contract exists as a set of rules, principles, boundaries, expectations, and consequences that govern the concrete document and abstract concept. It is preferable to write the concrete aspects of the contract clearly, simply, and positively. The power of the contract depends on how a class translates the abstract aspects of the contract into practical, accessible operational ideas and behaviors (Elias & Schwab, 2006).

Rules exist as words on paper or a whiteboard and remain just words, never becoming meaningful. Until they become a concrete and material part of the students' lived experience, they will have little influence on behavior. For those of us (especially the more practical minded) who tend to have great affection for rules and legalistic thinking, it is critical to shift our focus from the rule as written law to rules as values implying a larger purpose.

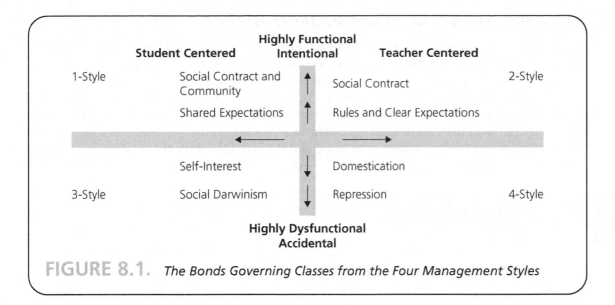

FIGURE 8.1. *The Bonds Governing Classes from the Four Management Styles*

In the same way, principles can remain mere abstractions and noble concepts that are never translated into action. We must continuously help our students understand how the abstract concepts that seem so clear to us can be applied and what they look like in practice. The discussion of expectations in Chapter Four should be useful in formulating concrete strategies for translating your abstract desires into tangible behavioral expectations that are clear to students.

WHERE DOES THE SOCIAL CONTRACT EXIST?

A social contract can begin as a document; however, the written document is not the contract. The social contract exists to the degree to which the stakeholders (teachers, students, and assistants) understand and commit to it (MacNeil, 1980). The knowledge component is foundational; no one cannot commit to something without understanding it. Likewise, if you do not commit to what you have ceremonially agreed to, you are not fulfilling your role, and consequently the social contract does not truly exist. Moreover, if the contract exists only in your head and not in your students' heads, it does not exist. Finally—and this point cannot be emphasized too strongly—if the students view you as (externally) imposing the rules on them, the contract loses power and effectiveness. If the students see the ownership of the social contract as theirs (internal), it will be powerful and effective. In other words, to the degree that it exists within the hearts and minds of students and not as an imposition from their teacher, the contract exists.

REFLECTION 8.2

Have you at some time observed what a leader of a group referred to as a social contract or a democratic organization but was truly a quasi-dictatorship? What was the reaction of the members?

IMPLEMENTING A CLASSROOM SOCIAL CONTRACT

Implementing a social contract involves a great deal more than explaining the classroom rules. The social contract functions to the degree that it is meaningful, internalized, and committed to by the students. It will be internalized and invested in much more if students feel a sense of ownership (Brophy & McCaslin, 1992). For that reason, it makes sense to have students involved in creating the class rules and the consequences of breaking rules. If you find yourself uncomfortable with the idea of students taking an active role in this process, you might discuss the rationale behind your thinking with them, and if possible involve them in problem solving any necessary modifications as the contract evolves.

8.3 | **REFLECTION**

Recall a situation in which you were involved in the creation of a set of guiding principles. How did your participation affect how you felt about the value of the principles?

Step 1: Decide on Terms for the Contract's Tenets

You need terms to express the basic tenets of your contract. While what I call the basic tenets are ultimately a matter of semantics, each of the assortment of possible options for these basic terms implies a somewhat different meaning. Choose the term that best represents the kind of thinking you want to define your contract. Here is a list of the most frequently used terms and their common meanings:

- *Rules*—implies codes of behavior. Usually they are very behavioral and do not have much room for interpretation.
- *Bill of rights*—implies what is required of each member of the group and what each can expect from the other members.
- *Principles*—implies generalized intentions for behavior. These can have lots of room for interpretation.
- *Policies*—a lot like rules but can include more suggestions for procedures.
- *Boundaries*—implies the behavioral lines that should not be crossed. These are easier to negotiate but more difficult to articulate in a contract.
- *Expectations*—implies desired behavior. They are usually general and open to interpretation, but are easiest to write in positive terms. As discussed in Chapter Four, we inevitably have dozens of expectations. If you use the term *expectations* in your social contract, you might want to refer to them as "general expectations" to help distinguish them from the countless operational expectations that you want to simultaneously promote.

It is certainly reasonable to consider using a combination of terms, such as *rules, bill of rights,* or *principles* for the few global pillars of the contract; *procedures* for the operational processes you need to have in place to help the class function smoothly; and *expectations* for the countless occasions when a shared understanding of what to do and how to act needs to be in place.

8.4 | **REFLECTION**

What do you think of when you hear the terms listed above? What are your associations with each term? What would you guess your students associate with each?

Step 2: Develop a List of Basic Tenets or Expectations

No matter how organic, negotiated, or flexible your vision of the social contract is, you need some concrete pillars to anchor the broader contract. These rules, bill of rights, expectations, policies, or boundaries should be put in writing and made visible to all members of the classroom society.

Keep in mind two suggestions that will help you down the road. First, make the list as short as possible—no more than three to five items (Doyle, 2003; Emmer, Evertson, & Anderson, 1980). Too many rules are difficult to remember and have the effect of making each item less powerful as more items are added (Emmer, Evertson, & Anderson, 1980). Second, they should be stated positively (Thorson, 2003). Our unconscious minds can understand only positive messages, so an item that states, "Do not talk when others are talking," sends a confusing message to the unconscious. Moreover, stating expectations negatively can have the effect of encouraging negative behavior. Restating the rule in positive terms eases the unconscious conflict and clarifies the expectation. A more effective alternative phrasing would be something such as, "Be attentive to those who are speaking, and expect others to be attentive when you are speaking."

REFLECTION

8.5

Consider times when you were involved in creating a group plan. How did your participation affect your level of buy-in and investment in the outcome? Compare those cases with those in which a set of rules was imposed on you. In which situation did you find yourself being more respectful of the rules? What do your conclusions suggest about the value of including students in this stage of the process?

Depending on the age of the students, you will need to guide the process accordingly. If they are very young (grades K to 3), you might want to primarily use questions. For example, you might ask, "What kinds of things would you say are important for all students to do if we are going to have a good class?" And then as you hear responses, you might pick those that are getting at the most important areas and paraphrase them for the approval of the whole group. For example, a student might offer the idea, "We should not hit each other." Let's assume that the idea identified a useful principle. To validate the student and achieve consensus, you might respond, "What do you all think? Should one of our four rules be, 'We keep our hands to ourselves and respect each other's space'? That rule would include not hitting. What do you think? Raise your hand if you want me to write that as one of our rules." If you undertake the process in this fashion, you maintain as much control of the outcome as you need to feel confident in the results of the process, but it is genuinely collaborative.

If your students are older (grades 4 to 12), you might begin by placing students in groups and then prompt them to generate two or three basic expectations for the class. If you have been using concept-building exercises previously, you can initiate the exercise in a familiar manner. In essence, you are asking your students to generate examples for the following overarching concept: *things that all students can do, that if we each did them, the class would function well and grow as a collective.* They will need to be reminded that their ideas should be stated positively.

As the students come up with their ideas, you can list them on the board or an overhead projector. You might take the opportunity to add items that you feel are critical and are not already on the list. Students are rarely offended if you think of things that they forgot or didn't think about. After all ideas have been recorded, then work with the students to find the three to five themes that emerge from the list. After the themes have been developed, synthesize each one into a concise phrase, with or without the help of the students, depending on your preference. If you do it alone, the phrasing may be a little better, but if the students take this on, it will likely lead to another elevation of their level of ownership for the process. One idea for including the students at this stage is to give each group one of the themes and have them work with it until they come up with an acceptable phrase. In the end, a majority of the class must approve each phrase that is submitted.

8.6

REFLECTION

Students with experience performing concept attainment exercises will be much more effective when it is time to work with the social contract. This strategy is described briefly in Chapter Eleven, but helping your students become experts in concept attainment will have a transformative effect on many areas of the class experience.

Step 3: Develop Consequences for Contract Violations

Developing clear, logical, and related consequences for contract violations is essential to the success of any social contract (Brady, Forton, Porter, & Wood, 2003; Elias & Schwab, 2006). Even though many people use the two terms interchangeably, there is a significant difference between what constitutes a consequence and what constitutes a punishment (Elias & Schwab, 2006). Logical and related consequences help students foster cause-and-effect relationships between their thoughts and actions and the outcomes of those thoughts and actions. These lessons lead to ever-increasing levels of responsibility and promote students' internal locus of control. Punishments lead to obedience at best, and more often to resentment and hostility. Few meaningful lessons are learned from punishments, and their use degrades the quality of the contract. Punishments externalize the causality of the event as the students associate the interventions with pleasing or displeasing the teacher rather than with the choices they made.

Developing consequences as a class is an excellent way to promote higher levels of ownership and understanding. It will take time to help students understand the difference between punishments and consequences, but the distinction is a useful one to make. In addition, it will help clarify the nature and purpose of the social contract. Using the exercise involving the student missing the bus in the following chapter would be a useful place to start. The degree to which you have students involved in the development process is up to you. However, keep in mind the trade-off. You want to maintain a sense of coherence and vision to the contract. That will come primarily from your ability to support ideas and outcomes that integrate well as a whole. Then again, more student involvement usually translates into more empowerment and buy-in.

If you want to support student involvement, consider using an inductive process to accomplish this. For instance, you might ask the students questions and then brainstorm ideas for the common problems the class might face. It is best to be proactive rather than reactive when doing this. For example, consider a case where a student begins to abuse the use of the pencil sharpener. If you raise the issue to the class as a whole after the event, the issue will be associated with the student and the discussion will feel like public shaming to that student. If possible, you should anticipate the problem and have the discussion before the problem comes up. To be effective, consequences have to be well understood and in place before you can hold students accountable for them. Until then, you can use warnings. But use warnings as infrequently as possible because they weaken the cause and effect in the contract.

Take the case of the class where the students begin to request going to the restroom more often than you feel they should, and you determine that their absence and moving in and out is distracting to the class. You might take the opportunity to brainstorm a policy with the students on how to solve "our" problem. If you want to guide the process toward what you feel is a sound idea, begin by offering a plan for them to evaluate and approve. Or you can have students choose an idea from those that they generated themselves. Once the class has voted a policy into place, you can make an assumption about the level of understanding and ownership they will have toward it. So when that expectation is raised in whatever form, it will not be unanticipated or feel imposed.

With very young students, you will need to provide a greater amount of assistance in the consequence development process, but it can still be a useful exercise. Young students can have difficulty recognizing an appropriate level of severity and tend to think in terms of punishment. They will struggle with the notion that the consequences need to be logical and related. They will also abstract themselves from the possible misbehavior. They often struggle to conceive that they may be the ones violating the social contract. As a result, when you ask for ideas from young students, you are often surprised at what they come up with. You might ask, "What should we do if someone comes back from recess late?" And the response might be, "They should be spanked," or, "They should have to stay after school." Again, it may be wise to offer alternatives and have students select from among them. This will promote ownership while supporting an outcome everyone can accept.

A policy, rule, or consequence that is not working well represents an opportunity to improve the social contract and provide students with the opportunity to engage in a democratic decision-making exercise. Students of any age can successfully participate in a class meeting if it is well organized. (We discuss class meetings and their benefits in more detail in Chapter Fifteen.) These meetings have value to the extent that they are well structured and effectively led, and that students take them seriously. Here are some basic guidelines for an effective class meeting:

- *Establish a time frame for the meeting to take place and achieve an outcome.* For small problems, that might be five or ten minutes, or it might be longer for more substantial problems, such as conflict among subgroups in the class.

- *Have a preestablished outcome.* In most cases, this is to answer a question. For example, you might instruct the class that they have five minutes to answer the question, "What are we going to do when people go over their time limit at the computer?"

- *Have a policy in place that ensures that only one person talks at a time.* You can use Robert's Rules of Order, or the concept of the talking stick, or any other method that you find that accomplishes this goal.

- *Have a well-established system for making decisions.* This can be a public vote, a private vote, or you the teacher assessing where the consensus lies and voicing the will of the group.

Students should feel free to suggest to you (privately is best) that the class is in need of a meeting to resolve a pressing problem. You may not think that every request is worthy of a class meeting. But the more this process is generated by the students and results in an increased sense of justice and mutual respect, the more it will strengthen the social contract. If you are inclined toward a 1-Style management approach, a useful goal is to make yourself redundant in the process as the students learn to take increasing control over the process.

Step 4: Make the Social Contract as Conspicuous as Possible

The initial process of creating the basic rules, expectations, and consequences for contract violations should happen as soon as possible in the term. And once it is in place, the social contract has a genesis. But it will fade in memory if it does not become a living document. It needs to evolve to meet the needs of its stakeholders and grow as the collective grows in maturity, since any social contract will exist only in the collective understanding of the participants. This understanding begins with familiarity. One idea is to use phrases from your contract as banners within the class. For example, "This class is built on respect," or "Attitudes become actions." Take advantage of the walls of your classroom. Student are bombarded by thousands of visual images each day, so make the ones in your class empowering.

8.7   REFLECTION

In what creative ways have you seen teachers use the walls of the classroom to promote the expectations of their class?

For grades 2 and up, one option is to send a copy of the contract home with each student and have each parent and the student sign it, signifying that they have read and understood it (see the sample social contract in Figure 8.2). This practice can have many benefits. First, it provides an opportunity for families to read the social contract, promoting their understanding of what you are trying to accomplish and their appreciation that your discipline system is proactive and positive. Second, it allows you to refer to the fact that the student signed the contract. This may be valuable when they feel tempted to distance themselves from their agreement.

An effective strategy to promote understanding of the written content of your social contract is to take time to discuss it and then quiz the students on it. Why expect the students to pass the social contract contents quiz before they are able to enjoy the privilege of taking part in the other aspects of the class? It may be as simple as requiring that the students are able to list the class rules and achieve a 100 percent score before they are allowed to use a specified piece of classroom equipment (a computer, gym equipment, lab materials, puzzles, library books, and so forth). However, use the idea of a quiz only if you judge that the students need help buying into the social contract.

Although the written word can be a powerful tool in promoting a social contract, a good number of effective social contracts exist almost entirely on an implicit level—as shared understandings between the teacher and the students. This is possible because the majority of the means by which the social contract is communicated are through teacher-student interactions. Recall the discussion of classroom expectations in Chapter Four. Students will respond to the degree that an expectation is clear and associated positively. Therefore, promote your social contract with effective methods and avoid ineffective methods. Beginning with the most effective methods (as outlined in Chapter Four), let's examine how each technique can be used to promote the strength of a social contract:

- *Purposeful action.* The most defining factor in the development and implementation of the social contract will be the degree to which the teacher is consistent and clear and follows through. This idea is explored in depth in Chapter Ten.

- *Positive recognitions.* "I just want to recognize how respectful and supportive you each are to the person presenting. How does it feel to be in a class that is so respectful of one another?" Let the students know when they are behaving in a way that is promoting the social contract and the common good.

- *Clarifying statements.* "We all have our full attention on Phang right now, and we are listening for some of the key details that he included in his story." This is a powerful way to remind the students of expectations without being negative or lecturing them.

I _____(student's name)_____ , a member in the class of ____(teacher and school)____ , hereby commit to being a responsible member of the class and doing what it takes to learn, grow, and help others learn and grow.

I have been part of our collective process for creating our social contract on _____. I understand and commit to the following rules:

We respect one another. This is shown in our 100% attention and listening. In raising our hands to speak. Being considerate of the needs of others. In saying only positive things to others in the class.

We are responsible. This is shown in our preparedness. It is shown in the choices that we make. We do our part to make the class a better place.

We do our best. This is shown in making a consistently excellent effort all day long. We do our best when things are easy and when they are difficult. We persist even when we are tempted to quit, either on ourselves or on others.

I understand that my role in the social contract is to live up to my agreement, accept consequences when I do not, and continue to work to become a more responsible person and contributor to the class. I understand it is my obligation to know the expectations and consequences that have been developed by the class and teacher. I understand that I have a right to voice my opinion about any rule, expectation, or consequence at any time. But I do accept that once they have been established, it is my responsibility to be accountable to them or accept the consequences.

By my actions and my signature below, I hereby commit to doing my best to fulfill my responsibility to the class and our social contract.

_____   _____
Student Signature   Date

_____   _____
Parent or Guardian Signature (optional)   Date

Suitable for grades 1–8.

FIGURE 8.2. *Sample Social Contract*

- *Mantras.* "In this class, we raise our hands before we speak," or "In this class, there are only hardworking, intelligent students." Mantras are words that can translate into actions eventually. Even if they are far from a realistic assessment at first, they will become actualized over time.

- *Clarifying questions.* "What is the consequence if we do not finish our work during class?" or "What is the expectation when we are at the computer?" Questions help students recall the aspect of the social contract without being told. They engender accountability and self-reflection.

- *Warnings.* Use when an expectation, rule, policy, or consequence is new and unfamiliar. After that, warnings only weaken the cause-and-effect relationship that gives the social contract much of its power.

Negative recognitions, lectures, put-downs, punishments, personal praise, and public shaming weaken the contract and undermine the relationship between the teacher and the students. This idea will be discussed further as we examine the use of punishments in the next chapter.

8.8 REFLECTION

Recall a class where there were few, if any, rules, but all the students seemed to be clear as to what was expected of them and what they could expect from one another and the teacher. How was this accomplished? Examine the list of methods above. Did the teacher use any of these to help support a shared understanding in the class?

Step 5: Practice and Teach the Expectations of the Class Contract

If a procedure needs to be improved, practice it. If the social contract requires a new set of skills, teach and model them. To promote a practical understanding of the contract, make the implicit aspects more explicit. If your contract has words such as *respect, responsibility, attention, attitude, cooperation, effort,* and *encouragement* (and it is desirable that it does), you must make those abstractions concrete and personal, or they will remain abstractions (Hickey & Schafer, 2006). So use practical behavior to help students inductively master the conceptual realities. Positive recognitions of behavior are both concrete and personal. They teach concepts quickly if you help students recognize the connection. For example, after an activity, you might say, "Our goal was to take care of our materials so that they would last; I see that they are still all here and in great shape. That kind of responsible behavior tells me I can trust you to go out and get more materials." Or, "I notice that all of the members of this group waited their turn to speak. That is a great example of respect." Use mantras, clarifying statements, and clarifying questions in the same way.

How you deal with contract violations will have the most significant effect on the integrity of the social contract. When you observe behavior that violates the agreement, you have three choices. Only one is helpful. The other two will quickly undermine the integrity of the contract. If you take action, follow through, and hold the students accountable, the contract is shown to have efficacy and integrity. If you ignore the behavior or if you are negative (for example, by becoming disappointed, shaming the student, or recognizing the behavior publicly), it shows the contract to be weak and randomly applied. When it is inconsistently applied, it becomes about the teacher (the external locus of control) and not about the choice of the student (internal locus of control), and therefore loses power.

8.9 REFLECTION

Recall the social learning model. What does it imply about the importance of consistency?

Step 6: Clarify Expectations and Roles (Ongoing)

The roles of the teacher and students within the social contract may appear obvious. However, you might be surprised at how much students vary in their view of their roles in the contract and what they view as your role. Depending on the style of leader you desire to be, you will need to remind the students what your role is, what it is not, and what their roles are and are not. Students will likely bring in a composite of the roles that they adopted from past classes and their home life. And they will assign you a role that mirrors that which they have experienced from others. Again, do not stay in thoughts of disappointment or insult. Be proactive. Continuously clarify the roles within the social contract. This will be an ongoing process that will require public reminders such as, "I am not going to come and fix the problems in your groups. You will need to work out your disagreements on your own." And it will also involve private encounters: "Etienne, it is your responsibility to bring the necessary materials." The social contract will work best if you take a facilitator role. Avoid being the judge, the police, or a passive shopkeeper. The importance of this will be reinforced in the following chapters.

As the expectations become more familiar and concrete to students, you can begin to use language that tests the degree to which the expectations have been internalized. For instance, if the behavior related to what defines the concept of a ready group has been internalized by students, you should only need to refer to the term. In this case, you might say, "I am looking for the groups that are ready." If you observe groups demonstrating ready group behavior, you know that the students grasp it. If they do not, you know it is time to clarify the concept a bit further and then assess the expectation later to see if it has been internalized yet. Again, clarifying questions are helpful in assisting the students to move from the learning stage to the performance stage. For example, instead of saying to the class, "Class, please say hello to our principal, Mr. Maroufi," you might simply ask the class, "How do we greet a guest in our class?"

REFLECTION 8.10

Recall our discussion in Chapter Four comparing the effects of the use of verbal instructions ("I need you to . . . ") with verbal-clarifying questions ("What would it look like if . . . ?"). Can you see the differential effect of the two strategies in the process of supporting the internalization of our social contract?

Step 7: Foster Community Relations (Ongoing)

The social bonds among the members of the class will become stronger if they are supported by communal bonds. Fundamentally, a basic social contract does not require the need for interdependence or a commitment on the part of the students to the common good, yet building those qualities into the logic of the overall contract will bring an added level of vitality to classroom relationships. Applying the following three principles will go a long way in promoting the communal bonds in your class:

- Promote respect, and be intolerant of disrespect.
- Promote teamwork and mutual interdependence.
- Show caring and pride in the groups' accomplishments.

Each of these ideas is examined in more detail in Chapter Fifteen.

Step 8: Shift Ownership of the Contract from Yourself to the Collective (Recommended)

No matter if your preference is for a more teacher-centered class (2-Style orientation) or a more student-centered class (1-Style orientation), your contract will become stronger to the degree that the ownership of it resides with the students rather than you. If the students come to view the contract as something that you are imposing on them, it will have a limited effect. However, if they view it as something that functions to make their class more effective and more emotionally safe and they appreciate the feeling of responsibility that it promotes, it will grow in efficacy and integrity.

To help promote ownership of the contract, gradually shift the focus of your language from the kinds of expected behavior to the value for one's self and the group when that behavior is exhibited. Especially if you are interested in developing a 1-Style classroom, helping students appreciate the values of consideration, self-discipline, and personal responsibility are critical to promoting a living and internalized social contract and will lead naturally to the development of communal bonds. We discuss the pathway to a 1-Style classroom and how to build a community on the foundation of the social contract in Chapter Fifteen.

Transformative Idea

Assessing the quality of student participation and behavior (as described in the online article "Developing and Implementing an Effective System for Assessing the Quality of Student Process, Participation, and Behavior," at transformativeclassroom.com) can work in concert with the development of a social contract. It can help to clarify and reinforce what demonstrating a high-quality investment means. Whereas the social contract can clarify high-quality behavior and address behavioral problems, assessing the quality of behavior can have the effect of improving it.

CONCLUSION

A sound social contract makes shared classroom expectations more concrete and observable and has the further transformative effect of preparing students to be active democratic citizens. The next chapter explores the importance of developing logical and related consequences for social contract violations, and provides helpful guidelines for doing so.

Journal Reflections

1. Do you want your expectations and social contract to come mostly from you or from your students? Why?

2. Discuss your thoughts about the following terms: *rules, principles,* and *expectations.* In your class, which of these will be more prominent? Why?

Activities

1. In groups, discuss your feelings related to the use of student input in the creation of the social contract. Do you think that it is worth the effort and loss of control over the outcome?

2. In groups, take five or ten minutes to brainstorm some of the rules and expectations that you would include in the social contract section of your classroom management plan. What terms are you going to use to describe the ingredients? Share your ideas with one another. Sharing your classroom management plan ideas with others will help you get more ideas and clarify and strengthen your own ideas as you have to explain or defend them to others.

3. Develop a social contract for a hypothetical class or one that you are teaching.

REFERENCES

Brady, K., Forton, M. B., Porter, D., & Wood, C. (2003). *Rules in school*. Greenfield, MA: Northeast Foundation for Children.

Brophy, J. E., & McCaslin, M. (1992). Teachers' reports of how they perceive and cope with problem students. *Elementary School Journal*, *93*, 2–68.

Curwin, R., & Mendler, A. (1986). *Discipline with dignity*. Alexandria VA: ASCD Press.

Doyle, W. (2006). Ecological approaches to classroom management. In C. M. Evertson & C. S. Weinstein (Eds.), *Handbook of classroom management* (pp. 97–126). Mahwah, NJ: Erlbaum.

Elias, M. J., & Schwab, Y. (2006). From compliance to responsibility: Social and emotional learning and classroom management. In C. M. Evertson & C. S. Weinstein (Eds.), *Handbook of classroom management* (pp. 309–341). Mahwah, NJ: Erlbaum.

Emmer, E. T., Evertson, C. M., & Anderson, L. (1980). Effective classroom management at the beginning of the school year. *Elementary School Journal*, *80*, 219–230.

Hickey, D. T., & Schafer, N. J. (2006). Design-based, participation-centered approaches to classroom management. In C. M. Evertson & C. S. Weinstein (Eds.), *Handbook of classroom management* (pp. 281–308). Mahwah, NJ: Erlbaum.

MacNeil, I. R. (1980). *The new social contract: An inquiry into modern contractual relations*. New Haven, CT: Yale University Press.

Scheff, T. J. (1997). *Emotions, the social bond, and human reality: Part/whole analysis*. Cambridge: Cambridge University Press.

Scott, J. (1988). Social network analysis. *Sociology*, *22*(1), 109–127.

Thorson, S. A. (2003). *Listening to students: Reflections on secondary classroom management*. Needham Heights, MA: Allyn & Bacon.

9

Developing Logical and Related Consequences Within the Social Contract—and Why to Avoid the Use of Punishments

In This Chapter

- What is a consequence?
- What is a punishment?
- What is wrong with the use of punishment?
- Creating effective consequences within the social contract
- Examples of effective logical consequences

An essential part of a well-functioning system of social interactions and classroom social contract is the development of a clear relationship in the students' minds between their actions and the consequences of those actions. Therefore, it is necessary to develop a set of logical and related consequences for student behavior that violates the contract. These consequences create boundaries and clarify expectations. Along with providing meaningful cause-and-effect connections, agreed-on consequences for violating the social contract act as a practical, concrete manifestation of accountability and what it means to be a responsible member of the class. Without consequences, a social contract is an abstract ideal and practically ineffectual.

WHAT IS A CONSEQUENCE?

Often we use the terms *consequences* and *punishments* interchangeably (Elias & Schwab, 2006). However, consequences and punishments are very different. It may appear that they are different variations of the same idea—doing something to or toward students to give them a disincentive to misbehave—but as we examine each more closely, we will see that they are very different and have dramatically varying effects (Brady, Forton, Porter, & Wood, 2003; Dreikurs, 1974; Nelson, Lynn, & Glenn, 2000).

To illustrate the differences between consequences and punishments, let's examine two cases related to what might happen if a student misses a school bus. As you compare the two cases, which example would you characterize as a consequence and which as a punishment?

In case 1, the student understands that the bus to school arrives at his stop at 8:00. He gets to the stop at 8:05. The bus has come and gone as scheduled. The student realizes the bus is no longer an option and that he must find another way to get to school.

In case 2, the student again understands that the bus stops at 8:00. The student arrives at the bus stop at 8:05, and the bus is waiting. The bus driver is very angry and lectures the student about the importance of getting to the stop on time. As the student moves to his seat on the bus, the other students berate and shame him for making them wait.

9.1 REFLECTION

In a group discussion or on your own, identify all the ways in which these two situations vary from one another. As you examine them more deeply, you will recognize many ways in which they do.

Reflect on the two cases:

- Which one is more likely to change the student's behavior in the long term?
- Which one teaches the more useful lesson for life?
- Which one builds the student's sense of responsibility and internal locus of control (LOC)?
- Who is in control in each case? Is that important?

As you likely identified, the first case would best be characterized as a consequence and the second case as a punishment. In the first case, a lesson was learned; in the second, the result was merely discomfort. Both cases may have had an effect on the student in the short term, but only the first one is logically related to the problem. The student was late (cause), and therefore the bus was no longer available (effect), as it would have been if the student had gotten to the stop on time. The lesson to be learned is clear: get to the stop on time, and you will not miss the bus. The ownership of the problem rests with the student.

9.2 REFLECTION

Recall a situation in which you missed a bus, flight, or deadline or arrived at a store after it closed. Did you learn a lesson? Did your behavior change in the future as a result of the experience?

In the second case, we find a lot of difficulty recognizing the logical relationship between being yelled at and not getting to the bus stop on time. It may seem like a common response to such student behavior, but it is not logical. In this second case, the lesson learned has little to do with a need to change behavior and has more to do with avoiding the discomfort that may (or may not) come from the bus driver. And like many other punishments, there was no real consequence for being late. The bus was still there. The student learned that he could be late to the stop, and the bus would still be waiting. There was a lot of sound and fury, but it signified very little. In this situation, the causality was external. It was dependent on the mood and the whim of the bus driver, so there can be little or no effect on the development of the student's internal locus of control and thus growth toward more responsible future choices.

REFLECTION

9.3

When most people reflect on their childhoods, they recognize that the disciplinary interventions that they received from their parents were primarily punishments. Is this true for you?

CONSEQUENCES AS CAUSE-AND-EFFECT RESULTS

In life, consequences generally happen as a result of actions. We may choose to describe them with such labels as "reaping what we have sown," "karmic reactions," "sleeping in the bed we have made," and "emotional bank accounts," among many others. But in the natural world, all causes have effects. Nothing happens in a vacuum. All thoughts and actions have consequences. And if we are perceptive, we begin to learn which actions and thoughts (causes) bring us the kinds of circumstances (effects) that we desire and which bring us unwanted outcomes.

In the classroom, students experience countless consequences each day. Most are natural and occur without any teacher intervention. For example, a student in a hurry or who is careless may make a spelling mistake or miscalculate a math problem. Or a student may be friendly to other students and as a result be perceived as likable. An infinite number of events act as consequences for each of us daily.

Most consequences related to most teachers are typically positive. For example, when the student works at a task, the teacher may offer a verbal recognition of effort or provide academic or emotional support. And in most classrooms, when the student raises a hand, the teacher recognizes him or her for a response. In each of these cases, there is a fairly apparent cause-and-effect relationship between the thoughts and actions of the student and the consequences he or she experiences. Moreover, a student who feels successful associates that sense of success to a great extent with the person who helped him or her get there, and that is usually the teacher.

As we will discuss in more detail in the next chapter, the most powerful means to developing a responsible mind-set in students is to help make them aware of this cause-and-effect relationship between their thoughts and actions and the consequences. A requirement for helping students recognize cause and effect is to create it within the logic of the classroom social contract. The keys to this logic are the use of cause and effect in your explanations for why things happen academically and managerially and well-established, natural, related, and logical consequences for positive and negative behaviors. In other words, students learn that when they make certain choices, a logical and related consequence will follow.

Ideally, the best consequences (and inherently most logical and related) are those that are naturally occurring (Dreikurs, 1974). However, when these are not sufficient given the situational demands, the teacher must create a manufactured consequence that is as related as possible to the situational behavior. For example, in the instance of the student who arrived late for the bus, the consequence was natural. No one had to implement it. And in that case, the only person affected was the student. In the absence of clear and direct natural consequences, the teacher (perhaps with the help of the students) must manufacture one. For example, the naturally occurring effect of a student getting up to sharpen a pencil several times a day is that others are annoyed and order is disrupted. Clearly in this case, the natural consequence is insufficient to meet the needs of the class as a whole. Therefore, a manufactured but still logically related consequence needs to be developed (Dreikurs, 1974). One of the many logical consequences in this case would be that a student might lose the privilege of using the sharpener for a while. The cause is the student's choosing to misuse a privilege; the effect is that the privilege is withheld for a time. The student may be given the opportunity to try again later, and the hope is that he will take a more responsible approach to the use of the privilege in the future.

WHAT IS A PUNISHMENT?

A punishment is an external intervention that is intended to give discomfort for the purpose of payback or out of the belief that it will change behavior (Curwin & Mendler, 1986; Schlosser, 1992). There are no natural or logical punishments. The locus of control of a punishment is the punisher. In nature there are only consequences, no punishments. For instance, if you take a wrong turn on a hiking trail, you may get lost, run into trouble, experience hunger, or feel frightened, but none of this could be defined as a punishment. It is always rooted in the laws of nature—in cause and effect. You made a bad choice—you did not prepare properly or underestimated the task—so consequently paid a price.

Punishments come in many forms. Some are overt and obvious, such as picking up trash, names on the board, detentions, being sent to the office, angry outbursts, having to sit alone, calls home, and losing class points. Some punishments are much more subtle: lectures, guilt throwing, public shaming, overt disappointment, being more critical of student work after the students have misbehaved, lowering of expectations, and so on.

In a punishment condition, the pain and discomfort inflicted on the punished are always calculated by an external agent: the punisher. With consequences, the cost or benefit is determined by natural laws, whereas with the punishment, the price is determined artificially. Consequences teach lessons; punishments teach avoidance of the punisher (Schlosser, 1992). Most consequences are understood before decisions are made and actions take place. Punishments are typically reactive (see Table 9.1).

What Is So Wrong with Punishments?

On the surface, punishments can appear to work: that is, they produce what appears to be a desirable outcome (Landrum & Kauffman, 2006). But as we examine their effects more closely, we will see that punishments either do not improve behavior in the long term or are not the portion of the intervention that had the desirable effect (Kohn, 1999; Schlosser, 1992).

TABLE 9.1. **Consequences Versus Punishments: A Comparison**

Consequences	Punishments
Intend to teach lessons	Intend to give discomfort
Foster internal locus of control	Foster external locus of control
Are proactive	Are reactive
Are logical and related	Are unrelated and personal
Work in the long term	Work in the short term
Promote responsibility	Can promote obedience (but more likely resentment)

Punishment may stop unwanted behavior in the short term, which contributes to the illusion that it works, but the lesson learned is not related to the problem behavior and so will not lead to learning or behavior change. For example, if a teacher angrily tells the class, "Be quiet!" the effect will likely be that the students stop talking momentarily. But if we return to this same class a week later, the teacher will still be required to yell for quiet. The lesson that the students are learning from this punishment intervention is to tolerate the teacher's yelling and anger for a while and then wait for the opportunity to go back to the behavior that meets their previous needs. There is nothing learned that relates to an appropriate use of voice or a respectful orientation to others' need for a peaceful learning environment. Without the fundamental learning (which consequences provide), the teacher's external and emotional intervention appears to be the only thing that works. But it stops the problem only for an instant. Worse, as the students become comfortable with the negative impact of the punishment, they become increasingly immune, so more frequent and more severe forms of punishment are required to obtain the same result (Kauffman, 2005). According to the saying about digging yourself a hole, the first step is to stop digging.

Some readers may say, "But my class is improving, and I rely on punishments." Let's examine typical practices in such situations and analyze what is making things better. It is a safe bet that mixed in with the punishments are a lot of high expectations and the implicit message that you believe in the students and will not accept poor behavior. In the end, these positive messages of caring and validation are having the positive effect (Kauffman, 2005). If this is the case, the use of punishments is only holding the class back from its potential. If you keep the high expectations but exchange the use of punishments for consequences, you may be surprised at how the students respond with a level of behavioral maturity that you did not think that they had. Moreover, you will find yourself experiencing an emotional ease and lightness that gives you more positive energy throughout the day.

Consequences build responsibility in students. Children who are fed a steady diet of punishment (especially guilt, shame, and lectures) do not learn responsibility because the locus of control in punishment is external and responsibility comes from an internal locus of control. Punishments for the most part promote either obedience or rebellion (Landrum & Kauffman, 2006; Schlosser, 1992). You might think, "Well, if it is obedience, then I am fine with that." Obedience may sound desirable on the surface, and it may seem to make life easier for teachers, but it can be a slippery slope down a path that leads to emotionally immature and dependent students (Kohn, 1999). It might be useful to put yourself in the position of the student (a useful cure for most teacher power trips, by the way), and consider whether you would want to be put in a position where you were expected to do only what you were told. You can see the benefit of this arrangement for the self-centered teacher, but it is difficult to see the benefits to the student. The primary skill a student learns from a teacher who loves to punish and demands obedience is how to play the game of pretending to be repentant. This is not the kind of skill that translates into high-quality relationships over a lifetime. So if our job as teachers is to teach and promote our students' growth, why would we incorporate a practice that fundamentally stunts personal growth?

REFLECTION   9.4

Think about how you would respond to the teacher who suggests that consequences are fine for small things, but for the big things, we need to use punishments. Do you find this to be sound logic? It may help to recall your answer to the earlier question related to the events that changed your life the most. Were they consequences or punishments?

Why We Love to Give Punishments (and Pain-Based Logic)

When we examine why someone would have a compelling attraction to use punishments, we find that it has more to do with one's mental conditioning than any evidence of efficacy. Often teachers (and students in teacher education classes) become upset after examining the consequence-versus-punishment dichotomy and feel the need to defend the use of punishments. They often use the phrase, "I have tried to use consequences, but my students understand only punishments, and they are working for me." On the surface, this sounds reasonable. But as we examine the logic more closely, we can see why these classes are not developing more responsible and desirable behavior and why the teacher spends a lot of time being emotionally miserable. At the heart of their thinking is a pain-based logic. This form of reasoning implies something to the effect that, "Because I was personally offended by the students' actions, to teach them a lesson, to motivate change, and to pay them back, I need to give them some pain. It's only fair."

It is possible to assume that somewhere in the past of the teacher who clings to a pain-based logic and cannot give up defending the use of punishments is an attachment to a past authority figure who used this logic and a lot of punishments. As a result, the teacher continually misinterprets the evidence. Although the effects of punishments are to the objective eye (and to a teacher's own inner conscience) not very desirable—little improvement of behavior, an increasingly hostile climate in the class, and a feeling on the part of the teacher that he or she is acting more as law enforcement than as a learning facilitator—the teacher continues to hold to the belief that the punishments are necessary. The inner dialogue is, "If I do not give pain for unwanted behavior, I will be viewed as weak and powerless." There is a fictional and faulty working assumption that suggests that people cannot be trusted and that they respond only to pain and domination. Within this mental fiction is misinterpretation of one's own past. If people regularly receive the message that they cannot be trusted, they come to internalize the belief that they respond only to punishment. This interpretation is likely giving the teacher a great deal less credit for being responsible and trustworthy than is warranted and giving the influence of the punishments far too much credit for promoting positive behavior. Moreover, and most important, it is keeping this teacher (or parent, or coach, or leader) from trusting his or her students and giving up the illusion that the use of punishments is doing anything positive.

Sometimes it is not what we do, but how we do it that distinguishes a punishment from a consequence. In practice, what distinguishes a punishment from a consequence can be in how it is perceived by the students (Curwin & Mendler, 1986; Dreikurs, 1974; Schlosser, 1992; Weinstein, 2003). If the student perceives an event as external (you were angry), reactive (you were fed up), or intended to give pain (you needed to teach her a lesson for what she did), it is punishment and has all the negative impact of a punishment—even if the intent is a clear and logical consequence (Schlosser, 1992; Weinstein, 2003). This might seem confusing. Keep in mind, however, that management success is not about being able to defend one's self. It is about the results achieved. Ask yourself after each consequence implementation intervention (discussed in detail in the next chapter), "What did the student learn from that event?" and "Who and what was it about?" If it was experienced as being about choice and supported the processing for how a better choice could have been made, it was most likely a successful consequence. If it was perceived as being about you the teacher, and the student left the situation feeling as though she got in trouble and was therefore given some discomfort, it could best be characterized as a punishment.

To illustrate a consequence situation that could be similar to a punishment situation, compare two interventions with the same basic elements:

- A review is being provided as a service to help students prepare for an upcoming exam.
- Students need to listen during the review or ask questions.

- The review will last as long as it needs to.
- The expectation is that students are quiet during an exam.

Given these basic elements, consider the following two cases:

In case 1, the teacher is reviewing the material with students. After about forty minutes, the teacher senses that the students are restless and says to them, "I am seeing less attention than I did earlier. Does that mean you have had enough review and we are ready to take the test?" Some students say yes, and others say no. So he makes a deal: "If you are able to be attentive and use this opportunity well, we will continue to review; if it looks as if you are getting bored and restless, that will tell me that it is time to hand out the test." After a few minutes, the students look restless. The teacher says, "Okay, let's take everything off our desks and get out a pen or pencil [and he gives additional instructive and supportive comments related to the material]. We have done well on this in class, so let's show it here. And remember that we need to be respectful of one another, so please be quiet until everyone is done."

In case 2, the teacher is reviewing the material with the students. After about forty minutes, the teacher hears talking. He tells them, "There is too much talking right now." After a couple of minutes, talking continues so he tells them, "If you keep talking, I am going to give you the test." After a few minutes, the teacher again becomes frustrated with the amount of talking and says, "That's it! You are getting the test now!" As he passes out the test, he angrily tells the students that if they talk during the exam, they will "get a big fat zero!"

The two cases are essentially the same in terms of the teachers' actions. In both cases, the teachers made the determination that as a result of the students' behavior, they seemed not to be taking advantage of the review and therefore were ready to take the test. But would you characterize them both as consequences? Or was the second a punishment?

REFLECTION

9.5

Reflect on the differences in the two cases. Although they were similar, there were significant differences. What would you label each intervention?

Case 1 seems to meet the qualification for a consequence. It was proactive, logical, and related, and the students were in control of the outcome. As a result, the students felt responsible for what happened. Conversely, case 2 falls into the classification of a punishment condition. It was reactive, the teacher was angry, and therefore the students perceived the case of the action as being related to the level of the teacher's frustration. As a result, the locus was shifted externally. Moreover, in the end, the test was used as a punishment. What does that do to the students' association with the purpose of tests and other assessments?

If the teacher in case 2 had not resorted to a pain-based logic, a much better result would have been manufactured. In case 1, tomorrow is going to be better as a result of the teacher's intervention today. The relationship here stays intact, and the students take a step forward in learning to be responsible class members. In case 2, the relationship is damaged. The teacher has withdrawn a great deal from the emotional bank account balance that had been accrued. In case 1, the lesson learned is that if the class wants to have the privilege of a review, they need to use the opportunity maturely. In case 2, the primary lesson learned was to do a better job of interpreting what does and does not make the teacher angry. In case 1 the expectation was strengthened. In case 2, because the cause and effect were not well established, the expectation will remain vague. And finally, how about the energy level of the teachers? Which teacher used more energy?

9.6 **REFLECTION**

Cases 1 and 2 seem to imply that interactions that are driven by a pain-based logic (anger, punishments, guilt, revenge, shaming, embarrassment) are more exhausting for the teacher. Is this true in your experience? Reflect on the last interaction that you would characterize as being driven by a pain-based logic. What was the emotional cost to the pain giver?

9.7 **REFLECTION**

Reflect on the following situation:

A teacher decides to let students work together on an assignment. After a couple of warnings about the noise level, the teacher reaches a point of intolerance and implements a punishment, angrily stating, "That's it! I am fed up! You are making too much noise. Everyone is going to have to do the worksheet on your own."

What in the teacher's reaction would you call a punishment? How could he or she have accomplished a more effective result with a consequence?

Rewards, the Other Side of the Punishment-Reward Coin

In his book *Punished by Rewards* (1999), Alfie Kohn makes the argument that rewards (prizes, preferred activity time, stickers, personal praise, awards, and even, to an extent, grades) are really just the other side of a punishment-reward coin. As with punishments, rewards are external and artificial, and they do a poor job of teaching lessons related to the learning event. What we learn from rewards is to do what it takes to continue to get the reward. The focus is shifted from the value of the process or even the accomplishment to an external and artificial object (Deci, Koestner, & Ryan, 1999). The source of the reward is not one's own efforts but someone else: the "rewarder." So whereas consequences promote an internal locus of control and a success psychology, rewards inevitably promote an external locus of control and a failure psychology (see Table 9.2).

TABLE 9.2. **Positive Consequences Versus Rewards**

	Positive Consequences	**Rewards**
Examples	Increased opportunities	Personal praise
	Achievement	Tokens and grades
	Recognition of effort	Preferred activity time
	Opportunities to contribute	Party at the end of the week
	Learning	Stickers and stars
Locus of control	Internal to student	External from teacher
Teaches	Responsibility and a clear cause and effect between effort and the outcome	To do what it takes to get the reward and to shift attention away from the value of the task to the value of the reward
Motivation	Satisfaction of needs	To get the reward

Also beware of the less visible but often more insidious version of this reward and punishment paradigm in practice: the use of love and withdrawal of love in the form of praise and disappointment. Many teachers say that they do not like rewards and punishments, but their interactions with students are defined by, "Are you doing what I want? Then I like you, and if you are not, I don't." Recall the discussion of praise in Chapter Six: it is an external, coercive, and manipulative reward given under the guise of positive reinforcement. And its sibling, disappointment, is an external, coercive, and manipulative punishment disguised as corrective feedback. Neither is effective in helping students grow or learn, but each is very effective at keeping them in fear of failure, dependent on praise to perform, and externalizing their sense of cause and effect.

You Just Don't Know My School

It is true that many students respond to punishment and a pain-based logic because it is familiar to them. We can hear it in their voices as we try to explain that their actions reflect that they have made a choice to violate the social contract—"Teacher, why are you getting me in trouble?" We state the situation as a consequence; they hear it as a punishment. It is likely that these students have never been supported in a cause-and-effect pattern of thinking about their choices and actions. They are often acculturated into a crime-and-punishment orientation toward those in authority. In many cases, this student is exhibiting a deeply conditioned negative identity pattern. Students with a negative identity are actually habituated to and desire punishment and pain (see Chapter Fourteen). While this may seem odd, it is critical to recognize if we are to help these students grow in a more functional and healthy direction.

Sometimes we will be given a class that is mostly full of such students. Often in these cases, these students will have friends and even family who have very real experience with gangs, crime, and violence. So to them, punishment is what authorities use in their real world. When we respond to their misbehavior or observe others responding with abusive language or pain-based penalties, they often react with repentance and improved behavior in the short term. And when we dangle rewards in front of them, we see a seemingly unmotivated student come to life and make a substantial effort toward the task. So the temptation is to accept that this is what works for these students.

In many cases, these students can be found in schools in which the discipline culture is defined by a 4-Style mentality. When we ask experienced faculty for advice, we often are told to become domineering, lower our expectations, and threaten the students with poor grades or calls home, and give awards to the top students to motivate the rest. The logic is that since the students come to us with a well-formed failure psychology that frequently includes a negative identity, we need to give them what they are used to.

While it may even seem as though we are getting results in the short term, there are several reasons not to revert to a 4-Style approach with this group of students:

- The behavior in the class will not get better and will worsen in the long run.

- We are perpetuating a failure psychology in the students. We are bringing them one year closer to taking that failure orientation on to the next grade and out into the world.

- Like any 4-Style teacher, we will struggle with a hostile, unmotivated, and irresponsible class as long as we keep up this form of practice. Moreover, we are ensuring that the level of student achievement will remain low (Shindler, Jones, Williams, Taylor, & Cadenas, 2009).

- We have lost a chance to make a difference in the lives of these students. We had a transformative opportunity and did not take it.

The fact is that students who are used to 4-Style management will adjust to a 1- or 2-Style management approach eventually. Furthermore, as they internalize the emerging success psychology that the more effective environment is fostering, they will recognize that the 4-Style environment was unhealthy. This was depicted well in the films *Freedom Writers* and *To Sir with Love*. In each film, teachers were assigned classrooms full of students who were hostile to the teacher's ideas and cultural difference. In both movies the teachers maintained a belief that all their students were capable of learning and treating each other well, even in the face of great resistance. By the end of each movie, the teacher's persistence paid off. I have seen this phenomenon firsthand in countless classes. Many of the students who come from dysfunctional contexts do not know how to operate in a 1- or 2-Style class structure at first. We need to teach them how. It will take time, but it is worth it for the reasons listed above and because we will get results and transform lives.

To begin, we need to understand the nature of the patterns in which students are operating. For example, there may be a negative identity pattern. There may be a helpless pattern, or an external locus of control, or other manifestations of a failure psychology. Maintaining a working knowledge of how to promote a success psychology is an invaluable tool in any classroom.

The rest of this chapter and the next describe practical strategies for creating cause-and-effect thinking, more responsible behavior, and the development of functional social bonds, and they offer a path toward a system that works rather than resorting to the use of punishments and bribes.

CREATING EFFECTIVE CONSEQUENCES WITHIN THE SOCIAL CONTRACT

Developing logical and related consequences is crucial to achieving a social contract that feels democratic and is built on promoting responsibility. Without logical and related consequences, students can experience teacher interventions as external and arbitrary. If students view consequences as arbitrary or subjective, the contract will have little meaning and will likely feel imposed and artificial. For the social contract to be effective, students must feel as though being faithful to their agreements to the contract is making the class better and helping them feel the satisfaction of becoming more responsible while achieving their goals of inclusion and achievement.

In the next chapter, we discuss the importance of how consequences are implemented. The quality and effectiveness of the contract and how successfully it evolves is contingent on the care and deliberateness of the implementation, but in conjunction with that, the success of the contract depends on the quality of the consequences built into it. The most successful consequences are those that are logical and related, built in proactively, reflect the buy-in and ownership of the students, and contribute to long-term growth and behavior change.

Use Logical and Related Consequences

It would be nice if all problems had naturally logical and related consequences built into them, like the example of the student arriving late to the bus. But the reality is that it can often be a challenge to find a logical and related consequence for some things. Nevertheless, taking the time and effort to come up with quality consequences (alone or with the help of the students) is well worth the effort. Reverting to punishments will undermine the success of any contract, and consequences unrelated to the problem behavior do not teach lessons and are essentially quasi-punishments. A consequence is by definition related to the problem. If it is not related, it is not a true consequence, no matter how many other teachers call them consequences (Dreikurs, 1974; Weinstein, 2003).

A well-intentioned and fairly common practice in many schools is to have a standardized set of consequences for incidents of misbehavior. This is a step in the right direction in many ways. It encourages the individual teacher (especially those with a 4-Style tendency) to take a less punitive approach and it builds in proactivity and clarity of the policy. Table 9.3 is an example of the kind of schoolwide policy chart commonly displayed on classroom walls in many schools.

As you can see from Table 9.3, the same consequences are applied for all types of problem behavior. The primary problem with this approach is that it eliminates the opportunity to have logical and related consequences. That means there is little, if any, cause-and-effect connection between the consequence and the behavior that warranted it. As a result, no meaningful lesson is learned from this set of standardized consequences. Moreover, it is a real stretch to characterize what are referred to as consequences in these school codes as true consequences. Undefined time-outs and detentions are at best merely quasi-punishments.

In Table 9.3, warnings are listed as the first-level consequence (discussed in Chapter Four). They have their use. When understanding or memory is the issue, a warning can be a useful tool to help improve behavior or cognizance of the social contract. They are characterized as favors from the teacher to help support students toward the development of functional behavior free of the need for reminders. But they are not consequences.

A more effective approach to developing consequences for a social contract is to begin with the most pressing problems. For each problem behavior, select a corresponding consequence that is as logically related to it as possible. Bringing in students may be a sound way to get them to buy into the fairness and legitimacy of each consequence and to take part in conceiving what would be related consequences. Expect this to be the most powerful and memorable concept attainment exercise that the students participate in all year.

For example, if you discover that many students are turning in their homework late, you might ask them what you can do to promote more work being turned in on time. Make sure that you instruct them to think in terms of logical and related consequences. Be patient, as this is likely new thinking for them. In professional life, the consequence for being late with work can be missing a deadline, causing others to be let down or to have our own efforts become less valuable. Therefore, a logical guiding principle could be that work needs to be in on time to get full credit. As a result, a consequence for late work could be that it would receive only partial credit. Or you could take a more hard-line stance and say that only work that is turned in on time will be accepted. Either of these options makes sense, as might others. Both are grounded in cause-and-effect and real-world precedent.

In practice, establishing the logic and relatedness of the consequences you ultimately choose will make all the difference in how well they are accepted by the students, help to improve their behavior, and strengthen the social contract. The time used in the development of creating class consequences is well spent.

Be Proactive: Build Consequences into the Contract from the Start

Effective consequences are built into the contract before they are implemented (Bluestein, 1999; Curwin & Mendler, 1986; Dreikurs, 1974). In the example of the student who arrived late for the bus, the consequence would not have been educational if the bus left at a different time each day or if the student did not know when the bus was supposed to leave.

TABLE 9.3. Common Schoolwide Policy Chart of Consequences for Each Misbehavior

Misbehavior	Consequence
First offense	Warning
Second offense	Time at recess or after school
Third offense	Detention or contacting parents, or both

Making sure students are very clear about the consequences before the fact has many benefits. First, it will make contract violations less common since students know what is expected. Second, it makes it possible to implement the consequence by simply recognizing that a choice was made to violate the contract, as opposed to the student's perspective of the teacher "getting them in trouble." Third, the focus of the student after the contract violation is much more likely to be on how to display more effective behavior rather than what the teacher said or did or feeling that she was unfairly penalized. Being proactive promotes internal locus of control. When we know what to expect, we have power; when the climate of the class is accidental, the need for power is unmet.

It is a good idea to put consequences in writing and post them. Review them and give general reminders when you sense that a little prevention could be valuable. But the most valuable teaching tool will be your actions. Recall Chapter Three and the social learning model; students will learn from what you do.

T → S / O   In addition, the use of verbal clarifications can be invaluable. For example, we might use the mantra, "In this class, we actively listen to the other members of our group and ask clarifying questions when we don't understand." Or use a statement such as, "If we do a good job of taking care of the equipment, we will continue to get the privilege of using it; if we don't, we will need to go back to using the old equipment until we can show that we are more responsible." Again, the words can only support the actions. Following through strengthens the expectation and understanding of the consequence; not following through weakens them.

Promote Buy-in and Ownership of Consequences

When students own and clearly understand the expectations and consequences in their social contract, they are much more likely to carry them out and respect them. There is no better way to do this than to have the students participate in developing the consequences. This is especially true for grades K to 8. For high school, periodic class meetings during which a problem is discussed and students are enlisted to brainstorm logical and related solutions and consequences for the problem can be a good way to promote buy-in. This cannot be emphasized enough: over time, the contract and the consequences built into it will be only as powerful as the students' sense of ownership of them. When they fully accept the purpose of the contract as being related to them and their welfare rather than being just the "teacher's set of rules," the results can be remarkable.

9.8 REFLECTION

Compare two classes that you have observed at some point: one in which there was a great deal of ownership and buy-in of the rules or social contract and one in which the rules were imposed on the students. Was there a difference in behavior? Were you able to discern a difference in motivation?

Contribute to Long-Term Growth and Behavior Changes

The test of a good consequence is what it does in the long term. If it does not teach the students to be more responsible and self-disciplined, it needs to be reexamined. It is simplistic to assume that a consequence that deters an immediate behavior is a good consequence. This illusion of effectiveness keeps us in the trap of using familiar but flawed consequences or punishments. A useful clue to the long-term effectiveness of a consequence is the reaction from a student when it is implemented. If the reaction implies, "I knew not to do that," it has a good chance to be effective. If the reaction is one of repentance, look for the behavior to be revisited; it is therefore not perceived as a consequence but as a punishment.

Ask yourself, "What is being learned each time this consequence is implemented?" If the consequence is logical, related, and built in proactively, it is likely that the student is learning a useful lesson related to the problem behavior. However, we can consider success only if the behavior changes rather quickly and for the right reasons, and makes "tomorrow" more healthy and functional. Since every class is different and every student in the class is different, finding the right consequences may take a bit of active research on the part of the teacher. It may also require some collective soul searching on the part of the class.

Increase the Level of Impact of Consequences for Each Problem Behavior

All contract violations do not have the same degree of damage to the class's health and function. Moreover, a particular student action does not necessarily imply that the student has a problem. Most contract violations are a result of forgetfulness or immaturity. Some indicate a need to examine why the behavior occurred or continues to occur. Some require that the student loses an opportunity in order to experience a clear consequence for an inability to be a responsible member of the group. It therefore makes sense to have within the social contract an increasingly more powerful series of consequences for particular problem behavior. If the problem behavior is minor and infrequent, a small consequence may be all that is necessary. If it is prevalent or a persistent problem for a particular student, more significant consequences may be necessary.

Let's take the example of a student who cannot resist talking to the student at the next desk when she should be attending to those contributing in a class discussion. It is not a major problem if it does not happen often, but if it happens regularly or the particular student cannot help it, it becomes quite significant. Here is one possible series of ascending consequences:

- *First offense:* The student turns to a neighbor to talk while the teacher is talking. *Consequence:* The teacher stops talking (when she is interrupted) and waits for 100 percent attention or says something to the effect, "I need everyone's attention, so I will start over with the directions." This consequence is simple but effective. It does not take a lot of time or energy, but it is active and gets the message across.

- *Second offense:* The teacher notices that the student is talking to a neighbor when he is supposed to be attentive to another student who is contributing. *Consequence:* The student comes up with a strategy to make sure he is able to pay attention when it is required.

- *Third offense:* The student does it again. *Consequence:* The student is moved to another seat.

- *Fourth offense:* The student has the same problem in the new location. *Consequence:* He has a conference with the teacher after school, resulting in a written contract.

Given that this series of consequences implies escalating degrees of power, the student is given logical and appropriate opportunities to solve his problem. It is unlikely that many students would require all four levels of consequences, but it is comforting for both the teacher and the students in the class to know that they are in place. Much of the stress experienced by teachers and the frustration experienced by students come from worrying about what particular students may do on a given day. Having clearly established consequences in place eases much of that stress. The ownership for making good behavioral choices rests with the students. The teacher simply needs to be a fair and consistent manager of the social contract.

9.9   REFLECTION

Are you asking yourself, "At what point do we include in the series of consequences something that will give offending students some pain to teach them a lesson?" If so, watch out for the tendency to make the consequences more negative (painful) rather than more powerful.

An important distinction should be made here between the increasingly powerful (consequences) and the increasingly painful (punishments). In pain-based logic, if one blow to the head does not do the trick, then maybe two will. The problem with this logic is that no lesson will be learned from the blow (standards, shaming, lecture, picking up trash, or something else) because it is not related to the misbehavior. Therefore, since the small amount of pain did not change the behavior pattern, a greater amount will work only to make the student more hostile and defiant.

There is often a misconception that consequences are easier on the student than punishments are. Even some teachers who are opposed to punishments for ethical reasons hold this belief. However, it is simply untrue. If you examine the most difficult and painful lessons you have learned in life, you will realize that nearly all of them came in the form of consequences. Close scrapes with nature, losing loved ones, missing the cut, painful relationships, lost jobs, and missed opportunities are all examples of life's consequences. Few of the punishments that have been imposed on us have had the same power to affect or teach. The power of consequences is that they are meaningful and require a real price to be paid. Punishments may feel bad, but in the end they merely need to be tolerated. Their only price is discomfort.

Beware of Punishments Disguised as Logical Consequences

The term *consequences* has become popular in discipline circles, especially in schools, partially because of the natural and logical concept and partially because it sounds less harsh or cruel than *punishment*. However, calling something a consequence does not make it so, just as calling something a punishment may not be accurate (Elias & Schwab, 2006).

Since the use of the term *consequences* is attached to all manner of teacher-imposed penalization in schools today, it is common to see punishments and punishment-based systems sold as assertive discipline consequences. Some examples are negative calls home, being sent to the office, picking up trash, or running laps. One of the most prevalent examples of this brand of punishment is the idea of writing the names of students on the board or its sibling, having students move their cards from the green level to the yellow level to the red level (Canter, 1992; Wong & Wong, 1991) in a card system. This practice is essentially a systematic shame-based punishment sold as a system of rational consequences. Not only is it a punishment or "pain-based" system at its core, but like all other punishment systems, it does not work. Check in on a class that uses such a system, and you will see the same names on the board or the same cards changed from green to yellow all year. Like other pain-based systems, its main function is to make the teacher feel better, but it will not do much to change behavior for the better and does a great deal of harm on other levels. Because of the widespread use of this procedure, the online resource article, "Why Not to Use Colored Cards and Names on the Board Behavioral Systems and What to Do Instead," at transformativeclassroom.com is devoted entirely to an examination of it, its fundamental problems, and a more effective and positive alternative.

9.10

REFLECTION

Observe a class at the beginning of the year that uses a colored-card behavioral system and then again months later. Do you see the same students with their cards on a lower color level? What does it tell you?

Avoid Giving Activities as Negative Consequences

Most of us can think of countless examples throughout our schooling where we were given an activity as a punishment. We had to run laps, memorize capital cities, clean up the room, pick up trash around the school, do push-ups, help the teacher at recess, or any number of other activities that were supposed to "teach us a lesson." And even today they can seem somewhat related to our misbehavior. But as we examine this practice more closely, we can see that in the long run, the use of activities as penalties is a step backward.

First, it is difficult to classify activities as something other than punishments. They are based on the principle that if students detest doing the activity, they will be deterred from making the same choice again. Recognize the pain logic? We are attracted to these types of penalties and even perceive that they have a desired effect because they appear to deter certain behaviors in the short term and produce the desired level of repentance in the students after the penalty. But are they really logical and related? What is the relationship between talking in class and having to write fifty times, "I will not talk in class?" Or what is the relationship between being tardy and having to run laps?

Second, the actual lesson that these punishments teach is to avoid the activity (Landrum & Kauffman, 2006). The message being sent is, "Since you did something that we want you to stop doing, we are going to penalize you with a behavior we would like to see you do more of." This acts to create a disincentive to engage in a desired behavior. In the long term, since no related lesson is learned, there will be no desired behavior change, except possibly some avoidance of getting caught. Yet we can be assured that the student will develop a negative association (and therefore a disincentive to perform) with the behavior. A student who is told to write the line "I will not talk in class" fifty times as a punishment learns that the act of writing is a punishment to avoid. (So much for all the time we spend telling our students that they should love to write!) Similarly, if we tell them they must run as a punishment, we are saying that the only reason that they should ever consider running is if someone forces them to. If we punish a student by having her help clean up, beautify the school, and so on, we are saying in effect never to do anything helpful, of service, or altruistic unless you are forced to.

9.11

REFLECTION

Recall a situation in which you were forced to do work (run laps, help clean, write, or something else) as a penalty for misbehavior. How did it affect your association with that activity at the time? Has that negative association carried over to the present?

A helpful guiding principle might be to use activity as a positive consequence and inactivity as a negative consequence. If the student has a great day, invite her to stay after school and help you clean up. Observe the effect this has on her. Most likely she will consider it an honor. If a student makes an exceptional effort in an area, give her an extra task that stretches and challenges her. Work that is seen as a reward reinforces the student's intrinsic sources of motivation. When work is seen as a punishment, students learn only to do what is externally rewarded.

Clarify this principle by creating a clear cause-and-effect relationship in your class. It may help to use such social frame clarifying statements as, "When you work hard and invest, I will give you more challenging work; when you show that you are not ready for the challenging work, I will give you work better suited to a less motivated and responsible group." "When you show that you can be responsible, I will give you more freedom and responsibility; when you show that you are not responsible, you will not be given the same opportunities until you show you are ready." Watch the student rise to the occasion. In this responsibility-based classroom, failing to earn the opportunity to take part is a powerful and related consequence, and if failure does take place, the presence of the clear cause-and-effect logic within the expectation provides an opportunity for reflection. Over time, the result will be the development of more intrinsically motivated students.

Developing social bonds can set the table for communal bonds, but it will not create them. Developing clear expectations, logical and related consequences, and a functioning social contract will ultimately lead to increasing levels of emotional safety, a sense of fairness, and behavior changes for the better, but they cannot by themselves create in a student a cause beyond themselves or community. Nevertheless, it is a wise and likely necessary starting point for most groups. The social contract can transform a class from a self-centered and dysfunctional group of individuals into a self-responsible and functional collective. However, if we want to foster the transformation of the group into one that is bonded, acts as a team or tribe, and puts the needs of one another first, we must make an intentional effort to promote a success psychology and foster communal bonds.

Table 9.4 lists some common problems that occur in a class, followed by examples of common punishments that teachers use and possible related consequences for the same problem. As you will notice, there is rarely a case when we are able to manufacture a consequence

TABLE 9.4. Consequences, Punishments, and Transformative Ideas for Problem Behaviors

Problem	Punishment (What Not to Do)	Related Consequence	Transformative Idea
Problem lining up	Disappointment Shaming Lost points	Practice lining up	Be positive, but help the students learn to be successful and take joy in their success. (See Chapter Twelve.)
Turning in assignment late	Public embarrassment Asking for an excuse	Loss of points	Project-driven work and meaningful assignments will reduce the tendency for students to neglect assignments. (See Chapter 13 for more ideas.)
Frequent talking out of turn	Writing lines Negative recognitions	Loss of opportunity to talk Problem-solve solutions to fix problem Loss of opportunity to take part in activity	The level of side talk is usually related to how engaging the work is and whether the teacher has created a culture of listening. (See Chapter Six.)

(continued)

TABLE 9.4. Continued

Problem	Punishment (What Not to Do)	Related Consequence	Transformative Idea
Group cannot refrain from conflict that leads to poor performance	Hovering over the group Splitting the group up Shaming the group	First intervention: clarify task, confirm understanding. Second intervention: clarify need to resolve conflict; confirm commitment to conflict-free effort. Third intervention: loss of opportunity to take part in an activity, potentially needing to reflect on solutions for future efforts, or need to complete work on own time. (See Chapter Twelve.)	Clear directions, assessing the quality of group participation, and inductive lesson designs will ensure more students are engaged more of the time.
Tapping pencils on desks	Public negative recognition Staying after class	Have students put everything down and have their hands free while listening	Meet students' basic need for power. Create engaging lessons and develop a culture of listening.
Cheating	Public humiliation	No credit for work	Teachers who project the expectation that to cheat is to lose out and that they have faith that no one will cheat usually have little cheating.
Using a cell phone	Public humiliation Angry power struggle	Confiscate phone for a time	Set an expectation early in the year that there is no reason to have a cell phone out. Zero tolerance early will save a lot of pain later.
Going to the restroom	Publicly questioning why the student needs to go Questioning students' intentions	Some set number of restroom visits per quarter	Student uses restroom privileges as he or she sees fit, and when they are gone, the student is out of this privilege. Help the students make wise use of the privilege.

as logical and related as the bus's being gone when the student arrived late at the bus stop, but we can attempt to get close. Finally, transformative ideas are offered for each problem—that is, strategies that one can put into practice that make the need for such behavior less necessary.

CONCLUSION

This chapter has clarified the distinction between punishments and consequences and has demonstrated why the use of consequences produces more desirable and effective outcomes. A thoughtful and intentional approach to the development of the consequences within the social contract will help in efforts to promote more responsible behavior and a positive classroom climate. The next chapter provides a step-by-step system for implementing consequences and the social contract.

Journal Reflections

1. In your experience, have teachers more often used punishments or consequences? How have these affected you differently?
2. Do you recognize the pain-based logic inside yourself and others? Reflect how in your own experience, pain is traded back and forth between parents and children, teachers and students, and those with whom you are in relationships. If this idea resonates with you, I recommend that you read Eckhart Tolle's *Practicing the Power of Now* (2001).

Activities

1. In groups of four, brainstorm two common student behavioral problems that you have seen recently or feel are pertinent. (This activity is more effective if they are not severe problems, such as fighting or disrespect, which are addressed in the previous chapter.) Pass them to the group next to you. Once you have your neighbor's two problems, develop consequences for them. Be sure that they are true consequences, not simply quasi-punishments. Refer to Table 9.1 to assess your answers.
2. Discuss the difference between logical and related (but manufactured) consequences and naturally occurring consequences. What criteria would you use to decide which is best in any given situation?
3. In groups, fill in the following chart with teacher practices. When you are done, compare your answers with the rest of the class.

	Positive	**Negative**
Healthy and effective	Natural positive consequences for good choices 1. 2. 3.	Natural and logical consequences for poor choices 1. 2. 3.
Unhealthy and ineffective	Extrinsic rewards 1. 2. 3.	Punishments 1. 2. 3

4. In groups, discuss the differences between the two conditions in the scenarios of the student who missed the bus at the beginning of the chapter. What are the differences between a punishment condition and a consequence condition?
5. In groups, have each group develop a list of two or three common social contract violations (don't make them too severe for now). When you are done, pass them to another group. This group will need to come up with logical and related consequences for each problem. This is more difficult than it sounds. It will be helpful to turn to Table 9.1, which compares consequences and punishments. Share your ideas with the whole group, and discuss why you felt each was a consequence rather than a punishment.

REFERENCES

Bluestein, J. (1999). *Twenty-first century discipline: Teaching students responsibility and self-management*. Belmont, CA: Fearon.

Brady, K., Forton, M. B., Porter, D., & Wood, C. (2003). *Rules in school*. Greenfield, MA: Northeast Foundation for Children.

Canter, L. (1992). *Lee Canter's assertive discipline: Positive behavior management for today's classroom*. Los Angeles: Lee Canter and Associates

Curwin, R., & Mendler, A. (1986). *Discipline with dignity*. Alexandria, VA: ASCD Press.

Deci, E. L., Koestner, R., & Ryan, R. M. (1999). A meta-analytic review of experiments examining the effects of extrinsic rewards and intrinsic motivation. *Psychological Bulletin, 125*, 627–668.

Dreikurs, R. (1974). *Discipline without tears*. New York: Hawthorn Books.

Elias, M. J., & Schwab, Y. (2006). From compliance to responsibility: Social and emotional learning and classroom management. In C. M. Evertson & C. S. Weinstein (Eds.), *Handbook of classroom management* (pp. 309–341). Mahwah, NJ: Erlbaum.

Kauffman, J. M. (2005). *Characteristics of emotional and behavioral disorders of children and youth* (8th ed.). Upper Saddle River, NJ: Prentice Hall.

Kohn, A. (1999). *Punished by rewards: The trouble with gold stars, incentive plans, A's, praise, and other bribes*. Boston: Houghton Mifflin.

Landrum, T. J., & Kauffman, J. M. (2006). Behavioral approaches to classroom management. In C. M. Evertson & C. S. Weinstein (Eds.), *Handbook of classroom management* (pp. 47–71). Mahwah, NJ: Erlbaum.

Nelson, J., Lynn, L., & Glenn, H. S. (2000). *Positive discipline in the classroom: Developing mutual respect, cooperation and responsibility in your classroom* (3rd ed.). Roseville, CA: Prima Publishing.

Schlosser, L. K. (1992). Teacher distance and student disengagement: School lives in the margins. *Journal of Teacher Education, 43*(2), 128–140.

Shindler, J., Jones, A., Williams, A., Taylor, C., & Cadenas, H. (2009, January). *Exploring below the surface: School climate assessment and improvement as the key to bridging the achievement gap*. Paper presented at the annual meeting of the Washington State Office of the Superintendent of Public Instruction, Seattle.

Tolle, E. (2001). *Practicing the power of now*. Vancouver: Namaste Publishing.

Weinstein, C. S. (2003). *Secondary classroom management: Lessons from research and practice* (2nd ed.). Needham Heights, MA: Allyn & Bacon.

Wong, H., & Wong, R. (1991). *First days of school: How to be an effective teacher*. Mountain View, CA: Wong Publishing.

10

Implementing the Social Contract and Promoting Student Responsibility

In This Chapter

- The big picture
- Delivering consequences
- What constitutes a successful implementation
- Step-by-step examples
- What if a student says no
- Why students make excuses
- How to foster student responsibility
- Comparing the social contract in the 1- and 2-Style classrooms

A social contract is only as good as its implementation. The most critical elements in the process of the development and use of a social contract relate to how effectively the teacher fosters an understanding of the cause-and-effect relationship between choices and outcomes and intentionally and effectively implements the agreed-on consequences within the contract.

IMPLEMENTING THE SOCIAL CONTRACT

Once the social contract has been developed, it will be defined largely by how it is implemented in the first few days. Whether it was developed with the involvement of the students or constructed by the teacher alone, the essence of the contract is that it defines the collective good. It says, in effect, "We are the contract, and it will work to the degree that all of us as members of the class community buy in and commit to it." Therefore, it is true democracy in the sense that its power comes not from the teacher but from the collective commitment of the students to their functioning as a body (Rogers & Freiburg, 1994; Watson & Battistich, 2006).

179

In the early stages of any implementation of the social contract, the teacher needs to clearly project the following fundamental concepts by both word and deed:

1. The contract is about the welfare of its participants, not the wishes of the teacher.

2. I [the teacher] am just a manager/steward/facilitator of the contract, not the police, boss, or judge of good and bad behavior.

3. When contract violations occur, I [the teacher] owe it to you [the participants] to hold you accountable for what you have agreed to.

4. You [the participants] do not need to be sorry when you violate the contract; you simply accept your consequence and make an effort to learn from the event.

5. Therefore, I [the teacher] will not ask for your repentance for what you did or apologize for the discomfort a consequence may involve.

6. I [the teacher] owe it to you [the participants] to implement the contract in a manner that protects and respects your dignity and as a result you [the participants] owe me [the teacher] recognition of the difficulty of my role.

7. It is okay for any member of community to raise a concern for the common good.

10.1 REFLECTION

Reflect on the vastly different expectations and management systems that students will bring into your class from home and from previous teachers. How long will it take to help all of your students adopt a set of shared expectations? get on the same page? Will you have the determination to be a beacon of clarity and not get too distracted by the growth pains that students exhibit?

Keep the Big Picture in Sight

Teachers must continually help each student recognize that the social contract is just one part of the overall effort to support his or her journey to becoming more self-responsible, disciplined, successful, and an integral part of the classroom community. One way to do this is to help students recognize that consequences occur many times a day, that the majority of them are naturally occurring, and that even those initiated by the teacher are primarily positive (see Table 10.1).

If we allow ourselves to be genuine, enjoy our students and the act of teaching, and invest in the emotional bank account of our students, just being present in our class will be a

TABLE 10.1. **Types of Consequences by Origin and Effect on Student**

Origin of Consequence	Effect on Student	
	Positive/Promote	**Negative/Limit**
Naturally occurring	Sense of accomplishment Growth Learning	Unhappy recognitions that a choice has led to an unwanted outcome
Logical, manufactured	Positive recognitions by the teacher Good grades More opportunities and choices	Lost opportunities Teacher-delivered consequences

substantially positive consequence (Osterman, 2000). Moreover, if we make a very intentional effort to use positive recognitions of our students' efforts, most of the interactions they have with us will be of the positive variety: they choose to invest in their work (cause or action), and we recognize this and give them positive, task-clarifying feedback (effect or consequence). In addition, it will be useful to support students' recognition of this cause-and-effect relationship. Therefore, when they make a choice that leads to a significant outcome, positive or negative, we supportively and caringly help them see how the choice they made has a result. Accordingly, when it is time to approach a student about a violation of his or her agreement to the social contract, it should be seen as just another means to help the student grow toward personal responsibility and accountability to peers (Hines, Cruickshank, & Kennedy, 1985).

REFLECTION   10.2

Recall the examination of the idea of the emotional bank account in Chapter Three. In your assessment, would it make a difference if a student were given a consequence by a teacher who had invested in the emotional bank account of their relationship as compared to not having invested? Is so, why would you feel there would be a difference?

Many students will be new to participating in a democratic classroom. If they have grown accustomed to classrooms managed by punishment, shaming, mandatory obedience, or the teacher as boss, it may take them a while to get used to being empowered (Manke, 1997; Weinstein, 2003). Using empowering mantras and language in general that continuously clarifies the roles of the participants is important, especially early on. You may need to remind them that "the class is made up only of talented, responsible, self-disciplined students." And repeat to them on occasion, "I am not the boss or the police in here, and I am not going to get mad at you. My job is to hold you accountable for what you've all agreed to and help you to become more self-disciplined and responsible."

REFLECTION   10.3

I recently observed a teacher-student interaction that I thought was instructive. It was the second month of school, and the teacher had developed a relatively sound set of rules and consequences. At one point, a student did something minor (but it was obvious to everyone in the class) to violate a rule; the teacher calmly told this student that the consequence was to lose a minor opportunity. At this, the student became irate and said loudly to the teacher, "How come you are always getting me in trouble!"

Where did the reaction come from? What would you do if you were the teacher in this class?

Although words are important to help clarify the conceptual framework from which the members of the class are operating, over time the power and effectiveness of the social contract will come from observation of your actions when you implement consequences outlined in the contract. Taking into account the nature of social and indirect learning, your actions will speak louder than words when it comes to students' learning about the integrity of the social contract and what to expect when violations occur.

Delivering Consequences

Consequences exist only as abstractions. It is how they are implemented that will define whether students experience them as fair and opportunities to learn rather than personal and punitive (Burden, 2003). Curwin and Mendler (1986) suggest, "Sometimes it is more how we say something than what we say. A lousy consequence delivered [effectively] is better than a good consequence delivered in a publicly humiliating manner." They offer a series of useful steps for implementing a consequence. Keeping each of these practices in mind when it is time to address a behavior that violates the social contract will help ensure that the intervention is effective and does not attack a student's dignity.

Curwin and Mendler's Nine Steps for Consequence Implementation

1. *Always implement a consequence. Be consistent.*
2. *Simply state the rule and consequence.*
3. *Be physically close. Use the power of proximity.*
4. *Make direct eye contact. [This could also be said as "make personal contact."]*
5. *Use a soft voice.*
6. *Catch the student being good.*
7. *Don't embarrass the student in front of the class.*
8. *Be firm but anger free when giving the consequence.*
9. *Don't accept excuses, bargaining, or whining. [pp. 94–97]*

Why Consistency Is So Important

When we examine what promotes function or dysfunction and movement up or down the effectiveness continuum, applying the social contract consistently shows itself to be essential in efforts to move up the continuum. The younger the students, the more significant this will be. At the heart of the social contract is the cause-and-effect relationship between choices and consequences. If students make certain choices, the teacher is given the responsibility by the contract to implement a consequence. The locus of control for the contract rests with the students. The purpose for the teacher's faithfully executing his role in the contract goes far beyond making sure the student "gets what she deserves." When the teacher does what is expected, the message is sent that the contract is working. It is not an arbitrary instrument but a real and living agreement. The message is clear that the contract governs all students, not just those whom the teacher feels need to improve behavior. With consistency comes a feeling of rightness, justice, and security that governs the class.

 Recall the social learning model. When the teacher applies the contract inconsistently, students learn that the implicit rules in the class include arbitrary teacher subjectivity (Doyle, 2006). They find that what and why consequences are implemented is not so much about the contract as it is about the unpredictable desires of the teacher. The result is a shift in locus of control away from the students to the external agent: the teacher. Of course, subjectivity and discretion will always be a reality, but when the students see variation in consequence implementation resulting from laziness, favoritism, unpredictable moods, retaliation, weakness, or just careless randomness, they lose some faith in the integrity of the social contract (Doyle, 2006).

Eventually most students will understand that there may be a need for exceptions and variation because students have different needs, and to best help the collective, the teacher must take each learner's specific circumstances into account. But no matter how noble the intentions, it will be difficult for many students to interpret differential treatment as anything other than inconsistency.

REFLECTION

10.4

In your judgment, when is it better for the teacher to be uniform in consequence implementation, and when is it fairer and more effective to fit the consequence to the situation and needs of the particular student?

Examining Privacy, Proximity, and Group Consequences

When you intervene with one student privately, your interaction is between that student and you alone. When you intervene with a student publicly, you include an audience and all that that implies. Privacy requires proximity (Curwin & Mendler, 1986; Wubbles, Brekelmans, Brok, & Tartwijk, 2006). When implementing a consequence to one or more students, be physically close to the students, and speak in a private tone. It may be useful to bend down to the student's level so as to reduce your position of dominance. The power of the event will come from the fulfillment of your job in the equation by holding the student accountable, not in any display of your toughness.

Students learn most lessons indirectly. They infer what will happen to them in a future situation by what they observe happening to another student in the same situation. There is a temptation to use the public dimension of an intervention with one student or group to send a message to the whole class. The logic goes something like this: if the rest of the students in the class see this student receiving a consequence, they will understand that the same fate could be theirs. When it comes to positive consequences, this is pretty useful logic. If a student is making a good effort, we recognize it; if a student needs help, we give them support; and if a student is risking sharing an idea, it can be very empowering to show publicly that we will validate the effort and the risk. But when we use a public context for implementing contract violations, we bring shame and embarrassment into the equation. This can seem inconsequential to us, because the interaction often feels the same from our perspective. But to students, public penalties hurt and can be experienced as attacks on their dignity (Elias & Schwab, 2006). And even if the public consequence does not produce much negative emotion, the public shaming component shifts the focus of the consequence from a natural and related outgrowth of the social contract to a weapon wielded by the teacher. Possessing the power of this weapon can make us feel influential, but giving in to the power trip will undermine our authority, the legitimacy of the social contract, and students' dignity in the long term (Watson & Ecken, 2003).

REFLECTION

10.5

Recall teachers you have had or seen who liked to publicly flex their "teacher power" and give public consequences or punishments. What effects did you observe it had on the class over time?

Group Contingencies as a Consequence

When a whole group contingency is imminent, individual students will feel an incentive (peer pressure) to act in a manner that benefits the collective (Robinson & Ricord Griesemer, 2006; Skinner, Cashwell, & Dunn, 1996). If all members of a group are put in a position in which something needs to be done (perform a task, exhibit a behavior, or refrain from a behavior, for example) or the entire group will be unable to meet its goal, each member will feel the weight of the whole as they consider their actions.

One typical example of the use of this principle is when a teacher says to the class, "Everyone needs to clean up their desks before anyone can go." In this situation, the pressure each individual student feels as a result of this arrangement is likely more related to the desires and expectations of classmates than those of the teacher. The teacher has essentially used the power of a social mechanism, peer pressure, to motivate individual students to behave in a collectively beneficial manner.

Following are some other examples of the deliberate use of peer pressure:

- The teacher looks for "ready groups" or groups that are demonstrating by their behavior that they are ready, given a prescribed characterization of "ready" clarified at an earlier time.

- The teacher stops and waits for individual students to listen and get on task. In this case, the message is that the group has to wait for an individual or two, so those individuals need to attend not only because of the expectation but also because the progress of the entire group is contingent on their actions.

These types of consequences can have a great deal of power and can be carried out relatively efficiently. As a result, they are attractive for a lot of reasons. We do need to distinguish between times they are working to support our long-term goals and times they are creating unwanted outcomes (Skinner et al., 1996).

10.6 **REFLECTION**

Consider teachers you have seen who have used a great deal of peer pressure and group contingency to motivate the students in their classes. Was it effective? Why or why not? How did it make you feel?

When Group Contingencies Are a Good Idea

- The stakes are small. A small loss of time will not have a lasting cost, but anything that affects grades, friendships, dignities, or material or learning outcomes should be avoided.

- It helps make an expectation more concrete and leads to more understanding and self-responsible behavior in the future. In other words, it is a good practice if you recognize that it is needed increasingly less over time.

When Group Contingencies Are Not Such a Good Idea

- They involve the same student repeatedly. When one student or small group of students repeatedly causes the group to pay a price, this can lead to the student's or group's becoming resented, marginalized, or having negative identity patterns encouraged.

- It is clearly not working to motivate better behavior or has become a crutch the teacher uses to obtain the desired behavior. If the students do not see and agree to the need for the behavior, it will be just a gimmick at best and at worst will lead to resentment toward the teacher or dependency on a threat condition to obtain responsible behavior.

- The majority of students feel that they are being coerced rather than challenged. This again can lead to resentment toward the teacher.

REFLECTION 10.7

Consider the costs associated with giving up some amount of group cohesion or the quality of your relationships with your students for higher levels of efficiency. This is not always the result when we use group contingencies, but it can be. When would you make this trade? How much sense of comfort would you trade for more efficiency and a feeling of accountability? Reflect on your answer related to the idea of what promotes a success psychology in the classroom.

For example, if we find that quite a few students in the class did not treat the lesson materials very well (in spite of being given a clear expectation of how they were to treat the materials beforehand) and we withhold those materials for a couple of days from the whole class, this can be an effective consequence. It demonstrates active follow-through. It also demonstrates a clear cause-and-effect relationship: respect the materials and you can use them; don't and you will have to wait to try again later. But if the penalty is the result of a few of the same students on a repeated basis, an implementation of group consequence becomes much less desirable (Robinson & Ricord Griesemer, 2006; Skinner et al., 1996). The majority of the class feels penalized for the actions of a few and can develop a growing resentment for them and a loss of trust in the teacher's sense of fairness.

The most telling evidence of the fact that group contingency is being effective is often expressions on students' faces when you make your request. Is it a sense of urgency and playfulness, or discomfort and impatience? If you see resentment emerging as a result of the practice, stop what you have been doing and try something else. In most cases, it is not worthwhile to trade the emotional quality in the class for more efficiency.

Delivering a Consequence to an Individual Contract Violation

As we examine the notion of how best to implement consequences, recognize that problems do not all come in the same size and shape. Table 10.2 describes three levels of student behavior problems and offers potential logical consequences for each. Level I problems are a result of student forgetfulness or lack of effort. Level II problems reflect deeply conditioned patterns of dysfunction or the rejection of the social contract. Level III problems reflect behavioral problems rooted in physiological dysfunctions.

In this chapter, we focus primarily on level Ib types of problems. These are the most common and involve most students at one time or another. In Chapter Fourteen, we explore levels II and III types of problems and how to deal with them.

Curwin and Mendler (1986) offer three pieces of advice when it comes to delivering the message to a student who has violated the contract: simply state the consequence, be firm and anger-free, and use a soft voice. On the surface, they all appear to be common sense. But the power of these ideas lies primarily in what they instruct us not to do. Since the social contract is fundamentally about each participant's commitment to an agreement, adding anything other than facts shifts the focus from the agreement (and locus of control) to the teacher (external

TABLE 10.2. **Levels of Classroom Behavior Problems and Examples**

	Description	Classroom Example	Potential Logical Consequence
Level Ia	A student or class displays a form of dysfunctional behavior that will likely become steadily more problematic if ignored.	Students failing to give another student 100 percent attention when appropriate.	Stop the class and ask the students to give the student their full attention. Ask the student to start over. (See Chapter Six for material related to technical management.)
Level Ib	Student actions that violate the classroom rules or social contract. Typically rooted in forgetfulness, lack of understanding, or carelessness.	Student carelessly leaves a mess at a work station.	The student is asked to clean up before moving on to the next thing.
Level IIa	Students knowingly reject their commitment to the social contract in words or actions. Typically rooted in defiance, a desire for power, or a cry for help.	Student refuses to clean up his or her area or deliberately continues to talk when the expectation is to be attentive to the speaker.	Remind students they are not part of the class until they can demonstrate a commitment to the social contract. The student may be required to complete and commit to an individual behavior contract. (See Chapter Fourteen.)
Level IIb	Students exhibit dysfunctional behavior on a regular basis. Typically rooted in a deeply conditioned pattern of thinking and ego defense.	Student tends to disrupt the work of other group members any time the task seems too challenging in an attempt to meet needs for competence and power or student exhibits a compulsive need for attention.	The student is brought to recognize the pattern (negative identity pattern) with the teacher's help. Demonstrate progress and commitment to the social contract, and potentially complete and follow an individual behavioral contract. (See Chapter Fifteen.)
Level III	Students experience a struggle with their behavior and have a biological or organic basis for their lack of self-control (for example, attention deficit hyperactivity disorder).	Student struggles to attend for long periods of time and feels a compulsive need to move and talk—even though he wishes he could attend and feels guilty that he cannot.	The student follows the plan laid out in his or her individualized education program and personal behavioral contract.

agent) and weakens the relationship. Adding a little guilt, shame, or lecturing or putting the behavior into a generalized context such as "this is the third time you have done this," or "if you keep doing this . . ." is not only unhelpful, but detracts from the power of the lesson. Although it may feel natural and common and our parents and teachers may have used this method, resist the temptation to add anything to the basic message that the student made the choice to violate the agreement and now must accept the consequence for that choice.

REFLECTION   10.8

Recall the last time you (or another teacher) were in the position to deliver a consequence (discipline a student). Did you or that teacher refrain from adding to the consequence with guilt, shame, or a lecture? In your assessment, why is it that we find it so difficult not to add something to the equation?

What Constitutes a Successful Implementation?

Keep in mind what you are trying to accomplish as you move to implement a consequence. First, the event should help strengthen the student's internal locus of control. That is, the student should feel that his choice is the cause and the consequence is the logical effect. Second, the student should maintain a sense that he needs to be responsible for the group, and making different choices in the future is not only possible but good for the entire group. Third, you should walk away having opened the door to the student's own internal reasoning process. You cannot make him learn a lesson. You cannot tell him he did learn a lesson. But you can do your job and trust the process and the student's sense of reason to result in his healthier choices in the future.

REFLECTION   10.9

Recollect the discussion of the construct for a psychology of success in Chapter Eight. When delivering a consequence, you might ask yourself, "Am I taking the opportunity to have a transformative influence on this student by promoting her psychology of success, or am I simply giving her what she deserves?"

You may see signs that behavior will likely not change in the future. For example, a student who is acting highly repentant and projects a shameful affect is likely to leave the interaction without having learned a lesson that will lead to long-term behavior change. This may be an unfamiliar notion, but as you examine the student's thinking more closely, you see that she is caught up in the "sorry game" instead of thinking of ways to do better next time. Second, the student has difficulty accepting ownership and projects an external locus of control. The student gets overly fixated on a perception of you as unfair, wondering why you are picking on her, and focusing excessively on the personal aspect of the event. It is likely that this student is used to punishments and will translate your clear cause-and-effect consequence language into your punishing her. To help this and similar other students grow and become better members of the community, you need to help them with their cause-and-effect processing, approach them with unconditional positive regard, gently help them understand that your intention is not to make them feel bad and that consequences are not personal, and that you are sincerely and steadfastly behind their efforts to make thoughtful choices.

STEP-BY-STEP CONSEQUENCE IMPLEMENTATION EXAMPLES

This section presents two cases in which students violate the social contract—one from an elementary level context and the other at the secondary level. Each case presents the student's behavior, the existing agreement from the social contract, and an effective step-by-step implementation of the consequence.

Elementary Level

Case: Interfering with others during a learning activity

Social contract agreement: "We give our attention to those speaking and keep our hands to ourselves when we are on the carpet. If we need to speak, we raise our hands. The consequence for failing to do so is removal from the activity. If the problem is chronic: an individual behavioral contract."

Student behavior: A teacher is leading a lesson as the students sit on the carpet. Liko is not listening and is touching and trying to engage other students near him.

Teacher intervention: For mild cases in which students simply appear to be fidgety or distracted and have lost focus (level I problems), it may be most efficient and helpful to use a combination of eye contact and a clarifying statement or clarifying question. For example, you may stop (an active consequence), give Liko a second to recognize that he is violating the contract, and then resume your lesson after you get active recognition that he understands and is ready to be more responsible (for example, he stops and demonstrates attentive behavior). You may also use a clarifying statement such as, "We all need to have our eyes up here right now" or "We are all giving José our undivided attention. José, could you start over, and we will all do a better job of listening this time?" Or you could use a clarifying question such as, "What would it look like if we were all doing a great job of listening right now?" or "Are we all listening like pumas right now?" Use a positive tone and avoid glaring at the student. As we discussed in Chapter Six, avoid all negative recognitions such as, "Liko, I need you to stop talking and pay attention." Negative recognitions may feel occasionally necessary at the beginning of the year, but eliminate them from your language quickly and completely. You will be surprised at how you do not miss them.

Who Owns the Social Contract?

The social contract is not intended to corral students or offer short-term solutions. It is intended to change awareness and patterns of responsible behavior. So solutions such as proximity alone, or what Jones (2000) refers to as "camping out," will most often stop the behavior in the short term, but it will send the message that the teacher is the police and no one should misbehave around him (as well as result in the need for an increase of the same intervention in the future). Also, the technique of using personal recognitions (discussed in Chapter Six) such as the phrase, "I like the way Hanna is listening right now," will have a limited and confusing effect and will lose power over time. It may be useful to ask yourself periodically "Are my interventions encouraging students to take ownership of their social contract, or are they mostly still about using my authority to keep them in line?"

Assume this is the beginning of the year and Liko is still learning how to be a functional part of a group. You may want to give him a break due to what may be a lack of understanding of the expectation. If it is not the beginning of the year, you may want to omit the warnings and move straight to the consequence. If eye contact and clarifications get the result you need, you should then make private and personal contact with the student. Subtly and without drawing the attention of the other students, you need to get close to Liko and help him understand the expectation and the consequences. You might say, "Liko, what is the expectation when we are all on the carpet?" There is no need to include any negative language. Liko may need some help, but at some point you need to hear him correctly state the expectation. Then ask him what the consequence is, which has been agreed to in the social contract, for failing to be self-responsible during time on the carpet. If he does not know, remind him (and again, not knowing is a defense that needs to be sincere and in any event cannot be used long). Warnings and reminders send the message, "I will assume that you did not understand what you did, and from now on, after this warning, you will." If this is the case, you might say to Liko, "So Liko, when I look back here later, what am I going to see?" Liko states the expected behavior. "And what is the consequence if you aren't able to show me that you can be a responsible part of the group?" Again, Liko needs to state the consequence. At that point you can smile genuinely at Liko and then shift your attention back to the group. You do not want to hover or get caught up in anticipation of what Liko is going to do. You need to be in the moment and let Liko make his choice.

In most cases, eye contact and clarifying recognitions do the trick. When that does not work, making personal contact and reminding the student of the expectation will take care of most problems. But you need to provide meaningful and related consequences that fit the severity of the situation. If you look back and see Liko talking to his neighbor, do not repeat the more subtle consequences such as eye contact. You asked Liko to act responsibly. He told you that he understood and was committed to fulfilling his responsibility. His behavior now demonstrates that he made a choice to violate his agreement. Therefore, the time for warnings and group consequences has passed and you move on to the next level of consequence.

Now Liko has lost his opportunity to be part of the group. Approach him and privately, speaking softly and plainly, tell him in so many words, "Liko, I just observed you talking to your neighbor. What was the consequence that we agreed to when one of us does that?" (Let Liko answer.) "That's right, so since you chose to talk, I want you to sit by yourself at your seat while we continue here on the carpet. Can you do that? Do you understand why? [Wait for recognition.] And when we are on the carpet tomorrow, you will have another chance to show that you can listen and keep your hands to yourself."

It is important in this case that you send the message to the rest of the class that you put your energy into those who are choosing to be responsible. If students see you putting a great deal of attention into Liko, those who are seeking attention may (usually unconsciously) conclude that misbehaving is a good way to get it. At some point during the transition to the next activity, send a quick private message to Liko: "Thanks for sitting quietly. I know that you will be able to do better next time."

REFLECTION   10.10

As you read the intervention, where is the locus of control? If you are Liko and have been asked to sit out of the activity, who do you feel is responsible for what has just happened? What would you guess Liko is thinking in terms of the choices that he intends to make in the future?

Secondary Level

Case: Abuse of the pencil sharpening privilege

Social contract agreement: "In this class, we use the pencil sharpener when absolutely necessary and do not disturb others when we sharpen. The agreed-on consequence is loss of opportunity to use the sharpener."

Student behavior: During one period, Nara makes three trips to the pencil sharpener at a time when students are expected to be concentrating on independent work. She also takes the opportunity to make distracting comments to some of her friends and other receptive students along the way.

Teacher intervention: If you interpret that the expectation is weak and that most students do not assume that there is any problem with using the sharpener multiple times in a period, you may want to take the opportunity to clarify the expectation and remind the class of the consequence. This is especially useful at the beginning of the year. A reminder is not a consequence, but you may need to take responsibility this time for a poorly understood expectation.

However, if the consequence is clear and well understood, you implement the consequence. If you feel Nara is in need of some help adjusting to the expectation, a personal reminder may help; however, reminders should be used sparingly as students get more mature and familiar with the social contract in your class. So let's assume this is not early in the year, and Nara should be clear about the expectation.

You approach Nara and create a private interaction. You may choose to make eye contact with her to show seriousness and sincerity, or you may want to let her drop her gaze to the desk and speak to a spot on the desk.

Eye Contact and Culture

Culturally eye contact can be problematic. It can make students feel threatened or disrespectful to be forced to look you in the eye. Try to become aware of what works with your students; it will probably be a variety of behaviors.

Speaking in a soft tone, try to help Nara see the cause and effect between her choices and why you are talking to her now. It is typically effective to ask her, "What is the expectation regarding sharpening pencils during class?" Depending on her answer, you may need to help her recall when the expectation was discussed and that she was present when the class agreed to the expectation and the consequence. Then simply state the consequence. You might say something such as, "What I saw was you making the choice to use the sharpener for entertainment; it distracted the other students and violated your agreement to them and our social contract. Therefore, the consequence is the loss of the use of the sharpener for the rest of the week. I can loan you a pen today if you give it back at the end of the period. And next week before you get to use the sharpener, I need you to assure me that you are going to take your commitment seriously." You may also add a final thought to the effect: "I know that you are a great kid, and I believe that you can do well."

In this scenario, it will be important to help Nara recognize that most of the interactions that you have with her are positive and most of the consequences in the class are too. So you may want to catch her doing something well and offer a positive recognition. Both public and private positive recognitions will have power as long as they are sincere. You may also realize that some of the responsibility for a student's desire to use a trip to the pencil sharpener to meet his or her basic needs for fun and belonging rests with your choice of instructional strategy. Too much independent work is going to lead to such problems.

10.11   REFLECTION

Ask yourself an honest question. If you were Nara's teacher, have you moved on from the situation when you walk away from Nara? Are you in the moment and present to the rest of the class, and will you maintain your positive expectation for Nara and respect her choices in the future?

Dealing with Bargaining, Pleading, and Whining

In the development of the social contract, bargaining can be healthy. As events arise where the students and the teacher recognize that a new expectation, rule, or procedure may be in the best interest of the collective, negotiating revisions to the contract or class expectations can be valuable (Bluestein, 1999). These are proactive, democratically developed changes.

Nevertheless, it is rarely a good idea to bargain after the fact with a student who is trying to make a deal to avoid a consequence. For example, either Nara or Liko may try to talk their way out of accepting the agreed-on consequence. In such a situation, one of them might respond, "Sorry, Ms. Brooke. I really am; I promise I won't do it again, really." Part of you may be tempted to say, "Okay, I can see you are repentant and basically a good kid. Just don't do it again." This may seem rather harmless or inconsequential, but it is not. The result is a degradation of the contract, a loss of respect for you and your role as leader, and a greater likelihood that the behavior will reoccur. And when it does, you will likely encounter an even greater intensity of bargaining and whining. This is because it has now worked once—the use of the strategy has been reinforced. Conversely, if you hold fast and follow through, it may feel as though the student is upset at you and could exhibit revenge behavior in the future. This might happen in a small number of cases, but if you are fair and your consequences are proactive, logical, and well understood, the result will almost always be that the student returns with a higher level of respect for you and will be less likely to bargain or repeat the choice.

REFLECTION

10.12

Have you ever told students no when they made a request for something that you had clearly let them know they could not do or have and seen the look of resentment in their eyes as they walked away? When they came back, was the look still there? You may have assumed that they would hold it against you, but did they? Did they respect you more or less in the future? What is your explanation for this?

When a Student Says No to You and the Contract

The more consistent you are, the clearer and more related the consequences are, and the more carefully implemented the consequences are in a way that preserves students' dignity, the more you will get a decreasing amount of bargaining, whining, excuses, and contract violations (Wang & Anderson, 1994). However, the possibility will always exist that a student says no to the contract and thus raises the problem to level II. Then your response needs to reflect the new level of the problem. As we will discuss in more detail in Chapter Thirteen when examining conflict resolution and power struggles, the contract cannot maintain its integrity if some students in the class deliberately disrespect it. A student has the choice to say no to the contract, but the choice leaves him outside the community until he chooses to reaffirm his commitment to the collective by way of behavior and living up to the agreement. You will never have to fear a student's saying no if you keep in mind that all you can do is offer choices to students and encourage their success. You cannot make students' choices for them.

STUDENT RESPONSIBILITY

It is difficult to conceive of a more important aspect of the job of teacher or parent than promoting a sense of responsibility in young people. Responsibility is basic to a psychology of success and being a member of a democratic society, and it is critical to achievement in and beyond school (Bluestein, 2005; Elias & Schwab, 2006; Watson & Ecken, 2003). Talent and intelligence are valuable, but more essential to students' happiness and success in life will be the degree to which they take responsibility for their thoughts and actions. The patterns that students develop have a powerful effect in shaping their destinies and determining the degree to which they become responsible adults.

10.13   REFLECTION

Do you know anyone you would consider highly irresponsible yet happy and achieving his or her potential? Do you know anyone who may not have been the smartest person in the class but today is happy and successful? Would you say this person is responsible?

At the root of a responsible attitude is acceptance—acceptance of our reality, acceptance that our thoughts will manifest themselves in behavior, and acceptance that we are the authors of our own fate. There is a great temptation to resist what is. Our minds, in desire for relief from discomfort, become skilled at the practice of denial, making excuses, shifting responsibility, and taking on the role of victim. If being responsible were easy, we would see more people demonstrate it. But it is difficult and takes a lot of practice and a lot of support from others, especially those entrusted to teach.

In an effort to operationalize the broad notion of responsibility, we can begin by breaking it down to its essential factors. These are the building blocks of responsibility:

- *A sense of cause and effect.* We recognize that what we choose to do will have consequences and what we think will manifest itself in our actions. Like the law of the conservation of energy, there is a natural law that what we think and do matters and will cause effects to come into our experience.

- *An internal locus of control.* If we see ourselves as the authors of our fate, we have the capacity to be intentional and become what we choose. Research in human behavior demonstrates a consistent relationship between one's level of internal locus of control and the degree of personal responsibility one exhibits (Chubb, Fertman, & Ross, 1997; Elias & Schwab, 2006).

- *The social frame.* The working social frame defined by the relationship between freedom and responsibility is essential to any functioning social environment (class, family, team, group) and fundamental to promoting responsibility. It sets out a clear agreement that the young person who demonstrates a sufficient level of responsibility has earned more rights and freedoms. Those who do not demonstrate it must wait until they show the necessary responsibility to earn those freedoms.

- *Making choices and learning from the consequences of those choices.* Most of this learning occurs naturally, but it can also include consequences that are manufactured within a situation, such as a classroom with a social contract (Doyle, 2006).

- *Being in the moment.* Responsible thinking is not rooted in the past or what may be in the future. It is grounded in what's important now.

Conversely, some factors can be considered responsibility destroyers:

- *An attitude of blame.* When we blame, we fixate on the past and an external cause.

- *A victim mind-set.* When our thinking goes to "poor me," we lose not only a clear sense of cause and effect with regard to the past, but in essence toss the law of responsibility out the window. We make the psychological trade in which we give up power and an opportunity for growth to get (temporary) pain relief.

- *Making excuses.* When we make excuses, we essentially externalize the cause and effect of the situation (Butler & Wittenbaum, 2000).

- *An external locus of control.* Basic to a psychology of failure is the externalizing of the cause of one's fate or "fatalism." The external LOC views life as a series of accidents, and there is nothing that we can do or could have done. As we look closer at this mind-set, we see an effort to avoid guilt and ownership (Butler & Wittenbaum, 2000; Wang & Anderson, 1994).

MAKING EXCUSES

If you deal with many students, you will find that some are constantly making excuses and others almost never do. The student's age, gender, cultural background, or learning style seem to make no difference when it comes to excuse making. So why do students make excuses? There are three primary reasons (Butler & Wittenbaum, 2000; Wang & Anderson, 1994): avoidance of guilt and an attempt to protect their self-image; a perceived benefit within the context or a desire to manage the impressions of others; or a practical response to achieving a desired result, for example, to potentially improve a desired outcome.

Protecting One's Self-Image and Feelings of Guilt

When students will not admit to themselves that they forgot their work, said the hurtful words, or made the mistake because they do not see themselves as the kind of person who would do something like that, they experience inner conflict such as cognitive dissonance (Butler & Wittenbaum, 2000)—in other words, "Only a dumb, irresponsible, or bad person would have done that, and I am not any of those."

An environment that promotes a success psychology will reduce students' inclination to make excuses on all levels. In this case, creating an environment in which making mistakes is acceptable will go a long way. Moreover, as you focus more on process and mastery than on a fixed view of ability, students will see choices as opportunities to learn rather than events that define who they are. In a success psychology environment, students increasingly adopt an attitude of self-acceptance and progressively release an attitude of ego management and shame.

The Context Encourages It

If the social environment is hostile and students are put down for making mistakes or blamed for things that they do, they will learn that excuses are a valuable tool for protecting their reputation and ego (Wang & Anderson, 1994).

To support less excuse making and blame in the classroom, create a "blame-free-zone" classroom. Encourage all students to take responsibility for everything for which they are even remotely accountable. Do not accept victim language from any student. Do not ask for excuses or put students in situations in which they must save face. Moreover, keep in mind that the most powerful lessons you can teach your students about responsible thoughts and action will come from modeling them.

An Excuse Would Help Secure a Desirable Outcome

When you say to the student who is late to class, "So, Alton, why are you late?" or "This better be good," you are saying that a good excuse will work as a substitute for being on time (or whatever the expectation was in the situation). When you ask for excuses, you encourage students to make them.

To promote fewer student excuses and more responsible behavior. first do not ask for excuses. Instead, build in ways in which students are held accountable. For example, give the students three bathroom passes or homework passes or late passes at the beginning of the year to use as needed. Watch the students become very responsible about when they need to go to the restroom. When you build in room for mistakes and forgetfulness, you put the locus of control in the hands of the students. When you act as the judge of good and bad excuses, you take the locus of control away from them. When you ask for excuses, you train your students not only to be irresponsible, but to improve the skill of lying their way out of trouble.

Let students know that you are interested in what is going on in their lives, but that an excuse is not going to improve their situation. You trust them and believe in them, and therefore trust that they can problem-solve their way out of trouble or be mature enough to learn from what they did. You like your students so much you are going to give them the great gift of being responsible. You can be empathetic, and genuinely concerned, and even share stories of your own life lessons, but the emotional connection that you make with them is not a game. You are neither getting played by them nor taking joy in their "finally getting what they deserve" for being so careless or irresponsible. You are staying in the moment, being present to them, and on some level recognizing that this is a transformational event in which they have been given the gift of another step on their journey toward personal responsibility.

10.14 REFLECTION

Consider situations in which you felt the need to make excuses (or situations in which you still do). Which of these three reasons played the largest role in how you felt or what you did?

USING THE SOCIAL CONTRACT IN 1-STYLE AND 2-STYLE APPROACHES

A social contract is an effective tool within both the 1-Style and the 2-Style approaches. Used within the context of either style, it will lead to a decreasing number of contract violations and increasing sense of ease and fairness on the part of the students. However, it will operate somewhat differently in each case. At the beginning of the year, both styles rely heavily on demonstrating consistency and follow-through. While the teacher attempting a 1-Style approach must make a greater commitment to student involvement in the development process, teachers in both cases will need to take a strong leadership role early. Over time, the success of the teacher using the 2-Style will be determined by the degree to which he or she shows consistency and fairness in implementing the contract. In the 1-Style classroom, the teacher must make a greater effort to help students internalize the purpose underlying the contract and its principles (Watson & Battistich, 2006). The ownership of the contract is shifted to the members of the class society as a collective and away from the teacher as authority (Rogers & Freiburg, 1994). The locus of control for the contract (for example, responsible, healthy, considerate behavior) in the 2-Style classroom will rest primarily with the teacher. Throughout the term, students will see the teacher as the agent who keeps the class functioning effectively. The locus of control in the 1-Style classroom will shift over time to the students (Baker, Terry, Bridges, & Winsor, 1997; Rogers & Frieberg, 1994).

Why not test the boundaries of the contract? The primary reason that a student in a 2-Style classroom thinks, "Why not?" is related to the teacher: the student does not want to elicit a consequence. Eventually the main reason that a student in a 1-Style classroom thinks, "Why not?" is that he or she would be neglecting a commitment to classmates and diluting his or her own personal growth. While students in the 2-Style class will feel secure in the judgment that their teacher has the ability to maintain a functioning classroom, they will remain limited in their democratic participation skills and moral development as compared to students in the 1-Style classroom. Moreover, as students in the 1-Style classroom learn to take ownership for their classroom social contract, the foundation is being set for their development as a community, a topic we explore in more detail in Chapter Fifteen.

CONCLUSION

The social contract can be an instrument of coercion or empowerment depending on how you implement it. The better you are able to keep the focus on the contract rather than yourself, the more successful you will be. In the next chapter, we examine the relationship between management and instructional choices. Effective instruction can make your social contract feel like a safety net, whereas ineffective instructional practices will keep testing your social contract and keep you thinking about discipline rather than teaching.

Journal Reflections

1. What are your feelings at this stage in your reading regarding whether a 1- or 2-Style class is more for you? What are your criteria for making your decision?
2. What are three things that you would like to change in your management plan or your current practice as a result of your latest reading and reflection?

Activity

In this activity, you will take part in a role play involving a student who violates the social contract and the teacher who must implement a consequence. If you are part of a class, it will be useful to divide the scenarios among six groups. If you are not in a class, you may want to find a small group to help you with one of the role-play scenarios or write out your script on paper.

Directions: Your group is to create a lifelike role play between a teacher and one or more students. You are free to use whatever rationale you choose to inform your thinking, but try to base your intervention on the principles outlined in the chapter. Your task is to develop two situations: one where the behavior is dealt with ineffectively and the other in which the behavior is dealt with as effectively as you would consider possible. Take your job seriously. You may want to script your role play. Have fun with each, but you will likely find that the "what not to do" scene is more fun. Go for it! And before you begin the role play, it may help your audience if you provide them with a bit of background as to what has happened up until the point of your play in your hypothetical classroom.

Situation A: The students at one table keep talking to one another while you are trying to present material. What do you do?

Situation B: A reliable source tells you that at recess, one student hit another student, and the recess supervisor took no action (in fact, he never saw it). The students are just returning to the class. What do you do?

Situation C: You have students sitting in pods of four. At one table, one of the more fidgety students is pestering one of the other students at the table by taking things off her desk and staring at her paper. You have warned this student to stop, but the pestering has not lessened. What do you do?

Situation D: You are asking your class deeper-level questions to help them process a lesson you are teaching. One of your students is acting particularly silly, raising a hand and offering flippant and irresponsibly incorrect answers. What do you do?

Situation E: One of the students has just loudly discovered that her special pen is missing from her desk. Another one of your students has taken things in the past, but has always explained why it was just a misunderstanding. You saw this student playing with the pen earlier, before recess. What do you do?

Situation F: You are giving a test and see one of your students copying answers from a neighbor. It is obvious that she is trying to cheat. You have a rule against cheating in your class. What do you do?

Situation G: As you are lecturing, three girls in the class begin to pass a makeup set among one another and use it when they think you are not looking. What do you do?

Situation H: As you are teaching, a handful of students find themselves being pulled into a negative interaction. It starts small with a minor put-down, but soon grows as each student escalates the conflict with greater and more significant put-downs.

Here are two options to this activity:

Option 1: As a class, discuss what you think is effective or ineffective about each role play.

Option 2: Develop your scenario in writing, and share it with someone else for feedback.

REFERENCES

Baker, J., Terry, T., Bridges, R. & Winsor, A. (1997). Schools as caring communities: A relational approach to school reform. *School Psychology Review*, 26(4), 586–602.

Bluestein, J. (1999). *Twenty-first century discipline: Teaching students responsibility and self-management*. Belmont, CA: Fearon.

Burden, P. (2003). *Classroom management: Creating a successful learning community*. Hoboken, NJ: Wiley.

Butler, J. E., & Wittenbaum, G. M. (2000). Relationships between self-construal and verbal promotion. *Communication Research*, 27(6), 704–722.

Chubb, N., Fertman, C., & Ross, J. (1997). Adolescent self-esteem and locus of control: A longitudinal study of gender and age differences. *Adolescence*, 32, 113–129.

Curwin, R., & Mendler, A. (1986). *Discipline with dignity*. Alexandria, VA: Association of Supervision and Curriculum Development Press.

Doyle, W. (2006). Ecological approaches to classroom management. In C. M. Evertson & C. S. Weinstein (Eds.), *Handbook of classroom management* (pp. 97–126). Mahwah, NJ: Erlbaum.

Elias, M. J., & Schwab, Y. (2006). From compliance to responsibility: Social and emotional learning and classroom management. In C. M. Evertson & C. S. Weinstein (Eds.), *Handbook of classroom management* (pp. 309–341). Mahwah, NJ: Erlbaum.

Hines, C., Cruickshank, D., & Kennedy, J. (1985). Teacher clarity and its relationship to student achievement and satisfaction. *American Educational Research Journal*, 22, 87–99.

Jones, F. (2000). *Tools for teaching: Discipline, instruction, motivation*. Santa Cruz, CA: Jones Publishing.

Manke, M. P. (1997). *Classroom power relations: Understanding student-teacher interactions*. Mahwah, NJ: Erlbaum.

Osterman, K. F. (2000). Students' need for belonging in the school community. *Review of Educational Research*, 70(3), 323–367.

Robinson, S. L., & Ricord Griesemer, S. M. (2006). Helping individual students with problem behavior. In C. M. Evertson & C. S. Weinstein (Eds.), *Handbook of classroom management* (pp. 787–802). Mahwah, NJ: Erlbaum.

Rogers, C., & Freiburg, H. J. (1994). *Freedom to learn* (3rd ed.). Columbus, OH: Merrill.

Skinner, C., Cashwell, C., & Dunn, M. (1996). Independent and interdependent group contingencies: Smoothing the rough waters. *Special Services in the Schools*, *12*, 61–78.

Wang, D., & Anderson, N. (1994). Excuse-making and blaming as a function of internal-external locus of control. *European Journal of Social Psychology*, *24*, 295–302.

Watson, M., & Battistich, V. (2006). Building and sustaining caring communities. In C. M. Evertson & C. S. Weinstein (Eds.), *Handbook of classroom management* (pp. 253–279). Mahwah, NJ: Erlbaum.

Watson, M., & Ecken, L. (2003). *Learning to trust: Transforming difficult elementary classrooms through developmental discipline*. San Francisco. Jossey-Bass.

Weinstein, C. S. (2003). *Secondary classroom management: Lessons from research and practice* (2nd ed.). Needham Heights, MA: Allyn & Bacon.

Wubbles, T., Brekelmans, M., Brok, P., & Tartwijk, J. (2006). An interpersonal perspective on classroom management in secondary classrooms in the Netherlands. In C. M. Evertson & C. S. Weinstein (Eds.), *Handbook of classroom management* (pp. 1161–1191). Mahwah, NJ: Erlbaum.

4

Good Teaching Practices Lead to Good Management

11

Transformative Classroom Instruction and the Pedagogy-Management Connection

In This Chapter

- Exploring the sociopolitical foundations of instructional inequity
- Five key areas in which pedagogical choices affect management outcomes
- Teaching and managing students with different abilities and learning styles
- Examining the relationship between assessment and management
- Matching instructional and managerial styles

Your greatest asset in your effort to promote high-quality classroom management outcomes will be how and what you teach because classroom management and instruction are interrelated (Gettinger & Kohler, 2006; Munk & Repp, 1994). As depicted in Figure 11.1, what and how you teach, what and how you assess, and how you manage your class all systemically affect one another. When you perform effectively in one area, the other two benefit, and when you engage in practices that are ineffective in one area, the other two suffer as well (Munk & Repp, 1994).

Research into classroom effectiveness finds that in almost every case, classrooms with management, behavioral, and motivational problems tend to be characterized by the use of instructional strategies that fail to promote engagement or are insufficiently needs satisfying (Shindler, Jones, Taylor, & Cadenas, 2003). In fact, the problems that resulted from the use of certain instructional choices were highly predictable. Where certain kinds of problems were found, there were correlating teaching choices. In contrast, when the teacher used certain instructional techniques, disciplinary concerns fell dramatically. When the relationship between pedagogical choices and the types and quantity of management issues that teachers face was examined, it was evident that each pedagogical choice was either contributing to or undermining the ability of the teacher to accomplish his or her goals.

Making wise pedagogical choices can promote or hinder the ability to meet each of the following goals:

- *Reducing management problems.* Pedagogy that fails to meet students' basic needs leads to management problems. Engaging, satisfying, well-directed, meaningful instructional

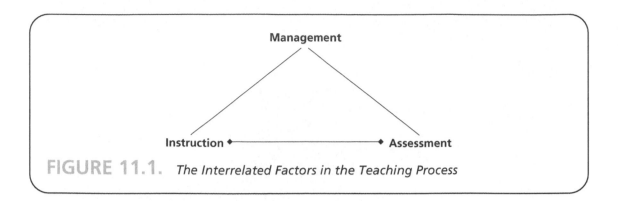

FIGURE 11.1.   *The Interrelated Factors in the Teaching Process*

activities can render misbehavior unnecessary (Gettinger, 1995; Gettinger & Kohler, 2006; Glasser, 1990; Shindler et al., 2003).

- *Promoting a psychology of success.* As discussed in Chapter Seven, each pedagogical action is either promoting or detracting from a student's psychology of success (internal locus of control, sense of acceptance and belonging, and growth-oriented orientation). Those that promote it will lead to a healthier classroom, and those that detract from it will lead to higher levels of dysfunction, behavioral problems, and student dropout (Hess, Well, Prindle, Liffman, & Kaplan, 1987; Shindler, 2003; Woods, 1995).

- *Acting as a transformative agent.* Each of us is being changed continuously by what and how we learn. In some cases, change is subtle, and in others, it is significant. For some, change leads to limiting beliefs or dysfunctional behavior. For others, it leads to empowerment and personal growth. What are your students learning in your classroom?

  - That knowledge is static and simply academic or is co-constructed and a source of power?

  - How to stick to thinking that is safe so as to protect their egos and narrow construct of what is familiar or how to take risks and develop an intrinsic love of learning?

  - To be resigned to a lot in life to which they feel they are limited or transcend their life circumstances and class barriers and become agents of change?

THE SOCIOPOLITICAL FOUNDATIONS OF INSTRUCTIONAL INEQUITY

It is no surprise that teaching practices vary greatly from school to school; however, it is remarkable just how much this variation is related to the socioeconomic status of the students in the school (Anyon, 1981; Duke, 2000; Hayes & Deyhle 2001). Anyon (1981) discovered that in a significant proportion of cases, the kind of teaching found in a school and the class of the students was correlated. In schools with children from working-class families, the work was characterized by an emphasis on following rules and directions and getting the task done. Conformity was encouraged, and there was little explanation for the purpose of work. Work was most often worksheet driven and did not promote critical thinking. In these schools, the emphasis was most commonly on rote and routine.

In schools with children from middle-class families, Anyon observed a greater emphasis on critical thinking; however, the purpose of learning was mostly defined by getting good grades and right answers. Students' interests were taken into account in the curriculum and management, but creativity was only somewhat encouraged.

In schools with children from affluent areas that Anyon referred to as "Affluent Professional" or "Executive Elite" schools, there was a much greater emphasis on student empowerment. Students were significantly involved in the decision-making process, and there was a deliberate attempt to make the learning meaningful and related to real life. Students' sense of self-responsibility and self-directedness were promoted. Management was defined more by reasoning than rules.

Typical Teaching Practices Found in Schools of Various Socioeconomic Levels

When Anyon (1981) examined the typical practices in various schools, she found the practices varied by the socioeconomic level of the school. She classified schools into four levels. The following practices were typical of those found at each of the levels.

Working Class Schools

- Emphasis on following directions
- Little explanation for purpose of work
- Worksheet driven
- Get task done rather than promote critical thinking
- Conformity
- Routine and rote preparation

Middle Class Schools

- Get right answers
- Get good grades
- Focus on text rather than student interests
- Little creativity
- Getting into college

Affluent Professional Schools

- Encourage student self-expression
- Apply learning to real life
- Negotiation between teacher and students
- Foster decision-making skills
- Promote a sense of responsibility for one's learning

Executive Elite Schools

- Develop analytical skills
- Make judgments about the best answer
- Independent project driven
- Reasoning instead of rules
- Promote self-directedness and self-confidence
- Preparation for life of leadership

Anyon (1981).

11.1 **REFLECTION**

Reflect on schools you have observed. Have you seen a relationship between the socioeconomic status of the students and the curriculum and instruction at the school? How would you explain your findings?

Use your notes on this reflection for activity 1 at the end of the chapter.

When presented with the findings of this research, few of my students are surprised, yet their reactions vary. Many react with resentment and indignation. Occasionally students deny the validity of the research. Quite often students who have experienced what Anyon characterizes as a working-class education feel that they were penalized educationally as a result of growing up in less-affluent areas. Consequently this leads to the tendency to assign blame. One could say that there is a lot of blame to go around (society, the economic system, parents, policymakers, and so forth).

Although the political implications of this research are profound and incendiary, few of us in the teaching profession are in a position to make wholesale changes to the systemic realities that contribute to inequity in schools. Nonetheless, we are in a position to change the lives of those in our classes. We can change the equation for the students with whom we come in contact daily by what and how we teach. In fact, we are the most powerful factor in the equation and are determining the future of our students by our pedagogical choices.

THE PEDAGOGY-MANAGEMENT CONNECTION

Each quarter, the first thing I do with my students during the class meeting dealing with the relationship between pedagogy and management is ask them to take a few minutes and (from their experience) fill in the blank in the following sentence: "Teachers who do _____ (pedagogically) have fewer management problems."

The ideas generated are consistently valid and insightful. This is no surprise, given that most of us can recall teachers who, because of how and what they taught, experienced few management problems. Conversely, we can usually remember more than a few teachers who because of their instructional style and choices found themselves dealing regularly with management issues. As you read this chapter, you may recognize practices that these enviable and unenviable role models used.

11.2 **REFLECTION**

From your observations, what instructional choices lead to fewer management problems? It may be helpful to recall teachers you have observed who have been so successful at getting students to learn that their classes have fewer than average discipline issues, as well as teachers who as a result of how they teach seem to have more discipline issues than most. Save your answers for activity 2 at the end of the chapter.

Teachers who produce effective learning outcomes also produce a desirable effect on classroom management and discipline. These practices can be separated into the following five key areas:

1. Effectiveness of lesson preparation, organization, and mechanics
2. Level of student engagement

3. Clarity of learning targets

4. Degree to which investing in the process has value and incentive for students

5. Degree to which the curriculum is relevant and meaningful to students

Effectiveness of Lesson Preparation, Organization, and Mechanics

Much of your success as a teacher will be related to your effectiveness with the many practical aspects of managing a lesson (Gettinger & Kohler, 2006; Good & Brophy, 2000; Harris, 1998). Difficulties with these small things can add up to substantial problems. Kounin (1970), in his examination of effective teachers, noticed that those who used certain instructional strategies had fewer incidents of misbehavior and that most misbehavior was the result of poor teacher planning and execution. He concluded from his research that it was better to be proactive than reactive when it came to classroom management.

Kounin identified areas in the technical act of teaching that contributed to more or fewer behavioral problems. One of the fundamental qualities that he observed in good teachers was what he termed "with-it-ness," in other words, being aware of what was going on in the class, or even having metaphorical eyes in the back of their head. If you are one of those who feels lacking in with-it-ness (you think that you miss social cues and are often unaware of the moods or mischief in the room), you may find teaching more frustrating than you originally conceived. However, you can be successful if you learn to develop the skills related to technical management (see Chapter Five) and effective lesson management described here.

REFLECTION

11.3

Reflect on your level of with-it-ness. Would you say that you have a great deal of it—that is, a good sense of what is going on even though unseen? Or do you often miss the cues and moods in the class? Some degree of with-it-ness is related to intentional factors, and some portion is innate and related to difference in processing styles. All teachers can be highly successful. However, whereas those teacher with more natural with-it-ness may find management a relatively natural skill, others may need to accept that it will take a bit more intention and skill development.

Kounin (1970) found that teachers who were most successful were effective in their management of the technical aspects of the lesson: maintaining the students' attention, using cues to alert the group to necessary information, and fostering accountability throughout the class, for example. He also found that teachers who were able to manage lesson mechanics had fewer problems. He broke this area into four skills:

- Overlapping—the skill of being able to attend to two or more things at once

- Managing movement—the skill of creating effective transitions and procedures

- Momentum—the ability to keep the lesson flowing without stops and starts, disruptions, or discontinuity

- Smoothness—the ability to create ease and clarity in the lesson and avoid jerkiness and confusion

Kounin found that an effectively orchestrated lesson led to more on-task behavior and less misbehavior resulting from student frustration and confusion. In addition, an effectively managed lesson makes the statement that the teacher cares and takes his or her role as the classroom leader seriously. So while on the practical level a well-managed lesson promotes efficiency, on an affective level, it promotes the bond between the teacher and students.

When reflecting on teachers whose pedagogy contributed to fewer management problems, you probably found that they exhibited some common skills and intentions. Teachers you judged to be highly effective lesson managers were most likely consistently prepared and tuned into the class, and they had effective strategies for dealing with lesson momentum and timing.

Be Prepared. Preparation does not ensure success, but it certainly makes it more probable (Good & Brophy, 2000; Munk & Repp, 1994). Teachers who are ill prepared or are asked to teach with a limited opportunity to prepare often experience a disproportionate number of management problems (Munk & Repp, 1994).

It would be nice if this were not the case. Time is difficult to find in the teaching profession, and finding the motivation to prepare is often challenging. Yet common sense, as well as the misery experienced as a result of those days in which we tried to wing it unsuccessfully, tells us that taking the time to prepare is worthwhile. Reflect on how you act when you are less prepared. Commonly those who are less prepared act more tentatively, use more words, pause to think more often, experience and project indecisiveness, change their mind more often, and are more likely to project weakness and fear. The result is what Kounin refers to as a lack of smoothness and momentum.

11.4 REFLECTION

Recall situations in which you have been asked to teach or present when you were not prepared. How did you feel? What was the pervasive emotion? Also, recall where your awareness tended to go. Was it more focused on yourself (self-consciousness) than usual?

Be Tuned In and Aware. Bring to mind the image of a master teacher you have observed. Where would you judge his or her attention to be: on the lesson, himself or herself, or the students? In most cases, master teachers are tuned in and aware of their students. It is very natural and common for new teachers to put their focus on the lesson plan and teach the lesson. But it is possible to be successful in teaching the lesson and fail to teach the students (Daly, Martens, Kilmer, & Masie, 1996; Wang, Haertel, & Walberg, 1993). Sticking to the plan may be effective in many cases, but to be successful requires teaching students rather than lessons. You should shift your awareness to what the students are doing, thinking, and feeling. Focusing more on learning outcomes and looking for evidence that those outcomes are being accomplished rather than thinking about where you are in your plan is a helpful mind-set, It is especially useful for student teachers and novice teachers to develop the intention to move their awareness outward while staying grounded inside.

Worrying about what the students think about you or being too slavish to the lesson plan will cause you to miss the essential reality in the class. In other words, you will be more successful when you are in the moment, present to your students.

11.5 REFLECTION

Reflect on where your awareness is located when you are confident and comfortable, and alternatively where it is when you feel threatened and insecure. What you are likely to recognize is that your awareness was located in very different places in each case. When we are confident and comfortable, we feel a sense of internal peace that allows us to be present and attentive. When we are threatened, our awareness stays outside ourselves on the perceived threat and draws us into a distressed and egocentric internal dialogue. As a result, when we feel threatened, we are likely to create a distorted and limited perception of what is around us. We should strive to promote a core of peace that will better lead to our ability to be open and attentive to that around us.

Promote Lesson Momentum and Timing. When you are aware, you are better able to read your students and promote lesson momentum (Doyle, 2006; Gump, 1974; Kounin, 1970). Ask yourself frequently whether students have reached what Kounin (1970) refers to as "satiation." Has your snappy lesson become stale? Have you asked students to take in too many details? Are you moving too fast and causing frustration? Ask questions, and read the students' body language; work to recognize when they are getting bored or frustrated, or are ready to move on. If these signals are present, you ignore them at your peril. If you absolutely must continue with a task that is causing boredom or frustration, let the students know that you recognize their emotional state and that there is a legitimate need to continue and when they can expect the task will be complete. But requesting that students deny their basic needs should be done sparingly, because it requires a withdrawal from the emotional bank account you hold with them.

Certain types of instructional methodologies lend themselves to greater likelihood of momentum problems (Gettinger & Kohler, 2006; Shindler, 2003). Recall the discussion in Chapter Six related to psychological movement. Lessons that contribute to the students' success psychology (internal locus of control, sense of belonging and acceptance, and growth-oriented orientation) will possess a sense of movement and momentum as they tap into internal sources of motivation.

REFLECTION

11.6

Imagine that a teacher has come to you for advice. He likes to teach courses in an exclusively lecture and test format because he feels that is the best way to accomplish his content outcomes. Yet he admits that he struggles with classroom management and that his students are frequently bored and restless, not to mention achieving poorly. He does not want to change how he teaches, but he wants his students to be motivated and well behaved. What advice would you give?

For many of us, especially new teachers, managing time is a challenging part of the job. It is not easy, but predicting how long an activity will last does become easier with experience. In general, it is better not to fight the clock but let your learning goals guide your decision making related to time. In addition, it is essential to be prepared for the potential situations that may arise. Being ready for anything will make time your friend. Having answers to the following questions in mind before you begin teaching a lesson will help you prepare:

- *What is the essential material or learning outcome in the lesson?* It is useful to have a sense of the learning goals that "must happen," "should happen," and "would be nice if they happened (but are less critical)." You will face countless situations in which you recognize that time is limited and you will have to cut something. Identify your priorities beforehand.

- *What should students do if they are done while other students are still working?* It is unfair to ask students to be still and unoccupied because they have completed their work quickly. Many behavioral problems result from pointless idleness. Therefore, have something for students to do when they complete the work, even if it is simply talking quietly or reading. As you consider activities to fill that time, keep in mind that when students demonstrate success, you should recognize them with something positive; *activity* is a positive consequence, and *inactivity* is a negative consequence. Therefore, it is best not to give students pointless busywork or just let them stand around. Encourage them to check their work. Have them help another student. Let them complete other homework. Let them work on the computer or play an educational game, or drill. Give them an activity that says, "Great job working hard to complete the task; as a result, you have the opportunity to get better or help others get better in the following way."

- *What will you do if the lesson takes less time than you initially planned?* Instead of stretching out the lesson and hindering the momentum or just letting the class hang out for the remaining time, use the time to accomplish something meaningful. That may mean doing a mini-lesson on something coming up the next day or after recess. It may mean playing a quick all-class game to send the message that when the class works hard, they fit in another activity—something just as fun as learning lessons. It may mean getting out journals, getting into groups for a discussion, or taking care of some unfinished business that has been waiting for a block of time. It will be useful to put this contingency activity on your lesson plan.

Promoting the Level of Student Engagement

Reflect on your own experience as a student. When you and the other members of the class felt engaged in an activity, how much misbehavior did you commonly notice? Conversely, when you felt a minimal level of engagement, were you and your classmates tempted to find other, perhaps less acceptable, ways to entertain yourselves? Consider these questions within the lens of students' basic needs: it will be apparent that engaging lessons are more satisfying. Preparing an engaging lesson also demonstrates that you care about student learning.

The term *engagement* is used rather broadly, and while we probably know it when we see it, it may be useful to examine the idea of engagement more closely. *Engagement* can be defined as the degree to which the students care about the topic or activity, connect with it, and feel cognitively "hooked in" and accountable when involved in the activity.

11.7   REFLECTION

Recall a time when you felt engaged in a learning activity. Did you care about it? Did you connect with it? What did the teacher do to encourage these qualities?

A typical lesson period commonly has the following sequence of events:

1. The students begin a lesson with hope and are relatively engaged.
2. Most students make an effort to understand and invest in the activity.
3. Over time if the lesson is too conceptual, becomes tedious, lacks interest to the student, or is not challenging enough, some students begin to get restless.
4. The teacher begins to exhibit negativity as a result.
5. The lesson ultimately descends into dysfunction, or the teacher begins to engage in an increasing number of disciplinary responses, or both.

While this sequence is typical, it is entirely unnecessary and avoidable. The problem is not the students. The problem is the lesson or lesson management (Wang et al., 1993).

To remedy this situation, begin by asking yourself how you are going to help students connect with the material or activity. Does it relate to their lives? How can you connect it to their prior knowledge? If it is conceptual, how can you make it concrete and practical? If it is practical, how can you give it broader meaning? In an effort to help students connect with the material, consider incorporating some or all of the following strategies:

Anticipatory Activities. We often lose sight of the fact that while we may understand the material that we are about to teach and have had the opportunity to process it and connect it to our larger knowledge or skill schema, students need some help putting their new learning into their own existing schema. So instead of jumping right in and presenting new ideas or demonstrating a new skill, incorporate an anticipatory device to help set the context for new material. Two effective examples of these are anticipatory sets and advanced organizers.

Anticipatory sets are activities that set the stage for the new material. They can be as simple as a question, a prop, or a movie clip. They help students connect with the idea in a more personal or concrete manner and so prepare them for the concepts to come. An advanced organizer is a graphic depiction of a concept, such as a diagram, a time line, an idea map, a table, or a chart. These help students create a preorganization for the material to come. They are especially useful when the content is highly conceptual or lacks a context. Anticipatory activities help all students process the coming material better and prevent a lot of "I don't get it" responses.

Matching Instructional Strategies to Content. If the same instructional methodology (for example, direct instruction) is used for all content, it will lead to problems with student engagement and therefore more misbehavior (Gettinger & Kohler, 2006). Just as it works best to run on land, swim in water, and fly in the air, students feel most comfortable learning in a mode that best fits the material that they are learning. In most cases, that means learning skills through direct instruction, concepts inductively, and facts within an applied context. Teaching material in a manner that works counter to the way that the human brain operates naturally produces frustration. We do not expect our students to swim everywhere, so why would we expect them to process all material with the same instructional format?

Providing Directions in a Manner That Meets All Students' Cognitive Needs. A good portion of students have a different set of cognitive style preferences than we do. It is common to find that after you have given directions, the students who are similar to us in style have understood, whereas those who are on the other side of the cognitive style fence have not (Myers, McCauley, Quenk, & Hammer, 1998; Shindler, 2005). Therefore, when giving directions, make sure that you meet all style needs. No matter your style, you need to be very intentional about making sure that all students understand the conceptual context (how the lesson fits into the broader sequence of unit, why it is meaningful, and where it is going in a general sense) as well as the practical aspects of the lesson (what the students are supposed to do, the steps involved, and what it will look like in the end).

Inductive, Problem-Based, or Inquiry-Based Lessons. Many teachers fear teaching in a manner in which they do not control the knowledge or content of the discussion. They avoid using such strategies as hands-on, discovery, or inquiry-based learning. Much like the monkey who cannot get his hand out of the jar because he refuses to let go of the apple, this effort at control is likely to produce an undesirable outcome. The thought is, "If I let the students do hands-on or inductive learning, I will lose control, and bad things will happen to my classroom management."

As in allowing students to learn cooperatively, these strategies may require some investment in helping students discover how to approach learning in a more investigative manner if it is unfamiliar to them. Over time, the level of engagement and the higher level of achievement will pay off in both learning and behavioral results (Hickey & Schafer, 2006; Russell, Kruger, & Schafer, 2004). Inductive learning has a built-in movement to it, is inherently engaging, and, unlike direct instruction, there are no gaps in instruction (where problems often arise). Off-task behavior is most often overt and observable, so there is little, if any, "checking out" on the part of students.

11.8 REFLECTION

Research suggests that the most significant predictor of a student's dropping out is academic performance (Hess et al., 1987). Many dropouts leave school because the work held no interest for them. In your assessment, how much of the dropout rate is related to ineffective instruction?

High-Participation Formats. Kounin (1970) found that high-participation formats encouraged student engagement. In his research, he noticed that when teachers used instructional formats that allowed the highest portion of students to be involved, fewer students were off-task or bored. These formats were contrasted to more passive forms of instruction, such as lecturing and procedures that include a lot of waiting in line or waiting for one's turn. In addition, high-participation formats meet the learning style needs of both introverts and extroverts in the class. The extroverts are energized by the collaborative element, and the introverts are provided an opportunity to speak in a smaller, more comfortable context. Bartscher, Lawler, Ramirez, and Schinault (2001) found that when teachers incorporated high-participation instructional strategies (for example, cooperative learning, peer review, creative writing) with middle school students, the result was both higher achievement and a lower incidence of discipline referrals.

Formal Concept-Building Exercises. The use of formal concept-building activities, such as concept attainment, can promote the concept acquisition skills of all learners and are especially critical for students for whom conceptual thinking is less natural (Shindler, 2005). Formal concept attainment is the process of helping students move inductively or deductively from the specifics of a concept to generalizations.

In an inductive approach, a class is led through an exploration of specific examples of a concept, followed by the generation of a definition, and finally by the opportunity to use that definition to classify further examples and nonexamples. A variety of effective strategies for promoting concept understanding exist. Survey the more concrete learners in the class, and they will attest that when the material gets too conceptual or abstract, they get frustrated or stop paying attention (Myers et al., 1998). Formal concept-building activities meet all students' learning style needs. They are satisfying to abstract learners and provide a concrete step-by-step process for the more practical learners.

Project-Based Learning and Providing Opportunities for Students to Put It All Together. Projects provide a number of features that promote higher levels of engagement, motivation, and satisfaction (Mergendoller, Markham, Ravitz, & Larmer, 2006). In contrast to the teacher-led direct instruction lesson, projects provide a natural momentum and context for synthesis. Students are creating something that does not exist until they produce it. The goal of the activity is concrete and built-in. Projects provide an opportunity for students to put it all together in a way that surpasses most other modes of learning. They afford countless places for students to relate previous knowledge to their efforts. In a project-based context, students have the added motivation that comes from knowing that they are going to show their completed effort to others. They own it, they are the experts, and they have concrete evidence of their effort that they can admire and feel proud of in the end.

11.9

REFLECTION

Reflect on the many people you have known who considered themselves poor students yet thrived in a project-based environment such as industrial arts, fine arts, drama, home economics, athletics, or auto mechanics. How would you describe the change in their personality from the typical classroom context to their preferred subject? Was there a change in their level of engagement, locus of control, or sense of competence? What implications do these stories have for you as a teacher?

Like inquiry-based learning and cooperative learning, project-based learning may be new to some students. Therefore, you will need to be patient and intentional about teaching the skills necessary for them to succeed. It may be necessary to keep the students mindful of the relationship between acting responsibly and being given greater freedom and opportunity. Over time, the inherently more engaging and satisfying nature of these learning strategies will provide the incentive necessary for students to treat them with the respect they require.

Cultivating a Culture of Listening. The level of engagement in a class will be higher when you have established a culture of listening (see Chapter Five), in which students have become accustomed to being attentive and respectful and to expecting the same from their peers. An integral part of the transformational classroom is a progressively higher level of awareness on the part of its members. Listening, engagement, and coming out of one's ego centeredness are intrinsically motivating; however, this satisfaction is usually masked by or competing with students' insecurities and mental conditioning (especially to flee the present moment). We need to be intentional in our efforts to help students feel secure and see the value in bringing their awareness outside their own "mental noise." One strategy that supports this goal is that of keeping students cognitively on the hook.

Keeping Students Cognitively Engaged and Accountable. When I am in the field working directly with teachers, one of the pieces of feedback that I give most regularly relates to the benefits of keeping students "hooked in" cognitively, that is, engaged and accountable. The way we manage questioning and class discussions can encourage boredom or cognitive engagement (Doyle, 2006; Evertson, Anderson, & Brophy, 1980). Evertson et al. (1980) found that effective teachers asked an average of over twenty-four questions during a fifty-minute period, whereas less effective teachers asked an average of eight.

The difference between effectiveness and ineffectiveness can also be more subtle and requires only minor adjustments in teaching technique. To achieve engagement, we first need to understand the dynamics and then incorporate a few strategies to keep students cognitively on the hook. For example, consider the following two scenarios:

Scenario A: The teacher asks one student a closed-ended question related to the topic—for example, "Armando, how many degrees are there in each angle of an equilateral triangle?"

Scenario B: The teacher asks one student a closed-ended question and then follows up with an open-ended question to the other students—for example, "Armando just said he thought that there were sixty degrees in an equilateral triangle. Do you agree with him? And how do you think he came up with that answer?"

11.10

Reflect on these two situations. It is likely that you have experienced something such as situation A many times as a student. When it was not your turn, where was your mind? Did you feel accountable? Would you have felt more accountable in scenario B?

If we compare the two scenarios within the dynamics of social or indirect learning, their differences become more apparent. In scenario A, the teacher (T) is interacting with the individual student (S) somewhat exclusively. The rest of the members of the class (O) are essentially spectators, or largely cognitively off the hook. Over time, this interaction pattern trains students to tune out when it is not their turn. And even when they are relatively tuned in, they are not likely to be attending to the desired cognitive processes. For example, it is more likely that they are thinking something along the lines of, "I wonder if Armando will get the answer correct?" or "Armando is one of the smarter students in the class. He should get this right." Attention to these tangential questions does little to promote the goals of the lesson.

There are many ways to bring all the students in the class into cognitive processing. In situation B, this was accomplished by simply asking a follow-up open-ended process question. As a result, the students felt accountable and included in the interaction. With this type of interaction, students quickly learn that there is an expectation that they will always need to be cognitively engaged. Everything that is said is part of a string of reasoning and reflection or metacognition, and anyone may be asked at any part to step in and join the enterprise.

The following strategies promote cognitive engagement:

- *Partner or group share.* Instead of asking a single student a question, ask students to share their answers with a partner or a group. Then call on one group or individual to share their answer. This format is more active and allows more students to process out loud.

- *Think pair share.* On determining that a question would be valuable if it were processed, first ask the students to spend a specified amount of time thinking about their answer (fifteen to forty seconds is usually adequate). Then instruct them to find another classmate with whom to share their thinking. To encourage more diverse pairing, you might ask them to find someone with a certain characteristic (for example, someone wearing the same color shoes). It will be useful to vary the pairing characteristic often to promote a greater degree of different pairings. This strategy combines both reflection time and collaborative processing and gets students up and out of their seats.

- *Use of personal chalkboards or whiteboards.* Instead of asking students to come to the board and write their answer to a problem or sentence or having them respond verbally, consider having students write their answers on a personal chalkboard or whiteboard. This can also be done in groups. More students are involved, and the answers on the boards provide an excellent source of assessment information.

- *Vote with fingers or by standing.* After one student has responded to a question, ask the others to stand up if they agree and remain seated if they disagree, or have them put up one finger if they agree and two if they disagree. Again, this provides excellent assessment information.

- *Wait time.* After asking a question, wait a few seconds before you take a response from a student. When a student has responded, wait for a few seconds before you make any evaluative statements. Alternately, you may just want to ask quietly, "So what do you think?" before waiting a while to give the students time to reflect and process. Wait time has been shown to increase engagement level in students (Tobin, 1987).

- *Using open- and closed-ended questions.* Typically open-ended questions encourage a deeper level of processing than closed-ended questions do—for example, "What do you think the _____ thought when _____?" (open ended) versus "What are the three states of matter?" (closed ended). Mixing open- and closed-ended questions together intentionally tends to create a greater level of engagement than using either one exclusively (Evertson et al., 1980).

- *Repeating the question.* Simply repeating the question after a response can work to encourage students to rethink their answers. Although it should not be used extensively, it can send the message that your role is not one of giving instant gratification after each answer and that you want to encourage the process of reflection.

REFLECTION

11.11

After reviewing the following actual classroom scenario, assess the problems with the teacher's lesson design as you see it, and develop an alternative strategy that you feel would be more effective.

The teacher decided to teach a lesson related to science to her first graders. The concept she was teaching was sea versus land creatures. She created an excellent set of hands-on materials, including pictures of both sea and land creatures. She divided the class into two lines and had the two groups compete. The student at the front of each line was asked to classify the picture as a land or sea creature. The activity worked very well for about the first three students at the front of each line. The classification aspect was effective on many levels. However, over time, there were an increasing number of disruptions in the back of each line, especially involving students who had already had their turns. After fewer than half of the students had participated, the activity deteriorated to the point where it had to be stopped.

Assume that the topic and classification aspect of the activity are worth keeping. What would you do to make the lesson work better so that there is a greater level of engagement and therefore fewer management issues?

Clarity of Learning Targets

Reflect on your anxiety level in the following two hypothetical situations:

1. You are a passenger in a car and you do not know where it is going or the purpose of the trip.

2. You are a passenger in a car and you know where the car is going and why you need to go there.

Given these two situations, it is likely that you would feel more anxiety in the first. When we do not know where we are going, we feel anxiety, and that anxiety manifests itself in some way. Commonly it takes the form of frustration. In some case, we might externalize that frustration directly by asking, "Where are we going?" And sometimes we might displace our frustration into disruptive or even destructive behavior.

As Stiggins (2001) suggests, when students have learning targets that are clear and standing still, they will reach them. Gettinger and Kohler (2006) state, "Clarity in instruction relates positively to multiple outcomes including learner satisfaction, achievement, and student engagement" (p. 88). When students do not have a clear sense of where they are going or what it will take to get there, they will be frustrated. Clear targets contribute to both better performance and better behavior.

Moreover, it is useful to recognize in the travel analogy that while the driver may have had a very good sense of where the car was going—which would have helped keep him or her from getting lost—it would not have done much to remedy the passengers' sense of frustration.

We rarely relate the quality of the learning objectives that we craft to the quality of the behavior in the class. But as we examine the connection more closely, it is probably stronger than you first considered. You may have viewed the notion of writing clear, observable behavioral objectives as simply a formality or even a luxury. However, when you determine the behavioral outcome that you want, you become a better teacher. When you are a better teacher, everything in the class runs more effectively.

Good objectives are learning targets that have been clearly and specifically stated, are as concrete as possible, and identify observable behavior or behavioral evidence of a learning outcome (Borich & Stollenwerk, 2000). When you have sound knowledge of the skill or cognitive operation or can visualize how it looks when the students can demonstrate that they have mastered an idea, you possess a tool that will help you promote success. Furthermore, you project and articulate that purpose to the students so that they know where they are going and how they are going to get there. When you know the topic that you are teaching but do not have clear learning outcomes, your students are like the passenger in the car who does not know where they are going or what the purpose of the trip is.

What teachers most often construct for objectives (when they do write them at all) could be classified into three basic types:

- Material to be covered. *Example:* "Cover page 34 and review for the final."

- Completion. *Example:* "Learners will complete division problems and begin homework on page 35."

- Cognitive-behavioral outcomes. *Example:* "Learners will (1) apply the process of division after it has been modeled in class to problems with remainders, (2) recognize what remainders are, and (3) be able to explain the concept of remainders in their own words and/or to peers."

Now consider the effectiveness of each to create effective learning targets that are clear and standing still. If you have written either material-to-be-covered or completion objectives, your questions as you teach are likely related to task completion, such as, "How are we doing getting done with this?" and "Who is done, and who is still working?" These questions are useful as secondary considerations, but they should not be the primary considerations. The primary attention should be placed on whether there is evidence that any particular student can demonstrate the ability to perform the cognitive operation needed to succeed in a task. You should be asking whether they are learning, not whether they are finishing the assignment.

Some teachers may say, "I do both, and while I may not write the cognitive-behavioral outcome down, I know what it is." That may be true. Nevertheless, when I observe teachers who have written completion objectives, in almost every case I see completion as their focus, and when I observe teachers who have taken the time to conceive and then write clear cognitive-behavioral outcome objectives, I see teachers who are looking for that when they check the progress the class or any individual student is making during the lesson. If you know what you are looking for, it should not be a lot of trouble to write it, so why not take the extra thirty seconds to do it?

REFLECTION 11.12

When you made the effort to write out behavioral objectives for your lesson, did you find that doing it was more difficult than you thought it would be? What does that tell you? It may be a useful reminder that we often make assumptions about how well we know what we are trying to teach, and those assumptions may not be sound.

Why Does the Type of Objective Affect Discipline?. Attention to learning goals rather than completion goals creates significant differences in teaching performance that will directly and indirectly influence the quality of your classroom management. One is that you teach differently. You have a greater sense of purpose, and you interact in a manner that creates goals and momentum, because it is learning driven rather than completion driven. When you have a clear sense of the cognitive operation or skill that you are looking for, you are more likely to use feedback language that supports the mastery of that objective. As a result, your engagement level is higher. You then consciously or unconsciously identify the importance to every step and component of the task.

Second, the students think differently. They pick up on your behavior and attitude. When they recognize that you are making an effort to help them reach goals related to learning rather than completion—applying a principle, synthesizing content, or mastering a skill—they respond with a greater level of investment in reaching those goals. Students who are focused on reaching learning goals have fewer episodes when they feel the need to misbehave or displace their frustration through negative behavior. Conversely, students who see the work as busywork assigned by a teacher who is just getting through the material have a much greater likelihood of misbehaving. When you communicate clear learning targets, your students have both a clear sense of the pathway toward and a vision of the successful end result. This is both motivational and focusing for them.

REFLECTION 11.13

Recall the discussion on basic needs in Chapter Six. How many basic needs are being met by the fact that a lesson has a clear sense of purpose? What happens when basic needs are not met? How many management problems that you have observed would you judge to be related to students' feeling a lack of purpose to their work?

Rubrics and Authentic Assessment. Most teachers have come to recognize the many benefits of using rubrics in assessment. Some of those benefits are well established and predictable. For example, when we compare one class that does not use assignment rubrics with one that does, we find that the students in the class with the rubric create consistently better-quality products (Gettinger & Kohler, 2006; Stiggins, 2001). However, few teachers recognize the relationship between the use of rubrics and the quality of the behavior in their classes. In fact, the relationship between assessment choices and the effects on student behavior is one of the most underexamined areas in education.

Consider these benefits of using rubrics on motivation and classroom management:

- Rubrics create another level of clarity to the learning targets (Gettinger & Kohler, 2006). In the example of the passenger in the car above, the rubric is like a train or bus schedule.

It puts the passenger in control of the trip. The passengers need to choose only where they want to go.

- A well-designed rubric can promote a greater degree of internal locus of control and growth-oriented orientation in students (Gettinger & Kohler, 2006). They support what Gettinger and Kohler refer to as the "effort-outcome linkage" (p. 88). A rubric that clearly spells out what constitutes a quality process contributes to each student's achieving success as a result of investment in the process as opposed to ability. This leads to the students' needs for power and competence being met to a greater degree, and as a result there are fewer incidents in which students misbehave in the attempt to get those needs satisfied.

- Clear rubrics contribute to a reduced need on the part of the students to ask questions, which gives the teacher more time to teach rather than constantly reexplain. Moreover, since rubrics create less ambiguity, there are fewer cases where students miss the target and feel the need to make excuses.

- Rubrics support reliability within the assessment. Reliability leads to a sense of trust and fairness in the process. When students feel that the process of assessment is fair, they are less likely to translate poor evaluations into hostility, resentment, or even revenge. The fact is that many students perceive the assessment process to be personal—about how much the teacher likes them or about how "good" they are. Rubrics bring objectivity, and therefore an element of fairness, to the process.

- Similar to clear behavioral objectives, rubrics provide the clarity that helps meet the learning style needs of both sequential and random learners in the class (Shindler, 2005). Sequential learners thrive on a transparent structure and well-articulated goals. They experience a loss of motivation and focus in the presence of a high level of ambiguity, too many changes, or a learning program that seems arbitrary. It is not uncommon for the sequential learner to interpret the lack of clarity in the class as evidence of incompetence in the teacher. In contrast, random learners are much more comfortable in an environment that includes flexibility and situational adjustments and as such are less concerned with drawing inside the lines if those lines are seen as inessential. When random learners' creatively interpreted efforts are met with a poor assessment by the teacher due to unclear learning targets, the result can be discouragement and tentativeness in future efforts.

- Rubrics enable us to better include process aspects of the product, performance, or skill into the assessment system. The benefits of this will be discussed in the next section.

Portfolios can have many of the same motivational benefits as rubrics, and although they may not accomplish the same level of reliability, they do promote the students' internal locus of control. Portfolios provide a concrete archive of students' growth over time and therefore offer a practical reminder that learning is about application rather than merely aptitude.

Incentives for Students to Invest in the Process

When we place value on the process, whether formally or informally, we put the power in the hands of the students. The result is a significant effect on the quality of behavior and motivation (Ames, 1992; Gettinger & Kohler, 2006). This effect is related to the following causes:

- When we emphasize the process, we encourage the basic needs of power and competence and promote an internal locus of control and growth-oriented orientation.

- When students see that success comes from their investment in the process, they are more likely to invest and make the effort. When they view success as related to innate ability, few students are motivated. Most take on an attitude of resignation that kills motivation and breeds compensation in the form of misbehavior. In contrast, value for the process has the effect of empowerment.

- When students put their attention on the process rather than the end result, a series of smaller, more immediate goals emerges. Instead of looking at the desired result and feeling intimidated, overwhelmed, or tempted to procrastinate, attention to the process shifts the students' attention to what is important now. "What small goal do I need to attend to at this time?" This strategy is especially valuable for students who have short attention spans or attention deficit hyperactivity disorder.

- When students get into the flow of attending to the process, their activities take on a natural movement and momentum.

REFLECTION

11.14

Reflect on why putting your attention on the process tends to produce a natural psychological movement to your effort. It may be illuminating to incorporate the lens of the three elements of success psychology (internal locus of control, sense of acceptance and belonging, and growth orientation, discussed in Chapter Seven) in this exercise.

You can encourage students to put their attention into the process in several ways:

- *Formally or informally assess process outcomes.* When you formally assess process aspects of the assignment and include them in the grade, you make the statement that the process is valuable in a real and material way.

- *Give process feedback to students.* Instead of giving praise or general feedback, make the effort to give positive recognitions of student process-related performance. For example, instead of saying, "The answers look good. Well done!" it is more effective to say, "I see you taking the time to outline your thoughts before you write. Smart idea!"

- *Use process workshops.* When you ask students to write a paper, create a product, produce a presentation, or perform any other complex task, encourage process investment by breaking the process down into stages. This can be done for individual or group products. An example of an individual product development series is that of the writer's workshop. which has these steps:
  - Prewriting
  - Drafting
  - Revising
  - Editing
  - Publishing

The next chapter examines a workshop process for a cooperative group effort.

When you commit to valuing and providing incentives for students to invest in the process, you will observe evidence over time that students are responding:

- A higher level of student investment from start to finish.

- Students displaying faith in the process rather than taking shortcuts or procrastinating.

- Students feeling freer to take risks and innovate. Many teachers hold the misconception that the way to encourage innovation is to give students a blank canvas. This may appear to be a reasonable assumption, but in most cases, it produces less creativity than it does intimidation. And it most often results in the majority of students simply reproducing the efforts of one of their peers. Process guidelines provide support and tools for the creative process.

11.15 REFLECTION

What have you found that promotes your creative process? Survey a few other teachers, and note what they do. What do your findings say about the kinds of strategies that can promote students' creative efforts?

Relevant and Meaningful Curriculum

Freedom Writers (a book and movie by the same title; Gruwell, 1999) is an effective portrayal of the true story of one class of students and their teacher, Erin Gruwell. When Gruwell arrived at her school, she found a group of students who functioned poorly as a collective, had a very low level of motivation, and exhibited what could best be described as a fundamentally failure-based psychology. Moreover, the students resisted her initial efforts since they viewed her as an outsider. Over time, she profoundly changed the dynamics and psychology in the class. Two factors of causation stand out. First, she instilled in her students a sense that she believed in them and cultivated a success psychology within the class. Second, she made a commitment to finding material that was meaningful and relevant to her students' lives.

I have visited the school in which the events of the book took place and many others like it. For every teacher like Gruwell, there are countless others who take a 4-Style teacher approach. They mistakenly trust that being strict enough, expelling enough students, and shaming students sufficiently will get results. These 4-Style teachers succeed mostly at confirming students' negative identity and adding to the staggering percentage of students who drop out of school. In fact, even if one's goals were simply a better-controlled class and fewer discipline problems, the path that Gruwell and those like her take would ultimately be more effective than being a 4-Style teacher. Most students drop out as a result of feeling that the curriculum has no interest or value to them (Hess, 1987; Woods, 1995). Students who do not care about what they are learning have little to lose. Threats of a poor grade or suspension have little power over students who think school is a waste of time.

I have yet to meet a student who did not desire a meaningful curriculum or who did not respond to being in a class where the curriculum was engaging, meaningful, and relevant to their lives. In research conducted in high schools, we commonly observe groups of students who act unmotivated, disruptive, and disrespectful in one class and engaged, responsible, and respectful of others in the next one. The difference between the two can be explained in most cases by the curriculum that the teachers in each class were using (Shindler et al., 2003).

Some of the ways to make curriculum more meaningful have been examined earlier in this chapter. Instructional strategies that promote engagement become inherently more meaningful, so it is impossible to separate the two. For example, strategies such as inductive learning, cooperative learning, and project-based learning all have the potential to make any material more meaningful. If we were to explore various classrooms, we would see countless ways that teachers create meaningful learning experiences—for example:

- Using culturally relevant material, such as literature that relates to students' personal experience

- Getting to know students' interests and gifts and making the effort to connect material to them
- Finding ways to make learning apply to practical applications that students may ultimately use in the future
- Teaching science in an inductive and hands-on manner
- Having students write their own goals (this is especially useful in physical education)
- Having students lead their own conferences
- Having students take part in service-learning projects
- Having students do ethnographic studies of their families and communities
- Including a unit of community (for kindergarten to sixth grade)
- Letting students choose books and topics that relate to their interests
- Relating curriculum to current events

REFLECTION

11.16

Take out a piece of paper and brainstorm some ideas from your experience (or that you have found through research) and continue listing ways to make the curriculum more meaningful and relevant from what you have observed.

SUCCEEDING WITH STUDENTS OF DIFFERENT ABILITY LEVELS AND LEARNING STYLES

Meeting the needs of all students is a challenge. There are few teachers who do not feel even a little guilty that their curriculum is not meeting all of their students' needs. One solution is to provide differential learning experiences for students depending on their needs and abilities (Wang et al., 1993).

Although this approach can encourage higher levels of success for many students, especially those at the high and low ends of the ability spectrum, it requires a substantial investment of time and energy on the part of the teacher. For this reason, it may be prudent to invest in strategies that meet the needs of all learners first and then supplement them with individualized strategies as necessary. Effectively executing the strategies in the first four sections of this chapter will promote success with more students more of the time, making differentiation less necessary. However, to provide the necessary support for many of your learners, you will want to find ways to differentiate instruction for different ability levels and teach for the success of students of all learning styles.

Succeeding with Students of Different Ability Levels

Many behavioral problems are rooted in work that is either too challenging or not challenging enough for some students. When the work is viewed as too difficult, students may quit and seek other means to meet their need for competence (acting out, getting attention, bullying, acting helpless, blaming others, and so on). This is especially common for students who have developed what Dweck (2000) refers to as a "helpless pattern." Conversely, when the work lacks sufficient challenge, some students become bored. In many cases, the greatest behavioral challenges are gifted and talented students who want a greater level of stimulation; not finding it in the curriculum, they attempt to find it through other means, such as challenging authority, rebelling, reinventing assignments, or picking and choosing when to tune in and when to tune out.

11.17 REFLECTION

How do you act when you feel that a task is too difficult? Too simple? Do you find yourself compensating in some way? What compensatory behaviors have you observed others use?

Succeeding with Students Who Have Different Cognitive and Learning Styles

When we know our own cognitive or learning style preferences, we are less a product of our conditioning and have an additional tool to keep from being unconscious of our default tendencies (Myers et al., 1998). When we know our students' cognitive and learning preferences, we have a window into how they learn best, how they tend to process information, and the kinds of learning contexts in which they will likely thrive and those they will find challenging. This knowledge is power. In our hands, this knowledge offers a glimpse into the human learning owner's manual. When we share it with our students, we give them a gift of empowerment for their own growth as learners.

Successfully Teaching Across Type

Once you have become acquainted with your style and those of your students, turn your attention to how your teaching can promote the success of students of all learning styles. To this end, keep in mind that you will be more successful with all students if you use the strategies described in this chapter. These strategies are effective in part because they work for students on both sides of each cognitive dimension. Next, recognize that no matter how well you know your own preferences and default tendencies, it will be helpful to be intentional about ensuring that students on the side of each cognitive fence are getting their needs met (Lawrence, 1987). Although you may not personally understand why students on the other side of a dimension have a particular set of needs, you can certainly show an appreciation that they do have such needs.

Most teachers find that considering the requirements of those on both sides of the fence makes them better teachers as well as more well-rounded human beings. Table 11.1 outlines a sample of ideas to consider when teaching students with opposing preferences. The online resource article, "Cognitive Style and Classroom Management," available at transformativeclassroom.com, offers a more extensive treatment of succeeding with students of different types.

All students need to spend some part of each lesson or day working to their strengths (Lawrence, 1987). While you may not have opportunities to provide different assignments for students depending on their learning style—nor would this be necessarily desirable—you can make sure that students have had the opportunity to work in their strength area at least some of the day. When students are forced to work in an uncomfortable mode for a prolonged period of time, you can expect a reaction. While this reaction will look different for different learning style types, it will appear as some form of distress. Table 11.2 briefly outlines the four possible student academic profiles (extrovert/concrete, extrovert/abstract, introvert/concrete, and introvert/abstract) and some of the needs of each type.

TABLE 11.1. **Effective Teaching Across Types**

Introverts Teaching Extroverts	Extroverts Teaching Introverts
Use group work and cooperative learning.	Provide individual tasks.
Use wait time with questioning.	Call on all students regularly.
Provide time for movement.	Provide written venues for thinking.
Value expression.	Value reflection.
Sensates/concretes teaching intuitives/abstracts	**Intuitives/abstracts teaching sensates/concretes**
Provide opportunities for creativity.	Provide hands-on activities.
Give students the big picture of their work.	Give clear step-by-step directions.
Use concept attainment and problem-based strategies on occasion.	Explain the practical application to work.
	Avoid long abstract or theoretical lectures.
Teach inductively on occasion.	Value the quality of students' work.
Don't overemphasize the details.	
Judgers/sequentials teaching perceivers/randoms	**Perceivers/randoms teaching judgers/sequentials**
Allow some flexibility in assignment format.	Provide clear written assignment guidelines.
Use variety.	Prepare students for changes in plans.
Provide clearly written assignment guidelines.	Try to keep to the agreed-on schedule.
Allow flexible time frames for completion.	Provide some routine in the day.
Value novelty and open-mindedness.	Value accuracy and punctuality.

REFLECTION

11.18

Locate your own style in Table 11.2. Does the description accurately characterize your academic tendencies? Now find the style opposite you. Do you have difficulty empathizing with students of this type? What implications does this have for your teaching?

EXAMINING THE RELATIONSHIP BETWEEN ASSESSMENT AND MANAGEMENT

Many teachers make the mistake of viewing assessment as a disconnected event that occurs after learning has taken place. When we examine the effects of assessment on classroom behavior as well as the learning process, we find that it has a powerful effect (Munk & Repp, 1994). For example, if you were to reflect on your own experience as a student, you will recall that how you were assessed influenced your experience to a great extent. In fact, what and how we assess defines what is success in a very real and material way for students. Therefore, keep the following principles in mind:

- *Never make grades public or use assessment for comparison purposes.* When you assess the quality of your students' work in relation to clear learning targets, you promote internal locus of control and growth-oriented orientation. Contrastingly, when you grade on a curve or make public comparisons, you make the statement that grades are partly about learning

TABLE 11.2. **Learning Profiles of the Four Academic Type Combinations**

	Extroverts (E)	Introverts (I)
Sensates (S)/Concrete Learners	Extroverted Concrete Learners Action-Oriented Realists (@35% of students) Let me work with my hands and create something practical. Some people may call me a "kinesthetic" learner, but I would rather call myself a "doer." I like to be part of a team and see practical results from my/our work. I have a strong need to contribute and be recognized. Don't just explain how to do something to me; at least show me, and better yet, let me try it out. I learn from doing and then reflecting on what I have done. If you want me to understand an abstraction, let me discover it inductively or I can have a difficult time integrating it into a big picture understanding. Written directions can be really helpful to me. If you expect me to continually sit and listen to a lecture and then do well on a test later, I will likely disappoint you much of the time.	Introverted Concrete Learners Thoughtful Realists (@25% of students) Let me work independently on tasks that are clearly spelled out. Let me work with facts and information, and I will be able to use my power of insightful realism to come to sound, well-thought-out conclusions. Give me a chance to be careful and thoughtful. I will be your most dependable and steady student if you give me work where the directions are clear and the desired outcome is understood beforehand. Give me recognition for my care and persistence since those are my strengths, and I may not draw as much attention to myself as some of the other students. When you give vague, careless directions or just expect me to "be creative" with no guidelines, I will likely feel some uneasiness and maybe even some resentment.
Intuitives (N)/Abstract Learners	Extroverted Abstract Learners Action-Oriented Innovators (@25% of students) Let me work in situations where I can use my communications skills in my learning. If I am working in a group where there are chances to be creative, I can get really motivated. I am a much better student when I am "into the task" as opposed to when I am "not into the task." I like to be inspired and see the purpose behind the work. I have an expressive energy that comes out when I am comfortable, and it helps me draw out my creativity and make connections across content. Talking, discussing, role-playing, debating are natural ways for me to tap that energy source. Peer tutoring, a subject that I am good at, is one of my favorite things to do. Projects where I can solve problems and draw energy from working with others and overcoming challenges are also areas where I feel very confident. When there are too many details, routines, lectures, or the same old thing all the time, I may turn my creative energies into behavior that you may not like.	Introverted Abstract Learners Thoughtful Innovators (@15% of students) Let me work in situations where I can come up with my own ideas whenever possible. I don't have as much trouble as some of the other students in being creative. I am often surprised when I see that I sometimes see deeper realities that other students miss. I like to come up with stories, draw pictures, or think of new ways of doing something. Some people call me a "visual learner" but I just feel more comfortable studying something for a while and understanding how it works before I try to do it or talk about it. I will be the last to volunteer usually, but I will work to master it long after the other students have moved on to something else. I need to be able make connections with the current subject and the previous subjects, so let me know the purpose behind what we are doing before you tell me what to do. If you ask me to do work that is pointless, inconsistent, or irrelevant then you will probably see me become at least a bit cynical or irreverent.

and also partly about rewarding or shaming students. These emotions tap into students' fear of failure and encourage their helpless orientation in addition to damaging the relationship of trust they have with you. Similarly, when you make grades public, you make the statement that each student's achievement is related to other students' achievements. As you examine that dynamic more closely, you will discover that there is never value to comparing one student's achievement to that of another. This strategy fails as both a motivational as well as an instructional device.

REFLECTION

11.19

Reflect on the following classroom scenario. The teacher has just completed an effective lesson in which he helped students of all ability levels understand and successfully complete a series of math problems. Some students were able to do all of the problems successfully, while others were only able to complete a few, but were encouraged that they got the idea and feel confident of their ability in the future. At this point, how do you think the students felt about their performance and their relationship with the teacher?

Next, the teacher takes out the grade book and asks each student to state their score out of 10. The students begin to report one at a time, "4," "5," "10," "2," "7," and so on. Now how do you think the students feel about themselves and their relationship with their teacher?

- *Assess process whenever possible.* Assessing process and other areas over which the student has 100 percent control promotes the student's internal locus of control and growth-oriented orientation (Gettinger & Kohler, 2006). Therefore, assessing behavior in the form of participation, process, cooperation, lab work, and effort can have a positive impact on classroom performance as well as behavior. However, if this assessment process is not done systematically, it will do more harm than good. For example, if you use a random and subjective process to give some percentage of each student's grade for participation points, it will work against both your management and motivational goals. It will most often be viewed by the students as a power play and another way to reward favorites. A step-by-step explanation for the development of a sound and effective process for assessing participation and process is outlined in the online resource article, "Developing and Implementing an Effective System for Assessing the Quality of Behavior, Participation, or Process," available at transformativeclassroom.com.

- *Give students as much control as possible over their assessment information.* Do not make grades and your evaluation of their progress a mystery (Mergendollor et al., 2006). Ask yourself, "Who is the assessment for?" When students have information, they have power. When they know where they stand, what it takes to hit the target becomes clearer. Rubrics, clear instructions, and anchor performances (product examples of different quality levels) all work together to promote a greater level of clarity of the target and lower the level of anxiety and sense of external locus of control (Gettinger & Kohler, 2006). Cohen et al. (2002, in Mergendollor, 2006) found that when the teacher incorporated the use of anchor papers that represented excellent levels of performance from previous students, sixth graders performed at a higher level and exhibited less off-task behavior.

- *Use assessment methods that match your instructional methods.* If you encourage process thinking, cooperation, and other more authentic outcomes but do not assess them, you make the statement that they are not valuable. Students will invest in that which you assess. Your assessment choices will send a message that is many times more powerful than your words. So if you assess primarily by tests and worksheets, students will quickly decide that the other (more authentic) outcomes in the class are rather meaningless (Munk & Repp, 1994).

11.20 REFLECTION

Complete the sentence, "The five most important things that I want my students to learn in my class are _____." Reflect on your list. Do you currently (or plan to) assess those things? Everything can be assessed. If you want help on how to assess more complex or authentic outcomes, refer to the online resource article, "Developing and Implementing an Effective System for Assessing the Quality of Behavior, Participation, or Process," available at transformativeclassroom.com.

MATCHING PEDAGOGICAL AND MANAGERIAL STYLES

"Can I be a 2-Style manager and a 1-Style instructor, or be a 1-Style manager but rely mostly on teacher-centered instruction?" It is possible to mix and match practices from different orientations into your class, but at a cost of incoherence or a lack of integrity in your methods. The pedagogy described in this chapter will promote the shift within students from passive consumers to active learners. Empowering students with pedagogy that puts them in control of their learning and validates their judgment and ability will foster their capacity to be successful within a self-responsible 1-Style classroom structure. However, it will also likely make them less willing to blindly follow directions without seeing their value. If you want to use a 1-Style management approach but insist on teaching with a heavily teacher-directed style, you will send mixed messages that will ultimately undermine your ability to bring about your management goals.

Achieving a 1-Style classroom requires a substantial commitment to creating a self-responsible, empowered, needs-satisfied group of students. Incorporating pedagogical and managerial strategies that promote these goals will act synergistically to bring about a more effective 1-Style classroom more quickly.

CONCLUSION

We do not need to look far for examples of teachers who are so effective with their pedagogy that they experience few management concerns. As you examine your own teaching carefully, you are likely to find areas where more effective instruction will lead to more sound management outcomes. In the next chapter, we examine the practice of cooperative learning, a strategy that can lead to higher levels of engagement and learning. Nonetheless, it requires a large number of management considerations, as you will discover.

Journal Reflections

1. Reflect on the research of Jean Anyon discussed earlier in the chapter. In your experience, do you see a differential curriculum and set of classroom management practices used for students of different socioeconomic classes? If so, what do you think are the main factors that contribute to the differences?

2. List two instructional practices that you use currently (or have seen others use) that you feel qualify as creating a psychology of success or meeting students' basic needs. Then list two practices that you use currently (or have seen others use) that you feel it would be better to stop using.

Activities

1. Discuss your answers to reflection 11.1 within your group.
2. Discuss your answers to reflection 11.2 within your group.
3. Incorporate your thinking regarding the relationships among instruction, assessment, and classroom management and discipline into your classroom management plan or classroom improvement plan. It may be helpful to include answers to activity 2 in addition to the following questions:

   - What do you do instructionally to meet students' academic needs?
   - What do you do instructionally to prevent students from needing to act out?
   - How does your assessment promote the goals of your management?
   - How do you allow for variable styles, cultures, and circumstances in meeting the diverse needs of your students, including those who are English language learners, have special needs, or are advanced learners?

REFERENCES

Ames, C. (1992). Classrooms: Goals, structure and student motivation. *Journal of Educational Psychology, 84,* 261–271.

Anyon, J. (1981). Social class and school knowledge. *Curriculum Inquiry, 11*(1), 3–42.

Bartscher, M., Lawler, K., Ramirez, A., & Schinault, K. (2001). *Improving student writing ability through journals and creative writing exercises.* Unpublished report, St. Xavier University, Chicago.

Borich, G. D., & Stollenwerk, D. A. (2000). *Effective teaching methods.* Upper Saddle River, NJ: Merrill.

Daly, E. J. III, Martens, B. K., Kilmer, A., & Masie, D. R. (1996). The effects of instructional match and content overlap on generalization reading performance. *Journal of Applied Behavioral Analysis, 29,* 507–518.

Doyle, W. (2006). Ecological approaches to classroom management. In C. M. Evertson & C. S. Weinstein (Eds.), *Handbook of classroom management* (pp. 97–126). Mahwah, NJ: Erlbaum.

Duke, N. K. (2000). For the rich it's richer: Print experiences and environments offered to children in very low- and very high-socioeconomic status first-grade classrooms. *American Educational Research Journal, 37*(2), 441–478.

Dweck, C. (2000). *Self-theories: Their role in motivation, personality and development.* Lillington, NC: Psychologists Press.

Evertson, C., Anderson, C., Anderson, L., & Brophy, J. (1980). Relationships between classroom behaviors and student outcomes in junior high mathematics and English classes. *American Educational Research Journal, 17,* 43–60.

Gettinger, M. (1995). Best practices for increasing academic learning time. In A. Thomas & J. Grimes (Eds.), *Best practices in school psychology* (pp. 943–954). Washington, DC: National Association of School Psychologists.

Gettinger, M., & Kohler, K. M. (2006). Process-outcome approaches to classroom management and effective teaching. In C. M. Evertson & C. S. Weinstein (Eds.), *Handbook of classroom management* (pp. 73–95). Mahwah, NJ: Erlbaum.

Glasser, W. (1990). *The quality school: Managing students without coercion.* New York: Harper & Row.

Good, T. L., & Brophy, J. E. (2000). *Looking in classrooms* (8th ed.). Reading, MA: Addison-Wesley.

Gruwell, E. (1999). *The freedom writers diary: How a teacher and 150 teens used writing to change themselves and the world around them.* New York: Random House.

Gump, P. V. (1974). Operating environments in schools of open and traditional design. *School Review, 82*(4), 575–593.

Harris, A. (1998). Effective teaching: A review of the literature. *School Leadership and Management, 18*(2), 169–183.

Hayes, M. T., & Deyhle, D. (2001). Constructing difference: A comparative study of elementary science curriculum differentiation. *Science Education, 85,* 239–262.

Hess, G. A., Jr., Well, E., Prindle, C., Liffman, P., & Kaplan, B. (1987). "Where's room 185?" How schools can reduce their dropout problem. *Education and Urban Society, 19,* 330–355.

Hickey, D. T., & Schafer, N. J. (2006). Design-based, participation-centered approaches to classroom management. In C. M. Evertson & C. S. Weinstein (Eds.), *Handbook of classroom management* (pp. 281–308). Mahwah, NJ: Erlbaum.

Kounin, J. (1970). *Discipline and group management in classrooms*. New York: Holt.

Lawrence, G. (1987). *Teachers types and tiger stripes*. Palo Alto, CA: Consulting Psychologists Press.

Mergendoller, J. R., Markham, T., Ravitz, J., & Larmer, J. (2006). Pervasive management of project based learning: Teachers as guides and facilitators. In C. M. Evertson & C. S. Weinstein (Eds.), *Handbook of classroom management* (pp. 583–615). Mahwah, NJ: Erlbaum.

Munk, D. D., & Repp, A. C. (1994). The relationship between instructional variables and problem behavior. *Exceptional Children*, *60*, 390–401.

Myers, I. B., McCauley M. H., Quenk N. L., & Hammer, A. L. (1998). *The MBTI manual: A guide to the development and use of the Myers-Briggs Type Indicator*. Palo Alto, CA: Consulting Psychologists Press

Russell, H. A., Kruger, A. C., & Schafer, N. J. (2004, April). *Analysis of transactional discourse during learning*. Paper presented at the annual meeting of the American Educational Research Association, San Diego, CA.

Shindler, J. (2003). *Creating a psychology of success in the classroom: Enhancing academic achievement by systematically promoting student self-esteem*. Classroom management resource site, California State University, Los Angeles. Retrieved September 12, 2008, from www.calstatela.edu/faculty/jshindl/cm.

Shindler, J. (2005). *Teaching across type: Five principles for succeeding with students of different learning styles*. Los Angeles: Paragon Educational Consulting.

Shindler, J., Jones, A., Taylor, C., & Cadenas, H. (2003, April). *"Don't smile until Christmas": Examining the immersion of new teachers into existing urban school climates*. Paper presented at the annual meeting of the American Educational Research Association, Chicago.

Stiggins, R. (2001). *Student involved classroom assessment* (3rd ed.). Upper Saddle River, NJ: Prentice Hall.

Tobin, K. (1987). The role of wait time in higher cognitive level learning. *Review of Educational Research*, *57*, 69–95.

Wang, M. C., Haertel, G. D., & Walberg, H. J. (1993). Toward a knowledge base for school learning. *Review of Educational Research*, *63*, 249–294.

Woods, G. (1995). *Reducing the dropout rate*. Seattle, WA: NWREL (Northwest Regional Educational Laboratories).

Effectively Managing the Cooperative Classroom

In This Chapter

- Designing an effective cooperative learning activity
- Assessment options for cooperative activities
- Managing cooperative learning effectively
- What to do when groups cannot function successfully
- Transformative ideas related to cooperative learning

Although a cooperative learning context does introduce unique management challenges, it can be managed as effectively as independent activities and offers a series of benefits that are impossible to achieve by other means, including higher levels of academic achievement (Gettinger & Kohler, 2006; Slavin, 1994; Slavin, Hurley, & Chamberlain 2003). Moreover, the reasons teachers are resistant to the idea of incorporating cooperative learning in their classrooms are typically founded in misconceptions. They may say, for example, "I tried cooperative learning, and it just turns into free-for-all social time" or "I want to do more cooperative learning, but I have too much to cover." Most of the causes of failure when implementing cooperative learning are explicable and largely avoidable. It is important to note that implementing cooperative learning successfully requires a commitment to doing it well and learning the skills to manage it effectively (Gettinger & Kohler, 2006).

WHAT IS COOPERATIVE LEARNING, AND WHY SHOULD I USE IT?

Cooperative learning refers to any form of instruction in which students are working together for a purpose. As we will see in this chapter, the effects will be more powerful to the extent that certain ingredients are present. The more any activity requires mutual interdependence, collective problem solving, and striving for a common goal, the better chance it will have at achieving the potential that cooperative learning offers (Johnson & Johnson, 1998; Webb, Troper, & Fall, 1995).

There are many reasons to decide that cooperative learning is worth the effort. First, it has been shown to have a positive effect on student learning when compared to individual or competitive conditions (Johnson & Johnson, 1999; Slavin et al., 2003). Second, cooperative learning has the potential to meet more learning style needs more of the time than individualized direct instruction (Shindler, 2004b). Third, the interpersonal and collaboration skills that can be learned in a cooperative learning activity teach skills that are critical for later personal and professional success. Fourth, it has the potential to produce a level of engagement that other forms of learning cannot (Slavin et al., 2003). Fifth, it can be a powerful tool toward several transformative goals, including building communal bonds, learning conflict resolution skills, learning to consider others' needs, and learning to be an effective team member (Watson & Battistich, 2006).

WHAT MAKES A COOPERATIVE LEARNING ACTIVITY EFFECTIVE?

As we seek to create the most valuable, engaging, and productive cooperative learning experiences for students, consider how learning within a social context is different from learning independently. Recall our discussion of the social learning theory in the previous chapters. The key to a successful collaborative effort is using the social aspect of the activity to the class's collective advantage. This will be true for both instructional and managerial goals.

12.1 **REFLECTION**

Recall situations in which you were asked to work with others. Brainstorm a list of elements that were present in situations in which you felt motivated and ultimately successful.

As we explore the practical aspects of effectively managing cooperative learning, you will undoubtedly develop a set of your own principles for an effective cooperative learning activity. The goals of effective management will be inherently relative to what each teacher wants to achieve. Teachers using the 1-Style and 2-Style approaches reading the chapter will likely differ in their management and instructional goals related to effective classroom management. Table 12.1 offers a comparison of elements that will lead to a greater opportunity for achieving what could be considered transformative results and those that will limit your ability to obtain such results.

HOW TO BEGIN

The starting point for building cooperative learning into your curriculum should be an examination of your learning targets and management goals. Teachers who think that they have "too much to cover" to include cooperative learning are likely working from the assumption that cooperative learning will need to be an add-on to their curriculum. Making this assumption is much like suggesting that a social contract is an add-on to rules and management procedures. Cooperative learning, like the social contract, is simply a tool to achieve teaching goals (Slavin, 1994).

12.2 **REFLECTION**

Think about these questions before you begin:

- What are my learning targets? Can the objectives that I am trying to reach be accomplished in a collaborative format?
- What benefits will the cooperative aspect bring to the learning?
- What will I need to change about my approach to teaching and management?
- Am I doing it haphazardly, or am I able to commit to developing a system for incorporating cooperative learning and making it work?

TABLE 12.1. **Effective and Less Effective Elements in Cooperative Learning Activities**

More Effective Elements	Less Effective Elements
Activity has a psychological movement toward a goal and meets many basic needs in the process. Students feel that they are going somewhere.	Students feel that the activity is a formality or may recognize that the task could be done more effectively as an independent exercise.
Emphasis on the quality of the process.	Emphasis on the quality of the final product.
Structure supports the cohesion and social development of group members.	Structure is either accidental or flawed and results in the perpetuation of the current social structure or rewards the advantaged students.
Expectations are clear on the implicit and explicit levels, leading to focused effort and low student anxiety.	Expectations are untaught or left vague and result in confusion or frustration.
Teacher interventions lead to the development of clarity and learning, with the goal of tomorrow being better than today.	Teacher interventions are reactive and act to solve problems only in the short term, if at all.
Leadership is defined by either a 1-Style teacher, who promotes an ever-increasing level of self-directed effort, or a 2-Style teacher, who promotes an increasing level of efficiency.	Leadership is defined by either a 3-Style teacher, who maintains an accidental climate defined by social Darwinism, or a 4-Style teacher, who maintains a level of threat in the room that provides the occasional illusion of order.
Students are able to share their outcomes with others, resulting in pride in their accomplishments and reinforcing the ethic that learning is a constructive process rather than merely a process of fact retention.	Students work to please the teacher, and the learning process is defined mainly by each student's being required to guess what the teacher wants and will think is "good."

Use your answers to these questions to make choices related to what you want to achieve in the area of cooperative learning. The following sections consider these topics related to the following:

- Designing your cooperative learning activity
- Managing your cooperative learning activity
- Dealing with problems that arise
- Using cooperative learning to achieve your long-term management goals

DESIGNING YOUR COOPERATIVE LEARNING ACTIVITY

Once you have identified learning targets that can best be taught within a partial or fully cooperative context, you need to make a number of design decisions: selecting a learning activity structural design or format, deciding on the best group structure, and developing an effective assessment system that aligns with the goals of the activity.

Select an Appropriate Cooperative Learning Environment and Exercise Format

The first item to consider when introducing a cooperative exercise is determining which structural format is best suited to the learning targets. There are several types of format options (Gunter, Estes, & Mintz, 2007; Johnson & Johnson, 1999). Each of the activity designs has different benefits and poses different challenges. Here I will reduce them to a few general types: group projects and performances, inquiry-based learning in teams, collaborative content processing, the jigsaw model, the graffiti model, collaborative assessment, and collaborative group work. A brief description of each of these formats is offered in Table 12.2.

When deciding which cooperative learning activity format is the best fit, reflect on your desired learning targets. Does the learning lend itself to inquiry (that is, can it be discovered inductively)? Is there a product or performance that would logically come out of the activity? Would processing the content collectively bring added benefits when compared to having students process on their own?

TABLE 12.2. Cooperative Learning Activity Format Options

Cooperative Learning Activity Format	Benefits	Challenges
Group products and performance. The group works together to create a product or performance that meets certain criteria.	The finished product is motivational. Provides the feeling of winning as a group. True interdependence is often required. Has a built-in quality of going somewhere.	High stakes create increased chances for conflict and therefore a need for conflict resolution skills. Assessment choices will have a dramatic influence on the way the project proceeds.
Inquiry-based, discovery, or lab activity. The group takes part in collaborative research using an inductive or deductive process.	Inquiry-based learning is inherently authentic as well as engaging. The skills learned in this kind of activity lend themselves to real-life applications and meet many learning style needs.	Inquiry-based learning may be unfamiliar to some students and must be well structured. The process will need to be taught before it can be assumed that students will be able to apply it effectively. It is possible that students can be left behind in the process if they are neglected.
Collaborative content processing. Students examine information together and discuss it; then they report their findings.	The quality of thinking is better as a result of having more perspectives and the opportunity to process verbally rather than just mentally (Slavin, 1994).	It is difficult for the teacher to be sure that the groups are discussing the academic content rather than something else. Having effective expectations in place is critical, especially for noise level, how to take turns, and listening effectively.
Jigsaw model. Students are divided into groups in which students learn a topic or skill; each group is then divided into new groups so that each group has a representative who can teach each topic or skill.	This method can be an effective way to present content. Students learn to become experts and to teach others. With large numbers, it can be more efficient than presentations.	The mechanics of the jigsaw are rather tricky at first and always require precise coordination. Assessment is difficult in that the teacher cannot observe each presentation of content, so must use some other means to ensure quality (Gunter et al., 2007).

(continued)

TABLE 12.3. Continued

Cooperative Learning Activity Format	Benefits	Challenges
Graffiti model. Groups are given a question or topic. For a set amount of time, each group writes answers to the question on a sheet of paper. Groups then rotate to the next sheet of paper. When all groups have completed each station, the original group summarizes the findings for their question or topic.	Groups are exposed to each question in the process. Insights from other groups help reinforce the benefits of working collaboratively. Each answer is completed with a depth that no single group could have accomplished.	Logistics need to be clearly established, or groups may be confused. Groups need to be encouraged to think independently, or they tend to replicate the comments of previous groups (Gunter et al., 2007).
Collaborative assessment. Groups are given a task and can work together to produce one product or independent products, depending on the choice of the teacher.	The quality of the outcome is usually better than work completed by an individual. The process itself promotes learning and deeper processing of the material. Can be done soundly and reliably (Shindler, 2004a).	Collaborative exams are recommended only for groups that have demonstrated advanced cooperative learning skills and levels of responsibility. Having individuals turn in independent products can be a useful compromise design.
Collaborative group work. Students complete independent assignments but are allowed to talk to one another and give and receive assistance and peer tutoring.	Students learn how to teach one another and explain material in their own words. Students are free to interact as much or as little as they need to for meeting their goals and needs.	Some students may use the time to socialize rather than attend to the academic task. Expectations need to be in place for what qualifies as an appropriate noise level, what constitutes cheating, and what actions qualify as an abuse of the privilege.

REFLECTION   12.3

React to the teacher who says, "Anything that I can teach inductively I will, and anytime I can incorporate cooperative learning into the unit or lesson, I will." Do you agree?

Design an Effective Task Structure

To be effective, cooperative learning activities need to be approached intentionally. Preparing a group of students for a cooperative learning activity is like preparing a team for a game. A famous saying among coaches is, "Failure to prepare is preparing to fail." Those who lament that their cooperative learning activity descends into a free-for-all are likely underestimating the requirements of the role of leader and the need to take an intentional approach.

A useful principle to keep in mind is to introduce only one new variable at a time. Never ask students to process new content and a new process at the same time. Pick one or the other.

Let the students work with content that is at least a little familiar and not too threatening when you ask them to focus primarily on developing cooperative learning skills. When the students have grown comfortable with the dynamics and expectations of cooperative learning, they will be ready to work with content of any kind. Getting there should not take long.

The task design elements to determine are the size of the group, the completion of the group, the time frame and nature of the task, and potential roles for group members.

An examination of the many factors involved in creating groups makes it readily apparent that this task needs to be undertaken thoughtfully. A good portion of potential management problems stem from careless group development (Lotan, 2006; Rubin, 2003).

Group Size. Two students do qualify as a cooperative group, but if possible, consider creating larger groups. Three or four members are typically optimal. Groups greater than four can be problematic. In almost every case of larger groups, some students end up being spectators or marginalized by the others (Slavin, 1994).

12.4 REFLECTION

When you have been part of groups larger than four members, was everyone an active participant, or were some members spectators?

Group Members. There are several configurations to choose from for grouping students: student self-selection, choosing groups by random, grouping by similar ability or mixed ability, or using a systematic method such as combinations of learning style types or manufacturing groups that you think will produce optimal results. Each produce dramatically different outcomes. Table 12.3 compares the advantages and disadvantages of each of the options.

It will be tempting to give in to the students' desires to make their own groups. It is usually easier and most students will be happier. However, when making choices here, consider how your choices work to promote the social frame that "when students demonstrate responsibility, [they] will be given freedom." In the short term, allowing students to self-select their group may seem innocuous; over time it will likely lead to clique formations and entrenchment of the social structure (Lotan, 2006). With each successive exercise in which self-selected grouping is allowed, students become more accustomed to the process and increasingly develop a sense of entitlement that it is their right. A common result is the teacher's eventual determination that there are too many negative effects from the policy of self-selected grouping. At that point, the teacher decides to begin the process of reassigning groups, not anticipating the strong and often defiant reaction of the students. This reaction is especially forceful from students who feel that they have the most to lose by a new arrangement. For example, a student who unconsciously believes that he is "too good" for other members of the group to which he has been assigned may act this out in immature and inappropriate ways.

These types of displays can take you by surprise. They can be spiteful and expose the lack of community and egalitarian sociopolitics in the class. While the temptation is to be angry toward the student who displays a sense of entitlement or discrimination, the fault actually lies with the choice made weeks earlier to allow self-selection of groups. The event could have been prevented. Moreover, it represents evidence that instead of promoting community, cooperative learning activities have been undermining the democratic values in the class (Rubin, 2003).

TABLE 12.3. **Common Cooperative Learning Grouping Techniques**

Grouping Format	Advantage	Disadvantage
Random. Students number off in a fixed pattern, producing groups that have a random composition.	Most likely creates mixed ability, mixed learning style, and mixed social group groupings. Can be done easily. Students see it as fair.	There is no control over the composition of the group. Groups may or may not be equal or desirable.
Similar ability. Teacher selects students, or students self-select into high, middle, and lower levels depending on the activity, skill, or subject. Group members have similar levels of ability.	Students can move at a pace that fits their natural inclination. Students who are low ability can be in a position to be leaders or major contributors. High-ability students may feel more challenged.	Group outcomes will vary widely. Students of all abilities will miss the opportunity to work with some students. It can create a climate of haves and have-nots. High-ability students lose the opportunity to be leaders to some degree, and lower-ability students lose the contribution and modeling of high-ability students.
Mixed ability. Teacher selects students who represent different levels of ability and creates groups that consist of students of all levels.	Sends the symbolic message that the class is egalitarian and classless. Higher-ability students are in a position to be experts, leaders, models, and teachers; lower-ability students get the benefits of having higher-ability students in their group.	Higher-ability students may not experience the stimulation or challenge that they would with other higher-ability students. Lower-ability students may feel perpetually in need of help rather than experiencing the role of leader or expert relative to the others in their group (Rubin, 2003).
Learning style similarities. Teacher creates groups that have similar personality types, cognitive styles, learning styles, or kind of intelligence.	Students feel a greater affinity for one another. Thinking may be more harmonious and familiar to each member.	Products may lack evidence of other types of thinking. Creative groups may lack practical ideas for execution. Practical groups may lack creative energies that would help generate ideas.
Learning style mix. Teacher selects students from a variety of learning styles for each group.	Groups will have a greater balance of types of intelligences and styles. Products will show evidence of more skills and perspectives.	Groups will have different ways of approaching the task and assigning value to ideas. Requires tolerance and some degree of appreciation for the fact that others have different learning styles.
Self-selected groups. Teacher allows students to make their own groups.	Relatively easy for most students to find a group. Students prefer this option and will be pleased that it was chosen.	Can lead to cliques and the maintenance of the social hierarchy and political structure in the class. Difficult to use other systems after students have gotten comfortable with this type (Lotan, 2006).

12.5

REFLECTION

Recall groups that you would consider to be "evolved" or that have developed the qualities of a genuine community. Do you see much evidence of cliques and a social hierarchy within the group? Why do you think this is the case?

A good standard to use in these cases is that when students stop caring about who is in their group, they are ready for the privilege of choosing their own. You could counter, "My students will always be concerned with who is in their group." Be assured that you may be surprised at their ability to grow out of their recalcitrance. One of the transformative effects of a high-quality cooperative learning process is that it helps students get past their preformed perspectives of one another.

When in doubt about which grouping to choose, default to mixed-ability groups. Ability grouping has its place, but it has some serious disadvantages. One is that it can quickly define a culture of haves and have-nots, thereby undermining the sense of community in the class. Mixed-ability groups have many advantages, including providing opportunities for stronger students to take on the role of peer tutor and weaker students to benefit from having the stronger students in their groups. If you do feel the need to group by ability, try to limit it to situations in which the ability level is mostly related to previous experience rather than students' perceptions of innate intelligence. For example, if you created groups of experienced computer users and groups of less experienced users and had students self-select, in this case it is less likely that students will feel stratified than if you placed them into high- and low-ability groups in an area that they felt represented a fundamental aptitude.

Random grouping often produces relatively desirable results and can be done rather efficiently. For example, with a little practice (and you do need to practice), students can get used to numbering off into groups quickly. The following sequence can be effective. First, count the students. Second, mentally divide the number of students by the number that you want to have in each group; that is your count-off number. Third, instruct them to count off. Be sure that the students say their group numbers out loud. This will save you the trouble of learning that when you say the numbers, the groups often end up with disproportionate sizes. Having students say their numbers promotes both memory and honesty. Another system is for you to create random groups before the event and then simply read them off.

Sample Direction Sequence for Numbering Off

1. Wait for 100 percent attention.

2. "We are going to number off into seven groups of four for the next activity. When we get into groups, I will explain what we are doing."

3. "Let's begin counting by sevens. When we are done, the ones should go [determine spot], the twos should go [determine spot]" [and so on.]

4. Students count off and stay in place until they are all done.

5. Early in the year or if the students have taken a long time to get into groups on their previous effort, say, "Okay. It should take us about thirty seconds to get into groups. Ready? Go!" When students have learned to move with urgency and efficiency to their group, you merely have to say, "Ready? Go!"

Roles for Group Members. Assigning students roles within the group has many advantages (Johnson & Johnson, 1999a; Slavin, 1994). First, it provides students a clearer sense of what to do in the process. Second, assigned roles make it more likely that the necessary roles and duties will ultimately be performed. For example, if there were no designated manager or recorder, the function of a group may be limited and certain tasks may never get performed. Third, students learn that roles are useful in the accomplishment of collective efforts. They come to understand that those who can fulfill a certain role within a group can often be more valuable than those who are highly talented but provide a less focused contribution. Fourth, if roles are rotated regularly, students have the opportunity to take on roles that they may not otherwise have chosen. Some students will feel very comfortable taking the role of recorder but may never volunteer to be in a leadership position unless that role has been assigned to them. And students who have expressive personas and comfort with a leadership role may always find themselves taking over unless they are expected to fulfill another role that requires other skills. While it may not be entirely comfortable for students to work outside their natural strength areas, it provides them an opportunity to develop areas that could use growth. An added consideration is the opportunity to learn appreciation for effective performance in roles previously avoided. This contributes to admiration for others when they perform those roles.

REFLECTION   12.6

Reflect on your own experience in groups. If you had your choice, would you take the same role each time? Have you experienced growth when you were required to take on roles that were not your preference?

In the early stages of development, it is usually most effective to assign roles to group members. This can be done randomly or purposefully. If different roles are assigned often and randomly, all students usually have the opportunity to take on multiple roles. However, if you are concerned that all students may not have the opportunity to take on each role—or you simply do not want to take chances—you may want to keep records and be purposeful about rotating roles.

A simple technique for assigning roles is to use physical objects on the walls of the room or yard. You can simply assign certain roles to those closest to certain objects. For example, one possible scenario may play out in the following manner: "Is everyone ready? I will pass out the directions shortly. But now that we are all sitting in our groups, let's designate roles [a reminder that everyone is going to get to serve in a leadership role at some point in the quarter or year]. Those closest to the clock are the managers [wait for reaction to die down if there is one]. Those closest to the window are the recorders. Those closest to the board are researchers, and those closest to the door are the mediators [or consensus builders]."

As with the group membership, there may be some students who are happier with the role that they have been assigned than others. Resist the temptation to feel sorry for students who did not get a role they wanted or apologize to them. Instead, project the message: "Remember that all roles are really important. Do your best to do a great job of your role and help your group. What's important now? What do you need to do to help your group succeed?" Raise their level of awareness of the possible resentment or passive aggressiveness the students may be feeling and challenge them to rise to the occasion.

REFLECTION   12.7

When would you choose to assign roles, and when would you let the students do what comes naturally?

Groups do not always need roles. A useful principle may be that they are not needed when students have shown that they have the skills to execute the task without them or roles are not applicable to the task. This requires your judgment and depends on the situation.

What are some typical roles students can take to contribute to the group's capacity to reach its goals most effectively? The answer is, "whatever roles the activity requires." It can be counterproductive to be too tied to any established roles that you or others have used. Examine the task and ask yourself what jobs are needed for the success of that particular task. The most meaningful roles should emerge. Here are some typical roles that can be useful in various cooperative learning activities (Johnson & Johnson, 1999a):

- Manager
- Reporter
- Reader
- Consensus builder
- Recorder
- Researcher
- Leader
- Mediator
- Monitor

It may be helpful to create an evolving written catalogue of roles and descriptions you can print for each substantive cooperative activity. Pasting that list into the assignment sheet will bring another level of clarity to the assignment. Later in the chapter, I introduce an effective method for making the job description of each role more concrete and meaningful and encouraging students to value the importance of their role.

Identify the Time Frame and Nature of the Task

Defining the time frame of the task may seem like common sense, but it is critical to the process (Slavin, 1994). Whether the activity is three days or thirty minutes long, students must be able to pace their efforts and adjust to the level of urgency or reflection required. What are the priority tasks that need attention? What needs to be done carefully? How much time is allowed for brainstorming or discussion? In most classes, some groups oversimplify the task and do it too quickly. These efforts are usually missing something that the teacher thought would be included or do not reflect the kind of deeper processing that he or she was looking for. Some groups will overcomplicate a task that was intended to be straightforward. They can become paralyzed by the idea generation process and never get to the execution. Especially early in the year, you may want to give time frames for the duration of each piece of the process.

Conversely, you may want to offer a time frame for when certain aspects of the process need to be complete, so that the group will have sufficient time for the later portions of the task. A useful tool in the effort to structure the task and time frame is to have students develop benchmarks for the product at intervals along the way.

Assess the Cooperative Learning Activity

The relationship between assessment and classroom management is a powerful nexus that is usually given only a fraction of the attention it warrants. It is especially significant for cooperative learning.

How and what you assess will define for the students what is important in the experience and shape the learning environment as much as anything else you do. What you assess tells the students what to care about and what constitutes success. You might begin by asking yourself a few defining questions:

- Do you want to assess formally or informally?
- Do you want your unit of analysis to be the individual student or the group as a whole?
- Do you want to focus more on the final product or on the process and level of investment the students make along the way?

Each of these choices will have a significant effect on the way that students approach the task and what they will infer to be a successful performance. Table 12.4 outlines the advantages and disadvantages of each method of assessment.

While all options have their benefits, some options contribute to more desirable results (Slavin et al., 2003). Using no assessment is clearly less trouble; however, it makes the statement that every effort is the same as every other effort. If this is true, incorporating no formal assessment is a valid option. However, if you are assessing other areas of achievement such as tests of knowledge or homework assignments but not the cooperative learning activities, you are making a statement that the quality of effort during the cooperative learning has little importance, regardless of what you may say.

Self-assessment can be an excellent tool for groups that have demonstrated a high level of responsibility and skill at the cooperative learning process. It can also be a useful adjunct assessment system to teacher-based assessment as a way of promoting more self-reflection. However, translating it into a grade is extremely difficult and should be avoided. It can be a valuable process for students to informally self-evaluate the quality of their performance and the performance of those in their group, yet when that evaluation is translated into a grade, it typically

TABLE 12.4. Assessment Options for Cooperative Groups

Type	Individual Accountability	Group Accountability
No formal assessment	Fine, as long as the task is inherently engaging and you want to promote internal locus of control. May not provide enough motivation for tasks that are less inherently interesting or for students who need a little external incentive.	
Formal self-assessment	Good for having the students reflect on their process effort. Shifts the locus of control of assessment to students. Problematic when trying to promote accountability.	
Peer assessment	Can be effective in that those doing the rating are in the best position to judge the quality of the other students' performance. However, this method often leads to one of the following problems: the reliability of the ratings are usually suspect due to social dynamics, and putting students in the position of rating one another is often perceived as unfair or uncomfortable.	
Process assessment	Helps motivate the student to put forth full effort and be cooperative. Does not penalize students for others' lack of effort.	Helps motivate the group to work through problems, collaborate, and use the prescribed process format.
Product assessment	Rewards students for their personal contribution and does not penalize them for others' lack of quality. Does not readily promote cooperation skills.	Helps motivate students to create a quality outcome, but may lack the ability to reward effort and desired process along the way.

leads to a great deal of damage. Your efforts to promote cohesion and trust within the group will be undermined as a result of students' feeling vulnerable and resentful of one another's ratings when including any feature of peer-based assessment. Moreover, it is likely that popular students will be graded more favorably by their peers than students who do not possess the same level of political or social capital. Typically many students are honest when there is no cost but much less honest when they recognize that they will be penalized for being self-critical.

12.8 REFLECTION

In your experience, would you say that when students fully invest in the process, the products usually work out well? Conversely, would you say that a good product assumes that a group of students has invested in the process fully?

Assessing process outcomes typically has the effect of promoting a greater level of student investment in the process. Moreover, when students invest fully in the process, the products they produce usually reflect their high-quality investment. Many learning targets during cooperative learning activities will be in the areas of processes, skills, and dispositions. If you have learning targets and goals in these areas but do not use an assessment system that supports them, you have in essence built failure into the instructional design. Many teachers who do not currently incorporate process assessment into their teaching dismiss its potential, yet teachers who do incorporate some process or behavioral-level assessment recognize the powerful effect it can have to shape the quality of student performance.

12.9 REFLECTION

Reflect on your experiences as a student in cooperative groups. How did you feel when you were graded on the performance of the whole group? Do you see the advantages and disadvantages of both individual and group grades for collaborative efforts? How will this understanding affect your decisions as a teacher?

MANAGING YOUR COOPERATIVE EXERCISE

If you have designed an effective cooperative learning activity, much of your work will be done. The task itself will create much of the energy and define the focus. So how do you manage it? Here are three principles to guide your thinking:

1. At any time, but especially in the early stages of developing a climate supportive of successful cooperative learning, make the social frames very explicit (recall Chapter Three). It is important to promote in the students' minds the cause-and-effect relationship by saying, "When you are ready for X, you will be able to do Y." Cooperative learning is just another teaching strategy, but it is also a privilege. Keep the students mindful that they need to continue to earn this privilege.

2. Assume that students need a great deal of support and structure until they show that they can succeed with less. To be effective, cooperative learning requires a deliberate use of technical management and skills development (Slavin et al., 2003). One of the benefits of cooperative learning is that if it is done well, increasingly less management is necessary over time.

3. Be aware of the presence of social and indirect learning when you make management choices.

When students are working in groups, messages sent to one group will affect the other groups as well. The actions that you take with one group tell the other groups what to expect. When you publicly recognize the successes of one group, the other groups will become wiser as a result (Bandura, 1986; Slavin et al., 2003).

The effectiveness of your management will be related to your ability to develop a culture of listening and provide clear directions, be an effective leader and teacher during the activity, teach the skills necessary for groups to function effectively, and respond to behavioral problems when they arise.

Developing a Culture of Listening and Providing Good Directions

A successful cooperative learning environment requires a culture of listening. Be sure the students understand the directions before they begin, and have an efficient, painless way to get 100 percent attention for short periods of time. It will be difficult to be fully effective in managing cooperative groups without the use of a well-established cue. The nature of cooperative learning requires that you frequently add information, process ideas, check for understanding, and ask questions quickly without being too disruptive to the process or requiring yelling or nagging (Slavin et al., 2003). Being a master of technical management in the development stages of the process is essential.

When possible, provide written directions or guidelines. These will save you and the students time, create another level of clarity, and improve the quality of the students' performance. Include this information in written directions or guidelines:

- Step-by-step procedures for the task

- Roles and role descriptions

- Explanations of cooperative group skills that may need attention

- Assessment instruments for the process or the product (or both)

All of these features except the first can be pasted into each new set of guidelines.

REFLECTION

12.10

Recall cooperative learning activities you have observed. What portion of the activity problems would you say related to technical management issues? What technical management strategies might have helped those teachers?

Being an Effective Leader and Teacher During the Activity

One of your most important roles as leader of the cooperative learning effort is that of the link among the groups. Your words and actions act as the mode of communication between each group. Without your words, each group is essentially working in isolation (Johnson & Johnson, 1999a; Slavin et al., 2003). A powerful principle to keep in mind related to the social learning model is that what can be communicated to one group will inform or improve the performance in the other groups.

When we examine the social learning diagram within the context of cooperative learning, we notice that most often the S represents entire groups. One of the monumental instances of a missed teaching opportunity is observing something good that one group is doing and keeping it to yourself. This is especially true with cooperative groups. Too often as teachers walk around from group to group, they are the only ones benefiting and becoming more informed. If you take the opportunity to communicate in a publicly positive manner what you have observed, each group will have the opportunity to learn from the other groups.

Keep these principles in mind as you provide feedback and direction during the cooperative group activity:

- When you recognize that providing additional information or clarification would be valuable for everyone, stop the whole group with a cue. Wait for 100 percent attention, and then provide the information in as few words as possible and as clearly as possible. Be sensitive to maintaining momentum within the groups, so do this as little as possible. Also, it will be easier to maintain attention when the information that you share is valuable and concise. Test your students' patience at your own risk.

- When you wish to share valuable information that is not necessary for every student to have, speak at a slightly higher volume (but watch your pitch, because students tend to turn off messages that are spoken in a high or panicky register).

- Move from group to group. Make sure that you get around to each group during each phase of the task. Do not take over when you are there. In fact, the less you need to intervene, the better.

- Be concrete and specific (recall from Chapter Four information on personal versus positive recognitions). You may find yourself saying, "Good job!" a great deal, which is fine. However, try to include specifics as well. For example, a more effective statement would be, "Great job staying with it. See, when you are persistent, the ideas do eventually come." Or, "Great idea! I see one group decided to make three columns on their paper and list ideas for each category."

- Make positive recognitions public, but make negative recognitions, criticisms, and consequence implementations private. Build the vision of a successful performance with your words, but use actions to change behaviors that need to change.

12.11 REFLECTION

Reflect on the instinctive words you use when you recognize a student's efforts. Are they encouraging and educational? What habits could you adopt to make your feedback more effective?

Teaching the Skills for Groups to Function Effectively

In almost every case, teachers whose students succeed at executing effective cooperative learning activities have taught their students the skills they need to do so (or have benefited from teachers who have done so previously). Teachers who assume their students have the skills to participate in cooperative learning activities without being taught those skills are usually disappointed. Put simply, you reap what you sow. Recall the discussion related to technical management. When you observe performance that lacks the quality you consider necessary, you have three choices: live with it, be disappointed and get negative, or change it.

Instead of starting off the year allowing students to fail and then being disappointed, a better idea is to start the year by building the skills necessary for success (Gunter et al., 2007; Slavin, 1994). Once students show the ability to demonstrate these skills, you can move on. This investment of time and effort early in the year will pay back many times over the course of the year in efficiency and positive emotion.

Students need to master these cooperative group skills:

- Listening
- Resolving conflict

- Communicating concerns
- Making decisions
- Performing a role
- Executing the necessary learning process
- Sharing

Before you begin the cooperative activity, you might select one or two skills that you judge to be the most critical given the needs of your class, and engage in a question-driven concept attainment exercise in an effort to clarify them, so that when the students take part in the task those concepts are well defined and understood. What is an I-message? What does it mean to be cooperative? What does a good listener do? These are all abstractions. If you do not make them concrete, they will remain abstractions and never be translated into behavior. It therefore makes sense to teach them in concept attainment exercises in which you are asking the students to provide examples and nonexamples of the concept. For example, you could ask them to identify examples and nonexamples of active listening. The exercise might look like this (Gunter et al., 2007):

Examples of Active Listening	Nonexamples of Active Listening
Eye contact	Looking away
Clarifying points	Daydreaming
Waiting until the speaker is done	Getting lost in one idea
Paraphrasing what you heard	Making assumptions

These can be as simple as a twenty-second question-and-answer activity or as involved as a formal concept-attainment-building activity.

Success will come from your ability to translate the concepts fundamental to effective cooperative learning from abstractions into practical recipes and then finally into behavioral habits.

The most powerful tool for helping students grasp the concept within practical behavior is to see it firsthand in themselves or in their peers. Too often students do not recognize quality behavior unless it is pointed out. It is essential that you are intentional about verbalizing examples of high-quality behavior. For instance, if you observed students successfully resolve a conflict, you might share what you observed with the other groups. It is not important to congratulate the group; the positive recognition will be praise enough. Instead, emphasize what they did that was effective. The subtext of your message is that if the other students make similar behavioral choices, their efforts will be more effective in the future.

The role that you choose to take in the process will depend to a great degree on your personal goals and teaching style orientation. Teachers using 1- and 2-Style approaches must be intentional about the process of creating clear expectations and taking on the role of the communication link among the groups. Either style will need to be an effective technical manager with groups new to cooperative learning. However, there will be differences, and those differences will likely widen over time. A 2-Style orientation will achieve increased efficiency and the level of comfort and enjoyment will increase along with it. The 1-Style orientation assumes that as efficiency is attained, the skills of self-direction are increasingly introduced. The ultimate goal of the teacher who is working toward a transformative effect will be cooperative learning that runs itself. The stages of evolution from a group new to cooperative learning to a group that can self-direct its own efforts is a three-stage process, as outlined in the box.

Stages of 1-Style Teacher Involvement on the Path to Student Self-Directed Cooperative Learning

Stage 1: Creating the Foundation for Success and Teaching Skills

- Be very clear about the vision. Create a clear set of expectations, protocols, and procedures for each type of cooperative learning.

- Be intolerant of behavior that will undermine the process: carelessness, abuse in any form, put-downs, helplessness, selfishness, or game playing.

- Explain to the students about if-then cause and effect: if they grow in their ability to self-direct, then they will be given more freedom and autonomy.

- Limit opportunities when the effort is not present, and do not hesitate to practice procedures, repeat an activity, or stop if the students abuse the privilege of cooperative learning.

- Define the purpose clearly. This is done by the following means:
  - A clear assessment system for each type of process
  - Use of deliberate feedback
  - Clear directions, guiding questions, and expectation mantras

Stage 2: Developing the Capacity for Self-Direction

- Shift focus from what you think should happen to the students' perceptions of support of their effectiveness and their needs.

- Recognize and encourage innovation in the procedures.

- Use fewer concrete explanations and more expectation cues.

- Reinforce cause and effect: students' ability to self-direct will lead to more freedom and autonomy as they recognize what they are doing and what they are getting as a result (and, if you feel it would be effective, what they are not doing, and what would happen if they did).

Stage 3: Guiding the Self-Directed Effort of the Students

- Encourage students to rely on their own interpretations of what constitutes success and quality, and allow them to solve their own problems.

- Use more self-assessment instruments and fewer teacher assessment instruments, or allow the students to use the assessment instruments to self-assess.

- Offer more resources and fewer answers.

- Offer fewer judgments and opinions, and ask more questions.

- Encourage more creativity and risk taking.

- Take time for student recognition of what went well (on all levels) and what they assess might need modification in the future.

Also, do a project yourself along with the students, and thus be a peer.

RESPOND EFFECTIVELY TO BEHAVIORAL PROBLEMS

No matter how effective you have been at designing an effective activity and teaching the necessary skills, you may have students who violate expectations and exhibit problem behavior. Therefore, ensure that the class social contract includes expectations, rules, and consequences related to cooperative learning contexts.

When dealing with contract violations and small-scale dysfunctional behavior, keep the social learning model in mind, that is, making tomorrow better as a result of what you do today (Lotan, 2006).

Your management actions are teaching lessons. What you do today will define what happens tomorrow. This is especially true early in the school year. So before you choose to act reactively or do the first thing that comes to mind, ask yourself, "What am I encouraging tomorrow, if I take this action today?" Table 12.5 outlines some common management strategies to avoid and replacement strategies in managing the cooperative group context.

TABLE 12.5. **Strategies to Do and Avoid Doing When Managing Behavioral Problems in a Cooperative Group Context**

Strategies to Avoid Doing When Possible	Strategies to Do When Possible
Don't reward with inactivity or punish with more activity. Giving activity as a punishment creates a disincentive to perform the activity in the future. So laps, standards, more work, or a more difficult assignment will lead to unwanted negative consequences in the long term. And giving inactivity as a reward makes the statement that the goal in the class is to get to do nothing.	Use the principle that inactivity is the negative consequence and activity is the positive consequence. So when a group has finished its work before the others, give its members a more interesting or challenging piece of work or allow them to finish something else. Even playing a game is something. When a group does not demonstrate the ability to live up to its responsibility to cooperate and function as a collective, the best consequence is the loss of privilege.
Hovering. Do not stand over a group that is struggling to perform or get along. It sends the message that they are incapable of solving their own problems and that the teacher gives attention to those who are misbehaving (and as a result creates the likelihood that more students will misbehave or become helpless to get attention).	Put your energy into the groups that are on task and making a quality effort. This sends the message that when students are trying, you will give them attention.
Nagging. Complaining about what should be happening sends a negative, passive message.	Take action if the students are not being responsible. Give consequences, problem-solve, or teach the necessary skills.
Public shaming. Public negative recognition toward a group that is off-task is not effective. It is passive and hostile, and encourages students who tend to game-play and engage in power struggles.	If you identify a problem, engage the group of students privately. Be constructive, and release the disappointment. Send the message that you know the group members are going to fix their problem and you are willing to help them do so.

(continued)

TABLE 12.5. **Strategies to Do and Avoid Doing When Managing Behavioral Problems in a Cooperative Group Context (Continued)**

Strategies to Avoid Doing When Possible	Strategies to Do When Possible
Don't react to internal group complaints (tattletales or passive-aggressive complainers). If there are members of the group who are unhappy with what is going on, taking the side of the displeased student will reinforce the behavior. This response makes it more likely in the future and limits the potential for conflict resolution by maintaining focus on the interpersonal dramas and personality clashes and away from the task and the skills needed for getting past the pettiness to improved group function.	When a group is unhappy or has members who are unhappy about the group dynamics, help them to shift their attention away from the pettiness and intolerance to what they should be doing at that point and the skills that would help improve the situation (conflict resolution, active listening, or raising the level of personal awareness, for example).
Perpetuating group drama. If the group has developed a negative dynamic, don't contribute to the reinforcement of that dynamic. For example, if the group calls themselves the "losers in the class," don't allow that label, or you will be enabling their problematic definition of their ability to succeed. If they have defined the situation as the "boys are being bad," don't buy into the roles that they have given themselves. If you do, the drama will undermine the success of their effort and inhibit growing out of their limited thinking.	Use affirming language and the language of responsibility to all group members. No matter what they say is happening, define the situation as one in which they are capable, trustworthy, and responsible. It will be useful to be specific about situations in which you have seen them persist and solve problems. Help them raise their level of awareness about what is going on internally or externally. It can be helpful to simply tell them, "Lose the drama," and think of ways that they can make the whole group better (this message will need to be worded differently for different age groups).
Fixing the group's problems. It is tempting to allow students to find an easier path to comfort than being patient and working together and to do what it takes to find solutions. But if we do, we often enable students and make them dependent.	Support the students with ideas and strategies, but allow them to work through the difficulties. As opposed to coming to the group and making judgments about what is happening, it is usually more helpful to ask questions and guide them to solutions.
Removing students from the group. It is tempting to relieve the discomfort of some students by removing a group member whom they dislike or do not want to work with. For the troublesome group member, it may be a convenient way to get out of having to look dumb or having to work with others to become bothersome enough that the teacher removes him or her from the group. But examine these dynamics from the social learning model. If we allow students to dictate whom they want in their groups by pouting, complaining, or being passive-aggressive, we reinforce that behavior in those students and teach the rest of the class that if they do the same thing, we will come to their aid and enable their intolerance as well. Students who are removed quickly become pariahs.	It may be necessary to remove a student who has become extreme in behavior, but unless real abuse is involved, help students recognize that it is their job to support one another and get along. It will be useful to change groups often and resist the students' desire to choose their groups for a while. Individual process grading can help each student feel less penalized by the others as well as encouraged to show excellent cooperation skills. It is a powerful lesson that we sometimes have to work with people who are difficult, and when we succeed at working together, we all feel like winners: we resisted the temptation to quit and have shown ourselves and one another that we can come out on the other side better. And the community is stronger for it.

REFLECTION

Many of the ideas in Table 12.5 could be considered counterintuitive. As you read the list of strategies to avoid, what was your reaction? If it included a great deal of resistance to the ideas, why do you think this was? Explore your emotions and practical concerns.

If you design a sound exercise and offer the kinds of support described, you should experience a decreasing number of problems during cooperative group activities (Slavin et al., 2003). Each intervention will lead to further clarity of the expectations, new skill development, and higher levels of collective group functioning. In fact, problems early in the year might best be viewed as teaching opportunities. Groups that experience conflict provide a concrete set of circumstances to examine within the lens of the conflict resolution principles. Groups that struggle with ideas of self-direction or investment in the process offer the opportunity to reinforce the structural components of the activity that support and require these.

For example, when faced with a problem that appears to result from a lack of understanding of what constitutes quality cooperative group process, we might take the opportunity to ask our students to assess their current level of performance on a group process assessment rubric. (For a sample rubric, see the online resource article, "Developing and Implementing an Effective System for Assessing the Quality of Student Process, Participation, and Behavior" at transformativeclassroom.com.) This type of intervention will have a couple of effects. First, it supports the group members' recognition that a system is in place for assessing quality process, which may be new to them. Many teachers come into a school where there has been little effective cooperative learning and introduce it to their students. Even if the teacher designs a perfect exercise, success will not come immediately. Too often the teacher creates clear and conspicuous expectations and then is impatient when the students do not respond immediately. It may be useful to assume that nothing in your system will have an effect until it has had a real and material impact on the students' lives. If you have consequences in place, you may need to implement them before they are taken seriously. If you are assessing process, you may need to take students through a number of activities from start to finish in which you assess process before they respond. Second, asking the students to self-assess will have the effect of promoting self-reflection. Early in the year, they may or may not take the rubric seriously, but until they use the values assumed in it to make judgments of quality regarding their own performance, the rubric will remain an abstraction and a formality. In other words, students will invest in the process to the degree that they value it and believe that doing so will benefit them. This perceived benefit can be either manufactured (their grade will be positively affected) or organic (they experience a greater level of satisfaction and level of function).

One intervention that can have a powerful effect, but should be used sparingly and avoided if possible, is to withhold the privilege of the cooperative context if a whole class does not approach it with care, responsibility, and appreciation. Consider a situation in which a teacher develops a cooperative inductive science lesson incorporating group investigation. If it is early in the year and the majority of the students in the class approach the lesson with a careless, entitled, or irresponsible attitude, the teacher might decide to withhold the lesson until they can approach it with the sense of value it warrants. After assessing the situation and deciding to take remedial action, the teacher might say to the class: "I can see that some of us were taking this assignment seriously, but many were not approaching the task responsibly. We can learn science in a number of ways. This way takes a lot of time to prepare and design and uses materials that need to be treated with care. I did not see evidence that we were ready for this kind of activity at this time. So I want you to put away these materials, move your seats back into their rows, and take out your textbooks. I am sure that we will be ready for an activity like this in the future; today we weren't."

An intervention such as this will likely succeed at building the cause and effect between the level of freedom given and the level of responsibility shown. However, make a substantial attempt to build the foundation of functional behavior with positive recognitions and skill practice before you take such a dramatic step.

12.13   REFLECTION

Put yourself in the position of a student who was being careless in the scenario above. How did you feel after the teacher took away the materials? Whom do you hold responsible? How will your behavior change in the future?

Not uncommonly, all groups but one or two are on task and functioning effectively. Keep in mind that three important things are going on at that moment: (1) on-task groups that need reinforcement from the teacher as encouragement, (2) a group or two that are off task and need help, and (3) an entire class that is watching and learning how you deal with the groups that are off task as well as those on task. Here we examine an intervention sequence scenario for dealing with a group that is struggling to function.

If a whole group is having trouble working together, keep the ownership of the problem on the students and provide interventions that include choices and consequences. All the while keep your intervention anger-free and constructive.

Your first intervention should assume that the students can succeed if they have a better sense of what they are doing. It may be helpful to begin each interaction with a sense of the result you need to achieve before you walk away. Intervention 1 thus asks, "What is the problem?" The goal is to clarify any misunderstanding:

- *What do they need?* Support to help them accomplish their task.

- *What do you need as a result?* Recognition from them that they have what they need to accomplish the task with an implicit commitment that they can do it now.

- *What you need to do:*

  - Support the process. Ask, "What do you need? What can I help you understand?"

  - Communicate the score at this point: "I must not have done a good job explaining the directions. Let me try again, and help me if you still do not understand."

Do not hover. Send the message that you trust that students can find a way to function more effectively, and then put your energy into the students who are on task and investing in the process. Give the group time to fix "their problem."

If you look over at the group again and notice that they are still experiencing dysfunction and their efforts have not produced sufficient change, intervene again.

Intervention 2 asks what they are going to do to fix their problem. The goal is to troubleshoot and gain commitment:

- *What do they need?* Strategies that they must agree to that will support their collective functioning. Also, they need to be concrete and specific about what should happen and who is going to do what to make the situation better. They need to acknowledge a clear understanding of the consequence if they do not achieve it.

- *What do you need as a result?* An assumption that the group has the strategies needed to solve their problems and the group's commitment to work together on the task and to overcome the dysfunctional dynamics. You need an explicit assurance that they can do it and a clear sense that the group understands the consequences for not demonstrating that they can function. For example, they can give you an answer when you ask, "When I come back, what will I be seeing from this group?"

Again you send the message that you believe in the group (no matter their history) and assume that it is just a matter of time before they will get on track. So move away from them, let them solve their problem or at least own it, and put your energy into the other groups. It is important to keep your energy supportive and positive and not let your disappointment sour your interactions with each of the groups. The high-functioning groups need the mirror of positive energy and enthusiasm to take them to the next level. Groups that are struggling need your trust, supportive attitude, and absence of negativity. Your negativity will only magnify any negativity in the group.

In nearly all cases, these two interventions will resolve any problems; over time, even these interventions will become less necessary as the process becomes more familiar and more functional and, as a result, more satisfying. But now what happens when you look over at that group and observe that they still cannot get past their dysfunctional dynamics?

REFLECTION   12.14

What is your instinct telling you to do at this point? What does common sense tell you to do? What does the social learning model tell you to do?

Ask yourself:

- What can I do in an intervention to make tomorrow better as a result of what I do today?

- What have the members of the group agreed to? What expectations have been put in place? What are the logical consequences?

Intervention 3 should have follow-through and promoting accountability as its goal. Ask yourself:

- *What do the students need?* Acknowledgment of their choices and accountability for their actions.

- *What do you need as a result?* Evidence that you have followed through and held the students accountable for their actions and the implementation of a consequence that will make tomorrow better as a result.

Given that the students have expressed commitment to having a clear understanding of the task (intervention 1) and have received a second opportunity to get it together (intervention 2), you can assume that the problematic behavior was a function of their collective choice to perpetuate the dysfunction. As a result, you are in the position of following through with a consequence. You need to send the message to the rest of the class that when a group chooses to hold on to a self-centered attitude rather than do what is best for others and themselves, they need a concrete reminder that it will not work in the future.

You can send this message in a number of ways. One consequence is to withdraw the group's opportunity to take further part in the activity. In addition, group members might be asked to write down ideas for how they are going to keep this kind of problem from arising in future situations. It is critical to implement a consequence that is active but keeps all judgment and shame out of the equation. The loss of the right to participate should be left on its own to teach the lesson. Moreover, your interactions with this group must be private. The hint that you are disparaging the members of this group to others will have a profoundly negative effect on your relationship with them and likely undermine any value your disciplinary action might have. If you notice that after a few minutes the group seems to show evidence that they have learned their lesson, you may decide to give them a second chance.

At some point in this process, your inclination might have been to split up the group. The effect of this choice will usually be that you feel better and the conflict stops. But examined from the perspective of the social learning model, it will become apparent why it may not be a good idea. If the students learn that you bail out groups by splitting them up when they do not get along, you will get more groups asking you with their words or actions to split them up and free them from a group of students they did not want to work with in the first place.

TRANSFORMATIVE IDEAS RELATED TO COOPERATIVE LEARNING

Cooperative learning is a strategy that has the potential to have a powerful transformative effect on a class. In fact, it may be impossible to achieve a significant level of community or a psychology of success without incorporating some form of collective effort. Among the cooperative learning strategies that have the most transformative effects are these:

- *Egalitarian grouping strategies* (whether grouping is done purposefully or randomly). There is a powerful effect on a group when they stop being concerned with who is in the group and become fully present to anyone with whom they are teamed.

- *Moving toward self-direction.* When your students demonstrate the capacity to take on greater levels of responsibility and self-direction, they reflect the transformative effects of your efforts to support a new level of functioning.

- *Self-assessment.* Help the students get used to making their own judgments about the quality of their effort. This has to come after they have nearly all demonstrated a mastery level in relation to your assessment criteria or as defined by your participation quality rubric.

- *Assess the quality of the investment and process.* The online resource article, "Developing and Implementing an Effective System for Assessing the Quality of Student Process, Participation, and Behavior" available at transformativeclassroom.com, outlines a system for assessing process. The ability for a well-crafted system to create a concrete and behavioral definition of quality participation or process translates into higher-quality student investment. These systems have a liberating effect on students who engage in dysfunctional behavioral patterns. Most of the time, students are oblivious to the reality that they are operating with a set of dysfunctional patterns that is keeping them from experiencing a deeper level of satisfaction from their work and their interactions with others. Clarifying what functional behavior looks like can be all it takes for most students to achieve it. Once they do, they find that it is much more satisfying than what they have defaulted to in the past.

- *Debrief the process after the activity.* One of the most powerful and simple yet underused strategies to support the transformation of a group from egocentric and dysfunctional to a raised level of awareness with qualities of a community is to use a purposeful debriefing process (Stolovitch, 1990). The goal is to create or reinforce the concept of "a good group member" and raise the level of motivation for all students at all ability levels. It can be accomplished in just a minute or two, but it is well worth the time investment.

Addressing the class as a whole, ask students for examples of other students in their group they have observed doing a good job of those things in the "good group member" concept—things that you consider important to making a successful group, such as a positive attitude, consistently making an effort, being cooperative, performing their role, working through conflict, working through a problem, or whatever else you think makes a group learn, succeed at the task, and function well.

Ask for one area at a time, and encourage students to give examples of what they saw that was valuable. Help a student who says something vague and general clarify what he or she observed specifically. For example, if one student says, "I saw Colby being a good group member," you might ask the student to say what Colby did that demonstrated he was being a good group member.

Expect that the first time you do this, students will look at you blankly. Give them time to think. The second time you will get a better set of responses, and eventually you will see all the hands shoot up.

When students hear one student positively recognizing another, they are given a positive and concrete behavioral indicator of what constitutes high-quality effort. This can have a powerful effect on making the abstractions in the concept for "quality participation or process" very practical. In addition, since students know these behaviors may result in positive recognition by the teacher or other students at some point, they have a greater incentive to demonstrate them.

Imagine the thought process within a group after incorporating this strategy a few times. Most students now are looking for and recognizing high-quality examples of good group effort, and they are aware that others may recognize their efforts. Moreover, with each iteration of the process, the students gain a greater number of concrete and personal examples of recognized behavior. Implementing the strategy provides the students with opportunities to compliment one another, which makes both complimenter and complimented feel good and builds community in the class. Imagine the transformative effects on the climate of the class when students are constantly attentive to opportunities to compliment their classmates and ways to "put each other up."

REFLECTION

12.15

Put yourself in the role of recognizer. How does it make you feel? Now put yourself in the role of being recognized. How does this make you feel?

Much of the power and transformative influence of cooperative learning when it is done effectively is that it naturally creates a success psychology and has a psychological movement to it. Recall the three factors from Chapter Seven that form the foundation for a psychology of success. As you examine cooperative learning in relation to these factors, its potential becomes even more apparent:

- *Locus of control.* In cooperative learning, students have greater control over their learning outcomes. Often the result is the creation or synthesis of something meaningful and original. Students are asked to make countless decisions of real consequence and as a result learn how to take greater responsibility for those decisions.

- *Acceptance and belonging.* In cooperative learning, students learn to work in teams to meet a goal. They come to recognize that they need one other in order to be fully successful. Groups that accomplish goals and overcome challenges together bond in a significant way.

- *Growth orientation.* In cooperative learning, you can make the process itself the primary goal and help students recognize that it is about what they put into the effort rather than simply what they bring to it. The structure of knowledge itself promotes a focus on what is possible rather than preoccupation with a fear of failure.

12.16 **REFLECTION**

Recall life situations in which you would say that you felt psychological movement and that things were going somewhere. Did the context involve collective accomplishment?

CONCLUSION

While creating an effective system for managing cooperative learning takes time and intention, the rewards are well worth the effort. Cooperative learning contexts provide benefits of which no other context is capable. In Part Five, we explore how to deal with conflict and students who have more substantial behavioral problems than others. Conflict need not undermine your progress toward your transformative goals. And taking a constructive approach with more substantive problems allows you to maintain your overall vision for success without reverting to interventions that perpetuate power struggles and negative behavior patterns.

Journal Reflections

1. Which types of assessment formats do you find most personally motivational? What formats are the most effective in the classes that you have observed?
2. When you envision leading cooperative activities, do you feel inclined to take a more teacher-centered (2-Style) approach with the students you will teach, or a more student-centered (1-Style) approach? Why were you drawn to that approach?

Activities

1. In small groups, brainstorm a list of the most common problems that teachers you have observed had when implementing cooperative learning strategies. What are some of the ideas that you would suggest to help them solve these problems?
2. In groups of three to five, develop a cooperative activity for a grade level and subjects of your choice, and later share it with the class.

   A. Brainstorm some activities that would fit well into a cooperative structure. Then select one around which you want to construct an activity.

   B. Decide on the structure of the activity:

      • Process and goal

      • Roles

      • Incentives

      • Assessment

   C. How are you going to communicate your expectations to your students on functioning in a cooperative group?

   D. What do you plan to do if there are groups that are not on task or are in conflict? What if it is:

      • One student in the group who is the problem?

      • A whole group mired in conflict?

   E. Present your idea to the other groups.

REFERENCES

Bandura, A. (1986). *Social foundations of thought and action*. Upper Saddle River, NJ.: Prentice Hall.

Cohen, E. G. (1994). *Designing groupwork: Strategies for heterogeneous classrooms*. New York: Teachers College Press.

Gettinger, M. (1995). Best practices for increasing academic learning time. In A. Thomas & J. Grimes (Eds.), *Best practices in school psychology* (pp. 943–954). Washington, DC: National Association of School Psychologists.

Gettinger, M., & Kohler, K. M. (2006). Process-outcome approaches to classroom management and effective teaching. In C. M. Evertson & C. S. Weinstein (Eds.), *Handbook of classroom management* (pp. 73–95). Mahwah, NJ: Lawrence Erlbaum Associates.

Glasser, W. (1975). *Reality therapy: A new approach to psychiatry*. New York: HarperCollins.

Gunter, M A., Estes, T. E., & Mintz, S. L. (2007). *Instruction: A models approach* (5th ed.). Needham Heights, MA: Allyn & Bacon.

Johnson, D. W., & Johnson, R. (1998). Cooperative learning and social interdependence theory. In R. Tindale, L. Heath, J. Edwards, E. Posavac, F. Bryant, Y. Suzrez-Balcazar, et al. (Eds.), *Theory and research on small groups* (pp. 9–36). New York: Plenum Press.

Johnson, D. W., & Johnson, R. (1999). *Learning together and alone: Cooperative, competitive, and individualistic learning* (4th ed.). Needham Heights, MA: Allyn & Bacon.

Johnson, D. W., Johnson, R., & Holubec, E. (1998). *Cooperation in the classroom* (7th ed.). Edina, MN: Interaction Book Company.

Lotan, R. A. (2006). Managing groupwork in the heterogeneous classroom. In C. M. Evertson & C. S. Weinstein (Eds.), *Handbook of classroom management* (pp. 525–540). Mahwah, NJ: Erlbaum.

Rubin, B. C. (2003). Unpacking detracking: When progressive pedagogy meets students' social world. *American Educational Research Journal*, *40*(2), 539–573.

Shindler, J. (2003). Creating a more peaceful classroom community by assessing student participation and process. *Online Journal of Peace and Conflict Resolution*, *5*(1).

Shindler, J. (2004a). Greater than the sum of the parts? Examining the soundness of collaborative exams in teacher education courses. *Innovative Higher Education*, *28*(4), 273.

Shindler, J. (2004b). *Teaching for the success of all learning styles: Five principles for promoting greater teacher effectiveness and higher student achievement for all students*. Retrieved October 9, 2008, from www.calstatela.edu/faculty/jshindl/ls.

Slavin, R. E. (1994). *Cooperative learning: Theory, research and practice* (2nd ed.). Needham Heights, MA: Allyn & Bacon.

Slavin, R., Hurley, E. A., & Chamberlain, A. (2003). Cooperative learning and achievement: Theory and research. In W. Reynolds & G. Miller (Eds.), *Handbook of psychology: Vol. 7. Educational psychology* (pp. 177–198). Hoboken, NJ: Wiley.

Stolovitch, H. (1990). D-FITGA: A debriefing model. *Performance and Instruction*, *29*(7), 18–19.

Watson, M., & Battistich, V. (2006). Building and sustaining caring communities. In C. M. Evertson & C. S. Weinstein (Eds.), *Handbook of classroom management* (pp. 253–279). Mahwah, NJ: Erlbaum.

Webb, N. M., Troper, J. D., & Fall, R. (1995). Constructive activity and learning in collaborative small groups. *Journal of Educational Psychology*, *87*, 406–423.

Remediation Without Coercion

13

A Win-Win Approach to Conflict Resolution and Potential Power Struggles

In This Chapter

- Examining the sources of classroom conflict
- A process for win-win conflict resolution
- Peer mediation
- Successfully resolving power struggles

Conflict is a natural part of any functional class; in fact, it is not necessarily a sign of problems with classroom management or the health of the classroom community. Nevertheless, it can often lead to unhappiness or discomfort, and some members of the class may emotionally withdraw or attack (Johnson & Johnson, 2006). Making sense of conflict and providing students with the skills, knowledge, and dispositions to process it effectively is essential to creating a functional democratic classroom.

SOURCES OF CONFLICT

Conflict originates from many sources and takes many forms. Sometimes it is brought into the class from the outside, and sometimes it is created within the class (Batton, 2002; Johnson & Johnson, 2006). Either way, when it is examined with a sufficient amount of awareness, it can be a useful means to personal and collective growth. Our job is to help students see that conflict can be an opportunity rather than just a source of grief. This section looks at the most common sources of classroom conflict.

REFLECTION **13.1**

In the classrooms that you have most recently observed, was conflict present? What form did it take? Who was responsible for initiating it or perpetuating it?

Students Have Competing Ideas

As you develop a culture of listening and respect, you have to help students separate difference of opinion from personal attack. Helping them learn the skills of self-expression while keeping the dignity and respect of others paramount is important. It can be useful to illuminate for students the concept that their ideas have changed over time and will undoubtedly change in the future. As they better distinguish their ideas from their identities, they will find it much easier to have discussions without getting defensive. You can allow students to disagree and permit them time to process those emotions. As they learn that not always being right or having others disagree is not the end of the world, they become more comfortable with self-expression and less fearful of conflict.

In addition, you need to help students express their ideas in ways that do not attack others. A good way to start is to help them use phrasing that identifies their idea as their opinion. I-messages are useful for this purpose (Batton, 2002; Gordon, 2006). For example, you might encourage a student to say, "From what I understand, I think a gas tax is a bad idea," as opposed to, "A gas tax is a terrible idea!" The first phrase does an adequate job of expressing an opinion as such, whereas the second expresses the same opinion as a fact. Practicing how to phrase opinions at the beginning of the year is time well spent. Leading the class in a concept attainment or classification exercise related to helpful ways to express opinions versus unhelpful ways to express opinions can help clarify the difference.

Putting the exercise on a large sheet of paper and leaving it on the wall for a few weeks for reference may be helpful. Keep in mind that the most powerful learning in this area will come from your modeling. Therefore, model what you want to see from your students. This will be more challenging than it sounds.

Students Have Competing Needs and Desires

No matter how clear your expectations, no matter how well understood your social contract, and no matter how well you promote community among the members of the class, there will be some level of conflict that comes from students' competing needs and desires (Johnson & Johnson, 2006). But the difference between a democratic classroom with an intentional process for dealing with conflict and an authoritarian classroom where the teacher acts as judge is this: in a democratic classroom, conflict is an opportunity for all parties to grow, while in an authoritarian classroom, conflict is a source of trouble for all concerned (Emmer & Gerwels, 2006). Moreover, in a democratic classroom, each conflict leads to more learning and skill building, which leads to more effective conflict resolution and less future pain and suffering. Teacher-based resolutions lead to dependent and passive students who learn little about how to deal with the conflicts that arise in their lives, in or out of the classroom.

Avoid these actions with regard to conflict between students:

- *Ignoring conflict.* This leads to the benefit of the advantaged. The powerful will ultimately use the vacuum of justice to get their way over the less powerful.

- *Acting as judge.* This sends the message that students are too immature to solve their own problems and impedes their moral and social growth.

- *Siding solely with the victim.* Be empathetic, but avoid being used as a tool to get back at an aggressor. This will lead to more dependence and a cycle of victimization for the weak party and an identity as a bully for the aggressor.

- *Don't encourage tattling.* The more you encourage it, the more you will get it. You encourage it by acting as judge, siding with the victim, or not encouraging students to seek their own solutions before they come to you.

Encourage the following actions with regard to conflict between students:

- *The use of a well-established set of guidelines for conflict resolution.* An effective and uniform system helps support a sense of safety and learning for students. (See the win-win conflict resolution guidelines below.)

- *Skills related to expressing and owning one's feelings.* I-messages and empathy are complex skills to learn, but they are effective and save a lot of pain and suffering.

- An effort on the part of the students. They should ask themselves, "What is the best thing for the class as a whole, and can I find a solution that meets my needs and is good for the group as well?"

- *An inclination to solve one's own conflicts.* It may feel difficult not to intervene at first, but you will be surprised at how empowering it can be for the students, especially those who have previously been dependent on adult interventions.

- *An inclination to think in terms of one's own behavior first and that of others second.* Too often conflicts escalate because students all feel the need to point out the misbehavior of other students. We have all heard countless phrases that begin, "Teacher! _____ is _____ing." Aside from the most severe cases, attending to these types of student pleas for your intervention will only increase the amount of conflict and encourage an external locus of control mentality. A useful phrase in these cases is, "If everyone takes care of themselves, we will all be fine."

- *An effort to recognize how much they are growing in their conflict resolution skills.* As with the other skills that you are trying to encourage, do not hold back your pride and respect for students who are making the effort to grow in a new and difficult area. (For ways to do this effectively, see the discussion of personal recognition versus praise in Chapter Six.)

- *Openness to modifying the social contract.* If a conflict or series of conflicts sends the message that something is not working, use the opportunity to brainstorm a contract modification. This activity can be a conspicuous opportunity to model the principle that conflict is an opportunity for growth.

REFLECTION   13.2

As you reflect on the most recent class that you observed, how many of the teacher interventions were consistent with the list outlining what to encourage, and how many fell into what to avoid? Did you see evidence of the effect they had over time?

Teacher's Negative Affect or Misguided Practice Leads to Student Conflict

If you are practicing any of the teacher behaviors identified as leading down the effectiveness continuum as outlined in Chapter Two, conflict will follow. It may take the form of resistance stemming from a feeling that basic needs are not being met. It may take the form of jealousy if you use extrinsic rewards or personal praise. It may take the form of mistrust if you are inconsistent with your consequences or use arbitrary punishments. In one form or another, student discomfort will lead to conflict. Be proactive. Create a safe, needs-satisfying, consistent classroom climate, and you will have to do a lot less conflict resolution and power struggle management.

13.3 **REFLECTION**

Reflect on the relationship between teacher action and student reaction. Visualize classrooms in which there is nearly no conflict and other classes in the same school in which there is a great deal. In your opinion, how much of the conflict in any class is created, directly and indirectly, by the actions of the teacher?

Students' and Teacher's Needs Compete

Even if you are successful at creating a healthy needs-satisfying classroom where expectations are clear, there are bound to be times when your needs and those of your students will be at odds (Johnson & Johnson, 2006). Sometimes just explaining the rationale behind your expectations can help students see why they are necessary. Sometimes it may be necessary to engage in a process of problem solving to achieve understanding.

For example, you may have a homework policy that seems to make perfect sense, but a number of students do not complete most or all of their homework. In situations like this, it is important that you listen to your students' needs. Ask what they would change in the policy to ensure that everyone came with their homework completed. After listening to suggestions, you can find a practicable compromise that works for all parties. Bluestein (1999) calls this negotiating "creating a boundary." She suggests that conflict is minimized when each party can accept a policy boundary that works for him or her. This process helps meet the students' basic need for power and brings another level of clarity to the expectations.

13.4 **REFLECTION**

Boundary setting can be a potent teaching tool to promote clear expectations and student empowerment, but it can also lead to an excessive amount of bargaining if it is not done intentionally and proactively. (You may want to review the discussions in Chapter Five and Eleven on this topic.)

Students Bring Displaced Anger from Outside the Class

Sometimes you have done a good job of developing a sound social contract and a fair and supportive classroom environment, but because one or more students feel the need to test you or "share their pain," potential conflict can arise. Following the steps outlined in the next section for dealing with a power struggle can help strengthen the social contract, keep you from getting hooked into destructive dramas, and lead to a growth opportunity for the students.

A SYSTEM FOR WIN-WIN CONFLICT RESOLUTION

Having a system for conflict resolution in place for your classroom or school can have many benefits. First, it will reduce the amount and intensity of the conflicts that do occur. Second, it will help students build useful skills to solve their own problems—skills that will be valuable within the school walls and in their homes and communities. Third, the conflict resolution skills will act to promote a deeper sense of responsibility, community, and success psychology among the student body.

Naomi Drew (2002) offers a six-step process for successful conflict resolution. It can be used by students for self-mediation or used by a peer mediator. These steps provide a useful framework for examining how to make a conflict an opportunity for growth rather than disharmony.

Step 1: Cool Off

Drew (2002) suggests that conflicts cannot be solved in the face of hot emotions. It is important for all parties within any conflict to take a step back and recognize the reactive pattern that wants to emerge and gain some distance and perspective. Help students develop the habit of taking a moment to turn their attention inward and notice that they most likely want to react out of a pain-based response whenever they feel they have been hurt, threatened, or wronged. Eckhart Tolle (1999) refers to the "pain-body" as a mechanism in each of us that feeds on painful emotions. This pain-body reaction blinds us to reason and actually incites more pain in an attempt to escalate drama and conflict. Helping students develop their awareness alone will save a great deal of suffering for all parties over time.

REFLECTION

13.5

Can you recognize this pain-body reaction within yourself when it arises? We all have a pain-body, and while the triggers may be different (insecurity for one person and rejection for another person, for example), the mechanism is rather similar. When the pain-body reaction arises, notice how you desire to hook into the pain and perpetuate the angry emotions. Seeing it within yourself will make you much more effective when you see it arise within your students.

Step 2: Tell What's Bothering You Using I-Messages

When each participant is ready to put energy into listening and problem solving and is no longer acting out of the defensive pain reaction, they are ready to enter into a process of communication. However, if the words used imply blame, attack, or indictment, not only is it likely that these are communicating the participant's pain; it probably will trigger the other participant's defensive reaction. The result will be an escalation of pain as each participant engages in a pain frenzy. On the surface, this may appear as communication, but in reality, it is simply people hooking one another to their inner pain mechanisms and ego defenses. This is what goes on in most arguments.

The language in the participants' communication at this stage needs to work to offer information and clarity rather than blame. A good technique for accomplishing this is the use of I-statements—phrases such as "I was waiting my turn and it seemed to me that you stepped in front of me," or "What I heard you say was 'I am a fool' and I did not think it was funny and I did not appreciate it." Drew (2002) recommends that when making I-statements it is important to avoid put-downs, guilt trips, sarcasm, or negative body language. The statements need to simply report information and one's experience.

It is important to remind participants that both events and feelings are useful information at this stage. The students need to maintain a win-win mind-set throughout the process. Information contributes to solutions, whereas blame, attacks, and victim language contribute to loss. This early step requires a great deal of trust on the part of the participants. They will be tempted to give in to a competitive win-lose mentality. In the early stages of facilitating this process, you will be required to provide a great deal of encouragement to your students to trust the process and their classmates.

Step 3: Each Person Restates What He or She Heard the Other Person Say

When both participants are required to restate what they heard the other say, they bring clarity and empathy into the process. Each is important. If there is no clarity, there can be little understanding, and solutions will likely be superficial. If there is no empathy, the opportunity for growth is lost. In addition, it is a sign that participants do not sincerely desire a win-win outcome. Successfully restating another's words shows an effort to come out of one's narrow point of view into a place of shared understanding.

In the example, one such restatement might be, "I heard you say that you did not think it was funny when I called you a fool. Is that correct?" This restatement introduces clarity and empathy to the process.

Step 4: Take Responsibility

It is important that participants in the process realize that blaming and faulting are counter-productive and avoid them. Blame is external and past oriented; responsibility is internal and present to future oriented. A conflict resolution process is an effective tool to promote internal locus of control and a consequent success psychology.

Encourage participants to embrace the attitude that they want to see what each can do to make things better in the future. This is in direct contrast to the attitude characterized by the statements, "It is not my fault," or, "It is your fault."

Step 5: Brainstorm Solutions and Come Up with One That Satisfies All Parties

Drew (2002) suggests that resolving conflicts is a creative act, and that there are many solutions to any single problem. Participants quickly learn that conflict resolutions are not about getting someone in trouble or deciding who is at fault. They are about how to make life better in the future. Sometimes this is a matter of compromise, sometimes it is a matter of finding a new and better way, and sometimes it is about one person realizing the need to change a behavior pattern.

For younger students, it can be immensely helpful for you to ask guiding questions to help the process along—for example, "What is it that each of you wants?" "What did you do today to try to get what you wanted?" "What happened?" "What could you do tomorrow to get what you want without one person feeling hurt?" As you guide this process, give students time to think after you ask your questions, and resist the temptation to give them answers unless absolutely necessary. After hearing a workable idea offered, you might ask, "Would that solution work for both of you?"

For older students, it may be effective to have each participant take some time independently or as a team if that makes more sense and brainstorm a set of ideas on paper. They should be encouraged to think of a series of ideas. As with any other brainstorming exercise, students should recognize that items further down the list often end up being the most insightful. Participants can then examine each list and agree on a solution that is most acceptable to them.

The conflict resolution process should be part of the social contract, but this does not imply that consequences for contract violations are ignored. For example, in the case of two students involved in a physical altercation, there should be some consequence for hitting. In a situation where one student hits another in response to a hurtful comment, a conflict resolution process should be employed, but the consequence for hitting still needs to be implemented. The conflict resolution process will help aid in supporting better decisions in the future and mend the relationship between the students. The class also needs to understand that when they violate the social contract, consequences are in place.

Step 6: Affirm, Forgive, or Thank

After a solution is agreed on, help participants develop the habit of shaking hands, thanking one another, and forgiving one another. Forgiveness and gratitude are powerful mind-sets for closing the process. These signify that what was most important about this conflict resolution process was that everyone grew and that the relationship was worth the effort it took to overcome the natural tendency to fight or withdraw.

Results of the Process

Every time the students successfully execute this conflict resolution process, their skills for dealing with conflict grow. If they can learn when they are young to recognize their defensive pain-driven mental reaction, become responsible for their actions, and forgive and move on, they will have acquired skills that are as valuable as anything else they will learn in school.

The conflict resolution process serves to promote students' psychology of success. Win-win conflict resolution skills promote each of these factors: internal locus of control, acceptance and belonging, and a growth-oriented orientation to learning. Moreover, this process can be a powerful tool in the development of a more responsible approach to problems within the class (Batton, 2002; Emmer & Gerwels, 2006).

PEER MEDIATION

When the involved parties cannot resolve conflict by using conflict resolution skills, it can be effective to enlist the help of a peer mediator (Johnson & Johnson, 2006). In a peer mediation program, third-party students support their schoolmates in solving problems (Freiberg & Lapointe, 2006; Johnson & Johnson, 2006). These can be problems in or out of the classroom. The peer mediator can be any uninvolved student, but in many programs, students are given special training to be "peacemakers" (Johnson & Johnson, 1999).

Using students rather than adults to resolve conflict offers several advantages. First, it is empowering to all parties. Students learn that conflict is a matter to be solved with a given set of skills, not simply misbehavior. Second, they learn to empathize with others' struggles, pain, and ego attachments. It is much easier to help someone else to look at a problem with a broad perspective than to do it oneself. When we see a pattern in another, we can better understand that same tendency within us. Third, it puts students with strong empathetic and personal skills in positions where those skills are used for the benefit of the whole. Conversely, it puts those with previously underdeveloped empathy skills in a position to work on them.

Johnson and Johnson (2006) outline the peacemaker process as having the following three parts:

Part 1: Understand the nature of the conflict.

Part 2: Choose an appropriate conflict strategy. Students are encouraged to keep in mind that the goal of the conflict resolution is to help the participants achieve their goals and help the parties maintain a good relationship.

Part 3: Negotiate a solution to the conflict. At this stage, the peer mediator needs to steer the process toward a win-win (integrative) rather than a win-lose (distributive) outcome. The mediator should help the participants:

- Describe what they want
- Describe how they feel

TABLE 13.1. **A Comparison of Transformative and Ineffective Peer Mediation Systems**

Peer Mediation in the Transformative Class	Peer Mediation That Misses the Target
Students feel empowered to solve their own problems (with or without mediator help).	Students believe that the peer mediator is another arm of the teacher's authority.
Students' recognition grows that every conflict is an opportunity to successfully use their conflict resolution skills and increase their ability to overcome problems.	Students see conflict as another form of bad behavior and something that they may "get in trouble for."
The teacher puts most attention on the process. The goal is to get better at conflict resolution.	The teacher puts most attention on the problematic nature of the content of the conflict itself and why it is so inconvenient.
Students realize that peer mediators are agents for help, even though they are not perfect, and they accept mediator influence as a learning experience.	Students feel peer mediators are know-it-alls who are ineffective and power hungry, and worsen conflict situations.
Over time there is a growing attitude of "you first," and "let me win by being the one who is more conscious and unselfish."	Over time, there is a growing attitude that some peer mediators are on the side of the teacher. To open up and talk about what they want and feel will get them in more trouble, so they should keep quiet.

- Describe the reasons for these wants and feelings
- Take the perspective of others into consideration and summarize his or her understanding of what the other person wants
- Generate options for a mutually acceptable solution
- Select one of the options that both parties can live with
- Make a record of the mediation

In many schools, the mediators, or peacemakers, wear identifying T-shirts. It is recommended that a class or school rotate the position frequently, so that each student has an opportunity to practice the role. I also recommend that formal processing be done on a regular basis—both conflict resolution training and job clarification training. Many times students consciously or unconscious slip into bad habits when in this role and often confuse their job with being a law enforcement arm of the staff. Peer mediation, however, works on trust. When the other students do not trust that the peer mediator holds helpful intentions, the system breaks down (see Table 13.1). Peer mediation has a powerful potential to be a transformative component in the class, but only if conducted with the right intentions.

13.6   REFLECTION

Imagine a school in which students are experts in conflict resolution. These do exist, and the results they achieve are often remarkable when it comes to reducing fighting, bullying, arguments, and the many conflicts that arise in collective spaces at a school. Consider encouraging a schoolwide approach to conflict resolution modeled after the steps outlined above.

> **Possible Phrases for a Wall Chart to Support Conflict Resolution Success**
>
> *In this class we . . .*
>
> - Deal with conflict constructively, thoughtfully, and deliberately.
> - Recognize that conflict comes from thoughts. We can change our thoughts and end or reduce conflicts when we so choose.
> - Understand that conflicts have solutions if we make the effort to look for them.
> - Use conflict as an opportunity to make us better as individuals and as a class.
> - See ourselves becoming more skilled at conflict resolution all the time.
> - Understand that conflict resolution is always win-win.

DEALING WITH CONFLICT WITHIN THE SOCIAL CONTRACT

A social contract exists to meet the needs of its members. If it is not meeting its members' needs in the most effective and fair manner, it should be modified. Conflict can be a signal that the social contract needs to be modified. If a persistent problem exists in the class, the solution is to go about a process of systematic problem solving and then adopt the new solution into the social contract. For example, if students argue over who gets to use the computers, you need a better system for computer use. The more democratic the process, the greater the sense of ownership of the outcome. When contentious issues arise among members of the class, it may signal the opportunity for a class meeting or at least a brainstorming exercise.

REFLECTION

13.7

What is your impulse when conflict arises in your class or within groups you are leading? Is it to take over, or is it to use the conflict as an opportunity for growth and problem solving? If you are attempting to head down the road of being a 1-Style teacher, you will want to find an efficient system for conducting class meetings. These meetings need not take more than a few minutes.

Power Struggles

As we examine the idea of power struggle situations among students, keep in mind that you are working within the social contract framework. In many cases, what is occurring during a power struggle is the students' testing the integrity of the social contract (Curwin & Mendler, 1986). They are, in essence, rejecting the class agreement (see Chapter Ten). When a student is openly defiant, you are naturally going to feel angry and offended, and the tendency (encouraged by your own defensive pain reaction) is to exert your power and show the student who is in charge. While this may feel satisfying in the moment, it produces a number of undesirable effects:

- Engagement in a power struggle. There is no power struggle until you buy into the challenge.
- Losing sight of the point. The point is that the student is to be responsible and fulfill his or her agreed-on commitment to the contract.

- Sending a message to the other students that the teacher can get hooked into a power struggle.
- Sending the message to the other students that when a student says no to the contract, he or she is given only short-term pain and not held responsible in a meaningful manner.

13.8 REFLECTION

How do you tend to respond when students challenge you? What happens when you take the challenge and engage the student?

What do you do to address level II cases in which a student challenges you other than to react unconsciously to the personal offense? Curwin and Mendler (1986) offer a process for dealing with a power struggle successfully. It provides a coherent and sensible approach to dealing with student-teacher conflict that will save pain and suffering. Considered within the context of the social contract, it has the following effects:

- Strengthening the social contract by reinforcing it
- Placing the responsibility on the student
- Indirectly teaching (social learning model) that living up to the commitment to the social contract takes precedence over selfishness

- Teaching that a game or emotional hook is not going to work to change the rules that are outlined by the social contract

Dealing with a Power Struggle

Curwin and Mendler (1986) offer seven steps to success when confronted by a student who attempts to engage in a power struggle:

Step 1: Do not manufacture power struggles by the way you teach. By and large, power struggles are a result of a student's attempt to satisfy an unmet need. Students who feel a sense of power and control, are making progress toward their goals, are supported by the teacher, have avenues to share concerns, and are given choices and not backed into corners by harsh directives will be much less likely to feel the need to engage the teacher in a power struggle.

Step 2: Move into a private encounter. If the encounter begins publicly, quickly move it into a private, one-to-one interaction. A public stage will put students in a position where they must defend their image and put you in a position in which you feel the need to demonstrate your power.

13.9 REFLECTION

Recall the social learning model here. What does public implementation create? How does the audience factor affect the student's thinking?

Step 3: Avoid being hooked in by the student. If the student tries to hook you in by making you feel guilty or responsible for his or her inappropriate behavior, ignore the hook and give the responsibility back to the student. A hook is intended to shift the focus externally to you or some other factor. The student is acting to shift blame and pull you in. If you become drawn in on a personal level, the student is in control.

Common Power Struggle Hooks

"You are not a good teacher."

"You do not like me."

"No one likes me."

"You are prejudiced."

"Other teachers let me do this."

"You let everyone else do it."

"I can see why people say you are such a _____."

"School is a waste of time, especially this class."

"I promise not to do it again. Just leave me alone."

REFLECTION 13.10

What hooks have you heard students use? Share your story with your colleagues or classmates. Reflect on what the hooks are intended to do and why it is so tempting to play into them.

Step 4: Calmly acknowledge the power struggle. It is counterproductive to show anger or flex your strength. Instead, calmly acknowledge that things appear to be heading toward a power struggle, which would surely make any eventual outcome worse. Ask the student to consider how the situation could end up in a win-win scenario.

Step 5: Validate the student's feelings and concerns. Use phrases such as, "I understand your feeling the way you do, but that does not excuse what you did," or "Those feelings make sense; I can see why you think that, but . . ." Feelings are important and valued, but they are beside the point. Throughout the process, project an unconditional positive regard for the student. You understand the student's feelings and concerns but at the same time maintain a clear understanding that he or she is accountable. If you become negative, the student will lose sight that the intervention is about his or her responsibility and see it as a punishment that is coming from an external agent (that is, the teacher).

Step 6: Keep the focus on the student's choice, and simply state the consequence (repeating if necessary). No matter what hook the student tries to use, keep the focus on the fact that the student made a choice to violate the rule or social contract ("I understand that you feel this is unfair, but you made the choice to do this. The consequence we decided on for that is . . .") The act was the student's choice. Therefore, the student must accept responsibility. If the student does not accept the logical or agreed-on consequence, he or she can choose to accept a more significant consequence, such as losing the opportunity to be present for part of the class or activity. Calmly repeating the agreement can reinforce the point to the student that he or she needs to make a choice or take responsible action. The rest of the conversation is secondary. Be careful not to badger the student. A calm or encouraging affect can be effective; aggressiveness will be counterproductive. There is no need to escalate or act out your power. In fact, you already have the very real power of the social contract and your rights as a teacher.

13.11   ## REFLECTION

When you visualize a power struggle with a student, do you find yourself naturally wanting to be either aggressive or feeling fearful? Take a moment to visualize a power struggle situation. What emotions do you feel? Now visualize the interaction without fear or aggressiveness; simply include awareness and clear communication. Can you feel your thinking becoming clearer, and can you see the student as less threatening as well?

Step 7: Put your emotional energy into constructive matters. After you have communicated the choices, it is not useful to dwell on the student's behavior. There is no need to hover or pressure the student. Shift your attention back to your teaching. Model constructive, rational, positive behavior.

Applying the Steps to a Classroom Situation

Let us apply the seven steps to a classroom situation in which a student exhibits level II misbehavior and challenges the teacher to a power struggle. Assume that the teacher has done an effective job of developing the social contract and creating clear expectations in the class. On this day, for some reason—perhaps displaced aggression from an earlier parent-child interaction—the student tries to engage the teacher in a power struggle.

Imagine that you have just completed an activity in which students individually complete a project requiring them to use paper and poster-making materials. You give the class a five-minute warning before asking them to clean up their desk areas and get ready to go. As you are about to dismiss them, you note that some paper scraps remain on one desk. According to sound technical management principles (and consistent with your social contract), you calmly repeat, "When all the desks are clear and all the materials are put away, we can go." On just about any other day, this would have been sufficient to motivate all the students to fulfill their responsibility to the class and the social contract. But today is different: one student does not move to clear the desk. Let's suppose that the student is hinting at his disposition on the matter by avoiding eye contact with you. As your blood pressure begins to rise, you remember that you need to be purposeful and deliberate and use this opportunity to take a step forward in your own conflict skills, toward better classroom relationships and improved clarity of the classroom social contract. You dismiss the rest of the class and ask the student to stay.

Here is how to apply the seven-step process in this power struggle:

Step 1: Consider if your actions may have been a contributing factor. Consider that there may have been an occurrence during the activity that the student may be reacting to. Did you possibly make an inadvertently derogatory comment about the work, or have you perhaps alienated the student in the past? If so, this is a good time to do some healing. However, no matter what has happened, the bottom line is the same—the student agreed to live up to the social contract, and part of that responsibility is to do his part of the cleanup. Your request was reasonable. You are the facilitator of the contract, so it was your job to make the request. It is not your job to judge, shame, lecture, or bring up anything in the past. As you approach the student, keep two ideas paramount: show real concern by helping the student's growth, and keep the focus of the interaction on the act and the responsibilities that go along with the choice to take action.

Step 2: Move into a private encounter. If a power struggle is forming, do not take part in the interaction in a public forum. The public factor will likely encourage the student to defend his dignity and impress his friends (and even enemies) and will encourage you to exert power in the face of a public challenge. So close the proximity gap and move near the student. Moving to a private location might be best. The fewer distractions and the more immediate the resolution, the better the outcome will be.

Step 3: Avoid being hooked in by the student. If the student is still sitting and has not taken the sensible step to clean up, it is a good bet that he is deliberately engaging in a power struggle. Remind yourself that the student is experiencing pain in some form and is intent on sharing some of that pain with you. If you shift into pity or defense mode, you will soon be in a power struggle. Keep your "relationship and responsibility" mantra going in your head if you begin to feel hooked in.

At this point, it makes sense to repeat the request again, calmly and clearly: "When you clean up your desk, you can go."

Without being condescending, use a "broken record" technique to clarify the contractual expectation. If your continuous response is some form of the message, "When you [fulfill your responsibility], then you will [be afforded the rights of those who are responsible]," the student understands the issue is regarding his contract obligations and not something of less significance.

The student may offer a statement intended to hook you in: "This is the worst class I have ever had," or "You are the worst teacher," or "You never make Julie pick up her stuff," or "This is because I am [ethnicity] and you do not like [ethnicity] students." Hooks may make you want to express your anger (by activating your pain-body reaction) or defending yourself. But the hook is not the point, so do not play into it. Once you respond to the hook, you are in an argument and the student has shifted the focus of the interaction toward his agenda and away from his responsibility. A useful phrase at this point may be: "That may be your perspective, but right now you have to decide what you are going to choose to do about the paper on your desk."

Step 4: Calmly acknowledge the power struggle. It may be useful at some point in the interaction to help the student become aware of the dynamics of the situation. A useful phrase may be, "You seem to want to argue or get into a power struggle right now. That is not going to help either one of us resolve this situation." Playing the psychologist may seem condescending, so try not to guess what is wrong. Just show empathy and awareness of the dynamic. The more awareness that can come into the situation, the more reasoned the thinking will be. A useful thought here is to mirror the affect that you want from the student.

Step 5: Validate the student's feelings and concerns. Without being too psychoanalytical, it is useful to let the student know that you understand that he has some pain that is causing this need to engage you. For instance, if the student makes the statement, "I know that you do not like me; don't pretend you do," he may or may not be expressing authentic feelings. The mistake would be to respond in an attempt to defend against the accusation of nonliking or ignore the idea completely, implying that the student is right. So you might respond in a way that attempts to validate the student but keeps the fulfillment of his or her responsibility in the foreground, such as: "You know I like you, and I get the feeling that there is more going on here than what is being said. I promise that we can talk later about your concerns regarding me and this class, but right now you have one job: to make the choice to fulfill your commitment to our social contract or accept that through your actions, you are rejecting your commitment." You need to fulfill your part of the social contract by following through and taking the time to listen to the student's concerns. You can control only the choices that you make; the student needs to take responsibility for his.

Step 6: Keep the focus on the student's choice, and simply state the consequence. In the larger context, the choice the student has made is to essentially say no to the social contract. However, your phrasing should point out the choice the student is making and the resulting consequence of that choice.

Early in the interaction, your language might be to the effect: "You made the choice not to clean up your desk area. When you choose to follow through on cleanup, you will be dismissed to go." At this time, the consequence may have increased to losing an opportunity to take part in an activity with the other students.

As time goes on, the student's decision not to pick up the paper implies a choice to defy his commitment to the social contract. Your statement after a few minutes of student inaction should imply that the student must somehow show a commitment that this will not happen again. You might say, "You made the choice to disregard your responsibility. Our social contract works only when we all live up to our agreements. You need to clean up your area and explain to me in writing how and why this is not going to happen again before I can consider you a responsible and committed member of this class."

Step 7: Put your emotional energy into constructive matters. Your physical actions throughout this process are also meaningful. Avoid hovering or standing over the student. Giving the student space sends the message that he is free to make a decision without coercion. Use eye contact and good listening skills when you are directly interacting with the student, but when allowing the student time to think, operate as you would if alone. Let your behavior send the message that you hope the student makes a good choice, but your job is to put energy into your work and the class. If the student wants to engage in something constructive, you will be present, but the student cannot get you to join in his pain session.

As long as the student chooses to dismiss or reject the social contract by exhibiting a level II form of misbehavior, he has made the choice to be outside of it until he recommits to being a responsible member. It may be the case that no student makes that kind of choice all year. If you do a good job of creating a healthy learning community, it will happen rarely, if ever. However, if there is fear of a student engaging you in a power struggle or rejecting a request, you will carry a bit of unnecessary anxiety. Your fear may lead you to such actions as ignoring or rationalizing a student's choice to dismiss the class contract or implementing a punishment that does not hold the student responsible for his or her choice, such as sending the student to the office. Keep in mind that a student always has the choice to be responsible or not responsible. If the student chooses not to be responsible, that is his or her right. Realize that rather than get angry or fearful, you can simply provide a clear context for future choices. It is possible that a student may at some point choose to step out of the class commitment and you will need to employ the tough love philosophy it takes to let him or her make that choice.

If you let fear or sympathy influence you to let the student off the hook, you have sent a powerful message to the class that when students say no to the social contract, you will not hold them accountable. Examined within the social learning model, the message is that the contract is neither sound nor sacred. Even if no other student wants to disrespect the contract, they will likely lose respect for it when they view it being disregarded and unsupported by your follow-through. It may not be conscious, but there is a correlated erosion of commitment to the social contract. Conversely, when we hold students accountable—no matter how difficult this may be—we send the message that the social contract has integrity.

REFLECTION

When a student says no to you, how have you typically been inclined to reply? How might you approach this possibility in the future?

CONCLUSION

Conflict exists in all classes. How you process it will define the effect that it has on your students. As we examine the process for creating the 1-Style classroom and the qualities of a classroom community in the coming chapters, we will see how conflict can be a growth opportunity. Moreover, it can provide a means to empowerment from the knowledge that awareness and intention can be maintained in the face of problematic situations. In addition, power struggles can become opportunities to learn responsibility and strengthen the social contract.

The next chapter addresses how to work with difficult students, building on concepts from this chapter. If you take the position that difficult students must be punished and put in their place, you will engage in perpetual power struggles, and your efforts will not support the growth of the students toward more functional behavior.

Journal Reflections

1. Recall the most recent power struggle you observed. Did the teacher use the skills and processes recommended in this chapter?
2. Reflect on the classes you have observed that seem to be conflict free. How did the teacher promote this condition? Conversely, reflect on classes that seemed to be mired in conflict on a regular basis. How did the teacher contribute to the situation?

Activities

1. In small groups, role-play power struggle scenarios. Have one member of the group take the role of the student who is trying to hook the teacher into a power struggle and one member take the role of the teacher who is trying to guide the interaction to a positive outcome. It will be helpful to pay attention to the steps Curwin and Mendler suggested. Here are some possible power struggle scenarios:

   - A student refuses to hand over an electronic device or phone (there is a no-electronics policy in the class).
   - A student insults the teacher in front of the class.
   - A student refuses to do work or line up.
   - A student refuses to put away materials.

2. After the role play, have all members of the group discuss what they would have done and whether they felt the intervention of the member taking the role of the teacher was effective and why.
3. The next time someone initiates conflict with you, practice applying win-win conflict resolution skills. Then reflect on the difference it makes in coming to a constructive outcome.

4. Conduct a Web search related to conflict resolution programs. In your search engine, put in the words *conflict resolution, schoolwide,* or *classroom,* and explore some of the sites that outline successful programs. What do these programs have in common?

5. In your group, role-play one of the following conflict resolution situations. Pick one member of your group to be the teacher and two others to be students.

> *Elementary school:* Student A comes to you crying and tells you that student B has been pushing him. Student B quickly comes up to your desk and tells you that student A was pushing her too. Help guide the students through a conflict resolution process.

> *Secondary school:* As you approach one group in your class, you can see that they are off track. Student A tells you that student B is not doing her job in the project. Student B says that she is doing what she was told to do earlier, but now everyone else in the group is changing their minds. Student A laments that student B is going to damage his grade and has been misrepresenting what he said. Student B is getting defensive and threatens to give up and let the others do her part. Help guide the students through the conflict to a more productive and amicable place.

REFERENCES

Batton, J. (2002). Institutionalizing conflict resolution: The Ohio model. *Conflict Resolution Quarterly*, *19*(4), 479–494.

Bluestein, J. (1999). *Twenty-first century discipline*. Torrance, CA: Fearon.

Curwin, R., & Mendler, A. (1986). *Discipline with dignity*. Alexandria, VA: ACSD Press.

Drew, N. (2002). *Hope and healing: Peaceful parenting in an uncertain world*. New York: Citadel Press.

Emmer, E. T., & Gerwels, M. C. (2006). Classroom management in middle and high school classrooms. In C. M. Evertson & C. S. Weinstein (Eds.), *Handbook of classroom management* (pp. 407–437). Mahwah, NJ: Erlbaum.

Freiberg, H. J., & Lapointe, J. M. (2006.) Research-based programs for preventing and solving discipline problems. In C. M. Evertson & C. S. Weinstein (Eds.), *Handbook of classroom management* (pp. 735–786). Mahwah, NJ: Erlbaum.

Gordon, T. (2006). *Teacher effectiveness training*. Solana Beach, CA: Gordon Publishing International.

Johnson, D. W., & Johnson, R. (1999). *Learning together and alone: Cooperative, competitive, and individualistic learning* (4th ed.). Needham Heights, MA: Allyn & Bacon.

Johnson, D. W., & Johnson, R. T. (2006). Conflict resolution, peer mediation, and peacemaking. In C. M. Evertson & C. S. Weinstein (Eds.), *Handbook of classroom management* (pp. 803–832). Mahwah, NJ: Erlbaum.

Tolle, E. (1999). *The power of now*. Vancouver, Canada: Namaste Publishing.

14

Changing the Negative Identity Pattern and Succeeding with More Challenging Student Behavior

In This Chapter

- Changing the negative identity pattern
- Bridging the gap with disconnected students
- Using reality therapy and student contacts for chronic problems
- Supporting students with attention deficit hyperactivity disorder

The problems you experience with one or a few students can cause you a great deal of distress; you may even feel that you are failing in general with a whole class. In this chapter, we examine how to take effective action in meeting the more significant behavioral challenges that you face so that you can promote more functional behavior and a healthier climate for all of your students.

REFLECTION

14.1

Recall classes you have taught or observed or in which you were a student. Were there students whose behavior presented a challenge to the teacher? How significant was the impact on the class? In what ways did these students affect the learning and the climate in the room? The answer to this question should underscore the importance of having a systematic approach to dealing with difficult students.

LEVELS OF PROBLEM BEHAVIOR

Chapters Eight through Ten examined the effective creation of a sound and functional social contract that included logical consequences and the implementation of action steps for cases in which students chose to violate their agreement to the contract (see Table 14.1). We could

TABLE 14.1. Levels of Classroom Behavioral Problems

	Description	Out-of-School Example	Classroom Example
Level I	Student actions that violate classroom rules or social contract. Typically rooted in forgetfulness, lack of understanding, or carelessness.	Person carelessly exceeds the speed limit or runs a stop sign because he or she was not paying attention.	Student carelessly leaves a mess at a work station or talks to a neighbor when the expectation is to be listening.
Level IIa	Students knowingly reject their commitment to the social contract in words or actions. Typically rooted in defiance, a desire for power, or a cry for help.	Person knowingly drives too fast and in a risky manner because he or she is late.	Student refuses to clean up his or her area or deliberately continues to talk when the expectation is to be attentive to the speaker.
Level IIb	Student exhibits dysfunctional behavior on a regular basis. Typically rooted in a deeply conditioned pattern of thinking and ego defense.	Person drives recklessly, using his or her vehicle as a means to work out aggression and for self-satisfaction without concern for the safety of others.	Student tends to disrupt the work of other group members anytime he or she feels the task is too challenging in an attempt to meet his or her needs for competence and power or student exhibits a compulsive need for attention.
Level III	Student experiences a struggle with his or her behavior and has a biological or organic basis to this lack of self-control.	Person is incapable of stopping and attending for long. He or she seems to need to continuously make some sort of noise.	Student struggles to attend for long periods of time and feels a compulsive need to move and talk, even though he or she may wish he or she could attend and feel guilty that he or she cannot.

refer to those situations as level I problems—students fail to comprehend expectations or make poor choices out of carelessness or immaturity. Most contract violations fall in this category.

However, we occasionally find ourselves confronted with problems that are more substantial than simple contract violations. These level II problems result from a student's deliberate choice to reject social contract responsibilities or a fundamental pattern of student behavior that will not likely change on its own and left unchanged may do a great deal of harm to the welfare of the class as a whole. These level IIb problems are typically rooted in more substantial deep-seated conditions (Robinson & Ricord Griesemer, 2006). The strategies to use to succeed with dysfunctional behavior that stems from these conditions will go beyond (but likely include) delivering clear and logical consequences (Walker et al., 1996). Organic conditions such as attention deficit hyperactivity disorder (ADHD) require a separate distinction. We can refer to these neurologically based conditions as level III problems.

LEVEL IIB PROBLEMS

Level IIb types of behavioral problems commonly include the following situations:

- Students who have developed a pattern of negative identity
- Students who have developed chronic, compulsive, or habitual inappropriate behavior

- Cases in which there is a pronounced disconnect or gap between the expectations, values, and desires of one of more students and those of the teacher

Often these more substantive types of challenges include students' exhibiting an external locus of control and consequent faulty sense of cause and effect, a failure psychology, or attempting to meet his or her basic needs with means that are unhealthy and will not work within what is good for the class (Walker et al., 1996).

At the heart of these level IIb behavioral challenges is a student who has experienced a great deal of dysfunctional conditioning beforehand. This conditioning is likely being reinforced outside the class as well. What stands between the student and functional behavior is your ability to help the student recognize and become conscious of the dysfunctional conditioning within himself or herself and to assist the student in altering it or at least working with it in a productive manner. While level I problems do not require much recognition of deep-seated patterns and unconscious conditioning, solving level II problems without this conditioning is impossible. You may say, "I am not a psychologist; I am a teacher." You do not need to be an expert psychologist to succeed with level IIb behavioral challenges, but it is important to recognize the difference between a student's conscious choice and something strongly influencing his or her behavior of which he or she is unconscious and does not seem to be entirely choosing (Robinson & Ricord Griesemer, 2006).

REFLECTION

14.2

Recall a student you would classify as a chronic behavior problem student. Would you say that the student was happy or at peace with himself or herself? The answer may seem obvious, but it helps us shift our focus to what is going on with the student rather than why what he or she is doing is a problem.

To succeed with level IIb types of problems requires an intentional, proactive, and positive mind-set. Therefore, you need to begin by doing the following:

- Stop owning the student's behavior or taking it personally. Stay in the present moment, and avoid dwelling on past events. It may help to focus on the success you are having with the rest of the students.

- Avoid self-limiting labels such as "bad student" or "behavioral problem." When you label a student even mentally, you reinforce the idea that the problem is a fixed condition. You take on what Dweck (2000) refers to as a "helpless pattern" approach to dealing with it. You turn a challenge into a plight and go from being a teacher to a victim.

- Acknowledge that you have the ability to change the pattern, or at least get things moving in the right direction if you are systematic and consistent. You need to let go of any resentment and fatalistic thinking that is so easy to do in these situations. Instead, you must take positive action. Action is the antidote to despair.

- Let go of assumptions that negativity, punishment, passive aggressiveness, or projecting disappointment are doing anything but making things worse. You need to look the student in the eye and send these messages: you like her and believe she can do better; what she is doing is going to change, and it needs to change soon.

- Avoid relying on external authorities to solve the problem. Sending the student to the principal or calling home may be necessary occasionally, but this sends the message that you lack the authority, desire, or ideas to make the situation better. Work with the student to solve the problem instead of outsourcing the problem to others.

14.3 | **REFLECTION**

When you recall the response by school personnel to troubled and behaviorally challenging students in your years in schools, how many of the interventions that were used would you say met the criteria listed? How many of those students ultimately improved their behavior? Do you see a relationship between the two?

THE NEGATIVE IDENTITY PATTERN

14.1 | CASE**STUDY**

Negative Identity Pattern Case Example

The teacher has developed a solid social contract in his class by the fourth week of the year, and most students are very clear about expectations. However, one student always seems to be testing the teacher. She constantly seems to find a reason to be off task and annoy other students. Whatever the expectation is, she seems to take joy in doing the opposite or something to hinder the other students' efforts. The teacher has implemented the level I consequences that have worked well for the other students and has made it clear that what she is doing is unacceptable. But things have not changed, as she seems to enjoy being a clown and a fool for the other students. The teacher notices Mondays are usually her worst days.

14.4 | **REFLECTION**

Do you know a student like the one described in case study 14.1? Keep her in mind as we explore the idea of negative identity.

If you approach the student in case study 14.1 from a crime-and-punishment paradigm or just hope that someday the behavior will improve, you will likely be engaged in a battle for the rest of the year. Moreover, no matter how much you explain to this student that her behavior is not acceptable and she needs to "straighten up and fly right," the behavior is unlikely to change. You cannot just let her do what she is doing either, as it is not fair to the rest of the class, good for your mental health, or good for the student herself. Instead, look inside the student's pattern, and undertake a process to change it.

The problem behavior depicted in the case could best be characterized as a negative identity pattern. The negative identity student can take many roles: class clown, antagonist, the failure or quitter, victim, perpetually angry, sadist, or the tough or bad kid. You may not have done anything to bring on the problem, but to avoid a perpetual struggle, you need to take purposeful and well-conceived action (Vitaro, Brendgen, & Tremblay, 2001). As the saying goes, "Nothing changes until something changes," and you will have to initiate the change process if you want to see improvement.

Changing the Negative Identity Behavior Pattern of a Student

Most students are trying to achieve success (performing successfully, learning, fostering friend-ships, achieving goals) using positive behavior, such as making an effort, being productive, or doing the "right thing." Most of us can relate to the idea of trying to develop a positive identity. The more we have tried to reach our goals, succeed socially, acquire skills, and attain some level of positive recognition from others, the more we attach those positive attributes to ourselves, thus forming some degree of positive identity. Although we all have unconscious patterns that keep us from acting with full awareness of why we do what we do, and some-times making choices that we are not happy with, we typically seek to be generally functional and productive. However, teachers occasionally have students who have developed a pattern of dysfunctional behavior. If the problem is not organic (level III problems such as ADHD, fetal alcohol syndrome, or a mental or emotional disability), it is usually related the student's having been conditioned into a negative identity pattern. All of us carry some form of this conditioning as a result of our ego's need to avoid feeling guilty, inadequate, unworthy, or unloved. For some students, this becomes a primary mode of operation. These students spend a great deal of time in a defensive or reactive mode that has come to feel normal to them but is in fact largely unconscious and self-destructive.

In many cases, this negative identity manifests in a student who would prefer to be the "best worst" rather than a "nobody" or a failure. While on the surface, this may not make sense, it makes a great deal of sense when we reflect that on a fundamental psychological level the opposite of love is not hate but indifference. Who wants to be a zero? Who is capable of surviving without getting the basic needs of love and belonging met? Moreover, as we dig deeper into most negative identity patterns, we will recognize that at the heart of the problem is a psychological comingling of pain and love. In the face of a deep-seated sense of worthlessness, inadequacy, vulnerability, or guilt, it makes sense that the ego finds a way to compensate for the unbearable condition.

Keep in mind that some students exhibit the negative identify pattern perpetually, and others are triggered by environmental factors only in certain situations. Students whose uncon-sciousness and negative identity projection is displayed almost continuously may go to great lengths to initiate conflict and drama to confirm their negative identity. Others' negative identity pattern arises in certain situations that trigger a reaction that activates their source of inner pain.

REFLECTION

14.5

It is helpful when understanding the negative identity student to reflect on times in your life when you have done destructive, ugly, selfish, embarrassing, or hurtful things in an effort to gain love, recognition of others, or acceptance of the group. Did you know that what you were doing was not very good? Your ability to ignore that voice should give you some compassion for and understanding of the negative identity student.

To make sense of the pattern, it is useful to examine its behavioral roots and explore the roles of reinforcement, shaping, and social learning in how it is formed and reformed. In a positive identity cycle, individuals' efforts are reinforced to some degree by a desirable outcome and therefore provide an incentive to continue positive behavior. However, in the negative identity acquisition cycle (Figure 14.1) attempts at positive behavior (attempting assigned work, trying to be liked, attempting a difficult task) receive little or no positive reinforcement (Figure 14.1, point 1). They may receive grades below their level of satisfaction, feel as though they do not fit in, or fail at a task. As a result, their basic needs for love, power,

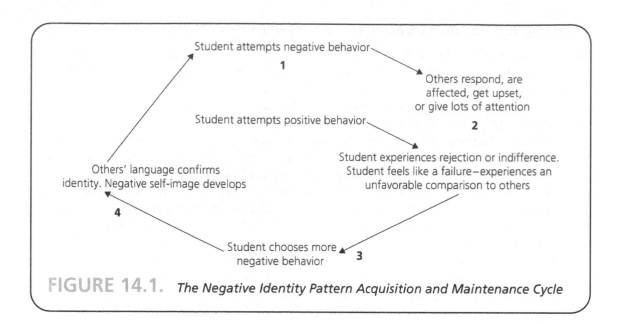

FIGURE 14.1. *The Negative Identity Pattern Acquisition and Maintenance Cycle*

and competence are not adequately met and the negative self-image is confirmed, triggering an internal feeling of pain related to a sense of worthlessness, inadequacy, guilt, or something else. However, they use their negative behavior (being annoying, failing spectacularly, disrupting the class) to gain attention and experience a feeling of satisfaction and power (Figure 14.1, point 2). When viewed within the lens of basic satisfaction, this reaction is understandable (remember that the opposite of love is not hate but indifference). The result is behavior that has been reinforced and is now more likely to happen in the future (Tremblay, Pihl, Vitaro, & Dobkin, 1994).

What feels like success is actually an addictive cycle that is digging the student an ever deeper hole. Aside from the negative behavior's being dysfunctional for all concerned, what is not understood is that while it may feel satisfying for the moment and even necessary to cope with a sense of inner pain, it will neither satisfy these students' basic needs nor ease the pain for long. In fact, the stronger the pattern becomes, the more likely the student will be in denial of the problem (Vitaro et al., 2001).

The early points of the negative identity cycle depicted in Figure 14.1 represent the reinforcement of behavior by others. Given the reinforcement for negative behavior, it is understandable that the student continues to choose it over more socially acceptable behavior (point 3). Moreover, as the student's behavior becomes more public and regular, he or she develops an identity and reputation that further satisfies his or her need for love and power (point 4). Over time, this public identity becomes a relatively stable (negative) self-image.

Helping the Student Change the Pattern

The key to transforming a negative identity cycle into a more positive identity cycle is to alter the system and then reconstruct it differently. There are two important variables in the process of ending the cycle and replacing the dysfunction with more functional and healthy behaviors: love and learning. The change must have a new mechanism for meeting the need for love and belonging and must involve learning new skills and ways to function—skills that may be currently foreign to the student. Success will necessarily involve replacing old behaviors with new ones and recognizing that those new behaviors achieve something more worthwhile and satisfying to the student. The stages of the cycle take place continuously, but we will deal with each phase separately here.

A good starting point is the use of extinction at phase 1. Extinction refers to the removal of a reinforcing stimulus (Kauffman, 2005). In this instance, the reinforcement motivating the student's negative behavior is probably somewhat complex, but it could include annoying teachers and students, laughing, being shocked, or giving pity after the student exhibits dysfunctional or inappropriate behavior. So while you might assume that getting upset, punishing the student, or even public scorn will work to discourage the unwanted behavior, these reactions actually reinforce the behavior (Kauffman, 2005). The student is seeking pain and confirmation of his or her negative identity, and these responses act to meet these needs. Therefore, you need to eliminate behavior that reinforces the negative identity–producing reaction.

REFLECTION

14.6

Reflect on what happens when you remove a long-standing reinforcement from an animal, including a human. If a behavior has been regularly reinforced, what happens when the reinforcement is removed? Does the behavior stop right away? Recall the classic example of the lab rat placed in a box and given a pellet of food each time it hits a bar: hitting the bar is the conditioned behavior, and the food is the reinforcement. When the researcher takes the food away, what is the rat's response? Like any other animal that has been conditioned, it will be to elicit the response (hit the bar) more vigorously. When the battery runs out on your television remote, what do you do?

Instead of giving in to the negative attention that the student is used to, recognize the nature of the pattern, determine the reinforcing stimuli the student is attempting to achieve with the behavior, and then go about removing them. In every case, if you want to effect change, it will be essential to stop showing anger, becoming negative, or implementing a pain-based form of response. However, since you are removing the reinforcing stimulus, be prepared for an "extinction burst," the intensity of which depends on the strength of the previous behavioral reinforcement (Kauffman, 2005). This burst or exaggeration of behavior is an attempt to elicit the desired response that has been removed. It will not last forever, but it may appear dramatic. For example, if the negative behavior was being annoying, the student will become especially annoying. If the negative behavior was to be a clown to get attention, expect the student to increase efforts to get a reaction if the audience stops laughing. Keep in mind that because the extinction burst can be so unpleasant, often efforts to change negative identity patterns are not able to withstand the discomfort the teacher or the class feels from the burst of negative behavior. Parents know how difficult it is not to give in to a tantrum. There is an encouraging note: after the burst, expect the behavior to eventually subside.

Why We Should Care About Helping Disruptive Students

Tremblay and colleagues (1994) found that students who become comfortable with a pattern of disruptive, aggressive, and antisocial behavior tend to maintain that pattern through later grades. Moreover, Robinson and Ricord Griesemer (2006) found that a pattern of disruptive behavior is strongly linked to adolescent and adult criminality. If we do nothing to help change a student's pattern, there is a great likelihood that that young person who cannot seem to stay out of trouble will be unable to get out of his or her rut and as a result cost him or her (and society) in the future.

You might be thinking, "I can't just ignore the student; his behavior is unacceptable and is disrupting the whole class." It is important to make a clear distinction here between discipline and the negative reaction the student seeks. In fact, they are unrelated (Robinson & Ricord Griesemer, 2006). Although you need to cease giving the student the pain and negativity that he or she has been conditioned to expect, you do not need to refrain from giving healthy, logical, and nonpersonal consequences when the student violates the social contract. As we will discuss later in this chapter, a personal behavioral contract with individualized consequences may be beneficial as well.

Exploring the Early Years of the Negative Identity Pattern Student

In many cases, a negative identity pattern is the by-product of an adult-child interaction that began at a very young age. When the child was young, most likely before she could speak and reason, an adult sent her the message that she was bad, worthless, or incapable. Being too young to be able to judge the validity of the message, the young person takes that information as fact. As a result she learned to believe the negative message and created a psychological connection between pain and love. Those who inflicted pain were also those who gave her love. As a result, she unconsciously connects the two feelings.

Over time her experience of pain becomes a familiar reinforcement that in a convoluted way is experienced as a kind of counterfeit love. This may seem odd, but recall that the young child does not have the processes to recognize the irrational nature of the relationship. The unconscious interconnection has been made, and the behavior pattern has been conditioned. Like a child born addicted to a drug, the negative identity pattern child has an early addiction to pain and feelings of worthlessness or inferiority that she experienced as a very young person. As a result, this child seeks out those feelings and tries to generate situations in which her negative identity will be confirmed.

When you become frustrated with the student's lack of progress toward more functional behavior, keep in mind that the mechanism that is supporting her negative behavior pattern is deep-seated and typically far below her level of awareness. Although it may be tempting to attempt to delve into the unconscious to help free the student from her false identity, it will be more helpful to support the emergent new identity and help the student recognize that she is good, valuable, capable, and accepted.

Early in the change process, it will be important to promote more positive behavior from the student. That means helping the student meet his or her basic needs, especially competence and love or belonging. Often a sense of inadequacy is at the heart of the problem. The student may not appear fearful and insecure and may even exhibit the opposite facade. That does not mean it is not there beneath the surface.

Also keep in mind that the most powerful reinforcement is going to come from peers. It may not be easy, but you need to create an emotionally safe classroom environment (Cone, 1997). Intolerance of put-downs and the development of healthy language is necessary. Mantras are helpful, such as, "In this class, we encourage each other to act only in ways that are positive for ourselves and for the class as a whole." Modeling by the teacher and student role models can be a valuable learning tool as well. Recall the social learning model: consistency is critical throughout the process. Responses that reinforce the negative identity can trigger a relapse and undo a great deal of your hard work.

To support the student in the effort toward more functional behavior, it may be useful to help the student identify a plan that includes behavioral goals toward which to work

(Robinson & Ricord Griesemer, 2006). The reality therapy process described later in this chapter can be useful in efforts with the negative identity students. This plan should define behaviors that are within the student's control and explicitly stated in behavioral terms, for example, through positive self-talk, persistence when frustrated, raising hand before speaking, and being considerate of others. The student needs to have a concrete understanding of and a commitment to his or her goals. This is where the practice of shaping will be critical (Landrum & Kauffman, 2006). The teacher needs to reinforce the student's attempts to achieve the goals of positive behavior even if they are not entirely successful. If the teacher reinforces behavior that is close to that desired, the student will be able to build up to full goal achievement. For example, if you observe the student demonstrating behavior that is a good effort toward one of his goals, take the opportunity to personally recognize him for that effort. In many cases, the student would not have realized that he had made progress unless you had pointed it out. In addition, public recognition of the student for positive progress can be powerful as long as it is sincere and well timed. Public positive recognitions can support both the student's need for love and his process of learning new ways of operating.

REFLECTION

As you begin to better understand the negative identity student, keep in mind that a part of this student wants to return to the familiar (albeit dysfunctional) negative behavior. At stage three of the negative identity intervention cycle, the student is like an addict who is on the wagon. He is sticking out his neck by trusting you. What would you predict the problems would be for a person making a life change from an old mind-set and set of behaviors to new and unfamiliar thinking and actions? What do you need to offer at this stage of the process and what should you avoid doing?

Watch out for the student's attempts to sabotage his or her own success. Help the student adopt the language of an internal locus of control and not to use negative self-talk or victim language, dwell on comparisons, or comingle academic performance with self-worth. Focusing on process and effort are good antidotes to the resurgence of a failure psychology. If the student experiences failure or a lack of support toward his or her goals at any time, he or she will be inclined to revert to the comfort of negative-identity behavior. And it should be emphasized that throughout the process, the teacher needs to maintain a high degree of trust with the student (Birch, & Ladd, 1997). Keep in mind that the addiction still exists and may do so indefinitely. Even if it is not readily apparent, it can be triggered by acute failure, rejection, humiliation, shame, or any other profound emotion that triggers the pain reaction familiar to that student.

As the student increasingly internalizes new goals and identity, it is essential that you guide the class in support of these efforts. You need to be intolerant of any labeling by peers or even the student that promotes a negative identity. You should use the power of labels to the student's advantage. Refer to the student with labels that support the process of transformation and the development of a success psychology. For example, you might use such confirming terms as *team player, winner, brilliant, persistent, selfless, scholar,* or *industrious,* for example. You may get a look telling you that you are being corny, but the student's private internal reaction will be powerful.

Send the message both implicitly and with explicit mantras such as this one: "In this class, there are no bad kids, fools, dumb kids, losers, failures, or helpless victims." To support the student's positive identity, it will be useful to put him or her in situations in which he or she is able to experience a sense of contributing to the welfare of others and, when possible, a leadership role. Encourage the ethic in the class that "when we support each other, we all win." This ethic was displayed powerfully in the film *Educating Peter* (Wurzburg & Goodwin, 1992), in which a class of fifth graders supported the growth and learning of a mentally and emotionally disabled classmate.

Table 14.2 outlines some of the forms of negative identity patterns and identifies the external trigger or reinforcer for each type of pattern. Students with patterns that are not as overpowering may need a substantial external event to trigger the inner ego response that perpetuates the negative identity. Other students' reactive patterns are activated almost continuously. These students are primed for something to trigger their negative reaction. For each type of pattern, a set of teacher supports is offered. It is possible that you recognize yourself in at least one pattern, and this is useful. The more effectively you deal with negative patterns within yourself, the better teacher you will be. The discussion in Chapter Sixteen addresses this process. Your own growth and self-awareness will be of value as you assist your students in their growth.

As you examine the various negative identity patterns in Table 14.2, you may notice some common ingredients. First, they all have a trigger, and promoting awareness of that trigger is critical to the success of the effort. Second, each pattern is masking something that the student fears. This is usually some sort of pain, and as the pattern gets more established, the student will fear the loss of the negative identity; it will feel like a loss of the self. The power of the addictive process makes it seem painfully true. Third, for each pattern, the solution requires promoting a success psychology within the student. The power of having basic needs satisfied in a positive and meaningful way will supersede the power of the addiction to negative attention. Conversely, the teaching practices that promote a failure psychology will reinforce and strengthen the negative identity pattern. If you do nothing else, take the practical action steps outlined in Chapter Seven for promoting a success psychology and avoid those that promote a failure psychology.

If nothing is addressed in this student's pattern, it may never change, and you will feel perpetually frustrated and resentful that he or she is in your class. Making the investment to change this pattern is worth the effort. I have seen many students change their mind-set from attempting to be the "best worst" to attempting to be an altruistic leader. The shift is not as impossible as it might appear. If the root of the problem is simply the student's finding a way to use his or her talents to meet his or her needs, then the change can occur relatively quickly and dramatically. Once the student realizes that he or she is capable of getting love, attention, and a sense of competence with positive behavior, he or she may take off in that direction. History is full of examples of those who have. Many students in my classes share that they were once the negative identity student and are now committed to much more positive goals, including becoming teachers. Before we give up on students and pass on the responsibility, keep in mind that it often just takes one understanding soul to change a life.

There are instances of turnaround everywhere, including former offenders. When asked what made the difference between a life of crime and a productive life in society, those who have turned around credit the support and faith of just one person. Often that one person was a teacher (Pianta, 2006).

14.8   ## REFLECTION

Recall examples that you know or have heard of someone who has gone from a negative identity pattern to working toward making a positive contribution in the world.

TABLE 14.2. **Types of Negative Identities, Triggers, and Related Teacher Support**

Negative Identity Pattern	External Reinforcement or Trigger of the Pattern	Teacher Support
Victim, poor me, or guilt complex. This student's ego tells him that life is unfair and that people are out to get him. The ego says that if he accepts responsibility for his actions, he will feel guilty and bad. Underneath is a sense of being unloved and unwanted. It shows up as an endless string of excuses and reasons that things cannot go right and a desire to have others absolve the student and confirm that "it is not his fault."	Pity from others. Confirmation that he has an excuse and is not responsible or to blame.	First, the student needs you to clearly communicate that you accept and believe in him. Second, you need to help the student recognize that he is asking for absolution from blame and responsibility. Third, you need to help the student accept responsibility for his actions and experience how it feels better in the end than avoiding blame.
Dangerous or intimidating. This student's ego says that by acting scary enough, she will be able to keep other people away. The student can attribute being alone to that, so she does not have to accept feeling unloved. Underneath it all is a desperate need to be loved and feel connected and a fear of rejection. It shows up as students who dress, act, and affiliate themselves in ways that make others want to steer clear. Her manner says, "Don't mess with me."	The intimidation of others. People seeming uncomfortable and uneasy around the student.	First, the student needs to know that you are a caring adult and see her as a good kid, but still a kid. Second, you define your relationship not by anything related to the student's external identifiers or reputation, but the positive goals, behaviors, and accomplishments that she makes in your class. Third, when the student tries to put on an intimidating facade, you ignore this and refocus her on the practical work of the class.
Failure, helplessness, or self-sabotage. This student's ego says that it is easier to quit than to deal with the pain of losing or performing below his own high expectations. What might look like inferiority is actually more likely an inner sense of superiority. Because the student has a need to feel better than others, he fears comparison and so finds ways to sabotage his efforts. If the student can tell himself that he did not try, it saves him from having to face failure. It shows up as an unpredictable and frustrating mix of excellent performance, self-sabotage, and quitting.	Comparison to others. Allowing the student to externalize his locus of control. Confirmation of his distorted view of reality.	First, minimize situations in which you publicly compare students. There is no educational benefit to it. Second, help the student recognize his pattern and take responsibility for finding more effective and conscious solutions to problems. This will include not buying into his helpless pattern language. You need to send the student the message that you believe in him but will not accept excuses or self-pity.

(continued)

TABLE 14.2. **Types of Negative Identities, Triggers, and Related Teacher Support (Continued)**

Negative Identity Pattern	External Reinforcement or Trigger of the Pattern	Teacher Support
Unloved, "look at me," clown. This student's ego tells her that unless she is getting a reaction from others, there is no evidence that she is lovable. So she acts out an endless part in which she tries to win the love that she feels she did not get earlier (probably from parents). The student becomes entirely dependent on external criteria for a sense of self. This is a losing battle, but works well to hone attention-getting skills. It shows up as a constant need for attention, reaction, and affirmation from others.	Giving attention when the student acts out. A sense of failure in another area.	First, let the student know that she will get a reasonable amount of attention, but that any attention-seeking behavior will not have the effect of obtaining more attention from you. Second, help the student build an internal locus of control and a self-identified sense of value. Third, you may want to find ways that the student can experience healthy attention from peers by giving her a format, letting her work in groups, allowing venues such as presentations, and giving the student a sense of responsibility in class. If you help this student feel that she is making a positive contribution, the student will feel less of a need to use inappropriate means to gain attention.
Best, best worst, inferiority complex. This student's ego says that he needs to win or is unworthy. The student interprets all events through the lens of competition. If the game does not work to the student's advantage, he will find a game that does. This same mechanism will create both the student who needs to get the highest score and the student who needs to create the most visible doodling or get the lowest score ever recorded. What it looks like is a student who acts and thinks only in comparisons and becomes overly joyful when he wins and overly miserable when he or she loses.	Competitive contexts. Public comparison.	First, reduce the unnecessary competition and competitive elements in the class. Ask yourself if they are valuable in the long term. Second, help the student recognize the tendency to want to see things in terms of comparison and that it is not necessarily a true representation of reality. Encourage the student to look at his learning as a process of growth rather than a measure of ability or self-worth. Introduce the student to the idea that success is more likely if he sheds the inferiority complex. It may seem useful, but it is not based in sound motivation. If it were, he e would feel satisfied more often, and it is a sure bet that he does not.

(continued)

TABLE 14.2. Continued

Negative Identity Pattern	External Reinforcement or Trigger of the Pattern	Teacher Support
Drama queen or king. This student's ego says that if she keeps the external dramas going, she will not have to deal with what is inside. What is inside is not nearly as scary as the student believes, but she sees it as an unbearable monster. The student allows her ego to run her life and finds whatever external stimuli, conflict, drama, offense, problem, disaster to attach to and engage in. The result is the development of coping skills that appear dynamic and occasionally effective. However, the failure to take personal responsibility for her actions and listen to what is going on inside create a series of ticking time bombs that explode eventually. It shows up as a student who always has a good reason for being prevented from achievement and for being in conflict with others and for why the rules need to be different for her.	High-pressure deadlines and outcomes. The thought that she will be exposed. Others buying into the drama and the external variables. Enabling the excuses or the drama stories.	First, do not buy into the drama. Second, help the student examine events within a practical lens. Help the student step back from the drama and recognize that there are many interpretations to events; the dramatic interpretation is just one subjective way of looking at it. Also, help her learn to look at the practical choices that led to the crisis. Could she have gotten started on the project earlier? Could she have planned for more time or cut out another activity to make sure that she achieved the desired outcome ? Third, help the student recognize that drama, conflict, and crisis are largely manufactured conditions. They do not occur without being created. Help the student evaluate how the latest drama or crisis that she experienced originated.
Pleaser, "Tell me I am good/teacher's pet." This student's ego says that if he does not have an external parent figure telling him that he is special, then he is insignificant. As a result, the student feels the need to be the "most loved," the "uniquely blessed" member of the class. While this may not seem negative on the surface, it is not healthy. At best, when you enable this pattern, you promote the student's lack of internal sense of adequacy and worth. At worst, if the student feels his need is unrequited, he may become a powerfully disruptive force in the class.	Giving praise each time it is requested. Treating students differently depending on how reverent they are. Playing into the student's game. Leading the student on.	First, project to the student that you like and accept him the way he is. Do give the student concrete and specific feedback and positively recognize his effort. Do not give the student personal praise, tell him that he is good because he has done good work, or buy into the student's requests for praise. Affirm the student's effort and give unconditional acceptance, but choose your words carefully so that the student does not hear personal praise. Second, help the student learn to validate his own work. When he asks what you think about something he

(continued)

TABLE 14.2. Types of Negative Identities, Triggers, and Related Teacher Support (Continued)

Negative Identity Pattern	External Reinforcement or Trigger of the Pattern	Teacher Support
Pleaser, "Tell me I am good/teacher's pet." (Continued)		made, ask the student what he thinks. Third, maintain healthy boundaries with the student. Stay professional, and avoid too much time alone with him.
Pain addict, chemical addict, destructive. This student's ego has become aligned with her pain-based internal physical reaction. The result is a student on the lookout for something to take as a personal offense, a challenge to her worth or honor, or anything that she can use to trigger the pain reaction. This shows up as a student who likes to challenge others, sees everything through the lens of being personally attacked and victimized, and is ready to fight back. In severe cases, this student is capable of unpredictable, risky, and destructive behavior.	Anger- or pain-based punishments. Making choices personal and attacking the student's dignity. Getting hooked into the student's efforts to personalize and create power struggles.	First, resist the temptation to engage this student in a power struggle. It will never end well. Also resist the temptation to get in the pattern of sending the student out after she has reacted badly to your ultimatum or threat. Second, follow the steps related to how to alter the negative identity pattern faithfully. You need to build a great deal of trust with this student and help her feel valuable and capable. Third, help the student find her talents, gifts, and strengths and reinforce her efforts toward cultivating them. Help the student find healthy addictions, such as exercise or creating or building things. Fourth, to the degree possible, allow the student to share what is inside, and let her know that you are there to listen and are on her side.

WORKING WITH CHALLENGING STUDENTS: BRIDGING THE GAP

- A student asks the teacher, "Do we have to take notes?" "Will you be collecting them?" "How many points is this worth?"

- A student nervously eyes his cell phone while the class is having a discussion. Inattentive to what is being said, he is lost in his anticipation of the chance to check messages.

- All the other students but one begin work. When the teacher asks her to get started, she gently smiles but continues to sit motionless.

In these cases, the student behavior is not overtly disruptive. These students are not technically hurting anyone and may not even be breaking any rules. They characterize a more subtle but significant kind of problem behavior: the disconnected student. If we do nothing, it is likely that these students will maintain their pattern, learn little, and the class will remain fragmented. As a result, these students tend to frustrate us most. They make us feel that we are failing, inadequate, and powerless, especially when we find that the same techniques that make us successful with other students do not seem to work with these students (Walker et al., 1996). While not as deep-seated as the conditioning at the root of the negative identity pattern, the problem here is also rooted in a conditioned pattern. The gap is maintained by unconsciousness; the key to the cure is bringing awareness into the equation.

REFLECTION   14.9

Recall classes you have recently observed. Did you observe disconnected students? How did you know they were disconnected? Keep those students in mind as you continue reading the chapter.

Recognize the Existence and Nature of the Disconnect

The problem when this kind of gap exists is that the teacher and the student are playing from a different set of rules. The term *rules* here does not refer to classroom rules, but rather rules that govern values and ways of being. Therefore, that which each party wants and expects intersects little, if at all, with the other. If each party continues to operate entirely within his or her own set of rules and agenda and remains largely unconscious of the rules of the other, the gap between them will remain. That gap will keep the teacher frustrated and feeling helpless and the students uninterested and uninvested. The first phase here is recognition.

Following are some of the common disconnects between teachers and students:

- The teacher's agenda is not satisfying to the students in terms of their needs. These needs may not be desirable or healthy or legitimate in class (for example, familiar forms of stimulation such as TV, the Internet, the cell phone, or texting; emotional or ego dramas; or addiction to instant gratification), but they define the world of the students, or at least the students' mental world.

- Performing at their minimum. Some students are very comfortable with a helpless pattern (Dweck, 2000) and are resistant to thinking about work outside that pattern. They see tasks as things to get done rather than opportunities to learn. They will make statements such as, "Do we need to do this?" "This is for points, right?" "I'm okay. I'll do it later." They have gotten comfortable essentially turning schoolwork into something that they must do to maintain their status as students to avoid dropout status or losing contact with their friends.

- Occasionally students adopt a mind-set that the teacher is the enemy to some degree (Wolcott, 1984). To them, the teacher may represent a hostile generation group, ethnicity, gender, value system, or class. There may or may not be anything to justify this perception, but it does seem real to them. As a result, they find ways to penalize the teacher, often in the form of poor performance, as in, "I will punish you by my failure."

REFLECTION   14.10

Do any of these situations seem familiar? Can you recognize the origin of the gap in rules for each type of student?

When you make a sincere effort in teaching and doing your best to help students learn yet experience a lack of caring, interest, or respect on the part of one or more students, the natural tendency is to get negative. You need to resist that negative temptation. Instead, focus on the positive only; allow the students to own their behavior, but take purposeful action to change the situation. Your first step, as always, is the realization that something needs to change and commitment to taking action without letting this student affect your attitude toward the class as a whole.

Raising the Awareness of the Disconnect

The second step is to raise the level of awareness in the dynamic. Nothing will change if both parties maintain separate sets of expectations. Like a generation gap, this gap will foster miscommunication and mistrust, so communication is part of the key to developing trust. Communicate to the student your awareness that a gap exists. Useful techniques here are I-messages, clarifying statements, and clarifying questions. For example, if a student is exhibiting a helpless pattern and suggesting that there is nothing he can do because he is not good at something in particular, you might raise his level of awareness with a clarifying question or statement such as this one: "I hear you saying that we should try only when we think we are already good at something." Be mindful that these messages need to be delivered in a sensitive manner. If you are perceived as judgmental or condescending, you will widen the gap and the message will not get across.

14.11 REFLECTION

Reflect on a gap situation you have observed. Did the teacher or the student recognize or raise the other party's level of awareness of the existence of a gap in expectations? Did the situation improve?

Closing the Gap—Start by Making a Connection

If you do not make an emotional connection with your students (recall our discussion of social frames in Chapter Three), the result is very often limited student motivation and the existence of "gaps." Are you only someone in the role of teacher or are you a real person as well? Are your students simply bodies in the seats or are they important to you? Remember that they "do not care what you know, until they know that you care." Your care for your students is expressed in many ways including being prepared, listening to them, and being genuinely and conspicuously interested in helping them be successful. In addition, you will need to connect in specific ways with students depending on the nature of the "gaps" that they experience.

"Different World" Students. In many cases, especially those in which the students feel the teacher does not "get them or their world," it may be essential to demonstrate your willingness to narrow the gap by coming to them. It helps to make a one-on-one connection with the student. You might find sources of commonality or pathways to mutual empathy or appreciation. This is especially important in cases in which students feel a disconnection between classes and that which is personally satisfying. Make a sincerely voiced effort to find out their interests. If possible, look for common interests or validate the student's interests. Later, just asking the student how that "something unique" is going can have a profound impact.

"Helpless Pattern" Students. To connect with students who exhibit the helpless pattern, first raise their awareness of it. You could comment, "I know that you really want to learn about vectors because you see the value and are fascinated by the concept, not just because you want to get the points." If you keep your process positive and audibly assign noble intentions, you will either help them recognize their pattern or open the door to discussion. Even if they deny your assumptions (for example, they could not care less about vectors), at least you have succeeded at helping them to reflect and have demonstrated caring. Over time acknowledge anything resembling growth-oriented orientation in their thinking, and provide positive recognition for it.

"Teacher-as-Enemy" Students. It can be difficult to know where to start with students who feel they need to conceptually reject what you represent. Remember to address this without hostility, as you would any mistake. Then make an effort to let them recognize that you have a lot more in common than they think. It will be helpful to be authentic and share at least a glimpse of your personal side. No matter the students' assumptions, you need to communicate that you care deeply about their success. As the students begin to respond, you can increasingly offer even more of yourself and develop rapport.

REFLECTION

14.12

As you read this last section, did you feel resistance to the idea of making the effort to come to the student? If you did, that is natural; however, examine that feeling more closely. The tendency to want to stay in your corner and hope things get better on their own is common, but that is usually just the fear of rejection or looking inadequate. Remember that you are the adult in the equation, and taking the bold step to break the ice will make you feel better about the student and your ability to handle future situations.

Community: A Gap-Resistant Climate

Do not underestimate the students' interest in being part of a safe, emotionally and intellectually fulfilling, needs-satisfying environment. They may project a hard shell and a quick habit of going negative on each other, you, and the course work, but in fact they want what we all want: a world where their basic needs are met. The more students feel safe to come out of their self-protective fortress, the narrower any gap will become. A classroom defined by a sense of community is by nature antithetical to the experience of disconnection on the part of its members. The desire to put the common good foremost is itself a powerful bridge. Therefore, your job is to help students:

- Recognize the desirability of an emotionally safe environment and build community (Chapter Sixteen)
- Understand that negativity is only a mental game that promises brief relief and short-term satisfaction and will never lead to true contentment
- Learn new skills and experience community in a concrete, hands-on way

Bridging the Gap with Engaging Work

As we discussed in Chapter Eleven, the type of work students are assigned will have a direct impact on your ability to manage the class. This is especially true for students who are disconnected or unmotivated or have learned to get by doing the minimum. Often students, especially those from large urban public school systems, get accustomed to a communicable mind-set that school is a waste of time. It may take a while to alter the conditioning, but you can. When students feel invested in a task, it brings them out of themselves and closes the gap.

Some useful ideas for promoting student investment in class work include:

- *Incorporate projects.* They help students feel a more concrete sense of accomplishment.

- *Focus on process and effort.* This builds a sense of internal locus of control and encourages the student to think about quality rather than just getting work done.

- *Incorporate problem-solving tasks.* This reinforces success as a function of investment and promotes a growth-oriented orientation.

Revisit Chapter Eight and the concepts of building a success psychology for more ideas.

14.13 REFLECTION

Take a look at a few classrooms. Do you see a relationship between the kind of work that the students are doing and the proportion of students who are disconnected from the teacher and their learning? How do you explain your findings?

REALITY THERAPY AND STUDENT BEHAVIORAL CONTRACTS

14.2 CASESTUDY

The teacher has created a culture of listening in her class, including very clear expectations. One day as she is giving directions, she notices Paul turn to another student and begin to talk to her. As is the teacher's technique in these cases, she stops, waits for 100 percent attention, and then begins again. Later, when another student is presenting, the teacher sees Paul talking again. She privately and calmly implements a consequence: she asks Paul to move to another location in the room. Moreover, she obtains an assurance from Paul that he understands the expectation and a commitment that he fulfills the part of the social contract related to listening and attention. Shortly after, the teacher again finds Paul talking to another student while she is giving directions.

The case of Paul illustrates a common example of a student with a deeply conditioned and chronic undesirable behavior (a bad habit). In this situation, Paul exhibits a compulsive need to talk to others during times that violate the needs of the rest of the class. Like other level II types of issues, simple consequences may not be sufficient to cure the problem. Punishments and detentions are unlikely to solve level II types of problems such as this or another negative identity pattern because they maintain an external locus of control. If the problem requires learning new behaviors and making new choices, you need to put the ownership on the student to solve his or her own problem. You need to stop owning the student's problems, but provide him or her with a means to grow out of them by his or her own volition.

A model that has proven effective for promoting more self-responsible thinking in students comes from William Glasser (1975). His work in the area of reality therapy offers a useful process to encourage students to make a commitment to more positive behavior. As opposed to models that assume change will come from increasing the level of consequences to the unwanted behavior, this process assumes that the solution comes from making the student responsible for changing his or her own behavior. Glasser offers the following series of steps for shifting the locus of the change process from external to internal, promoting responsibility, and ultimately achieving behavior change. In this process, the student gains awareness of the conditioned and compulsive nature of his or her behavior as well as the benefits of a more functional set of behaviors.

REFLECTION

14.14

As you reflect on the approach Glasser outlined, how do you find it differs from traditional or commonsense approaches? Where is the locus of control?

Step 1: Establish Involvement with the Student

You will not be very successful changing a dysfunctional pattern or closing a gap in expectations without demonstrating a personal commitment to the welfare of the student. The student needs to know that you care, can be trusted, and have his or her best interest at heart. If the student suspects that you are simply using the process to gain more solid ground for later disciplinary action, the result will likely be an insincere effort on the student's part.

No matter how it is implemented, this process will act to better define the terms of the necessary behavior change. But if you take an interest in the student, there is a greater opportunity to communicate intimately or authentically when the time comes, and the student is more likely to view the process as a means to genuine growth.

Step 2: Focus on the Behavior

To initiate the process, it is critical that the student understand that your goal is not a personal indictment, but the facilitation of more functional and positive behavior. Therefore, you need to maintain the focus on the behavior in question and not peripheral matters such as your frustration, the wisdom of the behavior, or past problems. You might use clarifying questions to help the student self-reflect, such as, "This is what I see [state the behavior]. How would you describe what is happening?" At this initial stage, you need to communicate the message to the student that you like him and believe in him, this behavior is not working, and you are going to work with him to change it.

Step 3: The Student Must Accept Responsibility for the Behavior

After the problem behavior has been identified, the student needs to accept responsibility for it. It is critical not to shame or blame the student. For students struggling with inappropriate behavior, there is likely a corresponding problem related to external locus of control. Promote the student's cause-and-effect reasoning: the cause is the problem behavior; the effect is unwanted consequences. It is important not to accept excuses. You are asking the student to accept the responsibility for choices she has made. You need to help her resist the temptation to blame others, become fatalistic, or see the process as a personal attack from you.

The student's affect will be a good indicator of the effectiveness of your intervention. If you see recognition (even involving consternation), you are on the right track. If you see a show of repentance or hear lip-service, you will need to help the student better focus on where the process is going: "I don't want you to be sorry or feel bad. I want you to know that we *are* going to work together to make sure this does not happen in the future."

Step 4: The Student Should Evaluate the Behavior

We typically overestimate the degree to which students evaluate the consequences of their choices. Students who tend to externalize the causes of their problems usually also resist constructive self-reflection. A student who spends time thinking about why she is "bad" is resisting reasoning how she can change unwanted behavior.

After the student has acknowledged responsibility, you need to help her evaluate her behavior in a nonpersonal and nonjudgmental manner. In a sincere and supportive tone, you might ask the student some thought-provoking questions, such as, "Would you consider what you did helpful or hurtful?" "What did it produce?" Help the student analyze the situation: "What do you think just happened?" "What will the result be if that interaction keeps happening?" "What will help you get what you want and be good for the rest of us?"

14.15 | REFLECTION

Getting to this level will be a huge win-win outcome for all concerned. In most cases, you will feel as if you have succeeded, and you have. Getting the student to evaluate his or her own behavior is significant and will have substantial benefits to both of you. But what potential problems can arise if stopping at this point? What happens if you walk away without a contract or at least a concrete commitment to behavioral change?

Step 5: Develop a Plan of Action or Behavioral Contract

Leading the student through the first four steps of the process may be sufficient to raise the desired level of awareness and consequent behavior change. However, if the problem is habitual or the student lacks motivation to change, a plan or contract stage is probably necessary. Working with the student, write a plan that details how the problem behavior will be remedied. The more this plan is written by the student, the more effective it is likely to be. Plans can take many forms, but you might want the student to include:

- A behavioral goal
- An analysis of why the problem keeps happening
- What roadblocks might be expected when the student tries to change the situation
- A time line (optional)
- Anticipated benefits of reaching the goal
- Self-initiated consequences for what happens if the student is not able to meet the goal and his or her behavior still violates the social contract

The plan becomes a contract when the consequences are included and the student commits to it and signs it.

Step 6: The Student Must Make a Commitment to Following the Plan

Throughout the process, help the student recognize that he is in control. If the student does not like the plan, it should be modified and written in a way that the student can accept, as long as it works for you and the rest of the class. The contract is not something that is being inflicted on the student. It is a support tool, and you are not going to beg, or nag, or take ownership for the student's choices. You are the student's leader and cheerleader, but you cannot make him do anything. You need to voice appreciation for the student's good intentions, but reiterate that what you need is behavior change. You need to see him "walk the walk" not just "talk the talk."

Step 7: Follow Up and Follow Through

A plan offers a number of benefits. First, you have a common language to use with the student as a result of the reflection process and the concrete plan that now exists. Second, you share clarity of expectation and consequences. Third, you have shifted the locus of ownership of the problem to the student. Your job now is to use those benefits to support the success of the plan.

The language in the contract will allow you to use fewer words when you want to recognize the student's success or see the student getting off track. For example, if one of the problems was disruptive behavior in cooperative groups and the contract outlines appropriate group behavior, you might only need to look at the student and say, "Role?" Before the behavior contract was in place, this interaction would not have been meaningful to the student. Now it will trigger a whole series of thoughts for the student: *The teacher is recognizing that I am straying from my intention. I need to ask myself whether I am doing a good job of my role. Have I crossed a line, and do I need to accept a consequence?*

If the process is working, the student should be doing most of the concerned thinking. Does the language in the contract need to change? Has the student reached her goal? You will know it is working when you see the student take ownership of the plan and you observe a change in behavior. If the plan is not working, it should be altered, and if the student does not meet her obligations, the consequences written into the plan should be implemented.

REFLECTION   14.16

Put yourself in the role of the student who has just gone through this process. How do you feel? Where is the locus of control? Are you looking in vain for someone to rebel against? Do you think you will make the effort to change your behavior?

LEVEL III CONDITIONS AND SUPPORTING STUDENTS WITH ADHD

Students who experience level III behavioral conditions, such as ADHD, fetal alcohol syndrome, emotional or behavioral disorders, and other biologically based behavioral issues present a substantive challenge in the area of behavior management. These students typically experience an organic difficulty maintaining focus and attention. As a result, they may be making a courageous effort to control themselves and maintain attention, but their chemistry makes it seemingly impossible. We need to recognize their organic limitations and needs and the corresponding conditioning that takes place as a result. In too many cases, students with organic difficulties such as ADHD develop a negative identity pattern to mask their struggles with the organic condition.

The primary symptoms of ADHD are persistent patterns of inattention, impulsivity, and hyperactivity when compared to others of similar age and developmental levels (American Psychiatric Association, 1994). According to the Centers for Disease Control and Prevention (2009), this pattern must adversely affect at least two settings, such as school, home, or work, and must have been present before the age of seven. ADHD has been the most common diagnosis for school-age children for many years, with prevalence estimates at about 4 percent in the primary grades and nearly 10 percent after fourth grade (Centers for Disease Control and Prevention, 2009).

Working in collaboration with the school counselor or psychologist is highly recommended. It will be essential to begin with a professional evaluation of the student's condition. ADHD, a kinesthetic learning orientation, compulsive attention-getting behavior, highly extroverted behavior, and a lack of personal behavioral control may appear similar in terms of behavior, yet each has different roots and requires somewhat different support behaviors on your part. One of the primary reasons that a student with ADHD presents such a unique challenge is that it will require you to think differently than you do with other students. This is especially true if you intend a 1-Style student-centered management orientation.

While goals for most students include self-responsible behavior, this goal may need to be reexamined for students with ADHD. Increasing these students' level of self-control will be a critical part of their growth, but you need to be sensitive to these students' limits as they progress in self-understanding.

We have discussed the encouragement of self-directed behavior for most students. Remember to limit extrinsic rewards and too much teacher dependence, especially in the 1-Style classroom. If you help students learn to stay present and attentive for ever-longer periods of time, they will become increasingly self-directed. However, this may be asking too much, too soon of ADHD students. In the case of ADHD students, techniques such as the use of rewards may be necessary to help them succeed.

Kirby and Kirby (1994) suggest that because individuals with ADHD often receive a substantial amount of negative feedback, it is important to structure the school day so that the chance for successful and positive feedback is increased. Most students can simply be challenged to work through difficulties and encouraged to persist in the face of demanding work or problem situations, but students with ADHD need more. They have a tendency to want to quit early on at the appearance of work that seems difficult or a lesson that requires a great deal of attention. Work that is too complex, boring, or repetitive will lead to behavioral problems with many students, and this is especially true of the students with ADHD. Therefore, you need to create a learning environment that contains both the perception and the reality of success.

Start with a diagnosis. Once you have a clear understanding of the student's condition, you will be in a better position to outline an intervention. Matching your interventions to the student's needs is most effective. Matte and Bolaski (1998) caution against the use of a blanket set of strategies for all ADHD students. For instance, a student whose predominant symptom is impulsivity requires different interventions from the student who is persistently inattentive (Rooney, 1995). Matte and Bolaski (1998) suggest that if a student is predominantly hyperactive, a kinesthetic approach to an academic exercise may be beneficial. Also, if a student is unable to channel the necessary mental effort into a single task, a tactile or group approach may help.

Partner with the student in the plan, and make it a team effort. A student who is aware of the plan and providing feedback on its effectiveness has a sense of power and ownership and is the best source of information. Make the plan as concrete as you can. The use of weekly or even daily schedules can be helpful. Keep in mind the success recognition frame (discussed in Chapter Three). The student needs a high level of recognition, and even rewards, for meeting the goals of the plan. The key is to keep the student feeling successful, or he or she will be tempted to quit, give in, and get fatalistic. Matte and Bolaski (1998) point out that ADHD students are often surprised by their own behavior and do not intend to act out in the classroom. They can be repentant one moment and out of control the next. Help them remove the guilt and shame from their condition and let them know they are supported. But they should also take responsibility for their own success by letting you know what is working and what they need from you.

Build in routine for these students. Find as many ways as possible for them to experience predictability and regularity in their work. The presence of ambiguity or change, or the need for learning new procedures or a large amount of interpretation, can trigger frustration and a desire to give up in ADHD students (Kemp, Fister, & McLaughlin, 1995). This routine does not need to be classwide; it only needs to apply to ADHD students.

Consider time of day in your planning. Matte and Bolaski (1998) suggest that academic work requiring a high level of attention is best scheduled in the morning, and other school activities that require less attention should be scheduled in the afternoon. Most students with ADHD are better able to control attention during the first half of the school day. This kind of schedule can decrease frustration for both the student and teacher.

Reduce the increments of time on task. Most students are capable of attending or sticking with a task for a good amount of time. This means more than fifteen minutes. For ADHD students, attending for five or ten minutes may feel like an eternity. We need to help them set small goals and feel achievement when they meet those goals. We might say, "Let's see if you can do problems 14 and 15 in the next five minutes. I will be back then, and we can see how you did. Do you think you can do that, or do you need more help before you get started?"

Consider incorporating the use of behavioral modification strategies. While it may go against your overall philosophy of classroom management, it will be helpful to become skilled at behavioral modification for the most challenging cases of ADHD. Again, this does not mean that you need to use any of the same techniques with the other students, but they can be invaluable in helping to structure the ADHD student's experience. When administered with patience and repetitiveness, they can be beneficial in improving classroom behavior (Kirby & Kirby, 1994). Matte and Bolaski (1998) suggest the use of the following behavioral techniques: withholding privileges as a negative consequence, recognizing and rewarding positive behavior as close to the successful event as possible, using checklists, and implementing a token system. They go on to state, "Students with ADHD struggle with basic causal relationships and they often fail to notice connections between behavior and consequences; therefore, for behavior modification to be effective, interventions must be consistent, repetitive, fair, and educable" (p. 41). Chapter Six outlines a series of techniques to make the use of extrinsic rewards more powerful and effective.

Think in terms of building a success psychology (as discussed in Chapter Seven). As with students who experience level II types of problems, you will be much more successful with ADHD students and those with other level III conditions if they experience empowerment and a high internal locus of control. Much of their sense of failure and guilt comes from feelings of being powerless to control their own behavior, along with their assessment that they are letting others down. Help these students recognize their successes as powerful, and make them partners in the effort so that they feel empowered.

You will be much more successful with these students if they feel that you accept them for who they are. They tend to feel that they are "bad." You need to communicate that you share a common challenge: growth and learning. Assure them that it is often difficult and failures will occur, but you will never stop caring about and accepting them, even when they do not meet your expectations. Finally, you need to help them recognize that things will get and are getting better as a result of their investment in themselves. Refrain from labeling them or letting them label themselves as "broken" or possessing a fixed view of their potential. You need to help them focus on how they are growing. The more concrete and specific you can be here, the better. The students will likely want to revert to a limiting self-image after they have had a rough day. Keep them focused on how they are making tangible progress and can make even more progress in the future if they continue to apply themselves.

CONCLUSION

Success with more challenging students can make all the difference in your effectiveness. Promoting growth in these students will lead to a sense of satisfaction as well as a better result for the student, the other students, and yourself.

The chapters in Part Six further examine how to go beyond the social contract to a more transformational form of management. Although challenging students may slow this process, they will also offer the other members of the class an opportunity to support the growth of one of the members of their community.

Journal Reflections

1. Recall a student who exhibited a negative identity pattern. Did the actions of the adults around him make his pattern better or worse?

2. When have you felt a gap, or disconnected, as a student? What was it that you wanted, and what were the rules of the game that you were playing? Why did you feel the gap? What did the teacher do that made you feel as if the two of you were playing from a divergent set of rules and expectations?

Activities

1. In small groups, share your experiences of negative identity students you have known. What was the reinforcement that the student was seeking? Did the student get the reinforcement for the negative behavior? Did anything or anyone intervene to alter the cycle and change the negative identity pattern, or did it maintain itself? What happened to that student eventually?

2. In small groups, select (or be assigned) one of the four gap conditions described in the chapter: (1) helpless pattern, (2) seeing no value to the work, (3) doing the minimum, or (4) the teacher as the enemy. Examine the causes of the problem, and then generate a list of strategies that a teacher might use to bridge the gap with this kind of student and support their reconnection with the learning.

3. View the video *Educating Peter,* and discuss the role of the other students in supporting the growth and adjustment of one especially challenging and troubled student. Peter has Down syndrome, but the implications of the video can be generalized to many other disabilities.

REFERENCES

American Psychiatric Association. (1994). *Diagnostic and statistical manual of mental disorders* (4th ed.). Washington, DC: Author.

Birch, S. H., & Ladd, G. W. (1997). The teacher-child relationship and children's early school adjustment. *Journal of School Psychology*, *35*, 61–79.

Centers for Disease Control and Prevention. (2003). Online Report. Retrieved July 25, 2009, from http://www.cdc.gov/ncbddd/adhd/data.html.

Cone, J. (1997). Issues in functional analysis in behavioral assessment. *Behavioral Research and Therapy*, *35*, 259–275.

Dweck, C. (2000). *Self-theories: Their role in motivation, personality and development*. Lillington, NC: Psychologists Press.

Glasser, W. (1975). *Reality therapy: A new approach to psychiatry*. New York: HarperCollins.

Kauffman, J. M. (2005). How we prevent the prevention of emotional and behavioral difficulties in education. In P. Clough, P. Garner, J. T. Pardeck, & F. Yuen (Eds.), *Handbook of emotional and behavioral difficulties in education* (pp. 429–440). Thousand Oaks, CA: Sage.

Kemp, K., Fister, S., & McLaughlin, P. (1995). Academic strategies for children with ADD. *Intervention in School and Clinic*, *30*(4), 203–210.

Kirby, E., & Kirby, S. (1994). Classroom discipline with attention deficit hyperactivity disorder children. *Contemporary Education*, *65*(3), 142–144.

Landrum, T. J., & Kauffman, J. M. (2006). Behavioral approaches to classroom management. In C. M. Evertson & C. S. Weinstein (Eds.), *Handbook of classroom management* (pp. 47–71). Mahwah, NJ: Erlbaum.

Matte, R., and Bolaski, J. (1998). Nonverbal learning disabilities: An overview. *Intervention in School and Clinic*, *34*, 39–42.

Pianta, R. C. (2006). Classroom management and relationships between children and teachers: Implications for research and practice. In C. M. Evertson & C. S. Weinstein (Eds.), *Handbook of classroom management* (pp. 685–709). Mahwah, NJ: Erlbaum.

Robinson, S. L., & Ricord Griesemer, S. M. (2006). Helping individual students with problem behavior. In C. M. Evertson & C. S. Weinstein (Eds.), *Handbook of classroom management* (pp. 787–802). Mahwah, NJ: Erlbaum.

Rooney, K. (1995). Teaching students with attention disorders. *Intervention in School and Clinic*, *30*(4), 221–225.

Tremblay, R. E., Pihl, R. O., Vitaro, F., & Dobkin, P. L. (1994). Predicting early onset male anti-social behavior from preschool behavior. *Archives of General Psychology*, *51*, 205–226.

Vitaro, F., Brendgen, M., & Tremblay, R. E. (2001). Prevention of school dropout through the reduction of disruptive behavior and school failure in elementary school. *Journal of School Psychology*, *37*, 205–226.

Walker, H. M., Horner, R. H., Sugai, G., Bullis, M., Sprague, J. R., Bricker, D., Kaufman, M. J. et al. (1996). Integrated approaches to preventing anti-social behavioral patterns among school age children and youth. *Journal of Emotional and Behavioral Disorders*, *4*, 194–209.

Wolcott, H. (1987). The teacher as enemy. In G. Spindler (Ed.), *Education and cultural process: Anthropological approaches* (pp. 136–150). Prospect Heights, IL: Waveland.

Wurzburg, G., & Goodwin, T. (1992). *Educating Peter*. PBS Video.

6

Adopting a Transformative Mind-Set

15

The Transformative Classroom

*Implementing a 1-Style Approach and Creating a
Classroom Community*

In This Chapter

- The 1-Style classroom as the natural state
- Defining *community*
- Stages of development for the transformative classroom

Marta is beginning her second year of teaching with high expectations for herself and her class. By the end of the previous year, she had developed a workable set of routines and did not feel as overwhelmed as she had at the beginning of the year. She has worked hard at classroom management and overall has had fewer problems than many of her colleagues. Marta has been clear about rules and consequences, and her students have responded to her clear expectations. She has avoided punishments and public shaming. Students trust and like her. However, as she considers her class, it seems too much about her. She feels the students respond to and depend on her direction. She enjoys the order and sanity in the class, but the long-term effects of her approach concern her. It bothers her that the students continuously ask for confirmation that what they are doing is "okay." Moreover, she feels that they make decisions tentatively and rely excessively on her to solve their conflicts. It concerns her when she overhears comments such as, "Look busy, or Mrs. Juarez is going to get after us!" She appreciates that students are aware of consequences and interested in being on task, but wishes they would see the value of good listening, being responsible, treating each other well, and working hard aside from being concerned about potential consequences.

Marta sees other teachers who allow students to make many of the classroom decisions and use self-directed learning strategies, but she worries about losing control of the class. Her perception is that teachers who hand over a great deal of power to students often seem to spend a lot of time disappointed in their students' irresponsibility. She does not want to spend all day lecturing about behavior or descend into a 3-Style approach like the teacher next door, who gives her students a lot of freedom and gets chaos as students take advantage. She has a sense that she could be more empowering and have a more democratic classroom, but she does not want to sacrifice order.

15.1 REFLECTION

Do you empathize with Marta? Why or why not?

Like Marta, many teachers intuitively sense that their classroom management could be accomplishing more than mere obedience and order. They recognize that a teacher-centered 2-Style approach to management—what Canter (1986) refers to as "assertive discipline"—is certainly preferable to taking an authoritarian 4-Style approach (Canter labels this the "hostile teacher"), but they do not see a teacher-centered approach leading to the kind of order and motivation they want to see from students. They receive an endless supply of advice about what "works" and how to avoid a 3-Style approach (which Canter terms "passive"). They find the advice either too teacher centered and gimmicky or too ill defined and unrealistic.

This chapter outlines a step-by-step process for creating a student-centered 1-Style classroom and a functioning community: the transformative classroom. It offers practical strategies for developing a more student-centered form of management and promoting a collective sense of responsibility and community.

READER NOTE

Some readers opened this book already possessing a commitment to a student-centered approach. Others may have been persuaded to adopt a 1-Style approach after some reading. For those readers, this chapter provides practical ideas to develop that approach. Other readers may find themselves attracted to aspects of the 1-Style approach yet remain most comfortable with maintaining a 2-Style approach. For those readers, this chapter should provide some academic interest. However, there are likely a good number of readers who intend to take a pragmatic approach to the management style they adopt. For those readers, this chapter offers ideas for making the shift from a 2-Style to a 1-Style management approach as the opportunity presents itself.

THE 1-STYLE CLASSROOM AND THE CONCEPT OF COMMUNITY

The natural state of learning is one in which students feel intrinsically motivated, a sense of belonging, and excited to learn and use their learning to make a difference in the group.

This natural state is transformative. However, few students learn in classrooms that promote this condition; in fact, over the course of their education, most students become increasingly removed from this state. The 1-Style classroom endeavors to promote a natural state of learning by using management strategies that empower students and create a needs-satisfying environment. Given that this natural state may be foreign to many students, developing a 1-Style classroom will require some patience as we help them adjust to it by awakening aspects that may have become dormant and developing the skills necessary to function in a democratic system.

The 1-Style classroom is possible at any grade level (Elias & Schwab, 2006). I have seen fully functional, self-directed classrooms of first graders, high school seniors, and all grades in between. I have seen 1-Style classrooms in all kinds of schools. We do need to be realistic, of course. Some students take to this style more readily than others. If you have been assigned a group of students who have developed a deeply entrenched failure psychology and a habit of externalizing their responsibility, you have a project on your hands. But if you have a group of students who are experienced at being self-directed and eager to take on responsibility, you will be able to shape them into a 1-Style community in a short period of time. Does one of these groups need your efforts more than the other? Does one of these groups deserve to learn in an empowering environment more than the other?

REFLECTION

15.2

Have you heard teachers tell you that getting their students to be self-responsible will not work? What are they saying about their students' future?

Characteristics of the 1-Style Classroom

While a 1-Style classroom management approach as defined in this book and a "classroom community" are similar, each has its own distinct qualities, outlined in Table 15.1. First, let's examine the qualities of the 1-Style classroom:

- *Teacher as facilitator and leader.* The teacher in the 1-Style classroom is not the boss, the police, or the attendant. He or she is a leader. The teacher's role is to create the conditions for students to achieve best. The 1-Style leader is neither permissive nor domineering. He or she is intentional in efforts to promote a shared vision among the members of the class and effectively facilitate and manage that vision (Brophy, 1999).

- *Self-responsible.* Students in the 1-Style classroom act responsibly because they recognize that it is to the benefit of the class and themselves. In contrast to a teacher-centered class, in which responsibility is defined by following directions, responsibility in the student-centered class is defined by making choices that are good for the group, demonstrating accountability to the agreed-on group goals, and contributing to higher levels of learning and function (Elias & Schwab, 2006).

TABLE 15.1. **Intersection of the Qualities of 1-Style Classrooms and Communities**

Qualities of 1-Style Classrooms	Qualities of 1-Style Classrooms and Communities	Qualities of Communities
Self-responsibility	Communal bonds	Traditions, rituals, and history
Culture of listening	Collective purpose	Shared identity
Efficiency	Group accomplishments	Shared socially constructed reality
Clear expectations	Shared values	
Success psychology	Caring leadership	
Self-directed	Sense of belonging	
Teacher as facilitator		
Social contract		

- *Clear implicit expectations.* In the 1-Style classroom, expectations are shared and understood on a deep level. Knowing the expectations is not simply remembering them; it is about understanding why they are valuable and why when everyone buys into them, things are better.

- *Learner-centered instruction.* Curriculum and instruction that engage and empower learners will help promote the goals of the 1-Style classroom more readily than more teacher-centered methods. Giving students ownership of their learning and ownership for management of their class produces the most transformative results (Watson & Battistich, 2006).

- *Self-directed.* The goal of the 1-Style classroom is for students to learn to self-govern and demonstrate self-discipline. Students learn that the only true discipline is self-discipline (Elias & Schwab, 2006).

- *Intrinsic forms of motivation.* The 1-Style class is structured to promote intrinsic versus extrinsic forms of motivation. Bribes and gimmicks are not useful in this environment. Just as students experience the needs-satisfying effect of doing meaningful work, they recognize that being responsible, thinking about the needs of others, and being given power over the decisions that affect them is needs satisfying as well (Ryan & Deci, 2006).

- *Group functions collectively.* As opposed to students responding to the will of the teacher, the group considers the good of the collective when making choices. The 1-Style class works like a team, with all members recognizing that they can achieve their potential only by working cooperatively with the other members (Kohn, 1992).

- *Intentional promotion of success psychology.* In the 1-Style classroom, the teacher maintains an awareness of how his or her actions are contributing to the success psychology of the students. The three subfactors of internal locus of control, acceptance and belonging, and a growth-oriented orientation provide a lens to guide decision making and assess the class's progress toward greater collective health (Dweck, 2000; Shindler, 2003).

- *Social contract.* The foundation of the governance of the 1-Style classroom is a well-established system of social bonds, expectations, and rules (Curwin & Mendler, 1986).

Characteristics of a Classroom Community

A classroom community has many of the qualities of the 1-Style classroom, plus the following distinct features:

- *Membership and shared identity.* Community members share a unique identity that creates a sense of belonging and membership. Each community has distinctive qualities that members adopt as their own (Watson & Battistich, 2006).

- *Common purpose and goals.* On some level, a community is working to accomplish something collectively. It has a purpose and a reason to be that works to the benefit of its members (McMillan & Chavis, 1986).

- *Communal bonds in addition to social bonds.* Communities, like any other functioning body, require social bonds (Chapter Eight). What makes them a community, however, are their communal bonds. Whereas social bonds address such questions as, "What is my responsibility to the group?" and "What can I expect from others?" communal bonds answer such questions as, "What can I do to make the community better?" and "When I have needs, whom can I count on?" Social bonds deal with issues of rights and responsibilities. Communal bonds deal with issues of relationship, obligation, and the greater good (Osterman, 2000).

- *Traditions, rituals, and history.* Over time, a community develops a history and a shared story. To mark this history, the community observes traditions and collectively remembers their past. Rituals and customs act to bond a community by creating a shared set of values and way of life (McMillan & Chavis, 1986).

Classrooms with Both Characteristics

As you can see, the 1-Style classroom and the classroom community have their own unique characteristics (see Table 15.1). Communities do not always possess efficiency and facilitative leadership, and one can create a 1-Style classroom without traditions, rituals, and a strong collective identity. However, these two types of entities share much in common. For teachers who desire either one or the other, it makes sense to create both simultaneously as they operate synergistically. For that reason, this chapter examines how to accomplish a classroom that includes the qualities of both.

REFLECTION

15.3

Which of the qualities listed in Table 15.1 do you find the most compelling? What are your essential goals for your students?

HOW TO CREATE A 1-STYLE CLASSROOM COMMUNITY

These are the basic requirements for creating a 1-Style classroom:

- *Intention.* To successfully lead a 1-Style classroom community, you must have a vision of what the collective wants to accomplish. The intention of promoting self-responsible students needs to be ever present in your mind and guide your actions. The 1-Style teacher is required to be purposeful in what he or she says and does far more than the other three management styles.

- *Awareness.* You need to be ever conscious of the covert and overt factors within the classroom environment that can undermine your success. The mental games (see Appendix E), the patterns within you that cause you to get negative, and the students' tendency to revert to failure psychology thinking all have the potential to hamstring your efforts and must be given sufficient attention. Being present and aware generally will also be critical. Being in tune with the state of mind of the group is a necessity.

- *Skills.* This and previous chapters provide many strategies to contribute to success in this effort. It is necessary to become familiar with the skills that students need in the process of becoming more self-responsible. And you must refrain from certain dysfunctional practices as you incorporate more effective practices (Watson & Ecken, 2003).

- *Commitment.* The 1-Style classroom requires commitment, patience, and perseverance. Students may initially resist your efforts (they have grown accustomed being dependent and dysfunctional), and you may even experience a strong desire to adopt a 2-Style approach or give up and adopt more of a 3-Style. You may find it necessary to take moments of reflection to recall why you are making this effort. Note that these efforts can be more successful and less stressful in collaboration with others who have similar goals for their classrooms.

Connecting with Like-Minded Colleagues

One of the disappointing realizations that many idealistic and ambitious teachers experience is that their efforts are not always appreciated by their peers. In some schools, this may take the form of a subtle competitive attitude; in others, there may be open resentment toward those who are attempting to do something positive and ambitious. The reasons this occurs are complicated, but it is more common than most of us expect. Attempting to create a 1-Style classroom may engender resentment from some of your colleagues. Consider connecting with colleagues who are supportive of your efforts and in whom you can confide. Most teachers who head down the road of the 1-Style classroom need some emotional and technical support.

Any group of students can become a functioning 1-Style classroom, though some groups require more time and effort than others. For some, a 1-Style of management will feel familiar to other contexts in their life (home, previous classes, after-school groups, and so forth). For these students, there will be little remediation required. You will not be working against a failure psychology or a hard, mistrusting emotional shell. You simply need to develop the skills at each stage of the process.

For other groups, a 1-Style approach will seem as unfamiliar as if you were speaking a foreign language (Baker, Terry, Bridges, & Winsor, 1997; Wolk, 2002). I have taught both kinds of groups. When faced with the more challenging task, even the most ambitious teachers are tempted to give in and revert to a style of teaching to which the students are accustomed (for example, to use 4-Style with a group of students who are used to being treated that way).

Nevertheless, there are many reasons to maintain your intention to create a 1-Style approach. First, it is possible. There may not be many who try it, but I have seen many 1-Style classrooms in schools where 95 percent of other teachers assumed that the only classroom management approach that would work was a 2- or 4-Style. It may take relatively longer to accomplish, and you may succeed only at creating a foundation. But if you do, you have had a transformative effect far beyond anything that you observe immediately. You may see only the tip of the iceberg of the changes that you have made. Second, creating a 1-Style classroom community has been shown to promote higher achievement, motivation, and commitment to school (Watson & Battistich, 2006). Third, the bonding and social skills development has been shown to decrease problem behavior in the classroom and beyond (Blum, McNeely, & Rinehart, 2002). Fourth, students are worth this effort. You have the opportunity to reproduce the normal dysfunction condition or to transform it. Do you want to be one more link in the chain of failure—or a catalyst for change?

CREATING THE 1-STYLE CLASSROOM COMMUNITY: A DEVELOPMENTAL SEQUENCE

Creating a 1-Style classroom community can be accomplished only in a developmental sequence. You will lead your students through three stages of development: formation, transition, and encouragement. Each stage requires the preceding stages to function successfully. You need to develop a foundation of trust and clarity before you can successfully promote self-directed behavior, and your students need to feel a sense of belonging and identity before the class can begin to look anything like a community. In the remainder of this chapter, we will examine development of a 1-Style classroom community in relation to the three developmental stages.

Stage One: Formation

The management goals of stage 1 are clarity and intention.

The foundation of the 1-Style classroom is built on clarity of expectations. A well-established cause-and-effect relationship needs to be promoted in the minds of each student: when we do A, B will follow. As facilitator of the process, be intentional about taking action and raising awareness that promotes clarity of expectations. High expectations are nice, but students cannot rise to a level of behavior that they do not grasp on a real and material level. Having high expectations is just a start, however. You must teach in accord with your expectations and include the skills required to function self-responsibly. You therefore need to be deliberate about creating the following features within the class:

- *Social contract and social bonds.* The social contract provides an opportunity for students to be responsible to the group; their collective contributions engender a sense of security. As each member supports the collective, everyone senses security for all. That security includes material and emotional safety. In Chapters Eight through Ten, I outlined the process of creating a social contract defined by well-established social bonds. A social contract exists to the degree that it is understood and shared. You know that it is working when you see students take ownership of the agreed-on principles of the contract. The communal sense of safety and faith in the contract will develop as you consistently take relevant action and implement consequences, both positive and negative.

- *Culture of listening and respect.* To function effectively, students should expect to be attentive and can expect that others will be attentive to them—in other words, they will participate in a culture of listening, which is a prerequisite for many of the more advanced stages in the development of the 1-Style classroom. (Chapter Five outlines a detailed process for creating this environment.)

- *Social frames.* From the first day of class, students should recognize deliberate and conspicuous social frames are operating in the 1-Style class. They should become increasingly conscious of the relationships between freedom and responsibility, success and recognition, and warmth and respect (see Chapter Three).

- *Operationalize conceptual expectations.* Concepts like responsibility, respect, cooperation, positive attitude, a full effort, risk taking, and creativity are abstractions that will remain so until they are operationalized and reified in students' experience (Hickey & Schafer, 2006). It is our obligation to make these ideas concrete and personally meaningful. Teachers typically assume that students already know what it means to exhibit these behaviors or that they will grasp these concepts as a result of a handful of verbal comments. However, they overestimate the degree to which their students have an operational working knowledge of the concepts used to describe good behavior. There are many strategies for making conceptual expectations concrete. First, you can use positive recognitions of behavior. When you see behavior that defines high-quality effort, for example, you can publicly recognize the practical action that you observed that characterized the term. Second, as discussed in Chapter Twelve, you can ask students to publicly recognize one another's positive behavior. Third, you can use a formal or informal assessment system. If you have a class that seems to lack both a conceptual and a behavioral knowledge of how to act in a responsible and functional manner, systems such as the one described in the online resource article, "Developing and Implementing an Effective System for Assessing the Quality of Student Process, Participation and Behavior," at transformativeclassroom.com, can be effective for promoting understanding and changing behavior. The community development section that follows will offer additional ideas in this area.

- *Put in place mechanisms for effectively facilitating cooperative learning, conflict resolution, and class meetings.* As early as possible in the school year, students should begin to practice cooperative learning and conflict resolution. (Strategies for doing so are outlined in detail in

Chapters Twelve and Thirteen.) In the first stage, the primary focus is on teaching these skills rather than being too concerned with how effective each appears (Johnson & Johnson, 1999). Avoid shortcuts. For example, maintain your expectation that cooperative groups follow the protocols that are set out even if students insist that they do not want or need them. When things devolve, it is difficult to reestablish original expectations.

- *Class meetings should be introduced when the group is ready for them* (Rogers & Freiberg, 1994). Use your own insightful judgment. A sound freedom-respect frame and a culture of listening and respect must be in place before attempting a class meeting of any substance. If the idea of a class meeting is new to your students, you might initiate the idea of democratic participation by holding votes on various classroom matters. You might start with shorter, less consequential topics for class meetings, such as whether to have the shades open or closed. In addition, the social contract development and evolution process can act to introduce class meeting protocol. In these early stages, keep class meetings short and efficient. Students will recognize they have an opportunity to be heard, but excessive complaining, spurious comments, or personal attacks are inappropriate. A process for facilitating class meetings is explained later in this chapter.

- *Establish your role and vision.* Unless students have come from a class in which a 1-Style of management was used, they will assign you a role similar to those adopted by their previous teachers. It may be useful to tell them, "In this class, I am not going to get mad at you, lecture you, shame you, wish you were different, or compare you to other students; nor will I accept excuses, poor efforts, disrespect of others, or selfishness. And soon you will not accept those things from yourselves or others in the class."

Expect students to question your resolve early in the year. They will ask you (and test you), "Do you really mean what you say?" "A few put-downs are okay, right?" "Making a mediocre effort is okay once in a while, right?" At some point they will learn from your actions that you are absolute about some things. Next, it will be useful to give them a sense of your vision: Where is this going? No matter the current state of affairs or the self-image with which students enter the class, they need to be sold on the idea that soon they will be respectful, responsible, self-directed learners and that you have no doubt that they are capable of and will ultimately accomplish that goal. The vision will eventually emerge from the collective, but at this stage, it needs to come from you so that you set out in the right direction.

15.4 REFLECTION

It is tempting to resent your students early in the year for trying to test you. But you need to give them a break and realize that they are responding the way they are used to. As things get better, they will forget these former ways. When that day comes, are you still going to hold it against them?

- *Development of clear expectations.* The 1-Style classroom is dependent on clearly established expectations. Expectations are rooted in the law of cause and effect. Students understand the concept of if-then—for example, if they listen with attention, then they will know what is going on and things will happen smoothly; if they do not, they will not know. In addition, there may be other consequences that you implement. However, if you explain things repeatedly, complain that there is too much talking, and are inconsistent with your consequences or use illogical punishments, no cause-and-effect relationship will develop in the minds of the students except, "When the teacher gets mad, she complains, but does nothing of consequence."

If you model and expect a certain type of behavior, for example, respectful interactions, the students will soon see that there is an expectation for such behavior. You show the value to using the behavior and a consequence when it does not happen. Lectures, guilt, preaching, and chronicling failure seem like action, but they are operationally useless. You must take real action. Model the behavior deliberately. Help the students recognize the value that behavior has to them individually and the class. No matter how repetitive it may feel, it is useful to promote mantra-type language—for example, "In this class we all try our best," "This class has only responsible learners," or, "The great thing about this class is that we always listen to one other and expect to be listened to."

The difference between expectations in the 2-Style and 1-Style approaches relates to what the students are responding to. In the 2-Style classroom, students are responding to clear and consistent consequences and modeling. They know what is going to happen, and the teacher follows through. The cause and effect is created in a systematic manner and reinforced each day. In the 1-Style classroom, the clarity is just as evident, but the cause and effect is located psychologically in the students' awareness of the purpose of the behavior. For example, if we all listen to each other, we develop respect and we learn more. It feels right on an intrinsic level.

In most cases, both the 1- and 2-Style approaches begin with much the same set of strategies. Eventually the teacher working toward a 1-Style approach will encourage a shift in students' thinking from the extrinsic consequences of an action to the intrinsic value of an action.

Community Development Goals: Safety and Belonging. When you look out at your class on the first day of school, the pervasive emotion in the room will likely be one of insecurity. On some level, most students feel apprehension and alienation from the other members of the class (Watson & Battistich, 2006). Simply put, the other members are still very much "other." This insecurity will work against the development of community within the group. First and foremost, community must be built within an emotional climate of safety and belonging.

You are the only one in the equation who can help the students past their insecurity and on the road to feeling bonded as a group. It will be useful to keep in mind that every member of the class wants the same thing deep down—the natural condition. In our core, we all want to feel safe, loved, valued, and connected (Glasser, 1990). When we do not get these basic needs met, we compensate. Each student's default compensation strategies will look a bit different (for example, acting cool or as a know-it-all, showing apathy, being overly accommodating, clowning). Maintain your awareness of the fact that your students' selves are not their compensation strategies. Moreover, avoid the trap of assuming that the existing dysfunctional group dynamics (social Darwinism, casual abuse, drama, obsession with "their thing," and so on) are natural. They may be normal, but they are not natural.

Natural is what is possible and feels the truest to our nature. *Normal* is what happens by accidental conditioning. If we do nothing toward achieving the natural, we get normal. Normal is characterized to a great extent by dysfunction.

Natural is what we fundamentally need. You can test this assumption when you have helped the group develop into a community. After you have helped students move from normal to natural, you can ask them if they would rather go back to the way that they were, or ask them if they prefer the climate in your class versus ones in which they needed to raise their defenses to survive the threatening and chaotic environment.

In stage 1 in the process of community development, there must be an intentional effort to create emotional safety, promote the individual membership and identity of each student, cultivate social bonds and a sense of fairness, and make a connection with each student.

Create Emotional Safety. Research has shown that verbal abuse and bullying have increased (DeVoe et al., 2004). In nearly every school, including those considered the safest and most affluent, students accept verbal abuse as a normal part of their experience during the school day (Shindler, Taylor, Jones, & Cadenas, 2003). While it may be common, it is extremely harmful. We have all experienced the deadening effect it has to the quality of life in a school.

This is an area where students need teachers and staff to be absolute. In your role of class-room leader, be absolutely intolerant of put-downs, verbal abuse, name-calling, and bullying. If you do not, students will not feel safe. They need to see enthusiasm for those things that you regard as unconditional. If there are acts of abusive speech or action, give consequences that send the message that there will never be a time when put-downs are okay.

It may be helpful to create an expectation in the class that "we say only things that make us better." You can call this anything that you like (*life-giving language, positive language, constructive language, affirming language,* or something else). It will be a good place to use a mantra such as, "In this class, we use only affirming language." Students will come to know that no matter what they hear when they are outside the walls of the classroom, they are safe from abuse within them.

15.5 REFLECTION

Reflect on the not unusual experience of a new teacher who is teaching high school English. Her goal is to create a student-centered class. As part of this, she asked her students to share their writing with one another to foster a community of authors. After two months, she was disappointed. Although her students were sharing with her and accessing their inner creativity, they did not feel comfortable sharing their work with one another. What would you say to this teacher? At what stage of the community development process would you put this class?

Promote the Individual Membership and Identity of Each Student. Many students spend their time in school feeling misunderstood, alienated, and as though they have no value (Rogers & Freiberg, 1994; Wolk, 2002). They look to friends, sports, clubs, and even gangs to fill the void that results from unmet needs. Before students can be expected to come out of their self-protective shell and consider the needs of others, they need to feel valued.

In this early developmental period in class life, send the message that every student is important and valued. Every student needs to feel that he or she has a meaningful contribution to make. Some of the strategies that support this goal are giving students roles and responsibilities, finding out who the students are, and beginning cooperative and collaborative activities as soon as possible in the school year.

Giving Students Roles and Responsibility As soon as possible, incorporate students into leadership roles. If an activity can be managed by students, take yourself out of the role of leader, and hand it over to them as soon as they show that they are capable. But recall the freedom-responsibility frame when doing so. Leadership roles are for those who have demonstrated the maturity and commitment required. Developing the expectations for being a leader requires the same process as those for other expectations. The following pedagogical sequence may be helpful: teach; recognize positive examples; practice in a low-threat situation; practice in a more intense situation; and recognize the value of demonstrating a high quality of the expectation (in this case, the skill of being a good leader). Some teachers assign roles to all students, but this can eliminate the sense that roles are for favorites. If you cannot find roles for all students, make sure that they know that all students will be rotated into a role eventually.

If you are having difficulty coming up with roles that students can take within your class, it may be useful to ask yourself whether a student would be capable of leading or managing a particular activity. Good examples of situations that students are fully capable of leading are classroom routines, calendar activities, dismissals, and recording simple data (milk counts or who has completed an activity, for example). We typically underestimate the contribution students can make in helping the classroom run well. Freiberg (1999) has identified more than forty developmentally appropriate jobs for students in the classroom. However, do not put students in situations that require them to make interpretations of value that affect other students' grades, social standing, or dignity.

Finding Out Who the Students Are   Each of us has a unique story. No matter how reticent we are, we long for others to know us. We want to be more than just a name and a physical appearance. We each have interests and experiences and dreams.

There are many effective strategies for helping students share more of who they are with other members of the class. In primary grades, a powerful experience is for students to write an auto-bio poem about themselves (see the box) or create a self-portrait (Alexander, Springer, & Persiani-Becker, 2006). Older students can put their mark on the room in a number of ways. For example, you can have them create a personal collage or write a paragraph about themselves as a caption to a drawing or photo of themselves.

Auto-Bio Poem Activity

One way to help students express who they are and allow others to get to know them is through the use of an auto-bio poem activity (Alexander, Springer, & Persiani-Becker, 2006). In this exercise students write an eleven-line poem about themselves. The teacher should begin by setting the context and modeling his or her own auto-bio poem. Here is one student's poem:

Line 1:	Your first name	Sandra
Line 2:	Four descriptive traits	Honest, caring, curious, energetic
Line 3:	Sibling of . . .	Sister of Graciela
Line 4:	Lover of (people, ideas)	Laughter, learning, challenge
Line 5:	Who feels . . .	Joy when playing with my friends
Line 6:	Who needs . . .	To laugh and sing
Line 7:	Who gives . . .	Friendship, encouragement, and smiles
Line 8:	Who fears . . .	Teenagers, getting in trouble, mean dogs
Line 9:	Who would like to see . . .	Peace on Earth
Line 10:	Resident of (your city)	Los Angeles
Line 11:	Your last name	Sanchez

It is also effective to find ways that students can self-express. Displaying and publishing their work sends the message that you care, they matter, and the purpose of the class is not simply to fulfill state standards but to grow as a community of learners.

Begin Cooperative and Collaborative Activities as Soon as Possible   In the first day or two of the new school year, have the students work in groups or teams. These kinds of activities set the tone of the class and make the statement that "we are going to work together; let's get used to it" (Johnson & Johnson, 1999). The Internet is filled with cooperative games and activities. Most are excellent, but be selective. Make sure that the activities you choose have no winner, are low threat, and can be performed by students of any ability level. Examples of first-week cooperative activities that have been effective are scavenger hunts, group foil sculptures, cooperative relays, creating a class logo in groups, and team-building activities. For younger students, activities with a large physical education parachute can provide opportunities that require cooperation and awareness of others. Recall the discussion of cooperative learning. It will work best not to expect students to perform a new skill (such as how to work in a team) and be responsible for processing new content at the same time. Also, recall that the social contract development process (described in Chapter Eight) can contribute to the goal of promoting group cohesion as well if it is done cooperatively.

15.6   REFLECTION

Reflect on situations in which you were part of a group whose members were unfamiliar to one another and in which there was no change over time; the members of the group remained anonymous to one another. How much connection did you feel? How much incentive did you feel to express yourself? Now compare that to groups where you were asked to contribute or share personal information. Did you feel more connected to the members of those groups after learning more about who they were?

Cultivate Social Bonds and a Sense of Fairness. Before students buy into the idea of the collective, they need to feel that the collective is safe. The class must be a predictable and fair place. Students need to feel that you are consistent and honest in implementing the social contract before they will be willing to work for the common good. If students perceive that you have favorites or see some students as "lost causes," they will not trust you as a leader. Moreover, if students feel that you are not interested in or competent enough to manage the social contract, they will lose respect for you and your vision. When the students can say to themselves, "This teacher has it together, he is fair and consistent, and he gets results," they will be ready to buy into the potential of the collective. If they do not, you will never get off the ground floor in your efforts toward community.

Make a Connection with the Students. A community requires caring leadership. To be an effective leader, you do not need to be charismatic or dynamic; you simply need to be clearly interested in your students' welfare. This is especially important for younger students. Some of the ways that you can show care include:

- Learning and using your students' names
- Asking students about their outside school interests and activities
- Keeping an open door for students who want to talk
- Being present and attentive when you have conversations with students
- Keeping positive recognitions public and negative recognitions private
- Eliminating all sarcasm, shaming, teasing, or embarrassment

Students need to know that you are on their side. Weeks of relationship building can be destroyed by a single act of perceived cruelty. For example, making fun of one student to other students can have the effect of making you an unsafe person to that student. Even if you think he or she should be "able to take it," any humor that causes pain is not safe or justifiable. Avoid victimizing humor, such as sarcasm, teasing, making fun of others, and comical put-downs. Instead, use humor that is safe. Being silly or self-deprecating, looking for irony, and making puns and victimless practical jokes are typical forms of humor that do not leave scars.

It will be useful to model self-disclosure and self-expression, but do this with care. You might start with safe sharing, for example, talking about families, pets, or hobbies. Then increasingly take opportunities to share your appreciation for the level of effort students are showing in their work or how much progress they are making toward being self-responsible. Finding opportunities to compliment students is powerful positive recognition and adds to the emotional bank account.

Concretizing the Concept of Community. Make the concepts that define your behavioral goals as concrete and practical as possible. The same thing should occur when it comes to the definition of community. The members of the community need to be explicitly aware that becoming a community is an active goal. Few students will be able to define community on the first day of school. You will need to undertake some form of intentional process for defining it. Initially create formal terms and language that define your concept of community. Nevertheless, no matter how elegant your definition is, it is still abstract language and will remain so until you make it meaningful. You can do this through:

- Teacher-student public recognitions (Chapter Four)
- Self-assessment of process and participation
- Student-student positive recognitions (debriefing; see Chapters Four and Twelve)
- A concept attainment exercise on terms that conceptually define community

Another method for making community themes more concrete is to focus on them in depth one at a time. This idea is explained in detail in the book *Tribes: A New Way of Learning and Being Together* by Jennie Gibbs (1995). In this system, the teacher or school as a whole selects one of the defining characteristics of community that has been decided on. For example, if you determined that community is made up of respect, responsibility, listening, cooperation, service, and effort, you would select one of these terms to use as a theme for the month. The term is integrated into the curriculum or serves as the focus of your recognition of positive behavior, class discussions, and student-student public recognitions. Each month (or week, if your group is fast to pick up the idea) you could introduce another term. Here are some examples of how themes could be displayed in chart form:

Concept: Listening

Looks Like	Sounds Like	Feels Like
Eyes on speaker Following directions	One at a time Encouragement	A culture of listening We care We want to learn

Concept: Cooperation

Looks Like	Sounds Like	Feels Like
Taking turns Sharing	Conflict being resolved Students on task Creativity at work	We are part of a team Everyone is necessary We've got "flow"

Concept: Responsibility

Looks Like	Sounds Like	Feels Like
Doing our job	Asking when we don't understand	We are mature
Being effective in my group role	No excuses, no whining	We can do it ourselves
Being accountable to the social contract		We trust each other

15.7

REFLECTION

When your own teachers used terms such as *responsible, effort,* and *respectful,* did you always know what they meant? Did all your classmates share the teacher's definition? Would it have helped if the class had a common working knowledge of the meaning of these conceptual terms?

Great Community Member Awards. Giving students awards can have a powerful effect. My recommendation is not to use awards or rewards in the 1-Style classroom. But if you are tempted to do it, do so thoughtfully. For instance, if you gave a regular "Student of the Week" award, it will typically have the effect of making the winner feel good and encouraging the other students to pay more attention to whatever it is that was being awarded. But if the award is for the student who gets the best grades, has the best science project, or is considered by the teacher to be the nicest, it will not help develop a community (Reeve, 2006). In fact, it will have the opposite effect. Most students view these sorts of awards as favoritism or rewarding the haves (and shaming the have-nots).

If you feel compelled to give an award, consider rewarding quality progress or improvement toward being a great community member. In this context, all students could potentially win. If students feel that they have a legitimate chance (internal locus of control) and are being rewarded for selfless contribution (promoting acceptance and belonging), the motivation level to earn the award will remain high over time. Reflect on the difference in the mind-set of students competing to be considered the most selfless contributor rather than the best student, for example. To deemphasize the competitive element, it will be more effective if the name of the winner is posted in an inconspicuous place rather than on a poster at the front of the room. It is also useful to include the names of some of the other students who had selfless weeks and list them as being awarded honorable mention. If you want to have fun with it, give similar awards to members of the school staff, community members, and public figures who exemplify what it means to be a selfless contributor.

Teaching Choices That Work Against Your Ability to Progress to the Next Stage. Before we explore what it will take to move your classes to the next level of 1-Style classroom community, consider those things that will work against your ability to get there. As we have discussed throughout the book, ineffective and destructive practices will do more harm than the effective practices will do good. Incorporating any of the following practices will undermine your ability to achieve a self-responsible classroom or the qualities of community:

- Randomness, inconsistency, and subjectivity
- Anger, punishments, or shaming

- Short-term fixes (being reactive rather than thinking about how to make tomorrow better as a result of today)
- Praise and rewards
- Shame-based behavioral systems (such as colored cards and names on the board; see the online articles "Why to Stop Using Colored Cards and Names on the Board Systems" and "What to Do Instead" at www.transformativeclassroom.com)
- Destructive criticism or fear of failure
- Creating a failure psychology (see Chapter Seven)
- A dysfunctional mind-set (see "How to Have a Generally Unsatisfying (Thinking) Day" in the next chapter)

REFLECTION

15.8

The most difficult thing to do as a teacher is to admit that something you do is working against your success. As you reflect on the list of practices above that will undermine success, do you find any that you want to continue despite your commitment to a 1-Style classroom? Your inner dialogue is probably protesting, "It works for me." This may be true, but refer to the examination of the phrase "it works" in Appendix C. Why do you feel compelled to hold on to the practice? Do you really need it? Will you really miss it? Is it really helping you reach your goals?

Stage Two: Transition Toward Self-Direction and Full Community

The management goal of stage 2 is to shift the locus of ownership and cultivate intrinsic motivation.

Once a foundation of clear expectations and social bonds has been established, increase your effort to shift the locus of decision making to your students. Encourage the class to increasingly take on forms of self-responsibility. The students should feel that they have their hands on the steering wheel. At the same time, they should increasingly recognize more internal sources of motivation and satisfaction in their learning. The contrast between the 2-Style teacher-centered class, in which students are encouraged to follow directions and become accustomed to extrinsic sources of motivation, and the 1-Style classroom should become evident at this stage. In the minds of students, choices will be less driven by the question, "What does the teacher want me to do?" and more driven by, "What can I do to learn more and help the class and myself get better?"

Empower the Students. It is true that you will never be in a position to abdicate the role of leader or facilitator of the social contract, nor will you ever want to put individual students in a position where they need to make personal decisions about other students. But at this stage in the process, there should be a distinct effort to transfer the steering to students to the degree that they are ready. As students come to recognize functionality and emotional safety in the class and gain trust in your leadership, you will be in position to progressively hand over decision-making power. You never want to put a student in a position to grade another student's performance, but you can empower the class as a whole to decide on a consequence for a particular contract violation or a format for presenting their projects.

Clearly, handing over the steering wheel to the students when they do not know how to drive is more foolish than courageous. In the absence of structure and clarity, expecting students to show self-regulated behavior is the definition of the ineffective 3-Style teacher.

Empowering students must be done with explicit recognition that they have shown the requisite evidence of responsibility. It will be useful to maintain a clear and deliberate awareness within the class that the responsibility-freedom social frame is operating: "When you are able to show me X, I will let you decide Y," or "Since you were able to do X, I think you are ready for Y." Should students fail to show the necessary level of responsibility, resist the temptation to show disappointment, shame them, or dwell on failure. Simply reduce the amount of freedom and responsibility you give them and explain they will have future opportunities to elevate their skills. Being explicit in your treatment of this relationship will help underscore the point that the empowerment process takes as long as it takes. It may happen quickly or take all year. It is up to the students.

As students show their capability, shift from doing all of the thinking to letting them do the thinking. The result will be that they will grow in the trust of their own ability to solve problems and take greater ownership over executing the solutions that are developed. The sequence of the transition should take the following form:

1. Teacher explanations
2. Teacher-led discussions
3. Student-led discussions when students have developed the skills
4. Student-initiated problem solving

Empowering students with decision-making authority will promote genuine self-direction as they take ownership of their classroom community.

15.9 REFLECTION

The more we give power away, the more power that we have. (Fitzclarence and Giroux, 1984, call this the "paradox of power.") On first examination, this idea may seem flawed or even absurd, but reflect on it. What is your reaction to those who try to control you? When they ask you to do something, what is your instinct? Conversely, when someone allows you to make up your own mind and respects your decisions, do you find yourself wanting to earn his or her respect? The idea of control is certainly complex and dependent on a number of factors, so challenge yourself to look past a superficial notion of power as you build your classroom vision.

Technical Management: Shifting from Extrinsic Recognition to an Intrinsic Awareness of Value. The intention and execution of your efforts in the area of technical management will have a profound impact on your ability to make a successful transition from stage 1 to stage 2 in the development of a 1-Style classroom. The goals of good technical management are smoothness, efficiency, safety (emotional and physical), and clear communication within a culture of listening (see Chapter Five). Although the level of efficiency within a 1-Style student-directed classroom will not likely be any greater than that within a more teacher-directed 2-Style class in the area of technical management, the 1-Style approach has two other important benefits: it can achieve a self-regulated class and require very little direction or energy from the teacher, and it will function to promote the other goals of a 1-Style classroom community, whereas using a more teacher-centered form of technical management will limit your potential to achieve these goals.

The key to moving from a more teacher-centered form of technical management to one that is more student centered is shifting the attention of the students from a possible consequence from an external agent if they do not act responsibly to having them consider the intrinsic value and benefits of being part of a respectful, safe, and efficient class. This shift is encouraged when students begin to recognize the value of being part of a system free of aggravation. This will happen quickly if you help students recognize this value. For example, as the students are listening to one of their classmates, you might briefly note how nice it is that people in the class listen to one another and expect to be listened to. And when they begin to naturally move with a purpose that reflects intentional consideration for others, point it out and encourage them to reflect on the value of their actions.

These recognitions can take any form that you feel is most effective given the needs of the students. One method is the use of simple reflective questions that are essentially rhetorical and therefore do not really need to be answered—for example, "How long did it take us to shift from the lab to our seats? I counted about forty seconds. At the beginning of the year, it took a lot longer. How does it feel to be able to trust that others will be ready when you get back to your seat?" Or "How does it feel to be in a class where you are listened to when you are speaking?" These questions shift the locus of control from the teacher to the students and create an awareness of the intrinsic value of the behavior. As the behavior takes on its own value and is associated with personal and collective satisfaction, the need for the teacher to maintain an extrinsic recognition or consequence structure becomes increasingly less necessary. Eventually the students should feel that they expect to have their hands on the wheel and may even feel a bit insulted that the teacher would need to take control with extrinsic interventions. However, during this transition to full student self-direction, it will still be necessary to implement consequences when students fail to meet expectations such as 100 percent attention.

At this stage, allow students to decide how best to execute routines, chores, and procedures (Freiberg, 1999). Allowing students to come up with plans builds understanding and ownership (Watson & Battistich, 2006). You simply need to help them set the standard for what qualifies as acceptable and fulfill your role as the one who ultimately makes the call when it must be made, as when delivering consequences, providing a global perspective, or recognizing the need for a change.

Cultivating Intrinsic Motivation. In the process of developing a 1-Style classroom, be very intentional about the type of motivation that you use for students. If you deliberately or unconsciously include many extrinsic motivators, you undermine the ability to create a self-responsible community (Ryan & Deci, 2000). Instead, find ways to promote more intrinsic sources of motivation within students. If the notion of intrinsic motivation is new, at least be aware of any tendency to revert to such strategies as prizes, praise, comparisons, emphasizing grades, awards, and challenging the students to impress you. This tendency is understandable, as most of the motivational strategies that were used with us as students were extrinsic in nature. But after building a foundation of trust and responsibility, you are in a position to open the floodgates of student potential. If you have done the groundwork in stage 1, you can now effectively help students tap into their inner sources of satisfaction, motivation, and love of learning (Ryan & Deci, 2006). It will be useful to strive to create the following conditions.

First, develop a pedagogy that encourages engagement, collaboration, inquiry, and flow. The most effective way to promote engagement and love of learning and tap into more internal sources of motivation is to structure the curriculum in a manner that encourages active learning (Devries & Zan, 1994). Learning is intrinsically motivating. Our natural state is to be continuously learning. We do not need to add anything such as prizes or threats of a bad grade. These work against the cultivation of intrinsic motivation and 1-Style classroom goals (Ryan & Deci, 2000). Allow students to solve problems, take part in inquiry-based activities, learn cooperatively, create projects and put it all together, publish and present their work, find out where their love and gifts lie, and take ownership of their own assessment and personal goal setting.

Our role in the process of empowering students is more cheerleader than dispenser of knowledge. We need to help students of all ability levels worry less about grades and more about learning. To do this, we need to make sure that grades do not penalize students for taking chances or being creative. One way is to try to encourage attention to the process as much as possible and the product as little as possible. Assessing process breeds internal locus of control as well as mastery orientation, and therefore more intrinsic motivation. Assessing product breeds fear of failure and a tendency to externalize the explanation for an outcome. Moreover, what we show caring about and what we model will have a profound effect on how students view their work. If we want externally motivated, helpless-orientation students, we should keep them concerned about making mistakes, make a big deal about who is doing better, get excited about displays of innate talent or cultural capital, and maintain an expectation that only a few students will do a good job. In contrast, if we want internally motivated, growth-oriented students, we want to show enthusiasm about progress and effort, project an expectation that all students can meet the targets (because they are clear and standing still), and encourage students to take risks, be creative, and make mistakes.

Second, develop structural conditions that promote intrinsic rather than extrinsic motivation. Sometimes it is not so much what we say but what the context promotes that determines how students think and act. For example, if we have created an inherently competitive context, no matter how much we encourage cooperation, taking chances, and being satisfied with doing one's best, students will be mistrustful, anxious, and attached to outcomes (Kohn, 1986; Watson & Battistich, 2006). If we instead create an environment free of student-to-student comparison, taking chances is encouraged, and knowledge is defined not by right or wrong answers but as a by-product of the process of discovery and research. The context itself sends the message that there is nothing to fear and a great deal to gain. In other words, the context itself is needs satisfying. When students find that they can meet needs in a context that produces a minimum amount of fear of failure, their sources of intrinsic motivation will emerge and blossom.

Cultivating a Vision Within Your Class. In stage 1 of the process of creating a 1-Style classroom community, your expectations needed to be clear and explicit. In stage 2, they will need to be just as clear; however, now you help students begin the transition away from focusing on you (the teacher) and them (the students) toward focusing on the collective "we." To do this, you need to create a collective vision. A vision acts to guide a group of individuals toward collective function and purpose. It says what you have agreed to and what principles you use to make decisions. In essence, the vision is the collective intention.

The vision in any class is recognizable to the degree that it is coherent, and that means someone has to manage it. In the classroom, it is the teacher. Vision has two parts: listening and articulating. The teacher must form the vision through listening to and assessing the will and needs of the group and then articulating that vision back to them. If you do not listen, the vision will represent your own subjective perspective, not the collective. If you do not articulate the emerging vision, it never gets communicated to students. Let's examine each of these aspects in more detail.

Listening You are the only person capable and positioned to interpret the big picture. You must be attentive to the needs and concerns of your students. They need to trust that you are paying attention and are perceptive enough to know when there is a need for action. This means being present to the students, being attentive to their needs, and asking questions. For example, if you feel there is an issue related to group dynamics, you might take a quick poll and ask who rates the group dynamics as safe and functional and who does not. Asking questions and taking flash surveys sends a message to students that you care and that their welfare is your first priority. Knowing that you are listening will help them trust that the decisions you make are grounded in good information and intended for the common good.

Articulating Concurrent with the process of listening, you should regularly articulate the observations, assessments, and concerns that you have, along with those that you have heard, being intentional that you are sincere in your efforts to help guide and resisting the temptation to be dogmatic or uninterested. When you articulate the vision, project a confident, proactive, thoughtful message. You are progressively encouraging students to take more control of the steering wheel. The classroom vision provides a clear map for your student drivers—a map that leads to a functional and satisfying learning experience. You can help students recognize and trust that the vision is leading them to a desirable destination by drawing their awareness to the beneficial places that you have already gone. For example, you might say, "I noticed that all of the groups were immersed in the task for the whole period. What do you think was the cause, and how did it feel?" In that statement, you project that your vision involves their approach to learning, and the learning activities themselves increasingly become intrinsically motivating.

The role of the teacher includes articulating the class's growth and articulating when there is a problem. Since you have been listening and have sampled student concerns from multiple sources, you are in a unique position to make assessments. Sharing your assessments with your students can support the vision building even more. For example, you might say: "I am hearing a lot of concern that the honor system we are using for equipment is being abused. Is that an accurate assessment? [Assume an affirmative response.] Okay, that was what I was hearing. So let's take five minutes to brainstorm better policies and then vote on the one that we like best." This interaction will have the practical benefit of fixing a problem that was causing stress. It also will have an additional symbolic benefit that you are proactive in assessing the direction of the ship and an effective leader in navigating the ship to a successful course. As a result, the level of trust from the students is raised. Not only do they learn to trust you a little more, they also gain another level of trust in themselves as a collective. Repeated incidence of vision-building interactions such as these act to develop the classroom social contract and shared vision to become increasingly more concrete, meaningful, and satisfying.

REFLECTION

15.10

Recall groups and organizations that you have been part of that you would say had vision. What did the leaders in those organizations do to promote that sense of vision? What lessons can you take from this situation into your classroom?

Community Goals: Collective Identity and Accomplishment. If you were successful in stage 1 of the process, the class should feel a sense of belonging and an acceptance of who they are by the other members. If this goal is accomplished, you will notice how much easier it is to achieve 1-Style classroom management goals. The next stage in the progression toward becoming a self-responsible community will be for the group to begin to take on a collective identity. As the group becomes increasingly loyal and other centered, the communal bonds within the group will be strengthened and each student's need for belonging will be met more successfully.

Nevertheless, a few cautions are in order. First, you need to make certain that membership does not become a call to conformity (Watson & Battistich, 2006). As students experience increased pleasure from being part of a "we," your job will be to help them understand that each individual (who possesses his or her own story, differences, and membership in other collectives) is valued not in relation to the degree he or she conforms, but simply because he or she is. Be intentional also about encouraging the members of your classroom community to embrace one another's ethnic and cultural identities. Help them learn how to be a "we" without having to create a "they." Kohn (1996) identifies the tendency for some collectives to become what he calls "pseudocommunities" that operate in fear-based oppositional identity rather than a natural state of belonging. Comparisons may be inevitable, but you should encourage students to resist temptations to feel superior, engage in unhealthy competition with other classes, or look down on other groups or teachers. Support an identity that is built on a collective effort toward growth rather than feeding a collective ego.

Promoting a Healthy Group Identity. These strategies will help promote your class's group identity:

- *"In this class" mantras.* When you use a phrase such as, "In this class, we use only affirming language," you help the class define itself in a positive way. These mantras act to shape the identity of the class over time. You will know that they have been internalized into the collective identity when you hear the students use them with one another.

- *Branding: Mottos, logos, songs, and nicknames.* Some degree of brand identification can strengthen group identity. It is possible to overdo this, and it should not be undertaken in a contrived manner, but it can be a fun way to build community. Would the class benefit from a logo? What about a logo design contest? Would the class benefit from a motto or a few slogans? Again, if the students pick up the idea and run with it, it will be more meaningful to them. Any branding must be positive and needs to come from the students. Does the class have a favorite song? Can you find ways to use that song to bond the group? For example, if the group has just accomplished something meaningful, singing the class song afterward sends the message that "we have an identity and we have a song."

- *Traditions and rituals.* Promoting the development of rituals and traditions accentuates the shared quality of the group's experience. Again, these will be more powerful and more fun if the ideas for them come from students. They can take many forms and look different at different grade levels and for different subjects. In a primary class, you may have the tradition of the children saying "good morning" in unison to you, a guest, or a student calendar activity leader. In a secondary class, you may develop the ritual of giving polite applause after presentations. You may put a trivia question on the board each morning for fun. One powerful ritual (described in more detail in Chapter Twelve) is to have students give positive recognitions of other students after a cooperative learning activity. One way you will know that your traditions and rituals have taken hold is when the students feel cheated when they miss out on the opportunity to take part in them on a particular day.

Encouraging Collective Accomplishment. When students succeed collectively, their communal bonds are strengthened. Moreover, they develop a positive association with one another and with you, who helped lead them to the accomplishment. Winning breeds liking, and liking breeds more winning. If asked, "When do your students win together?" most of us would be at a loss for an answer. Upon examining how students experience collective accomplishment more closely, it is clear they can feel that they are winning together quite often. While some of the means may be manufactured, most of them are naturally occurring.

Students win together when they work together and succeed. When you make a positive articulation that they can now collectively do something that they could not before, you let them know they won. They like themselves more, they like each other more, and they like you more as a result. For example, if you tell them that they used to struggle to put all the equipment away before the bell but now do it quite efficiently, you are in essence saying that they are winning. When students cooperate to put together challenging projects or presentations and as a class you recognize how well "we" did, you acknowledge that you have won. The class attempted something that they could not have done alone, could not previously do as well, and succeeded. As the class moves more completely into stage 2 of the community development process, this feeling of winning becomes increasingly attached to doing things for the common good. The students find that when their actions are informed by how things work best for the collective, outcomes that are good for everyone follow.

Students can also win in more traditional, albeit manufactured, ways as well. They can be judged the best in a contest or in comparison to other classes in some way. They can contribute to a school victory in sports, a knowledge bowl, or a fair. You can point out that they have better behavior or test scores than other classes. But be careful not to create "theys" just to make a stronger "we." It might seem beneficial in the short term but will undermine your community in the long run. Winning has to come from a win-win mentality rather than a win-lose mentality. When you get caught up in a win-lose mentality, you introduce fear of failure, enemies, and divisions within your own community. Whenever there is a collective win within the context of a contest, keep the class focused on the process aspects of the task rather than the outcome. To emphasize this, ignore the notion of the win and get excited about the teamwork, process execution, and the level of effort.

REFLECTION
15.11

What are some of the ways you have seen teachers help students develop a collective identity? What are some ways that you have seen students win together as a collective? Were they ideas that you feel are healthy and effective? Share these ideas with your group in class as part of activity 2 at the end of the chapter.

Class Meetings and Tribal Councils. One strategy that will promote a self-directed class and the development of communal bonds is the class meeting. Useful models for class meetings are offered by Donna Styles (2001) and Jeannie Gibbs (1995). The class meeting provides a concrete opportunity for students to display their self-responsibility and communal relationship. Once students have demonstrated the ability to listen attentively and actively and to use positive language (refraining from put-downs and personal attacks and instead using I-messages), and a commitment to solving problems as a responsible collective, they are ready to run their own meetings. Styles (2001) suggests that at this point, you take the role of scribe so you are sure that the ideas are represented neutrally. She also recommends that you let the students know that you will maintain the right to veto ideas that you feel are bad for the community or simply cannot be done for one reason or another.

Establish a clear protocol for class meetings. You can do your own research to find a system that works best for you and your grade level. However, here are some common features of most class meeting protocols:

- Students make suggestions for items to be discussed at the meeting. These can be problems to be addressed or ideas for class improvement.
- Students sit in a circle or at least in a configuration in which everyone can see each other.
- Meetings have a time frame.
- Meeting records are kept.
- Once action items have been decided on, identify those responsible for carrying them out.

Meetings need rules, and rules should be sacred. The rules suggested by Gibbs in her book *Tribes* are:

1. Attentive listening
2. Appreciation and no put-downs

3. Right to pass

4. Mutual respect

The process of development as a community is empowering. You will see evidence that students are growing in their sense of self and developing a psychology of success. Being part of a community provides a powerful sense of belonging (Rogers & Freiberg, 1994). The increasing amount of responsibility acts to foster each student's internal locus of control, and the emphasis on contribution as opposed to talent promotes the students' growth-oriented orientation (Dweck, 2000).

Be aware of these things, which undermine your ability to progress to the next stage:

- Being insincere or sending the message that you do not really trust students and your acts of empowerment are simply exercises.

- Bailing students out, hovering, or taking over when they struggle.

- Neglecting your active role in the process and descending into a 3-Style approach.

- Assuming bad days mean that your goals are wrong. Use problems as a form of assessment for what needs to improve.

- Focusing too much on either the top-performing students (those who are taking the idea of community and enthusiastically running with it) or the low-performing students (those who are resistant to buying into the idea of being part of a community). If you neglect the most functional, they will revert to the mean. If you neglect the least functional, they may jump ship completely. Help each level student grow at his or her own pace.

Stage Three: Encouragement

The management goals of the final stage are facilitating vision and self-direction.

Let's envision what is taking place at this stage (which very few classes achieve). Students have internalized the value of high function. They have taken ownership of the social contract and demonstrate high levels of self-responsibility. They have learned the skills for solving their own problems and raising issues to improve the effectiveness of the social contract and class procedures. They have also made a significant shift toward thinking in terms of what is good for their growth and the welfare of the class as opposed to what you want them to do. So what is left to do? It is true that the heavy lifting is behind you, but you are just as essential to the process of the class's continued growth and development as you were before. Your role now will be less about molding and more about reflecting back to students how they are doing.

Most important, at this stage you need to be the facilitator of the class vision. No matter how functional the behavior, it is only a few bad days away from reverting to a lower form. The reason it does not is that the students recognize the value and meaning in the ways that they are growing. Jealousies, entitlements, pride, insecurities, and old habits always want to resurface. You need to help students continue to see that what they have created (the natural condition) is better than the alternative. That can be difficult because just about every other source of influence (television, friends, entertainment, and professional sports) tells them the opposite: that it is best to do as little as possible to get rich, you should think only about yourself, and it is okay to use others to get where you want to go. Nevertheless, you have powerful influences on your side. The 1-Style classroom community is more satisfying on a deeper level and is free of the stress and struggle that can be so pervasive in students' lives.

You promote this vision by articulating the essential reality in the class: "You are getting better, and it shows!" No matter how they have improved, no matter their grade level, no matter how intrinsically they feel the improvement, there will be a tendency to overlook its significance or take it for granted. We have all seen sports teams begin to take their winning ways for granted and quickly turn into losers. You need to say out loud, "Look at how far you have come, and think about how you feel now as compared to before."

It will be natural for students to periodically revert to externalizing their responsibility. It is normal. We all do it. Be gentle and intentional when this happens. You do not want to reinforce the act of externalizing (wanting you to solve their problem, telling on others, or making excuses or acting helpless, for example) by solving their problems or buying into their helplessness. Empower them with an answer such as, "I know you can do it" or "That sounds like a difficult problem. How are you going to solve it?" Of course, you do not shame students for showing a little weakness once in a while or act condescending when they do not make the progress that other students are. That would be counterproductive and likely result in a total reversion. Instead, help students recognize they have solved problems like this before (demonstrated an internal locus of control), have persisted through frustration before (demonstrated a growth-oriented orientation), and there is a process to incorporate to get to their goal. It may be your conflict resolution procedure, or the social contract, or the steps to doing the project, or any number of processes that you have put in place. It will be useful to shift the students' awareness from their negative unconscious thinking to the moment: "What is important now?" "What is the first step in the process to getting the problem solved?" Within this interaction, your goal is to be empathetic, help them raise their level of awareness, and encourage a psychology of success.

When a large portion of the class seems to be operating from a fixed ability/helpless mind-set, use the same process as when working with an individual. Your fundamental message to the group should be, "I hear you, I empathize, and I will do my part to help, but I know that you can solve this problem. So what should we do first to move toward a solution?" If the directions are not clear or students have not been taught the skills to accomplish a task, your job is to provide clarity and guide skill attainment. If students have what they need for success but still act helpless, answer their helpless questions with guiding or clarifying questions. For example, if a student says, "We're stuck. What do we do?" you might answer, "Have you read the directions carefully?" or "Have you made sure that in the second step you listed and then classified all the qualities of the object?"

In examining the preceding interaction within the social learning model, notice that sending an empowering rather than an enabling message to one student gives the other members of the class the opportunity to learn that you are not in the enabling business and a way to think about solving any problems they may have had that were similar to the question that was asked.

Another powerful act of modeling for the teacher developing a 1-Style approach is engaging in the task along with the students. This assumes students have reached a level of self-direction in which they do not need the degree of monitoring or attention that they would have previously. When you are able to work side-by-side with your students, they can see how you approach a task, solve problems, and interact with other members of the group. Your modeling as the most attentive, positive, other-centered member of the class has a powerful influence on the students. It says that when you said, "This is our class," you were sincere; you are not above the spirit of the social contract; and the class still runs smoothly if it loses a teacher and gains nothing more than another great classmate. It can be fun and instructive to put a student in the role of teacher when you take the role of student. It offers you an opportunity to model exemplary student-teacher interactions.

REFLECTION

Have you ever observed a teacher take the role of the student? What happened? Did it result in the chaos that most people would presume?

Community Goals: Encouraging a Cause Beyond Oneself and Becoming a Tribe. If you have been successful in developing a foundation of community, students will be open to thinking about their role in a different way than they traditionally might. As they grow in their realization that it feels better to think about other people rather than about their own narrow needs and wants, the idea of community becomes less of an abstraction and more of an organic reality (Kohn, 1996; Rogers & Freiberg, 1994). In stage 1 when you asked, "What can you do right now to help the class as a whole?" most students likely heard *the teacher wants us to be nice to each other.* In stage 3, they hear that question differently. They feel the communal bonds that have been cultivated telling them that other members of the class are worth serving. They hear their basic needs telling them that when they put others first, more basic needs are met and they experience a greater level of satisfaction. They feel the power of being able to contribute in their own unique way and use their special talents and gifts to make their mark.

In this stage of the process, we have to help students translate these realizations into practical action. This applied action will happen at different levels. First, students find new and more effective ways to contribute to the group as their individual personality emerges within the collective. Second, they will be ready to make a difference within the school as a whole. Third, they will begin to connect the feeling of being part of a classroom community to being part of the global community and as a result will want to find ways to make a contribution to the world in some form.

What Does the Group Need from Me? Once students have developed an intrinsic appreciation for being part of a community, you simply need to encourage their energy and ideas as they arise. Given that it is a true democratic community only if it reflects the will of the students, you will not want to put too many of your fingerprints on things at this stage. You do not want to make cookie-cutter replicas in each of your classes. As much as possible, help ensure that the process occurs organically rather than predetermining outcomes (Kohn, 1996). Moreover, make sure that the community development process is not being co-opted by a few big-personality students

When things are going well, bring that to the students' attention. For example, you might simply mention, "Over the past week, I have seen four students use conflict resolution strategies really successfully. It looks as if you don't need adults to help you solve your problems any longer. That has got to feel good." When you make these statements, students recognize that they have a good thing going and the group needs them to continue to invest, take responsibility for themselves, and look for ways to make the group better. Once the students have taken on that mind-set, you need to do very little directing.

What Does the School Need from Me? Once the students become accustomed to looking for ways to contribute to the classroom community, they will be more open to making a schoolwide contribution (Elias & Schwab, 2006). This will happen organically as students recognize that the functionality, quality of life, and communal bonds that are occurring inside the class should be shared with those outside the class, and they feel impelled to make a difference in the school. However, if the reality outside the class is dramatically different (there are mostly 4-Style classroom cultures, a high level of conflict, or a failure psychology in the school, for example), this will likely cause consternation for students. This inner conflict has been evident in schools in which a teacher has created a working community. The students feel good within the class, but do not know how to begin to spread their positive experience to others.

15.13   REFLECTION

If you find your students have developed an effective working community inside your class and you are looking for ways to have them translate that behavior outside of the class, be patient. Help the students recognize and process their challenges. It might be empowering and comforting to point them to events in the civil rights movement in the United States and elsewhere.

One of the powerful ways that students can make a contribution to their school is to take on the role of formal or informal conflict resolution leader or peer mediator (Chapter Thirteen). Many schools incorporate a team of students in this role. Student leaders and peer mediators have the capacity to be many times more effective than adults in this function. Moreover, this role gives them an opportunity to make a significant difference as they develop valuable leadership and interpersonal skills (Johnson & Johnson, 1999).

If you succeed in promoting a love of making a difference in your students, they no longer see their efforts to improve the school as chores but as opportunities to make the school better. Ideas for school improvement are best generated by the students themselves. As they increasingly recognize the value of thinking in terms of the common good and observe a growing disparity between how things are in the class and outside the class, ideas for making a difference will come naturally to them: school beautification, creating a playground, planting a garden, making inspirational posters or artwork, or raising money with a recycling drive or rummage sale, for example. Ideas can also take the form of exhibitions of the work of the classroom community. Some ideas for these might include a gallery walk for other classes, a book sale or store run by the students, a science fair, a readers' workshop exhibit, or a field day they referee and organize your students.

Students in the intermediate grades can attain a great deal of intrinsic satisfaction from peer tutoring. This requires the cooperation of another teacher, but it can be a win-win: the younger students get positive role modeling and one-on-one tutoring, and the older students get to experience learning by teaching.

What Does the World Need from Me? As students grow in their level of responsibility to others and experience the satisfaction of making a contribution, a natural next stage is to think about how they can contribute on a broader scale. When students recognize that they can make a difference, they grow in the recognition that they have gifts, talents, and skills that are of value in the world, and they will want to find opportunities to use those gifts.

As the work of Anyon (1981) and others points out, many of the problems with teacher-directed curriculum and obedience models of management are that they rob students of any sense of power or value. When obedience and conformity are held up as the highest form of behavior, students' sense of worth, power, and uniqueness die a slow death. In the 1-Style classroom community, students grow in their sense of self-worth. No matter their socioeconomic status, they learn to make a difference, and in making a difference, they realize their gifts and their power to change the world. Being part of a nurturing community has the effect of raising students' career expectations and helps them find their passion. If school has taught students only how to take orders, they will look for jobs where all they do is take orders. If school has taught students to be self-responsible change agents, they will look for careers that will allow them to use their gifts to make a difference (Elias & Schwab, 2006).

You can support your students' interest in making a difference at this stage in the process by promoting such activities as service-learning, community activism, and engaging in the social issues with concrete, relatable goals and activities. Depending on the grade level and the community environment, you might look for opportunities for your students to engage in the larger community. You might have them volunteer or integrate a service-learning project into your curriculum. You might include ways for students to make personal social commentary within your assignments. Do your students need to be exposed to aspects of society that they have not yet encountered? When students experience new places together, their bonds strengthen. When we discover together, we win together.

CONCLUSION

Is a 1-Style classroom community possible with any group of students? Yes. But it will take longer with students who have not been given a great deal of responsibility in the past. Can you use some of the ideas but not others? Yes. You can borrow one or more of the ideas presented in the chapter (for example, holding class meetings), but if you take a piecemeal approach, you may find you do not get superior results. A successful 1-Style classroom requires a systemic approach. Its components need to be integrated with one another and constructed in a developmental progression. It requires significantly more intention and thought than the other three management styles. At first glance, it may not feel familiar or normal, but the closer you examine it and the more you experience it, you discover that it is natural. It is one of the delimited pathways to help your students reach their full potential. In essence it is the transformative classroom.

In the next chapter, we examine the relationship between your thinking and your effectiveness as a classroom manager. No matter the effectiveness of the strategies, your efficacy will be limited if you have dysfunctional habits of mind. When you become more conscious, aware, and intentional, you will experience greater enjoyment and success.

Journal Reflections

1. When have you felt community? How does that experience contribute to what you want to accomplish as a teacher?
2. After exploring this chapter, reflect on what you found to be useful. Do you have any reservations about attempting a 1-Style classroom?

Activities

1. In groups, share your answers to the Auto-Bio poem in this chapter.
2. Reflect on your own classroom. Answer the following questions:

   - How will I ensure a safe emotional climate?
   - How will I help make the concept of community more concrete and operational?
   - What are some of the ways that my students can win together?

REFERENCES

Alexander, B., Springer, S., & Persiani-Becker, K. (2006). *The creative teacher*. New York: McGraw-Hill.

Anyon, J. (1981). Social class and school knowledge. *Curriculum Inquiry*, *11*(1), 3–42.

Baker, J., Terry, T., Bridges, R., & Winsor, A. (1997). Schools as caring communities. A relational approach to school reform. *School Psychology Review*, *26*(4), 586–602.

Blum, R. W., McNeely, C. A., & Rinehart, P. M. (2002). *Improving the odds: The untapped power of school to improve the health of teens*. Minneapolis: Center for Adolescent Health and Development, University of Minnesota.

Brophy, J. (1999). Perspective of classroom management: Yesterday, today and tomorrow. In H. J. Freiberg (Ed.), *Beyond behaviorism: Changing the classroom management paradigm* (pp. 43–56). Needham Heights, MA: Allyn & Bacon.

Canter, L. (1992). *Lee Canter's assertive discipline: Positive behavior management for today's classroom*. Los Angeles: Lee Canter and Associates.

Curwin, R., & Mendler, A. (1986). *Discipline with dignity*. Alexandria, VA: ASCD Press.

DeVoe, J., Peter, K., Kaufman, P., Ruddy, S., Miller, A., Planty, M., Snyder, T., et al. (2004). *Indicators of school crime and safety, topic: Elementary and secondary education*. Statistical Data Report. National Center for Educational Statistics. Rockville, MD.

Devries, R., & Zan, B. (1994). *Moral classrooms, moral children: Creating a constructivist atmosphere in early education*. New York: Teachers College Press.

Dweck, C. (2000). *Self-theories: Their role in motivation, personality and development*. Lillington, NC: Psychologists Press.

Elias, M. J., & Schwab, Y. (2006). From compliance to responsibility: Social and emotional learning and classroom management. In C. M. Evertson & C. S. Weinstein (Eds.), *Handbook of classroom management* (pp. 309–341). Mahwah, NJ: Erlbaum.

Fitzclarence, L., & Giroux, H. (1984). The paradox of power in educational theory and practice. *Language Arts*, *61*(5), 462–477.

Freiberg, H. J. (1999). Consistency management and cooperative discipline: From tourist to citizen in the classroom. In H. J. Freiberg (Ed.), *Beyond behaviorism: Changing the classroom management paradigm* (pp. 75–97). Needham Heights, MA: Allyn & Bacon.

Gibbs, J. (1995). *Tribes: A new way of learning and being together*. Windsor, CA: Center Source Publications.

Glasser, W. (1990). *The quality school: Managing students without coercion*. New York: HarperCollins.

Hickey, D. T., & Schafer, N. J. (2006). Design-based, participation-centered approaches to classroom management. In C. M. Evertson & C. S. Weinstein (Eds.), *Handbook of classroom management* (pp. 281–308). Mahwah, NJ: Erlbaum.

Kohn, A. (1992). *No contest: The case against competition*. New York. Houghton Mifflin.

Johnson, D. W., & Johnson, R. (1999). *Learning together and alone: Cooperative, competitive, and individualistic learning* (4th ed.). Needham Heights, MA: Allyn & Bacon.

Kohn, A. (1986). *No contest: The case against competition*. Boston: Houghton Mifflin

Kohn, A. (1996). *Beyond discipline: From compliance to community*. Alexandria, VA: ASCD Press.

McMillan, D. W., & Chavis, D. M. (1986). Sense of community: A definition and theory. *Journal of Community Psychology*, *14*, 6–23.

Osterman, K. F. (2000). Students' need for belonging in the school community. *Review of Educational Research*, *70*(3), 323–367.

Reeve, J. (2006). Extrinsic rewards and inner motivation. In C. M. Evertson & C. S. Weinstein (Eds.), *Handbook of classroom management* (pp. 645–664). Mahwah, NJ: Erlbaum.

Rogers, C., & Freiberg, H. J. (1994). *Freedom to learn* (3rd ed.). Columbus, OH: Merrill.

Ryan, R., & Deci, E. (2000). When rewards compete with nature. The undermining of intrinsic motivation and self-regulation. In C. Sansome & J. M. Harackiewicz (Eds.), *Intrinsic and extrinsic motivation: The search for optimal motivation and performance* (pp 13–54). Orlando, FL: Academic Press.

Ryan, R. M., & Deci, E. L. (2006). Self-determination theory and the facilitation of intrinsic motivation, social development and well-being. *American Psychologist*, *55*, 65–78.

Shindler, J. (2003). *Creating a psychology of success in the classroom: Enhancing academic achievement by systematically promoting student self-esteem*. Retrieved October 11, 2008, from www.calstatela.edu/faculty/jshindl/cm.

Shindler, J., Taylor, C., Jones, A., Cadenas, H. (2003). Don't smile 'til Christmas: Examining the immersion of new teachers into existing school climates. In S. Ulanoff (Ed.), *Online yearbook for the American Educational Research Association Urban Teaching and Learning SIG* (pp. 24–29). Los Angeles: California State University.

Styles, D. (2001). *Class meetings: Building leadership, problem-solving and decision making skills in the respectful classroom*. Markham, ON: Pembroke Publishers.

Watson, M., & Battistich, V. (2006). *Building and sustaining caring communities*. In C. M. Evertson & C. Weinstein (Eds.), *Handbook of classroom management* (pp. 253–297). Mahwah, NJ: Erlbaum.

Watson, M., & Ecken, L. (2003). *Learning to trust: Transforming difficult elementary classrooms through developmental discipline*. San Francisco: Jossey-Bass.

Wolk, S. (2002). Being good: *Rethinking classroom management and student discipline*. Portsmouth, NH: Heinemann.

16

The Transformative Mind-Set and Making Your Thinking an Ally

In This Chapter

- Connection between thought and classroom management outcomes
- How to have an unsatisfying day
- Exploring the fundamental factors in your thinking that affect your experience
- How negativity in thinking manifests itself in classroom management dysfunction
- Changing your patterns of thinking
- Adopting a "yes" mind-set
- Beyond a positive attitude
- Cultivating your sense of purpose and, as a result, a transformative mind-set

READER NOTE

This chapter is intended to challenge you to reflect more deeply on the relationship between your thinking and how it translates into your classroom management. Through this examination, you will find that the thinking that you do, how you feel throughout the day, your effectiveness with students, and the source of those things that you refer to as "problems" are all connected. I do not ask you to take any of this on faith or adopt any specific set of values. In fact, I encourage you to be skeptical and question every idea in this chapter. If the ideas are valid, you should experience their validity firsthand. None of the content in this chapter is intended to be philosophical or ideological. It is intended to be practical and to explore the technical aspects of how your thoughts affect your work as a teacher. Some of the ideas in this chapter may seem unfamiliar, so it may be helpful to allow yourself time to reflect on them. Changing patterns of thinking takes time and intentional practice.

"Some days just seem to drag on forever."

"Those students make me so mad sometimes, and I bet they do it on purpose."

"It is odd: I am around people all day, but a lot of the time I feel isolated and lonely."

"I thought teaching was going to be more satisfying, but for so much of the day, I just feel dissatisfied. I am beginning to understand how people get burned out."

"I am doing my best to teach these students, but they seem to always be letting me down. I feel disappointed in them so much, with the exception of a few who are my hard workers."

Chapter One characterized the natural state in the classroom as one in which you and your students work in harmony in a functional and satisfying environment. As you have explored the previous chapters, you have likely recognized that a functional classroom environment does not come about inadvertently. With an intentional investment, a sound set of tools, and enough time, you can bring function to nearly any context. Your natural state of mind while teaching is one in which you are at ease, in the moment, engaged in your work, and feeling connected with your students. However, just as the natural classroom condition is uncommon, so is this natural state of mind. What is more normal is a state of mind that on some level is stressed or bored; feeling some degree of threat from students, parents, or administrators (or all of them); wishing to do something else; looking forward to the end of the day; and feeling isolated and alone. This normal but dysfunctional state of mind contributes to problems with your classroom management as well as your personal happiness.

While teachers have many challenges and real problems to face while teaching, most of the experience of things being problematic during the day takes place in our minds (Tolle, 2001). Teaching is difficult work, but doing that work is not the reason that you feel distress. Most of what gives you grief comes from how you think about things rather than the challenges that you deal with. This chapter looks at some areas of teacher thinking and examines how mental processes can make all the difference to how you experience and interpret your job and your students and what you find meaningful.

16.1 REFLECTION

The implication that the difficulties of your job are just in your mind can seem patronizing. The purpose of the chapter is not to condemn the way that you think, but to find ways to free you from those thoughts that keep you from enjoying your job.

16.2 REFLECTION

Informally construct a map of your emotions throughout your most recent day of teaching or working with others. What were the most common emotions? What were the repetitive thoughts? Keep these thoughts and emotions in mind as you continue with the chapter.

HOW TO HAVE A GENERALLY UNSATISFYING (THINKING) DAY

Typically we judge a day of teaching as better or worse relative to how well the students behave. Granted, students do have better days and not-so-good days, but as Haim Ginott (1972) observed, the teacher "makes the weather in the classroom." And we interpret the events and give mental labels to what goes on in our class. Our interpretation of the thousands of events that occur in a day will have a great deal to do with the lessons that we take away from those events, as well as the way we feel about them.

Moreover, to a great degree, our thinking will define our experience in how we subjectively and objectively feel about things: the affect we project, how we perform, and the effect we have on others (Friedman, 2006; Friedman & Farber, 1992). It may not be immediately obvious, but with certain kinds of thinking, we ensure that we have mostly unsatisfying and uneasy days; with other kinds of thinking, we ensure that we have a mostly enjoyable and contented experience in a class day. To examine this idea more concretely, consider the two descriptions in Table 16.1, and reflect on the powerful effects each type of thinking can have on the experience of teaching (or coaching or parenting).

REFLECTION

16.3

As you examine each list in Table 16.1, which one better characterizes how you typically think over the course of a day? What was your emotional reaction as you read the lists?

As you compare the lists in Table 16.1, keep in mind that both columns refer to a comparable day in a comparable school. There was nothing different in either context. The descriptions had nothing to do with location or who was taught. As you read the experiences described in each column you will note dramatic differences between them. The approach of the orientation on the left is certain to produce a sense of unease, stress, and dissatisfaction. Interestingly, the experience characterized on the left most closely resembles the normal state of mind for many teachers. As a result, the longer one teaches under this laborious mind-set, the less one wants to (Farber, 1999). In contrast, the column on the right depicts what we might characterize as thinking that will lead to the natural condition. This condition is unusual yet realistically attainable. In this chapter, we examine steps toward finding that natural state.

FUNDAMENTAL FACTORS IN YOUR THINKING THAT AFFECT YOUR EXPERIENCE

To make sense of why each of us can have such a dramatically different experience in a day of teaching, let's examine various potential thought processes, patterns, and reactions that take place. To begin, it will be useful to explore three factors that are fundamental to determining the quality of your thinking: your approaches to time, causation of events, and awareness.

Your Approach to Time

Most of us rarely consider our thoughts relative to the moment. In fact, most of us assume that our attention is in the present. So try this: check in on yourself at various points during a typical day and observe where your thinking is in relation to time. Probably your mind drifts between thinking about what has happened in the past and what might happen in the future. Most of us give very little real attention to the present. So what is the problem with that? Everything.

The only place that you can find peace, a clear sense of intention, and freedom from the mental noise that fills your head is in the moment. The past is where regret, blame, guilt, obsession, victimization, and resentment live. Those feelings can exist only if you allow your mind to dwell in the past. You will not find peace of mind in the future either. The concept of the future holds anxiety, boredom, fear, dread, anticipation, and projection of problems, as well as the delusion that the future will somehow bring relief from problems. The future has not happened, yet we allow ourselves to experience negative emotions in manufacturing a future reality that is unpleasant. Just as mistakenly, we miss the moment because we

TABLE 16.1. Comparison of Thinking That Leads to a Largely Unsatisfying or Largely Enjoyable Experience from a Day of Teaching

Thinking That Leads to a Higher Degree of Unease and Dissatisfaction	Thinking That Leads to a Higher Degree of Peace of Mind and Contentment
Begin the day by thinking about how long and predictable it will be, how much you are looking forward to its being over, and how relieved you will be when you can go home.	Begin the day grounded in the moment. Enjoy the processes and tasks in which you find yourself, and be present to and aware of your students.
Picture other classes or other schools where you envision the students being much better than your students. Compare your students to these past classes or other students, and look for their faults.	Accept your students for who they are. Do not judge them as better or worse; just accept where they are at this point in their learning and personal growth, and attend to what you can do to help them succeed in your class.
Begin to wonder what your "problem" students will do today to irritate you. Look for things that they do that confirm your expectations.	Assume all of your students are going to do the best they can given their conditioning, what they are reacting to in their lives in and outside school, and, above all, the relationship that you have previously developed with them.
Let your emotions be dictated by your reactions to external events. When a student does something that you do not like or when students are not meeting your expectations, assign them bad intentions, and let yourself get angry and disappointed.	Be aware of the connectedness of all events throughout the day. Keep in mind what you are projecting to the class. Try to project a positive expectation for all students. When things do not go well, assume responsibility for changing the cause or helping improve the situation. Take on a "yes" mind-set.
Hold resentment for students who are making your life difficult "on purpose." On the surface, pretend that everything is fine, but allow your inner dialogue to blame and judge the students who are causing you misery. Resent that they are in your class, and tell yourself how they are to blame for how you feel.	Keep in mind that you choose your emotional reactions to events. What you feel manifests in your interpretation of events. Watch carefully for feelings of defensiveness and threat. Be aware of what you are defending. (It is usually something petty.) If you shed the need to defend your self-image, the students stop being the enemy.
At lunch, find another teacher or staff member to complain to. Tell this person how the students are acting the same inappropriate, inattentive, and disrespectful way they did the day before. Paint a vivid picture of the parents as a useless and unsupportive lot who are ultimately the cause of all of your problems. Reflect on how if it was not for how they raised their children, you would not have half the problems that you do.	At lunch, take the opportunity for at least a moment for yourself. Find the present moment and allow yourself to just be, eat, and enjoy the company (or the solitude if you so choose). Spend only a moment or two reflecting on what happened in the morning and what adjustments you want to make. As you think about the rest of the day, keep your awareness of the present, and do not let your head get in the habit of being lost in thoughts of past events or future uncertainties. Plan in the moment, eat in the moment, and when it is time to return to class, maintain your awareness in the moment.
After lunch, keep your locus of control as external as possible. Hope the students act better, and look forward to times in the day when you do not have them with you. Anticipate that things will go poorly and when they do, let yourself react with habitual anger, shaming, blaming, and lecturing	As the students come into the room after lunch, take a moment to appreciate how unique and talented they are. As your attitude of respect and appreciation grows, you can see it being reflected back to you. As you begin to feel more connected and closer to the students, you feel the sense of responsibility for their

(continued)

TABLE 16.1. Continued

Thinking That Leads to a Higher Degree of Unease and Dissatisfaction	Thinking That Leads to a Higher Degree of Peace of Mind and Contentment
your class. Show your passive-aggressive disappointment and sense of superiority. Phrases such as "When will you ever learn?" will make you feel less responsible and justified in caring less.	welfare. You can then shift your attention away from you and your ego as "the teacher" and back to the moment, the task, and being fully present to the students. You focus on doing one thing at a time, doing a good job of each task, and letting the outcomes take care of themselves.
As students respond to your attitude of judgment and disapproval (which you thought you disguised) with aloofness and lack of respect, be sure to assign them the traits of lazy and disrespectful when you make assessments about their character. When you assign these qualities, keep the locus of causality and responsibility on the students; do not consider what part your attitude played in creating their response to you and the unsatisfying classroom climate. As feelings of loneliness and isolation creep in, long for situations in your life where you are loved or classes that gave you the love you deserved.	Focus your teaching on what is successful. Show respect for your students by projecting high expectations for their performance and their interactions with one another. Do not keep your positive recognitions (see Chapter Eight) or your appreciation to yourself. Use the power of the collective sense of ownership and responsibility to the community to guide your thinking in matters of behavior. Show your pride in the group, and give them concrete examples of the progress that they are making. No matter how successful you are, avoid thoughts of comparison to other teachers. You recognize that once you begin to judge and compare, you poison the well.
When you go home after a long day of teaching, run over and over in your mind all that students have done to you: the willful disrespect, the lazy and unmotivated performance that reflects badly on you, the intentional misbehavior. Be sure to assign the students bad intentions for their actions. Give yourself reasons to justify your defensiveness, but unconsciously beat yourself up for being inadequate. Alternatively, recall bad episodes from the day, and long for the next vacation or at least the weekend. Dread that you have to go back and teach tomorrow. Pretend that you "just leave it all behind" when you go home. Ignore the way that your negative feelings affect the way that you feel physically. Try not to notice how your unconscious mind does not want to give up the negative thoughts and the need to defend yourself. Just ignore the way your mind tries to compensate for your sense of disconnection and inadequacy, and attempt to fill it with some diversion or addictive behavior.	When you go home, practice being in the moment. If you have planning or grading to do, do it when you can. Do not ruin the moment with worry about what you need to do. It leads to resentment of the task and the habit of worrying instead of doing. When you are not engaged in school work, be in the moment. It may be tempting to cycle your day through your mind, but as you notice what you are thinking about, you will find that it is pretty repetitive. It is much better to be present to whom you are with and what you are doing. It will make your time away from teaching much happier and your time as a teacher more effective.
Tell yourself that everything is fine, and do not pay any attention to how easily your body and mind react with anger when someone or something says or does something that triggers one of the many things that irritated you during the day.	When you are grading papers, be in the moment. No matter how repetitive the papers are, enjoy each one. Avoid trying to "get through them." As you learn to enjoy the task and be in the moment while grading, you will find that time does not drag as before, you enjoy the task more, and you do not carry the resentment of grading back to class the next day. And it is a great exercise to practice staying in the present moment
If you have grading or planning to do, let yourself wallow in the resentment you feel for doing it. Put it off, but complain up to that point about how you have to do it.	

anticipate something in the future that we misperceive as more important. You need to make the present moment your friend. Denial of it is the cause of most of your perceived problems and suffering.

16.4 REFLECTION

If you are having difficulty recognizing where your attention is at any moment, try an exercise. Sit in a chair for fifteen minutes or longer, try to eliminate all distractions (the computer, TV, others, radio, and so on), and let your mind go where it wants. Observe your mind, and notice where it goes. How long does it take before it wants to think about the future (what you need to be doing, what event is coming up) or get caught up thinking about a past event (what happened that morning, other times that you have tried to sit quietly)? Then try to stay in the present and see how long you can do this.

What did this exercise tell you? Were you surprised at how little time your mind wanted to spend in the present?

Your Approach to Causation

The primary factor in the teaching style continuum as discussed in Chapter Two, making up the vertical axis related to function and effectiveness, is the degree to which there is an internal or external locus of control (LOC). This is arguably the most predictive characteristic of the success of a teacher (Shindler, Jones, Taylor, & Cadenas, 2003). Effective teachers attribute the causes of their successes and failures to an internal LOC related to what they do. However, to be effective and enjoy peace of mind, you need to have an internal LOC related to how you think as well. It is important to take responsibility for your thinking and recognize the cause-and-effect relationship between it and literally everything else, including your success, the quality of your environment, and your level of peace of mind and job satisfaction. If you believe that the "real world" (see Appendix D) is unsatisfying, that something external will always thwart your best efforts, and that "those students" will always disappoint you, those beliefs will cause it to be so in your experience (Friedman, 2006). But if you recognize that most problems are caused by your own mind and self-limiting thinking and that in a very real way you create your own "real world" by your attitude, you find that things not only seem better, they work out better.

Your mind in survival mode tells you: *If I take responsibility for what is, it will be too overwhelming. My students' needs are endless. This job is endless. It is so big. I can never really succeed. If I accept that I am responsible, I will feel inadequate, guilty, or overwhelmed. I cannot be held responsible for what happens to my students. It is not my fault. I cannot control everything.* These thoughts can torture you; they can make you feel guilty and inadequate and find reasons to become less responsible. There is a temptation to externalize, blame, complain, become negative, procrastinate, tune out, and view the students as the problem (Farber, 1999). Although this is understandable and normal, it is still dysfunctional.

To achieve peace of mind rather than externalize responsibility to cope with a sense of unease (a strategy that will not provide a sense of peace for long), changing your patterns of thinking is more effective (Larrivee, 2006; Tolle, 2003). The first step is to take responsibility for your own thoughts. You are the only one who can do this for you. You can develop the skill of recognizing the messages that want to come in. Practice drawing your awareness to this very moment and what's important now (WIN), and move away from the urge to fight what is. You do not have to take responsibility for everything that is happening in the situation; you just need to take responsibility for yourself and remember that the present is all you can control.

Second, when you access and focus on the immediate present, a clearer sense of intentions will follow. Moment by moment, there is nothing you cannot cope with. The future can seem overwhelming when you allow it to supersede your thinking, but it is not in this moment or in the next. Habits of mind are difficult to change at first but become increasingly easier. What is right, necessary, and important will ultimately come to you as you free your thinking from the habit of creating thought problems and making this moment into something that you need to run from (Tolle, 2001).

Third, trust your intentions and give up the desire to control. When we look clearly at the need for control, it is not so much a function of necessity as it is the ego trying to make the world consistent with its own picture. Deepak Chopra (1994) identifies the ability to shed "attachment to the outcome" as one of his seven spiritual laws of success. When we let go and stop clinging to outcomes, we free ourselves from the torment of guilt. Our egoic thought patterns insist that we need to be attached to the outcome, or things will not turn out well. It is useful to recognize this ego-based message for what it is: a mental fiction. On closer examination, we find our need to make things consistent with our idea of how things should be is fear based. Letting ego attachment dictate how things should work out will not improve outcomes but will go a long way toward making you miserable. It is a never-ending struggle with no peace.

REFLECTION 16.5

Reflect on the events of your day. When did you feel attached to things turning out a certain way? How did it make you feel: stressed, nervous, guilty, helpless, inadequate, upset at others? Did your feelings of attachment make things turn out any better?

Your Approach to Awareness

Where is your awareness throughout the day? Is it on the many negative thoughts that recycle through your mind on a continuous basis? "That student is such a problem." "How did they score so poorly on that test? I did a good job of teaching it to them." "Why is it so hard to get them to listen?" "We would be so much better off without this principal!" "How am I supposed to teach effectively without the books I need?"

Count the number of times in five minutes that you have these negative thoughts or others. You will be surprised at the number. Then count the number of times in a day that the very same handful of negative thoughts recycles through your mind. Note that you do not even try to bring them into your awareness; they find a way of dominating your thinking unless you create change within.

REFLECTION 16.6

Reflect on the following questions:

1. How much time am I spending with my awareness being truly in the moment?

2. Am I letting compulsive and negative thinking pull me out of the moment into a past defined by resentment, regret, and irritation or into a future that represents either dread or illusory relief from the current situation?

3. If my conscious mind is filled with this compulsive thinking on a continuous basis, what am I programming into my unconscious? And what will it look like when it surfaces in my behavior?

Reflect on how often you shift your awareness from what is important now (your students, investment in your teaching, appreciating what is good about the moment, and so on) to an imaginary audience. It is common when teaching for your mind to leave the present moment and allow the ego to become the audience. One of the manifestations of this is becoming self-conscious. Instead of being attentive to your students and the task at hand, you shift your attention to how you think you appear in the eyes of others. The practical result is action that is stilted and tentative.

Another manifestation is the commiserating ego. Our egos are a highly attentive and appreciating audience. The ego always commiserates with us when we have disparaging thoughts about students ("they are just not that smart," "they are not as good as other students," or "how are they not getting this?"). They are amused at the backhanded comments that we make to students who are not aware that they have just been put down. They are always there to listen to complaints about how our job is not as good as it should be, how things are unfair, and how, since it is not our fault, we are justified in daydreaming and entertaining ourselves in whatever way will allow us to cope with this unsatisfying moment. Playing to an imaginary audience is a clear sign that you are not in the moment and are acting unconsciously.

16.7   REFLECTION

Reflect on the last time that you played to your imaginary audience. What thought forms did it take?

Keep your awareness in the moment, on what you are doing right now, as much as possible. You may be planning operationally for the future or analyzing the past for helpful ideas, but if you do this in the moment, your ego is less likely to take charge of the process. When your awareness is in the moment, you will feel it in your body. Your breathing will become deeper and slower, and you will feel an ease and clarity.

16.8   REFLECTION

Now intentionally move your attention into the moment. Focus on being completely present to the task in front of you or the people you are with. Notice how you feel when the mental noise slows down and your attention is in the now. What else do you find in this state? Keep it in mind for later.

WHAT TO DO WHEN YOU RECOGNIZE THE VOICE OF NEGATIVITY EMERGING

Many times a day you will be tempted to give in to the voice of negativity within you. Yet, if you grow in your awareness of how this voice emerges, and the forms it takes, you can increasingly free yourself of negative thinking and action. Incorporating the following suggestions will help you move from reactive and negative thinking to constructive thinking and positive action.

- *Do not fight it.* Accept these emotions. You do not need to blame yourself or others for negative feelings. Just become aware of the thoughts. When you are in the act of noticing negative messages, you see them for what they are: simply thought forms and nothing that you need to listen to. In your noticing the feeling, it will lose power and control. This is in no way denying what you feel. Denial is counterproductive in transitioning your mind-set.

- *Listen to what negativity is telling you.* Treat negative thoughts coming in as information. Ask yourself, "What button just got pushed?" "What am I defending?" "Is there some inadequacy I feel the need to project?" "Is there some hurt or vulnerability at the root of the emotions?" Let the emotions tell you what is at the root of your negative reactions. Emotions are the most accurate window into the mind. Refrain from labeling emotions "good" or "bad"; just accept that they are there for now. They are real, but they are not your identity. What can you learn from your emotions?

- *Choose positive action.* In any situation we have only three functional or healthy choices (in contrast to many dysfunctional or unhealthy choices, such as going negative or becoming reactive and unconscious):

  - Accept the situation. Stop fighting the idea that things need to be different. Say yes to what is.

  - Take action. Tap into your intentional vision, and do something that improves the situation. Taking conscious, deliberate action will feel positive and lead to solutions.

  - Remove yourself from the situation. Take a time-out. Find another place to be. Wait until you have renewed inner peace and the negativity is not doing the talking.

EXAMINING THE EFFECT OF YOUR MENTAL SCRIPT

We all have a series of mental scripts swimming around in our unconscious minds (Nelson, 1999). Most of them are subtle, but some can define our entire outlook. Most of these scripts are formed very early in life and are often solidified in adolescent years. It has been said that we often select teaching as a career to rewrite the scripts of the years we would like to change or relive. Whether or not this is true for you, examining the underlying scripts in your unconscious can be enlightening and hold the key to dealing with your ongoing struggles.

These scripts can be healthy, unhealthy, or neutral (Nelson, 1999). For example, you may be carrying around a generally positive script that says, "If I work hard, good things will happen to me." Or when you were young, someone might have inspired you to believe you are capable; as a result you developed a script around that concept. Whether these scripts are healthy or unhealthy, true or false, once they are accepted truths in our unconscious minds, they are burned into our self-image and require strong counterprogramming to alter.

Commonly in the course of teaching, we discover that less-than-healthy scripts tend to define our thinking. One of the realities of teaching is that it is difficult to disguise who we are, and that includes the contents of our unconscious. In most cases, teaching will bring it out, even if we would prefer not. Some of the more common problematic mental scripts include these:

"I don't deserve respect."

"I will never get what I want."

"I am no good."

"You can't trust people. They are selfish and dishonest and will always let you down."

"If I act impossible to please, it will shift the attention away from me and my sense of inadequacy."

"If I am not likable, nice, and agreeable, I will lose others' love."

"Popular kids will hurt me."

"I am a fraud, and I will be found out at some point." This is probably the most common script that teachers (and many others) have.

Simply becoming aware of these scripts is the most effective strategy. Awareness alone will go a long way toward the ability to shed scripts limiting your growth and performance. In addition, it will be useful to self-program your mind with healthier, accurate messages. For example, if you recognize a tendency to doubt your own legitimacy or lovability, you may want to reprogram your thinking with a message such as, "I deserve love and respect." Simply repeating the message silently can have a powerful effect on unconscious beliefs over time. Becoming aware of the concrete evidence that contradicts these unhealthy scripts will be helpful too (Nelson, 1999). For example, if you believe that you must be likable or others will abandon you, you might be intentional about recognizing the evidence related to those students, friends, and family who like you no matter what, and for a lot of reasons other than your efforts to be nice.

16.9   REFLECTION

Examine the scripts in your unconscious. What messages are they telling you? What effect do you see them having on your teaching? What are the countermessages with which you want to reprogram your thoughts to be happier and more effective?

CHANGING YOUR PATTERNS OF THINKING

Cultivating more functional and harmonious forms of thinking does not require special skills or help from others. To begin, it is beneficial to acknowledge that dysfunctional thinking is not unique to you. All teachers (and everyone else) have some level of mental negativity that is holding them back. You must resist the temptation to deny that negative thoughts and tendencies exist at all. This is counterproductive. Denial fuels the unconscious; it may alleviate pain in the short term, but it compounds it in the long run. It is not useful to fight your feelings or be hard on yourself for having certain feelings. As we discussed earlier, feelings are simply information. They clarify a great deal, including what you need to work on. Moreover, you do not need to dissect the past to bring about change. You simply need to keep focusing on being in the moment. It is more effective to practice being more and more conscious and to place attention on forming new patterns than revisiting the past for answers.

Two things simultaneously start to occur when you become more in the moment and increase your level of awareness of how your thinking is affecting you and your classes. First, you notice how much that thinking has caused the suffering you have experienced, and in the act of noticing you see how the patterns that have brought you grief can be changed. Second, you notice that the students become less frustrating to work with, less threatening, and more enjoyable to be around (Tolle, 2001). As you begin to change, your situation changes along with you. In other words, your real and imagined problems begin to lessen.

In the next sections, we examine avenues toward promoting habits of mind that will bring you peace and make you more effective with your students. These avenues include cultivating an attitude of "yes," encouraging a positive energy flow, finding your inner voice of intention, and developing a sense of purpose.

Taking on a "Yes" Mind-Set

One of the most effective ways of making the shift away from whatever negative thought or state of mind that you are experiencing, into a place that is going to be more functional and enjoyable, is to take on a "yes" frame of mind: one in which you say yes to what is. You say yes to the moment. Tolle (2003) refers to this inner yes as one of the portals to accessing the present moment. It is a state of acceptance. You say yes to the life that surrounds you rather than wanting things to be different or wanting to be in the future. A yes frame of mind says that you are going to rise to the occasion and take action, as opposed to putting it off or being passive. You are saying yes to quality and acting with intention.

The artist needs to say yes to the moment to be able to access the creative energy within himself, or what is created will be uninspired. The athlete needs to say yes to the moment and commit to what she is doing or perform poorly, make mistakes, or even increase the chance for injury. The yes does not need to take any extra effort. It is not about trying harder. It is about being in the moment and tapping into the life force in that moment. In effect, you are saying yes to life itself.

Without being consciously aware of it, we approach most things with a subtle or not-so-subtle "no" mind-set and a rejection of life. While we tend to view our mental activity as neutral, on closer examination we see that almost every thought is defined by either a yes or a no attitude. Most of the time the effect is subtle, but each of these small thoughts adds up to larger and more significant outcomes such as a mental outlook or a physical manifestation in our bodies and is ultimately projected onto the classes that we teach. Table 16.2 lists some of the ways that a "yes" mind-set contrasts with a "no" mind-set.

Taking a yes orientation is by no means being passive or always agreeable. When you say yes to life, you have to say no to a lot of other things. It means saying yes to action, which means that you will need to walk away from some unhealthy situations or take an assertive position against something that you believe is wrong. When you say yes to life, you say yes to the fulfillment of potential, and that means you are saying no to hanging on to mediocrity and irresponsibility.

Is working from a mind-set defined by yes the same as being optimistic? Not really. Being sunny and optimistic is probably preferable to being sour and pessimistic, but neither optimism nor pessimism is rooted in a yes attitude. A pessimistic perspective says, "I know things will turn out badly. I just expect it to be that way, and I am usually right." An optimistic perspective says, "I hope things turn out well. I like it when they do, so I have faith that a good outcome will occur and I will get what I want." Do you hear yes in either of those statements? A yes mind-set has little to do with believing that we will or will not get what we want. It is not about the outcome but the process. Both optimism and pessimism are basically ego-based mind-sets. Neither will lead to long-term growth or fulfillment.

Exploring the Idea of Being Positive

Does being positive come from a yes attitude? Certainly having a generally positive attitude can potentially be rooted in a yes mind-set. When it comes to the job of teaching, sending out positive energy has many benefits. For one, it produces repeated deposits into the emotional bank account of relationships we have with others (Covey, 1989; see Chapter Three, this book). The positive energy that we radiate will come back in some form. The result is a positive effect on our lives, teaching, and relationships within the school. Offering positive energy to others tends to be worth it. We find evidence for this when we observe others who project a positive energy. What we usually notice is that they seem to be surrounded by positive energy from others.

TABLE 16.2. **Characteristic Thoughts of a "Yes" Versus "No" Mind-Set**

Thoughts Characterizing a "Yes" Mind-Set	Thoughts Characterizing a "No" Mind-Set
"I am in the moment. The moment is good."	"I want to be something else or to be somewhere else."
"There is endless wonder in the world around me if I only notice it."	"I already know how things are going to go. I have been there and done that."
"When I say yes, I feel an ease and clarity in my thinking. As a result, I find my intention more evident. I feel a clearer sense of direction."	"I want a diversion. I am bored. My work feels tedious."
"I see the human possibility in my students and others with whom I interact. I see learning all around me."	"I see all the limitations that keep my students from doing what I want them to do. Why do I have to work with such a flawed group of people? After a while, each group just seems like the last. I already know how they are going to act. And I am usually right."
"When I look out at my situation, I feel thankful. I get to do a meaningful job and make a difference. The list of blessings is endless when I really look at it."	"I never get what I want. I feel that others are always letting me down. Maybe the worst part is that I am sure they all know what I want, but no one cares enough to do it."

16.10 REFLECTION

Bring to mind someone you know who has a positive attitude. How would you describe the way that others respond to him or her? What are the implications for teachers and coaches?

While there is an undeniable value to projecting a sincere positive attitude, we need to take a close look at where it comes from. It may sound contradictory, but a positive attitude is often the flip side of negativity from the same dysfunctional coin. The earlier discussion on negativity noted that the mental act of being negative is rooted in a "no" of some kind and a denial of what is. In the same way, a positive attitude can be a mask for a deeper sense of nonacceptance. A person can be acting in a positive and socially acceptable manner while struggling inside with authentic thoughts and feelings. You can test this. After spending a class period trying to be positive, do you feel joy and ease and as though good energy has moved through you? Or do you feel that it took a lot of effort to "act" positive? The reality is that on some days, it may be necessary to act, but if you do this consistently, deeper insight is required. Acting is exhausting and difficult to maintain; no matter how much we deny it, our students can sense when we are acting. When we get home from a day of "acting positive," we feel drained. Moreover, whatever we were disguising through the day is there to greet us.

Why do we feel the need to act? The answer is complex and subjective, but typically it relates to the wish for acceptance. Ask yourself, "Though I pretend to like the students, do I really?" "What is keeping me from letting myself really care about them?" "I act committed to the classroom social contract. Am I?" "Am I afraid to be real with the students?" "What is the unease provoked by being myself?" The answers to these questions can bring some difficult emotions, but if you refuse to acknowledge them, your inner conflict will take its toll on you, your energy level, and your effectiveness with others.

Making the transition to more authentic engagement involves an intention to be in the moment and present to your students. It is a strange paradox: your ego tells you that if you did not put on an act, a negative, depressed, boring, dispassionate, or inappropriate person would be revealed. But when you say yes to the present, you do not have to act as if you are engaged because it happens naturally. When you are in the moment, you are focused not on your own problems but on the action that you are taking. There is no room for boredom. When you are aware and tuned into the reality of what you are able to do in a moment of teaching, you will discover an inherent joy. Any job that is done with an attitude of yes can be joyful, and teaching is especially rewarding because of the profound experience of promoting the growth of young people.

My Experience

Our attitudes go a long way in defining our situation. Remember that we make the weather in the room. We can confirm this idea by examining any classroom. What we find is that over time, the students and the climate of the class will mirror the attitudes and dispositions of the teacher.

I experienced this phenomenon firsthand a few years ago. After teaching many sections of classroom management pretty successfully, I began the next quarter with the attitude that I could just show up and the students would somehow receive the quality of instruction that the previous students had. I have to admit that my attitude had deteriorated: I had spent a great deal of time in schools and had become frustrated with the classroom management practices that I had seen, as well as with what I interpreted as the faulty assumptions that were at the root of those practices.

On the first day of class, as I interacted with the students, I heard many of those flawed assumptions coming out of their mouths. And without being aware of it, I began to treat this class with less respect and put less effort into it. I found myself complaining about them to others (breaking a rule that I now swear by: never to talk about students negatively) and developing negative expectations. Predictably they responded in kind. They took few risks when responding and did not laugh at my few efforts at humor. In the end, the quality of their work was subpar and uninspired.

As I read the course evaluations, I was shocked. I thought that I had done my usual excellent job teaching and that I was a likable and positive person. Above all, I thought that I was able to hide my unconscious lack of respect for these students. I clearly had not. I learned a painful but powerful lesson that quarter: when we give respect, we get it back; when we do not give it, we should not be surprised when we do not receive it.

I knew I needed to change my attitude. I started the following quarter by validating each new group of students. I did not rest on my previous performance but made an effort to make the content of the class meaningful and fresh. I projected a positive expectation and a respect for students' ideas. As I changed my attitude, my situation changed along with my mind-set. The students put more energy into the class. They listened better and stayed more focused on the task. They volunteered more and took more risks with their ideas. They reflected my respect. As a result, I was able to respond to the positive energy that I received with an increased positive energy of my own.

I enjoyed the quarter a great deal, and by all indications so did the students. The class's written comments read as though these students had had an entirely different instructor than the students from the previous term did. In many ways, they had.

CULTIVATING YOUR SENSE OF PURPOSE AND DEVELOPING A TRANSFORMATIVE MIND-SET

What do you use to guide your actions instead of all the mental noise and the reactive voice of the ego in your head? You need to listen to a deeper source. When you clear away all the noise, the fear, and the distractions, what emerges is a lucid sense of intention. When you say yes to the moment, you have access to this inner source of motivation: your inner life force. You could call it many things, but here I refer to it as the force inside you that provides you with intention. It exists between fearing and wanting, future and past. It is at the heart of your innermost self. When your mind is clear and you ask yourself, "What is important now?" (WIN), your intention is waiting with an answer. When you access your true intention, you access your true state—your natural state.

Each time you access this present-moment intention, you get a clearer sense of your larger sense of purpose. In that sense, intention and purpose work together. You could say that your intention answers the moment-to-moment questions, whereas your sense of purpose answers the larger questions. When your actions are guided by this clear intention, even challenging or menial activities do not feel pointless, insignificant, or mercenary. You get something out of everything you do. When the voice of your inner intention is audible, you get a glimpse of a larger sense of the meaning of what you are doing. Your intention illuminates your gifts and uniqueness. It clarifies how you can best make a contribution. Your true sense of purpose is a reflection of that illumination.

Just as your work will feel boring and unsatisfying when your ego is fighting the present moment, when your purpose is rooted in ego, you will struggle to achieve job satisfaction. If the motivation for teaching includes enjoying control of others, needing to feel important, rather than responding to the moment, you may be motivated but never satisfied. When your sense of purpose is ego driven, it leads to feeling separate, alone, unsatisfied, and the perception that your work is meaningless. Many teachers feel dissatisfied and search externally for a sense of purpose. They believe that when they attain a more powerful position, transfer to a better school, or get a raise, they will become satisfied and complete. What they usually find is that the sense of meaninglessness follows them to their new situation (Fallona & Richardson, 2006).

You can find your sense of purpose only by listening to your intention. The more you listen to your intention, the more you learn about what you truly care about and value. Moreover, you discover your gifts and the ways that you can make a difference. Fullan (1993) found that the most successful teachers were those who reported feeling a sense of moral purpose in their teaching. Wolk (2002) wrote, "There is no separation between the content we teach and issues of character and morality. They are just as intertwined" (p. 2). It is true that you may get the same salary without approaching your work with a sense of moral purpose, but will your work be as fulfilling and meaningful?

When your action is guided by a clear sense of purpose that grows from present moment intention, your work will be transformative. Whether you are alone, working with a single student, or teaching a room full of students, you will raise the level of awareness around you. You become a light to others. Your inner yes affects all that you do. Mahatma Gandhi said it best: "Be the change that you want to see in the world." When you act with present moment intention, you change the world one action at a time. It is much less important to invent a grand image of your ideal future than it is to simply be the change in this moment. When you do what you love and love what you are doing, meaning and purpose emerge naturally.

CONCLUSION

The job of the teacher is a great instructor. It provides us with an avenue for growth that few other professions can. Our teaching mirrors us to ourselves and so opens up doors for growth that are invaluable. Much of the time, we would have never volunteered to learn the lessons that we do. However, when we take advantage of the opportunities to grow and avoid the temptation to resign ourselves to perpetual coping, we find that these opportunities for growth, though often temporarily painful, are in fact true gifts. We come out the other side more compassionate, mature, and conscious. When we become more conscious, it is reflected in our teaching. When we say yes to our jobs, we find that they say yes back to us.

Journal Reflections

1. Reflect on how you see your purpose as a teacher and how it has evolved. What are the areas in which you would like to grow and improve? What do you see as internal and external roadblocks to your goals?

2. What forms of negativity do you recognize arising in yourself on a regular basis? Have they become part of your identity (victim, complainer, critic, angry person, dissatisfied person)? In other words, do they thread through the story line of your life?

Activities

1. As a group, discuss your recent classroom observations. Did you notice a relationship between the amount of negative thinking on the part of the teacher and the quantity of the behavioral problems or lack of motivation on the part of the students? What forms did the teacher's negativity take? How, in your assessment, did the negativity translate into problems within the class?

2. When your parents were upset, stressed, overburdened, or angry, how did they behave? How did your parents view human nature? Do you share their view (consciously or unconsciously)? Did the parent with whom you identify more have trouble setting boundaries or being consistent? Imagine that parent as a teacher. What advice would you give so that his or her tendencies did not sink them?

3. Reflect on some of the parent tapes that run through your mind—for example, "you are not smart," "you are the special one," "you are in the way," "if you do what I want I will love you," "if you mess up I will shame you." These tapes turn into buttons that students can push to trigger our insecurities or pain reactions. What are the parent tapes that you need to be most aware of?

4. Examine common states of mind you may have in a day. Pay special attention to the states of mind you take on when you are tired, stressed, or under pressure. Share with your partner some of those that you consider to be beneficial as a teacher and those that you judge to be less beneficial (for example, victim, overly critical, disappointed, blaming others, acting superior, acting helpless). What might you do to keep these kinds of unconscious tendencies from undermining your effectiveness or sense of satisfaction?

5. Steven Covey in the book *Seven Habits of Highly Effective People* describes a useful exercise for clarifying your sense of purpose: boil your life purpose down into as few words as possible (see whether you can state your purpose in thirty or fewer words).

6. One of the most effective exercises for counteracting negativity is to reflect on those things for which you are thankful. You can do this at any time—for example:

   - When you feel exasperated with your job or your students
   - Before you go to bed at night
   - Right now. See how many you can list in five minutes.

7. It is difficult for some of us to recognize the degree to which the noise machine in our head controls our thinking and how difficult it is to stop compulsive thoughts. It may all seem normal.

A useful indicator of how much our mind is in control is when we try to stop thinking. There are very few people who are able to go even ten seconds without an involuntary thought entering their mind. Test this for yourself. Try to stop thinking for ten breaths. Every time a thought enters your mind, start over. If you are like most other people, you will get the point of the exercise long before you ever reach ten breaths without thinking.

REFERENCES

Chopra, D. (1994). *The seven spiritual laws of success*. Novato, CA: New World Library.

Covey, S. (1989). *Seven habits of highly effective people*. New York: Simon & Schuster.

Fallona, C., & Richardson, V. (2006). Classroom management as a moral activity. In C. M. Evertson & C. S. Weinstein (Eds.), *Handbook of classroom management* (pp. 1041–1062). Mahwah, NJ: Erlbaum.

Farber, B. A. (1999). Inconsequentiality—the key to understanding teacher burnout. In R. Vandenberghe & A. Huberman (Eds.), *Understanding and preventing teacher burnout* (pp. 159–165). Cambridge: Cambridge University Press.

Friedman, I. A. (2006). Classroom management and teacher stress and burnout. In C. M. Evertson & C. S. Weinstein (Eds.), *Handbook of classroom management* (pp. 925–944). Mahwah, NJ: Erlbaum

Friedman, I. A., & Farber, B. A. (1992). Professional self-concept as a predictor of burn out. *Journal of Educational Research*, *86*(1), 28–35.

Fullan, M. (1993). *Change forces: Probing the depths of educational reform*. London: Routledge.

Ginott, H. (1972). *Teacher and child: A book for parents and teachers*. New York: Macmillan.

Larrivee, B. (2006). The convergence of reflective practice and effective classroom management. In C. M. Evertson & C. S. Weinstein (Eds.), *Handbook of classroom management* (pp. 983–1001). Mahwah, NJ: Erlbaum.

Nelson, K. (1999). Event representations, narrative development and internal working models. *Attachment and Human Development*, *1*(3), 239–252.

Shindler, J., Jones, A., Taylor, C., & Cadenas, H. (2003, April). *Don't smile 'til Christmas: Examining the immersion of new teachers into existing school climates*. Paper presented at the annual meeting of the University Council of Educational Administrators, Pittsburgh, PA.

Tolle, E. (2001). *Practicing the power of now*. Novato, CA: New World Library.

Tolle, E. (2003). *Gateways to the now*. New York: Simon & Schuster. Audio.

Wolk, S. (2002). *Being good: Rethinking classroom management and student discipline*. Portsmouth, NH: Heinemann.

APPENDIX

Questions and Answers on Transformative Classroom Management

Q: *Most of the teachers at my school are 4-Style (with a few who use 2-Style). I would love to incorporate transformative practices at the school, but I have no support. I feel that I would need to be at a different school before I could do what is in transformative classroom management (TCM).*

A: You are in a challenging situation. Teaching can be a lonely job in a school like that. Often the actions of other teachers consciously or unconsciously push you to give in and take on an attitude that resembles theirs. It can feel sometimes as though you cannot win in this environment. If you give in, you will feel that you have betrayed your mission as a teacher. At first it may seem that if you take on a different style, you will miss the benefits of being part of the collective. In some situations, there is an initial resistance to new ideas and leadership. Approach the situation with a mind-set that there are no enemies, just challenges. It is okay to listen and be present and respectful to your peers while maintaining your own boundaries and ideas. It is very important that you communicate with your principal, and help him or her understand what you are trying to accomplish and how it fits into the goals of the school. And it will really help if you can start by finding at least one other member of the faculty with whom you can share your experiences and ideas.

Q: *This all sounds good, but aren't there some students who just need a 4-Style teacher?*

A: No. Certainly some students are challenging, and it is tempting to give in to a tendency to become reactive when you run out of positive ideas; reactivity or power struggles will just make things worse. It is true that some students have been raised on a model of 4-Style adult relationships, so they may be used to them. They may seem to initially respond most obviously to the 4-Style. It may "work" on some basic level to keep them in line. However, it is not healthy and will not lead to their positive growth and development. It will never lead to true discipline or higher levels of functioning in the long term. It may be useful to compare continuing 4-Style teaching practices because students are accustomed to them to giving addicts their usual drug. It may temporarily halt the withdrawal symptoms, but it will not improve the situation in the end.

Q: *I teach special education. Can I use TCM ideas in my class?*

A: Yes, but you will need to be realistic and selective. Your teaching goal should be to lead all students to the level of self-direction and self-responsibility of which they are capable. In many cases, it is most realistic and sensible to incorporate a greater number of behavioral conditioning techniques when teaching students with moderate to severe developmental disabilities. Issues of safety, control, and appropriate social skill development typically require a great deal of direct instruction followed by clear rewards and consequences. However, all students will learn best and make the most progress in an environment that is free of pain-based logic and encourages the highest levels of self-discipline and self-esteem.

Q: *I went to a teacher training workshop, and they showed us how to use the colored-card system and how to use a reward system for promoting desirable student behavior. They said these strategies work. It seems that they contradict what is in this book.*

A: These strategies are very popular. In some cases, whole districts have adopted them, which means people have concluded that they "work." I would encourage you to look more deeply at each idea. Chapter Six, related to the use of rewards, is a good beginning. Also it may be helpful to read the online resource article, "Why Not to Use Colored Cards and Names on the Board Behavioral Systems and What to Do Instead," at transformativeclassroom.com, as well as testimonials online (a simple Web search for "colored-card systems" or "token economy" will lead to you to them) from teachers who have tried these strategies. What you will find is that they appear to "work" for a while, and then teachers either realize these strategies are just making things worse or they begin to rationalize that they are "working" despite evidence to the contrary. These teachers' stories of awakening are compelling.

Q: *Isn't it true that people all just have their own individual personality? Isn't it all relative? Shouldn't teachers just do what works for them and their personality?*

A: Yes, and sort of. We need to feel that what we do as teachers fits with who we are and what we are about. But we need to keep in mind that we are operating in a world where the physical laws are fixed. We cannot change gravity or even ignore it if we do not like the concept. It is true that we can adopt any set of beliefs we choose, but this does not mean those beliefs are based in reality.

Consider this idea within the context of the sport of golf. We can want the ball to go far and straight each time. We can use a style that we feel is most comfortable for us. We can believe that we know how best to hit a ball. But none of that makes any difference to the ball. It behaves only in relation to the forces that act on it. No belief, desire, style, or personality will have any effect directly. The only thing that makes any difference is what happens when the club hits the ball. Likewise, as teachers, we can believe that some things are good for our students or act in a manner that suits us, but that which is affecting our students will be consistent with the cause and effect that exists in natural law. In fact, everything we do has an effect on our students. Similar actions have similar effects. Above all, we need to ask ourselves whether this is about us or the students. Teaching should not force us to become someone we are not, but holding to the belief that the natural laws that govern human behavior will at some point conform to our personal tastes will lead only to frustration and ineffectiveness. Our journey will be a great deal more effective if we become students of those natural laws.

Q: *I am substitute teaching right now. Can I use the ideas from TCM to help me?*

A: Yes and no. The ideas in TCM can be useful in a substitute teaching context. Being aware and intentional and using clear, positive language with students will make you more effective in any situation. In addition, understanding how to promote healthy boundaries and deal with students who want to hook us into power struggles will be helpful. However, much of TCM is built on the principle that what we do today is setting the stage for a better next day. In most substitute teaching situations, teachers are placed for only one day or so. It is therefore difficult to build relationships and a foundation of cause and effect. You can learn a great deal about developing a teacher presence as a substitute and gain an understanding of the students, but your thinking should be very different if and when you begin teaching full time.

APPENDIX

Sound Versus Faulty Assumptions

Much of the practical as well as emotional dysfunction that teachers experience in the area of classroom management stems from faulty assumptions about the role of the teacher. Here we examine a few of them.

Faulty assumption: I have to choose between being strict or easy.

Why it is faulty. This is a false choice. There is a third option: be effective. Attempting to be strict (4-Style approach) or easy (3-Style approach) will be inherently stressful, and neither will be particularly effective. Choosing a 1-Style or 2-Style approach will lead to effectiveness and eliminate the need to think in these terms.

Faulty assumption: I have to choose between being nice or mean.

Why it is faulty. Effectiveness has little to do with being nice or mean. It has everything to do with consistency, clarity, and the use of effective strategies. Trying to be mean or nice is born out of fear. Any strategy that is fear based will eventually breed dysfunction. Students work hardest for teachers they like and respect. Gaining respect through being mean and feared robs you of effectiveness over time, limits your ability to bond with the students, and depresses the motivational level in the class. In the end, it is simply counterproductive. So when you hear the advice, "Don't smile until Christmas," offered by someone with good intentions, disregard it.

Faulty assumption: It's me against them.

Why it is faulty. It is not true. Seeing the students as the enemy is a mental projection. If you believe they are against you, they will be against you. If you believe that they are on your side and you let them know that you are firmly on their side, they will be, whether immediately or eventually.

Faulty assumption: It's the students' fault.

Why it is faulty. In most cases, the conditions that produce the problem behavior and classroom dysfunction are manufactured in large part by the teacher. While maintaining a clear expectation that each student is responsible for his or her own behavior, you must not lose sight of the fact that you make the weather. And while you will promote functional behavior by helping students learn to be accountable for their actions and choices, your effectiveness will be directly related to the degree to which you take responsibility for the conditions in the class that are contributing to problems. Therefore, in operational terms, much of your stress will come (unnecessarily) from taking on ownership for your students' behavior. Correspondingly, a great deal of your ineffectiveness will come as a result of externalizing the cause of the problems (and for how you feel as a result) to the students and (mistakenly) blaming them for the lack of function in your class.

Faulty assumption: Being passive-aggressive will work eventually.

Why it is faulty. An indirect means to "get back at students" is a cowardly and ultimately ineffective strategy. If you fear confrontation or following through with what you have set out, the social contract is destined to fail, and dysfunction will result. Moreover, no amount of complaining about your students to others (commiserating in the faculty lounge or to friends and family, for example) will improve the students' behavior.

APPENDIX

Examining the "It Works" Fallacy

As discussed in Chapter Two, beware of any phrase that includes the term "it works." This phrase can serve as a red flag. Phrases such as "This is what works with these students," "It is the only thing that works," or "Well, it works for me" are indicators that the practice should be carefully reconsidered. If you are looking to achieve greater levels of management effectiveness, the question should not be whether a particular practice works but whether it achieves a truly desirable outcome. Even if the outcome seems to be desirable in the short term or within some narrow perspective, it may require a broader examination or a consideration of what that practice is producing in the long term that is necessary to recognize the function or dysfunction of any practice.

In the list below, the first column represents the practical and psychological foundations of the phrase "it works" as it relates to classroom management practices. The other column outlines the concept of the empirical reality of classroom management practices that lead to desirable outcomes—those that actually work:

The "It Works" Fallacy	What Actually Works
Practices that are justified by such phrases as "it works for me," or "it works with my students," or "it is the only thing that works with the students at this school."	Practices that demonstrate efficacy in theory and practice.
Based in mental constructions and concepts.	Based in empirical reality.
Practices that make the teacher feel that he or she is doing something and having an effect.	Practices grounded in the laws of human behavior and cause and effect. Take into account human needs and nature.
Helps the teacher reinforce and confirm his or her constructed view of reality—usually characterized by a fatalistic concept of the "real world."	Through trial and error, praxis, hypothesis testing, and a process of reflective analysis, the teacher learns what produces desirable effects.

(continued)

(Continued)

The "It Works" Fallacy	What Actually Works
Typically produces a short-term effect that only superficially confirms a desired effect.	Produces a long-term positive effect—in essence, makes tomorrow more functional as a result of what was done today.
As with other coping mechanisms, there is some cyclical relief from the perceived problem condition as a result of implementing the strategy. But the cycle (problem, relief, dormant period, reappearance, or need for coping mechanism) will repeat itself unless the teacher experiences a need for it to change (usually coming from an external cause) and breaks the cycle.	As with any other functional behavior, teacher interventions are consciously and freely chosen to meet the specific demands of the situation. They are neither reactive nor compulsive.
Familiar enough to students that they do not resist or question the logic. Often this is due to the strategies being similar to strategies used in the students' home lives.	May or may not feel initially familiar to students, but after a period of use, inherently more satisfying and recognized for their ability to promote more functional and healthy behavior and relationships.
Practices typically achieve the (often superficial) appearance of having an emotional impact. Practices work to display the power of the teacher on a surface level.	Practices lead to real learning on the part of the students and therefore eventually true behavior change and maturity. Practices work to display the teacher's intentions to promote more functional behavior.
Requires an ongoing cognitive rationalization to self and others to maintain. Therefore, conscious awareness is essentially an enemy, as it illuminates the faulty reasoning and unconscious motivations behind the strategy.	Is consistently confirmed in both principle and outcome. Therefore, conscious awareness is essentially a friend in the process. It leads to greater levels of understanding.
Examples: punishments, public shaming (names on the board or colored cards), teacher as boss or judge, use of excessive extrinsic rewards, personal praise, and disappointment.	Examples: promoting a success psychology, meeting basic needs, taking meaningful action, promoting responsibility, promoting clarity of expectations, promoting intrinsic motivation.

Invariably the use of practices defined by the "it works with my students" mentality is accompanied by a corresponding view of human nature and the nature of classroom management. This view is characterized by a fixed view of ability and behavior and an external view of causality. This mentality is defined by phrases such as, "Students just are [a certain way]"—for example, "These students just have trouble listening." This external and fixed ability and intelligence mentality assumes that problems are inevitable and perpetual. As a result, the teacher accepts the practical reality that solutions will require a form of continually necessary short-term interventions and the psychological reality that it is the best that one can do. The result is maintenance of an external locus of control and a dispositional millstone that keeps the class heading downward on the effectiveness continuum.

Much like phrases that include the words "it works," phrases that include the words "it does not work" can be based in flawed logic. Sound practices will work. Someone is currently using that particular sound practice to get positive results with students in a similar situation or environment. When we use phrases such as, "I tried that but it did not work," especially related to strategies that characterize the 1-Style approach, we might listen for one of the following justifications. First, are we implying that we have a lack of commitment to the practice? Second, are we trying to conceal that we lack the skill necessary to make it work? Third, are we suggesting a lack of understanding of the practice or a picture of what it looks like when it comes to fruition? With enough time, commitment, skill, and knowledge of what we want as a result, any truly effective practice will work with any set of students, with very rare exceptions.

APPENDIX

Examining the Use of the Phrase the "Real World of School"

We often hear teachers use the phrase the "real world," as in, "That idea sounds nice, but it would fail in the real world." On first listening, it sounds like the voice of experience. These teachers have been around the proverbial block of classroom life and can attest to how the real world operates. The phrase "the real world" and its relation, "it works" (see Chapter Three and Appendix C), are signals to listen carefully to the messages beneath the words. In essence, the speakers are instructing us to adopt their worldview. It is certainly a convincing rhetorical device. If someone states, "Boy, my students have a hard time being honest in class," we might think, "Gosh, that teacher is struggling with that issue in his class. Good luck to him." However, if someone declares, "In the real world, people lie whenever they get the chance," this sounds like a fact with global import. We could feel that we should stop trusting our students and any we teach in the future. But the truth is that the real world is rarely defined by adages that include the phrase "the real world"; the use of "the real world" usually indicates a worldview that is jaded and fundamentally dysfunctional, and students are likely paying the price for this.

The following list represents a side-by-side comparison. The left column characterizes the use of the term "the real world," implied as representing a reality. The right column represents an effort to honestly characterize the nature of reality:

The "Real World": A biased perception of what is achievable, given beliefs, experiences, fears, and biases	The Real World: What is possible given the laws of nature and human behavior
"The way things are" is fixed.	"The way things are" is socially constructed over time and can change as a result of the collective and individual choices and actions of members of the group.
Students bring problems and deficiencies to the class that make certain teacher responses and behaviors inevitable.	While students can certainly bring certain energies and conditioned behavior into a class, in the end the teacher "makes the weather" in the classroom. Just about anything is possible with enough time, desire, and skills.

(continued)

(Continued)

The "Real World": A biased perception of what is achievable, given beliefs, experiences, fears, and biases	The Real World: What is possible given the laws of nature and human behavior
Some students are incapable of learning. Therefore, having positive expectations for them is futile.	All students can learn given the right conditions. Moreover, the level of expectations the teacher has will affect the relative success of every student (see the discussion of "Pygmalion in the Classroom" in Chapter Three).
"That practice will not work here. I tried it and it did not work with my students." Or, "The only thing that works with these students is . . ." (see Chapter Three).	A sound practice will work anywhere. For every teacher who claims that it did not work, there is another who found great success with a similar population of students, often in the same district.
"These students respond only to external reinforcement and punishment, so I have no choice but to continue to use that."	Students do get used to certain kinds of treatment and adult interactions, but they will respond to what feels right and what the situation calls for.
Usually a mental construction that one forms to escape feelings of guilt and inadequacy.	Inherently empirical. The more perceptive and aware we become, the more we can see the real world clearly.

As you examine each perspective, consider why so many teachers espouse the "real-world" view characterized by the left column. These vocalizations are examples of what is referred to in cognitive behavioral psychology as a reaction formation: a basic human defense mechanism in which the unconscious mind, confronted with unpleasant feelings (for example, guilt, inadequacy, helplessness), seeks relief through the creation of a reactive belief in an effort to compensate for that feeling. In other words, we create a belief structure that says, "My worldview is right (or at least makes me feel better), even if it is not supported by empirical evidence or reality."

The real-world view will correspond to a shift to an external locus of control (LOC). As you listen to the plea of the teacher defending this perspective, listen to the tendency to externalize causality. The opposite of this view is characterized by an internal LOC in which the teacher feels a responsibility for the outcomes that occur in class. The 1-Style (facilitator) and 2-Style (conductor) teachers use an internal LOC, and the 3-Style (enabler) and 4-Style (dominator) teachers use an external LOC.

It is not difficult to see why the challenging task of teaching and exposure to other externalizing individuals can lead a teacher to externalize his or her view for the way things are. In the short term, there may be a sense of relief, but at a cost. In the long term, it breeds misery and ineffectiveness. Teachers who cultivate an attitude of internal LOC will be happier at their jobs and more effective with students.

APPENDIX

Common Sources of Classroom Drama

Unconscious psychological dramas operate under the level of awareness (see Chapter Three). Drama can take the form of subtle or not-so-subtle power plays, social systems, and manipulative behavior patterns. They may seem necessary, but they exist only if the participants keep them active. Moreover, in many cases, they can seem harmless, such as an occasional exchange of sarcasm or verbal sparring. But as you examine the psychological games and dramas that follow, you will see that in many cases, the destructive effect can be significant. Some teachers confuse these games with the class "personality" or the existence of a "dynamic" atmosphere. But these are inherently lose-lose games.

Power Struggles

Power struggles are typically less about power and more about pride. They exist because the participants are attempting to defend something that is illusory (ego) and take their awareness off the goal (the best outcome for all concerned or accountability for actions). With enough clarity and awareness of one's reactive tendencies (defensiveness, insecurity, need to be right, need to be seen as important), power struggles do not need to exist (see the discussion of conflict resolution and power struggles in Chapter Thirteen). Moreover, although conflict resolution skills are useful, there is no substitute for the awareness of what our egos are telling us when we get the urge to engage a student in a power struggle. Ultimately the ability to choose constructive action over the reactive tendency to give in to defensiveness is the most effective way to achieve positive results.

Social Darwinism

We could also refer to this phenomenon as the "survival of the fittest." As depicted so vividly in William Golding's book, *The Lord of the Flies*, in the absence of a functioning social structure, the advantage goes to the advantaged. In the case of school-aged children, this often takes the form of the popular oppressing the unpopular, the strong oppressing the weak, and the haves oppressing the have-nots. This drama may be natural, but it is not much fun for those on the losing end and produces a psychologically damaging set of lessons for all concerned. The intensity of social Darwinism is often exacerbated by the actions of the teacher. When the teacher plays power games, promotes a competitive climate, and incorporates what could be described as a pain-based logic, this triggers the students' instinct for survival and self-defense. The result is a climate characterized by a cycle of attack and defend, where no members of the class are spared. Given a climate defined by a success psychology and a functional set of social bonds, the level of social Darwinism can be substantially mitigated.

Psychological Games

Most unconscious psychological games are played not to win but to meet a need. And unfortunately for the player, these games cannot be won. As we look closer at the dynamics of each of these games we see that the need that is motivating the players will never be satisfied. These games are lose-lose. Here are a few examples of such psychological games:

- *Sarcasm.* A teacher may say, "Hey, I can't believe it: a boy in this class finally got an answer right." It can seem funny and be amusing on the surface. However, examine the underlying message of sarcasm: "I will put you down to get a laugh from the class and show that I am powerful enough to put down you or someone else because it feeds my ego." The truth is that the use of sarcasm is a sign of insecurity. Moreover, it creates an underlying fear on the part of the students that they will be victimized. Negative energy always returns to its source.

- *I can top that.* Many teachers subscribe to the notion that students need to be shown who is boss. Instead of clear expectations and explicit boundaries, these teachers rely on the tenuous reality that that they can be cleverer than their students. The belief is that if the students recognize that the teacher is wittier and sharper, they will learn that they cannot win, will give up their attempts at testing, and feel respect in the process. While on the surface it may not seem so, this game is fueled by a sense of inadequacy on the part of the teacher. Like all other psychological dramas played out in the classroom, the result will be the win of an occasional daily battle but a war that can never be won.

- *Who can best justify the role of victim.* Many teachers come from families and external relationships in which temporary high ground can be won by the individual who can express the most injury and is therefore most deserving of sympathy and reparations (for example, "They changed the schedule again and did not tell us until today, so how am I supposed to teach with all this craziness?"). This victim drama, like the others, may achieve a desired short-term effect. It may encourage students to leave the teacher alone for a while and provide a momentary respite from one's sense of persistent guilt and responsibility. Over time, the effect will be a weakening of confidence in the teacher and a license for students to use the role of victim themselves to avoid responsibility. In the extreme, we could refer to the effect as producing a failure psychology.

- *My negativity will lead to your positive outcome.* Most of us have spent a great deal of our lives believing that negativity is useful and necessary. Whether it takes the form of complaining, chronicling failure, put-downs, shaming, punishments, disappointment, guilt, or something else, negativity will never produce long-term positive outcomes. As discussed in Chapter Two and Appendix C, it may "work" for us, but it will never produce effective results. It is a mental game that makes one feel a little better for a little while. Once in a while, it has the short-term effect of modifying student behavior, but the negative long-term effect nearly always outweighs any apparent positive result. Negativity begets negativity. Spend ten minutes in a class where the teacher uses a great deal of negativity, and you will feel the negative climate, see it on the faces, and hear it in the words of the students. Teachers who cannot believe that they can live without the use of negativity should try it for a week. They might be surprised.

"I don't do those things," you say. Wonderful! Nevertheless, challenge yourself to pay attention to the dynamics in your class for a week. What kinds of expressions do you notice on students' faces that you did not pay attention to before? How many times do you find yourself getting defensive or reactive? How many times do you find yourself unconsciously using negativity? As you begin to recognize the presence of the games, be cognitive of their price.

Effects of the Games

What is the harm done by these social and psychological dramas? Here are a few examples:

- They stunt the development of the effectiveness of classroom management in the future, dragging down the effectiveness and function continuum.

- They stunt the growth of the individual members of the class and impede the development of self-responsibility and conscious awareness.

- They stunt the growth of the collective. They work against your efforts toward collective functioning and the creation of a classroom community. A community requires a climate of emotional safety, security, and risk taking to thrive.

- Psychological dramas create a threatening environment and keep students confined to a state of self-defense and survival.

You may be asking, "If I give up all my reactive dramas, won't the class be uneventful and dull?" No. If you are having trouble conceiving of management without dramas and games, then it may be a good time to reflect on your approach to teaching.

What is left? The answer is more of the natural condition: the learning, joy, appreciation, creativity, a sense of ease and emotional safety, true relationships, respect, self-responsibility, motivation, and achievement with less stress and struggle throughout the day.

Transform Your School: A Schoolwide Student Discipline, Motivation, Character Building, and Peer Mediation Program

The principles of transformative management can go beyond the walls of the individual classroom and be used schoolwide. The program examined here is Transform Your School (TYS). It is aligned with the Alliance for the Study of School Climate (ASSC) and the School Climate Assessment Instrument (SCAI) and the principles from this book. The ASSC SCAI offers an assessment process and improvement system for moving a school from lower to higher levels of overall function and climate quality.

The TYS program provides a comprehensive plan for behavioral improvement that includes discipline, motivation, character development, and peer mediation and conflict resolution. It is designed for schools at the K–8 level. Information about the TYS program and how to begin implementing it can be obtained at www.calstatela.edu/schoolclimate.

Features of the Program

- Combines student behavior, character building, and peer mediation and conflict resolution into one comprehensive schoolwide program
- Promotes long-term motivational and behavioral improvement
- Promotes school pride, a positive climate, and a sense of school community
- Encourages whole-staff coherence and schoolwide continuity of behavioral expectations
- Integrates expectations across the classroom, physical education, special subjects, playground, lunchroom, and other school functions
- Builds students' internal locus of control, and success psychology contributes to students' academic achievement and social growth

Contrast to Other Schoolwide Discipline Programs

- No use of bribes and limited use of extrinsic rewards
- No use of public shame or comparison
- Minimal cost to maintain
- Shifts focus from the negative to the positive
- Peer mediators are leaders rather than junior police

System Themes

This program takes a positive approach to building a concrete, specific, and personal understanding of quality behavior. It features a few strategic behavioral themes. These themes can be modified to suit the needs of a particular school but typically include most of the following concepts:

- Cooperation
- Effort, trying
- Respect, sportsmanship
- Attention, listening
- Responsibility
- Positive attitude

Within the TYS program, these themes are taught, modeled, assessed, and reinforced throughout the students' experience across the school. Recommended applications of the themes include the following:

- Incorporated schoolwide as part of a "theme of the month" focus
- Incorporated within the class to promote higher levels of performance and improved behavior quality
- High-quality behavior recognized with the use of positive recognition of desired behavior cards (for example, using the school's nickname or mascot, such as "cougar cards") as well as other forms of positive recognition
- Reinforced on the playground to encourage high-quality behavior and related concepts across different school environments
- Incorporated in physical education and other special subjects to reinforce character and behavioral expectations and provide continuity
- Uses trained student peer conflict resolution leaders in conflict resolution

The TYS programs has these features:

Classroom-Level Features

- A rubric for assessing behavior or participation, or both
- Lesson plans for different character areas and conflict resolution
- Concepts built into lessons and discussions by monthly theme
- Facilitative teacher role (positive recognitions and reinforcer of concepts rather than giver of punishment or shame)

Playground Level

- Playground staff give positive recognition and cards (for example, "cougar cards")
- Loss of time used as a negative consequence
- No shame, no negative use of the system, and no public recognition of undesirable behavior

Physical Education, Special Subjects, and Out-of-Classroom Interactions

- Participation rubric as the primary focus of assessment
- Use of themes in projects, games, and activities
- "Catch a student being good" capacity for all adults on campus

Conflict Resolution and Peer Mediation

- Incorporates principles of the nationally recognized CRETE (Conflict Resolution Education in Teacher Education, Temple University) program
- Student peer conflict resolution leaders on duty at recess
- Conflict resolution lessons taught in classes
- Schoolwide expectation that students possess the capacity to solve their own problems and learn from their conflict

Program Implementation and Application

The TYS program is designed to meet the needs of schools at all levels of functioning:

Stage 1: Schools that see student behavior as a weakness and need a system to improve it

Stage 2: Schools that want to become more consistent with their expectations across domains of the school

Stage 3: Schools that want to move toward 1-Style classrooms for students who think more self-responsibly and want to shift toward a community-type school climate

The following resources can be used to support the program:

- Workshops and readings
- Transformative classroom management
- Conflict resolution training for students and teachers
- Classroom behavioral assessment systems including sound rubrics (see the online resource article, "Developing and Implementing an Effective System for Assessing the Quality of Behavior, Participation, or Process," at trasformativeclassroom.com)
- Healthy use of rewards (Chapter Six) and how to use cards effectively
- The fundamentals of building a success psychology in the school (Chapter Seven)

Training to Implement the Program

The following elements can be used in a training program:

- Whole school development and decision making related to essential terms and elements of the system
- Support of staff use of recognition cards
- Teacher workshops related to basics of transformative classroom management and use of behavioral rubrics in the classroom
- Peer mediator training in conflict resolution

Advanced training in the following topics can be useful:

- Building a schoolwide community
- Creating a success psychology in the classroom
- Working with challenging students

The SCAI can be a valuable asset in the process of implementing the TYS program. Deriving a plan of action from a systematic climate and function analysis typically produces a sounder and more sustainable set of outcomes. Administering the SCAI often identifies critical areas for improvement that are necessary to ensure the TYS program is successful.

The goal of the TYS program is meaningful behavior change and sustainability. For a system to be truly effective, it must work in the long term to change the behavioral culture at the school in and out of the classroom. An effective system must work to teach new skills and make high-quality behavior more desirable and satisfying for students. Moreover, it must make teachers' lives easier. The TYS program endeavors to do this.

Key TYS Areas

To see the difference between the TYS system and others, it is useful to examine it more closely in a few key areas: motivation, core concepts, changing undesirable behavior, and long-term effects.

Motivation Within the TYS Program. The goals of the TYS system are an increase in motivation to behave in positive, healthy ways, with more motivation coming from intrinsic sources. Strategies to meet students' basic needs and recognition for displaying high-quality behavior provide the means for this. Each student has five basic needs (see Chapter Six): power, freedom, belonging/love, competence, and fun. The system promotes the satisfaction of these basic needs as well as the behaviors that will help students attain what it takes to meet them throughout their lives.

In contrast to other systems of behavior, the TYS system uses positive recognitions to support behavior change and growth rather than bribes for desirable behavior. While the TYS system uses cards to symbolically recognize high-quality behavior, the use of the cards varies dramatically from other systems. In many behavioral systems, students are given cards as extrinsic rewards to be turned in later for prizes relative to the number of cards they obtained. The TYS system uses the recognition of the behavior as the reward. What is in it for the student? It depends on the way the school wants to manage this, but it includes the satisfaction of being recognized, the pride in telling parents and teachers of the recognition, and a concrete and material reminder of a behavior that was valuable in and of itself.

Chapter Six contrasts the healthy use of extrinsic rewards to the less healthy form defined by bribes and tokens. The problem with the approach to motivation in many other systems is that it is based on getting students excited about turning in their tokens for a prize. Inevitably over time, the prize becomes the purpose for the action. As time goes on, the prizes lose their impact, and the familiar conditioned behavioral patterns return. Now students are demanding more prizes because they have gotten addicted to extrinsic rewards for doing something healthy. In the students' minds, these systems built on bribes send the message: "You would want to make a high-quality effort, treat others well, or act responsibly only because adults will give you something." In stark contrast, TYS motivational philosophy changes behavior in a sustained way because it is driven by intrinsic sources—it is meeting basic needs.

Core Concepts of the TYS System. At the heart of the TYS system are core principles. These principles, agreed to by the faculty and staff, can range from five to twelve concepts. These core concepts typically include values such as effort, positive attitude, respect, responsibility, listening, and being prepared. Successful character-building efforts make these abstract concepts both concrete and personally meaningful. In the TYS system, the school's core concepts are taught and reinforced across the various aspects of the school day and even brought home. When these concepts are made concrete and meaningful, students recognize that they are on the pathway to a more satisfying experience at school. When they are recognized for demonstrating them, they learn that the school genuinely values them when they are doing their best and is not simply concerned about test scores and the students who misbehave.

Creating Rubrics and Making the Core Concepts Clear. The core concepts in TYS should be clear and consistently applied across the school. A useful practice for doing this is to create detailed rubrics for behavior. (See the online resource article, "Developing and Implementing an Effective System for Assessing the Quality of Behavior, Participation, or Process," at transformativeclassroom.com.) These rubrics can be used in the regular classroom, physical education, art, music assemblies, field trips, and on the playground. They provide the language for reinforcing behavior and a clear set of criteria for assessment. In contrast to behavioral systems that are based on recognizing negative behavior, TYS focuses on what is desired, not on what is not desired.

Dealing with Misbehavior. In the TYS system, there is no use of public recognition for unhealthy or undesirable behavior. If a student's behavior violates classroom, school, or playground rules, the student deserves to be given a consequence. The use of withdrawal of privileges or opportunities to participate is the primary form of consequence in most cases. School beautification, helping teachers, doing tasks for the office, and other service-related activities should be left for students who have earned the right to contribute as a reward. Those who make an effort and act responsibly are given an opportunity; those who are not ready to handle responsibility are not given an activity.

Behavioral contracts and individualized support for students who are struggling to make healthy behavioral choices are also recommended. Working with challenging students is outlined in Chapter Fourteen.

The TYS system offers schools the capacity to implement transformative classroom management schoolwide. It is grounded in principles that will promote better behavior and a set of shared schoolwide expectations in a manner that encourages ever increasing levels of student responsibility and sense of community while supporting the efforts of teachers in the classroom.

APPENDIX

Classroom Management and Student Achievement

In a study of twenty-one urban K–12 schools (seven elementary, seven middle, and seven high schools), high-quality classroom management was found to be strongly correlated with student achievement (Shindler, 2009). The sample of schools reflected a diverse range of student demographic populations. Schools were assessed using the Alliance for the Study of School Climate (ASSC) School Climate Assess Instrument (SCAI) by both students and teachers at each school. Dimension 5 of the SCAI, which measures the quality of classroom management, was used to rate the quality of practice. High-quality practices were defined by 1-Style/transformative classroom management practice (see Figure G.1).

The results showed that school climate and classroom management were highly related to student achievement. The correlation coefficient between the dimension 5 SCAI measure for classroom management and student achievement as measured by California State Academic Performance Index (API) was 0.7. When the API score was adjusted for the socioeconomic status of the students at each school the correlation increased to 0.8. In other words, there was an 80 percent relationship between the pattern of API and classroom management quality scores (as seen in Figure G.1). Moreover, the study found that when schools with similar student populations used more transformative classroom management, their achievement levels were higher.

The scatter plot diagram (Figure G.2) shows the relationship between student achievement and the rating of the quality of the classroom management (SCAI dimension 5) at each of the twenty-one schools. On the vertical axis, API scores range from 200 (low test scores) to 1000 (high test scores). On the horizontal axis, classroom management quality is rated between 1 (low quality) and 9 (high quality).

As Figure G.2 shows, when schools used practices closer to those described in TCM as transformative/1-Style and fewer 3- and 4-Style teacher practices, student achievement was higher.

Figure G.1 represents classroom management practices as represented on the ASSC SCAI dimension 5 in relation to the transformative classroom management teaching style matrix. The ASSC SCAI was designed to reflect high function/success psychology/transformative practices as most desirable and highest rated, and low function/failure psychology/accidental practices as least desirable and lowest rated. Extrapolating from the scatter plot correlations, predicted achievement scores can be derived from the data. Higher API/student achievement scores could be predicted for the use of high-function 1-Style practice, average scores could be predicted from use of traditional/low-function 2-Style practice, and low scores could be predicted from the use of 3- or 4-Style practice.

363

		High Function/Intentional Internal Locus of Control						
	Student Centered				Teacher Centered			
		9 SCAI @800+						
1-Style		8 SCAI @800						2-Style
				7 SCAI @750				
					6 SCAI @650			
						5 SCAI @550		
						4 SCAI @450		
					3 SCAI @400			
3-Style				2 SCAI @350				4-Style
				1 SCAI @300				
		Low Function/Accidental External Locus of Control						

FIGURE G.1. *SCAI Classroom Management Ratings and Corresponding Predicted API Score Correlations as Depicted by the TCM Teaching Style Matrix*

Source: Shindler, J., Jones, A., Williams, A., Taylor, C., & Cadenas, H. (2009, January). Exploring below the surface: School climate assessment and improvement as the key to bridging the achievement gap. Paper presented at the annual meeting of the Washington State Office of the Superintendent of Public Instruction, Seattle.

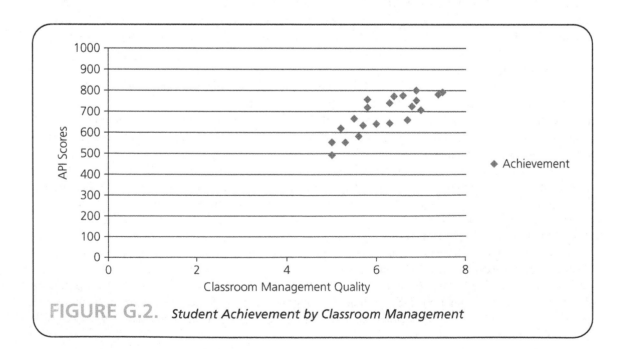

FIGURE G.2. *Student Achievement by Classroom Management*

REFERENCE

Shindler, J., Jones, A., Williams, A., Taylor, C., & Cadenas, H. (2009, January). *Exploring below the surface: School climate assessment and improvement as the key to bridging the achievement gap.* Paper presented at the annual meeting of the Washington State Office of the Superintendent of Public Instruction, Seattle.

INDEX

CPSIA information can be obtained
at www.ICGtesting.com
Printed in the USA
LVOW03s2331070916

503684LV00020B/132/P